Compleat

A Journey from Insanity to Humanity

Runner5150

Copyright © 2022 – Runner5150

All rights reserved. No part of this book may be used or reproduced in any manner whatsoever without written permission except in the case of brief quotations embodied in critical articles or reviews.

Thank you for buying an authorized edition of this book and for complying with copyright laws by not reproducing, scanning, or distributing any part of it in any form without permission. You are supporting writers and their hard work by doing this.

DISCLAIMER: NAMES AND LIKENESSES HAVE BEEN CHANGED TO PROTECT THE IDENTITIES OF THOSE DEPICTED IN THE STORIES.

Published in the United States of America

First Printing Edition, 2022

Table of Contents

A Foreword By runner5150   v

A Brief History of runner5150   v

Compleat: A Journey from Insanity to Humanity   vii

Part I: Growing Pains   viii

Terror In the Dark   9

Children Learn What They Live   20

Of Cats & Dogs   20

Wrong Way   25

Back to The Beginning   29

A Childhood of Sexual Misconduct   38

Spare the Child & Spoil the Rod   47

River   50

A Secret Fear of Horses   52

Breaking Things   57

Through The Ice   59

Haunting The Library   62

Fourth Grade & 2001: A Space Odyssey   66

gEnIuS   72

Sal & The Fear   74

A Note to God   81

Insanity   82

The Choir & The Teachers   86

Walking Man   106

Fran Was the Name of My Other Mother   109

The Dove & The Turtle   114

On Broadway   115

The Girl & The Devil in His Day   119

How Do I Separate Sex and Love?   122

People   139

Just a Thought   144

If You Truly Love Someone   147

The Eyes   148

Unworthy!   151

Completely Different Kind of Asshole   158

Uncle Sam's Misguided Child   159

Breaking Hearts   167

New Songs, Old Pain   170

Part II: The Middle   clxxiii

For the Ageless   113

The 10 New Commandments   114

Sobering In Japan   116

Buddha at the Bottom   120

3 Cameras for a Chevy   125

Pirates Into The Den   129

On God & The Loss of The last of My Humanity   134

The Miracle of Steve Elliott   155

Brig: The First Experience   163

The Lost System of Justice in These Un-United States   169

o d e P   173

Brig: The Second Experience   181

The Desert: The Diary Inserts   186

Stoney Moore & Empathy   214

Will Wonders Never Cease   218

How Religions Exclude What God Would Include   221

Ananias, Sapphira, and the Foundation of the Christian religion   227

Table of Contents

Special Things   230

The Awakening: Vess Moments for Everyone   231

Meeting Death   252

The Damned   255

You're Fired   258

Compleat   265

More On Sex   279

Shame Isn't Natural AKA Sin   286

Miss Martha   301

Science the Religion   310

The Bane of Humanity is Religion   312

On God   329

Balaam's Ass   334

Regina Myrtle Dixon   336

Betrayer of Trust   339

Stay Out!   346

Family   351

The Red Rose & The Blue Rose   357

Definition of Nightmare   366

Whole Humanity   370

Non-Nobility   376

Insight Into God   378

Simply Put   382

Where Was God Before Then?   387

Chicken or the Egg Answered At last   392

When Was the Last?   395

The Second Son That Almost Wasn't   399

Daddy Magic   406

Batter Up!   411

The Life and Death of Buck - Mr. Fuller   414

Two Out of Three is Bad   421

The Burden   423

And The Message Was Clear   425

The Angel & The Bad Man   427

Of Magic & Miracles   435

On a Life   442

What was the Beginning of my Insanity?   449

The Second Perception of Insanity   457

I Am Not A Crook   460

Falling or Failing   467

Punctuation   475

Whatever   480

Aside from Being Human   483

Around & Around the World, It Goes   486

Going Postal   496

Mad Man At McDonald's   501

Jaws   504

The How & The Why   506

Minding A Tricky Think   512

Privileged, The   517

Of The Women in My Life   523

Battling Ego   531

What He Said   537

Of Dogs & Cats   546

Gifts For the Giving   551

Table of Contents

Immortal Me   554

Non-Poetry   558

Thorns 560

Childish Man   562

On Women   563

When I Die   564

An Island   566

Smells 567

The TV is Still On   570

Modern Days   574

The Bus 576

My Normie Friends Say 579

12-Step Meetings   584

Let's Talk About God… 588

The Child Inside 614

Notes   619

Barring the Way to Eden 621

One   627

An Answer From God   628

A Letter from God   629

I Understand or I Die   632

A Last Note on Myself and My Love for Megan   635

The Craftsman & The Tool   637

Looking with God Eyes 639

What's Your Story?   642

The Final Story 644

Ravings & References   dclii

Runner's Ravings   dcliii

References   dclvi

The Medical Report   657

Compleat

A Foreword By

runner5150

I chose the handle 'runner' not because I can still run 3 to 5 miles a day (I quit that after college although I probably should have and could have kept it up) but because I read somewhere that back in the days of ancient kings, the royals would use runners to carry messages from city to city or king to king.

While these 'runners' needed to be physically fit (definitely not an apt description of me lately) they also needed to have the values or principles of courage, loyalty, and honor.

Why? Because they represented the royal, they were carrying the message for the other, making them surrogate 'royals' or maybe that's what was meant as being noble.

That's why honor was so important.

Loyalty would also need to be a part of their character because they could be carrying messages that contained important information that other kings would pay to know or even prevent from being delivered.

And that reasoning applies to courage as well, for two reasons. One, they put their lives at risk, running great distances to deliver a message that anyone might kill them for in order to obtain the information within the message or prevent it from being delivered.

But there was a second risk in carrying messages from one royal to another. If the receiving royal didn't like what was contained within the message or was angered by it, there was no guarantee that they wouldn't send the 'runners' head back to the original sender as an indicator of what they thought of the message.

Out of that came the old adage, "don't kill the messenger, just the message" and later "listen to/for the message, not to the messenger".

As for the "5150" part of my handle, it's a longer story that perhaps I'll tell you a little later on. But the short of it is that the California Penal Code for inmates that were found 'not guilty by reason of insanity was just that – CPC 5150 back in 1988 when I first experienced being in a maximum-security institution for the criminally insane. Like I said, a VERY long story behind that one.

I put the two handles together and defined them for myself as representing:

Introduction

runner5150 = one crazy messenger, who's not afraid to die to deliver a message that needs to be delivered. In a nut (pun intended) shell, that is who I am.

Whenever I've mentioned to people that I'm writing a book there are two questions that invariably follow that announcement.

The first is almost always "What is your book about?" And I find that question balanced between disgusting and amusing, because if they were truly interested in knowing what it was about – they'd read the book. No amount of explanations and descriptions, not even a foreword or jacket cover summary could explain what the true intent or purpose of a book is, and only by reading it could a person hope to grow to the knowledge of what the author was attempting to express.

The second question I'm inevitably asked I am more than willing to share an answer to, though not for the purpose of selling the book or promoting it.

I'm asked: "What is the name of your book?" And with every inquiry as to the title of this book you might be reading, I cannot help but laugh inwardly because I chose the title for many reasons and with the intent to allow human beings to do what they seem to do best – disagree on the meaning of the words.

Compleat: A Journey from Insanity to Humanity is the title I selected, although if I am fortunate, as Dostoevsky was with his "Notes from Underground," both publishers and the public will interpret the book as they see fit and I'll be laughing aloud when overhearing their discussions.

Why did I choose the archaic spelling (Old English) of Compleat? What was my intent for naming it a Journey? Was the Journey from Insanity a comment on my own mental illnesses or was it a guide for those who also suffer from mental illnesses, so that they could follow the path I shared and find relief from not just the stigma of mental health issues but also the issues themselves? Even the punctuation I chose to use will probably be either ignored or mishandled. And how the title is expressed will come under question simply because of how it could have been expressed.

Compleat A Journey! From Insanity to Humanity! could come across as a suggestion or direction, possibly even a command if anyone were to look at the stories I've shared and see the implications behind the ones I've written regarding religion and humanity's relationship with god and one another.

Compleat: A Journey, From Insanity to Humanity could be used to express a letter from the Insane to the Humane, or from one insane individual to all of humanity.

Compleat A Journey From Insanity to Humanity appears to be simply a title, leaving its interpretation totally open for the reader to decide what exactly the author intended for it to mean.

And of course, there's the title I selected for the book itself. Open to interpretation but with the colon placed exactly where it will put the edge of my intent under scrutiny for any reader who might relate to my reasoning.

Like Dostoevsky, I wrote the title the way I did for a reason. And as I already stated, his book "Notes from Underground" has been butchered by publishers and readers and booksellers to include a word he never intended to be there: the title of his book is NOT "Notes from THE Underground." But that's how readers, publishers, and sellers of books often refer to it.

I find that it's a sad world that cannot comprehend what the author's intent was in selecting a title for their works. It's even sadder that many won't ever even consider this fact.

Compleat

A Brief History of

runner5150

Of 1,000 inmates of the hospital 85% return to incarceration after just 6 months. Of the 15% left, which equals 150 out of the 1,000 only 1% are able to stay out of trouble after being out for 2 years. So, 1% of 15% would be what? 15 guys? The point is that out of 1,000 inmates released most return or are incarcerated for crimes, either the same type or other, within 2 years. I, on the other hand, have been on the streets since January 23rd, 1993. 29 years without repeating or violating any other laws.

Writing my stories here isn't about me trying to glorify any or all of my past mistakes or even my recovery from those mistakes. Nor am I out to make a profit from sharing them, and I am certainly not seeking to become some kind of prophet claiming enlightenment that might save us all from ourselves. What I am trying to share is what I honestly was like, what happened to and with me, and how the change came about in my life from a most unusual source; one that even I find difficult to embrace as being real.

This is, to put it simply, a collection of true stories. I can only hope that in reading it others might find a portion of what I have found through all the experiences I share here, the life of being a human being.

m. "runner5150"

Certified Alcohol and Other Addiction Specialist

Jan 11, 2021.

Compleat

Compleat: A Journey from Insanity to Humanity

Compleat

Part I: Growing Pains

Compleat

Terror In the Dark
_.._.._.._.._.._.._.._.._.._.._.._.._.._.._..

The details of what I remember from having been raped and stuck in a closet at approximately two years of age are both sketchy at best and difficult in recounting them in the stories where I mention the event.

As a two-year-old, I could remember the pain, but could never remember the name of the person who raped me. It would be years later that my younger sister, Violet, would reveal to me that his name had been Tom and that he had been one of our mother's many husbands … which I never would have thought of her until years later because she was our mother and I had no concept of her behaviors during that period.

* How my younger sister came to know of the event and the perpetrator remains a mystery to me but is one I choose not to investigate simply because his name really didn't matter in the scheme of things that happened. *

What I still retain to this day and age of my life beyond the pain was the terror I felt in the dark place in which I was placed as punishment for crying about what had been done to me. The closet where I was confined was totally dark, without any light coming into it from under the door or any cracks that might have allowed it alongside the edges or door handle, as there was no keyhole and I couldn't see what was in the closet with me, only feeling around myself as I stumbled and tried to force the door open against it being held shut.

I recall that I didn't feel any clothes, no coats or clothing hanging inside it, and perhaps there weren't any, though it was possible that there were, but I was too small to reach up and touch them. What I did feel were the edges of objects, hard and with pointed corners, perhaps boxes that were made of wood or metal but definitely sharp and not comforting in the least when I finally gave up my struggle to gain a release from that confinement and tried to find a place to sit down on the floor.

I found that I had been wedged into a place of harsh edges and points in the darkness and was terrified not simply by the pain that had been inflicted upon me. More terrifying than the pain itself was having been told that I would never be released from that place of darkness until I promised to not tell anyone about what had been done to me and stopped crying. I was afraid because I couldn't see that I would be able to stop crying and thought that I would be kept there forever. Forever. For a two-year-old, that concept of time was something I couldn't escape any more than I could force open the door to that closet. And that experience was perhaps the foundation of my perception of time itself being an illusion because, after hours of crying, I became so exhausted that I actually did stop crying. Who released me after that I cannot recall. Perhaps it was the man who raped me, perhaps my grandmother, whose closet it had been. But the foundation of my realization that time is an illusion had been laid, though I would not discover that fact for many years, and the realization that nothing stays in the static state that human nature labels as forever. Not even my own pain and terror.

Compleat

Children Learn What They Live
_._._._._._._._._._._._._._._._._..

Although this saying is an old adage from so long ago that its beginnings are lost in the currents of the illusion known as time, this platitude holds a place of truth for me. I truly believe that if a child is beaten into conformity and obedience it will grow to beat and force its own offspring into obedience and compliance to the acceptable norms of the society around it and them. Or, like myself, that beaten child will find itself an outcast from its surrounding society, family, and peers. Rejecting and fearing everything and everyone around them.

If that child is nurtured, respected, and instructed in how to discover the world around it and all the beauty therein, that same child can and will grow to see beauty in every aspect of life, caring for itself and others, and sharing or instructing its own offspring (and oft times the offspring of others) in learning to see or perceive their world in that same manner as well.

And while there are other means and methods of raising children, my experience with the process is limited to my own upbringing and my failed attempt at fatherhood to my then stepchildren and first-born son. That remains one of my greatest regrets and owed amends, but that story is told later in this book.

For now, I am expressing that in my childhood I experienced both the beating and attempted forced compliance, along with and in combination with moments of nurturing that, even so small, they would stand out as monumental due to their infrequency.

But there was another, insidious and even more harmful method that would grow to be the formative means by which I experienced being raised.

*

Being ignored

A child that grows to maturity having been ignored through its formative years and subsequent adolescence develops survival skills and the means by which its ego will be nurtured without the need for input from others. And thereby that child forms less self-esteem along with greater ego than either of the other two means I have mentioned prior to this one.

Compleat

This is a truth I have often tried to share with others.

Children cannot be treated as possessions without losing their 'glow', joy, and newness to the parent(s) who brought about their births. And the only result of an object not being new, exciting, and enjoyable is for it to become less likely to be paid attention to, eventually becoming ignored and possibly resented.

This simple, ironic, and – in my experience – 'unnecessary' need to be taught truth holds true for much of what the human race experiences within itself.

From other types of relationships all the way down to objects of material wealth. Even a Rolls Royce becomes just a 'car' eventually and those who can afford one find themselves wanting to buy the next newer one because the 'old' one has lost their interest.

Treating a child as a possession, many individuals find themselves having and wanting to have more children because the wonder of that first child has faded and they need to experience the wonder again, losing the experience of the person that first child is becoming.

Now, please allow me to ask: Do you have fears from your childhood? Not the ones of being beaten and abused. I already described some of those here. I'm talking about simpler fears. Like fear of the dark or secret fears like my fear of horses. I'll talk about that second one first, trying to avoid talking about more sexual abuse simply to take a break from writing about stuff that triggers both emotional pain and anger in myself.

I come from a family that loves horses. My Aunt Melanie owned a quarter horse ranch and I cannot think of another member of my family that has a similar terror as I experience in their company. So here is the story of how I believe I came to fear horses and my only family member that ever treated me as an equal, even though I was still a child. (Swap layout – consult catalog).

Compleat

Of Cats & Dogs

I have said this in other places but I have never fully explained the 'why' of my having said it. My 'pop' (god is only his title though some seem to think it's his name) gave humanity dogs in order to show us exactly what unconditional love looks like, in order that we might learn how to treat and respond to one another, they give us the perfect example to follow.

My experience is in this story, just as all these stories are real life-incidents, and if you are a dog person you may find reading this particular story as difficult as my relating it has been for me.

When I was a child of about ten years of age there came to the yard of my home a male German Shepard, a huge, tan, and black, beautiful dog. Around his neck, someone had placed a 'choke chain collar made of steel links and a length of rope where his previous owner must have had him tied up to prevent his running away.

That chain collar had twisted and tightened to the point that it had torn its way deep into that dog's neck. The depth of the wound suggested his efforts to free himself must have been monumental and the smell from it announced that the wound wasn't a new or fresh one either. It had festered and grown green with a gangrenous infection and there were maggots crawling through his flesh, making the stench so powerful that it could be detected from over twenty feet away.

Compleat

It was obvious to me that this dog's previous owner had stopped caring for it long before, for whatever reason. I tried at the time to give them the benefit of the doubt, thinking that perhaps they had grown old and died, leaving this poor abandoned creature to suffer.

He is the example I mentioned though: that dog suffering, neglected, and alone came to me, laid his head in my lap, and wanted only that I would choose to love and care for him. For him there was no past, no neglectful owner, no abuse or starvation so awful that he would choose not to love again. That need and willingness are what unconditional love looks like, and as anyone who has ever loved a dog or any animal can tell you the spirit of an animal is as close to pure love as humanity can find sometimes.

My parents eventually had that dog put down, not because of the severity of his wounds, but because the bill for having the wounds themselves treated would have been substantial and the maintenance for an animal of that size would have been a financial drain.

I wonder sometimes if my care and the financial repercussions of providing for me could have been avoided by having me 'put to sleep' would have entered their minds, given the chance and opportunity.

Since I lost both my cats, first Miss Pri (I read that it is the Sanskrit word for love) and more recently James Kat (aka Jimmy K.) I thought I should include this example of the reason god gave humanity cats.

Most people tend to joke about cats being lazy, aloof, gross, or always eating, sleeping, making a stink, or noises. With all the complaints about cats, some folk might wonder why would god give humanity cats, after all. We already have dogs to teach us what unconditional love looks like. Questions about whether they are really our secret rulers – four-footed kings and queens that command us to care for them? Or are they simply useless burdens that humanity has tolerated for thousands of years because they purr at frequencies that humanity enjoys?

Neither of those answers is the truth, however. Though seeing the 'why' with them might be a bit harder than it seems to be with dogs. My experience with cats came from a dark upbringing and being raised to hate cats of any kind. My family shared a story that a cat had crawled into a baby's crib and suffocated that baby by trying to lick the milk from the baby's mouth after his bottle had fallen away. Like most of the stories that promote fear and hatred, I had no idea of its lack of substantial proof or evidence.

Compleat

Years later I learned the harsh truth that it was more of a probability that the baby had died of SIDS (Sudden Infant Death Syndrome) and that the cat, sensing something was wrong had tried to revive or awaken the baby, much in the manner of a mother cat trying to wake a kitten that has died after being newly born.

I was taught that hating and killing cats was something my 'family' did on a regular basis. My so-called cousin, Boots, and his father Uncle George had a barn on their property where every stray cat they had come across had been killed, skinned, and had its pelt nailed to the inside of the doors of that barn. The doors were substantial and there was hardly a single space that didn't have a cat skin nailed upon them. While I never skinned a cat, I too was guilty of killing cats, just for their existence.

It wasn't until after I had taken my own life and been sent back that my perception of cats changed. If god had given us dogs to show us what unconditional love looked like, what then were we to learn from cats?

Cats are here to give us practice for what we learn from dogs. It's that simple, really. A cat is aloof, ignores those it owns unless it wants something from them, and almost always times its demands at the most inopportune time imaginable. A cat will seek unwarranted attention, howl, yowl, and scream if it doesn't get its way in anything. Sound familiar? Two-year-old humans have a lot in common with cats, though honestly a two-year-old could learn a lot from a cat when it comes to throwing a temper tantrum.

We are not their slaves nor are we their owners for that matter. Pop put us here as stewards of all life on this planet and they, cats, are the most difficult to care for, next to ourselves as human beings, but that is their purpose for existing.

So, we learn from caring for cats how to care for one another. Aloof, distant, demanding, selfish, self-centered, and especially almost always crying out for what we want/need/must have/cannot and do not want to live without we simply do not understand why we are told "no." Human beings must remind my pop of cats, there are so many of us that are just like them in these ways. So, we need cats to practice on, so we can learn to live with one another.

I offer this one small suggestion, though I am not telling anyone what to do or how to live their lives:

"Learn unconditional love from dogs, they display it every chance they get. Practice unconditional love on cats, they offer opportunity in every encounter.

Then take it one small step further and practice what you've learned with one another. I know you will be glad you did.".

Compleat Wrong Way

How do I tell the story of my heart being broken for the very first time in my life? The images come into my mind as I make the attempt, putting pen to paper, typing them into a document for others to read, and sharing them online with others. But the question isn't about creating the story, it's about reliving the trauma and suffering as if I were the child who witnessed the tragedy and was powerless to do anything about it.

Many apps and websites require those secret questions and the answers to them to verify a person's identity. And one of the most common questions they use is to ask: "What was the name of your first pet?" I honestly cannot answer that question though. Because the first pet I ever loved was a brown and white Cocker Spaniel whose name I cannot remember. I remember her face, her long ears flapping as she ran after sticks that were thrown for her to chase and bring back. I remember her colors being on her ears and across her back, like a small saddle and reins, and that her tail would wag so hard when she was happy that her entire body would wave back and forth, and that she would jump side to side in anticipation as she waiting for me to throw the ball or a stick for her to fetch.

And I remember how she died, barking at cars, on the east side of the street in front of the home we shared, on Ohio Ave in St. Louis, Missouri. She was protective of cars that went by and the ones that had loud mufflers or played extremely loud music were her nemeses. Her small body would tense up and she would roar her bark out as if she was so big that she could frighten vehicles into slowing down or being quiet as they passed the house.

Yet it was one of those cars, a convertible with three teenage boys in it, that took her life. They were driving south, on the west side of the road because here in the States they drive on the right-hand side of the road. She stepped off the curb on the east side barking her warning against the loud music those boys were playing and got their attention apparently. I cannot remember the exact song they were playing, only that it was some get drunk and have a good time Country-Western music they must have taken to heart.

I remember calling to her, trying to get her to come back into the front yard, small as it was, in front of the duplex of houses we shared with other families. And I remember watching those boys drive over onto the wrong side of the street and deliberately hitting her with that big, white-roofed, convertible car, killing her instantly and then driving away laughing loudly at what they had accomplished. They really were just having a 'good' time.

And all I could do was stand there suffering, seeing her crushed body and watching as they drove away. I can't remember how old I was, what the make or model of that convertible was, the license plate number, or what color the car itself was although I do remember that the convertible top was down and that was white. As were the three boys who drove on the wrong side of the road, just to run over and kill a small dog in front of a young boy and then drive away laughing about it.

That I do remember and, in writing about it, I relive the pain of that loss - the terror of watching as someone I loved die needlessly. I remember the rage I felt because I couldn't protect her. And I relive it inside myself every single day. Maybe with everything that has happened in my life, all the rage and fear, and anger I've felt came from being dropped on my head as a nine-month-old baby. But witnessing what to my mind was the murder of someone I loved is one of the greatest hurts I can recall and honestly don't want to keep experiencing even as I write about it.

I'll try this way.

Imagine if you can and will:

A four-year-old boy, playing in the limited front yard of a three-story, four-home duplex in St. Louis. With him is his family dog, a young cocker spaniel female, brown and white, with long floppy ears that flap in the wind as she runs after the sticks he throws and her entire body wags when she returns it to him, waiting for him to throw the stick again.

Their play and pleasure interrupted only when loud cars, with mufflers that were made to make the cars sound more powerful than they really were, or playing music so loudly that the pup would take notice and stop her play just long enough to bark ferociously as if she were guarding both her home and her boy from all intruders.

Then imagine that up their street came a car, big, loud, a convertible top that was white but down so that the occupants, three teenage boys, listening to some country western song on the car's radio at max volume came cruising past their yard. The pup, being brave would bark so loudly and ferociously that she would step off the curb and barely into the street, challenging this noisy monster to battle in her efforts to protect what was hers to defend.

On the opposite side of the street, going in the other direction from where traffic was meant to flow, the occupants of the vehicle came to notice their diminutive challenger over the music blaring from their car's stereo.

They came to swerve, crossing to the wrong side of the road and going in the opposite direction to hit, run over, and instantly kill the small dog, laughing every moment and driving away still laughing ...

leaving the crushed body of a puppy and the broken soul of a small boy.

Is it any wonder that I grew to hate country music and that it took me years of recovery to realize that it wasn't the fault of the music that brought that sorrow into my existence? And it wasn't even the fault of the teenagers that drove away laughing as if they had done something fantastically amusing.

It was the way of humanity – to view them, the world at large, and animals as less worthy than human beings – that brought about an end to someone that loved unconditionally. And to this day, that boy inside still hurts, still cries, and nearly rages at the injustice of it all.

The world doesn't have to be this way, but until all of humanity chooses not to act against itself, these things will happen. And young boys will cry needlessly, powerless to change what is.

Compleat

Back to The Beginning
_._._._._._._._._._._._._._._._._._.._

I've mentioned a girl several times so far and I'm not sure I have the right to speak of her now, but to know the truth of who I am I am forced to mention her here and by name. To do any less would be hiding from the person for whom I was willing to sacrifice all that I could have been, to protect her from who I saw myself as becoming.

In 1972 I was in love with a girl named Megan Abby (nee) Kaiser. And yes, we were both young, I was sixteen and she was even younger, by four years almost. This story doesn't address that, it just relates why I feel the way I do now and did then and what choices I made that led to my complete insanity.

We became a couple because my older brother had dumped her, for whatever reason he chose, and her younger sister – who I had been trying to be a 'boyfriend' with since everyone else in the neighborhood seemed to have one – had rejected me for being too overtly interested in being sexual for her tastes.

Megan and I were sitting in her parent's basement, both angry and I guess one could say, smarting from having just been 'dumped' and as the resentful, childish boy I was I thought to ask her, "Know anyone that could use a slightly used boyfriend?" Somehow that made sense to her as well and we agreed that 'paying them back' would be our version of justice toward both of our respective siblings. So, we started playing the part of being boyfriend and girlfriend to one another.

Compleat

We rode bikes together, walked hand in hand in front of them both at every opportunity, and kissed and cuddled with one another whenever either of them was around to witness what we were doing. And along the way, through all that playacting and spitefulness, I believe we fell in love, I know for a fact that for me it was the first time ever.

We were as physically intimate as we could be, with her parents being very devout Catholics - and mine being more than a little insane on the subject of sex. It seemed we never really had any time to be alone together or we might have done more than we did, but through what we did do actually get around to doing, I'd suggest that we learned what love combined with physical attraction can cause in the developing bodies of two young lovers. Although we never engaged in intercourse, never had or shared oral sex with one another, we learned, through kiss and touch and holding one another, about one another and our bodies and hearts all at the same time.

In the years leading up to us becoming what we were, my life experiences were less than favorable to having a relationship with a young lady, for such is what I viewed her as, the love of my life, a lady to be protected, cared for, provided for and loved until the end of time. I even wrote in my eighth-grade graduation book (not even sure anyone remembers those from that time) that I'd rather be damned to hell for all eternity than not love her for even a moment's time. Having suffered physical, mental, emotional, and sexual abuse, I had developed rage and self- defense mechanisms in order to protect myself pro-actively.

But then, one day, reality came into play in our lives. Her father, who already didn't like me because of our age differences, witnessed one of my outbursts of rage. This one was directed at my parents and my older brother, and I was using language and threats of violence beyond anything he had ever witnessed in grown men, let alone a boy my age at the time.

The result of his witnessing it was him telling me that I would never be allowed to see Megan again, and I knew he was telling me the truth, both in that he could prevent my seeing her and in the fact that my rage, directed outwardly toward those who I considered my 'tormentors', was actually an expression of the hatred I held for myself and had no place in her life. While I couldn't resist being around her, sneaking every chance I could just to sit and talk with her, I knew then that it couldn't last and wouldn't ever be allowed to happen for either of us.

Compleat

I had an awakening that day, not spiritually or in a healthy way, but still, I became aware that my learned and self-destructive nature had no place being around her. Ever. And so, I consciously devised a plan to prevent my insanity from ever having a chance of her being subjected to it by being in close proximity to me.

I decided to quit high school at the end of my sophomore year, honestly telling my parents and the school counselor that I was bored with school. I explained to them the part of my plan that I knew would be acceptable in that period of time. I intended to join the Marine Corps and go to Viet Nam to 'fight for my country.'.

And they bought the lie, my mother even stating, as her brother, Caden, had told her, that the Marines would "make a man out of me." The joining the Marines part was enough of the truth that they didn't see past it to the lie behind it. I could have cared less about my 'country' at the time. My uncle had come back from Viet Nam, shot up and carrying a piece of a friend's skull embedded in his own -, put there by a mine blast from something called a 'Bouncing Betty' in the jargon of that war and my family saw him as a hero.

My real reason for wanting to go? I wanted to go to Viet Nam, to vent all the rage I held inside on to towards other people by killing as many human beings (we called them gooks around my house back then) and hopefully to die myself somewhere in the process. What better way to leave and be forgotten than as an 'American' hero who died serving his country, was the thinking of my sick, by then seventeen-year-old, mind.

The best- laid plans of seventeen-year-old boys don't often come to fruition and the same could be said of my plan. Basic training for the Marines was a joke to me. I went through it with a smile on my face the entire time, to the point that the drill instructors thought I was mentally disabled or 'stupid' as they liked to put it. While there I witnessed an overweight boy, who may have wanted to be there for the right reasons, kicked worse than we would a dog that had stolen a ham off the table. He was then, shouted at and called a pig, and told to crawl like the 'pig' he was – all the while crying his heart out because he was being kicked out and made to feel as if he would never measure up to their 'standards'.' And still, I smiled and slid through it all without even needing to put forth the minimum effort they supposedly required of anyone who joined and wanted to be a Marine. In short, I never even broke a sweat. I realized that I would never be a "Marine." And going to Viet Nam was a waste of time.

Yet, it was while I was in basic that the second stage of my plan developed into the next solid step toward ending my relationship with Megan. It actually even helped that I came down with pneumonia the last two weeks of basic. I was able to write and tell Megan I wouldn't be coming home at the time we had expected. And then, I contacted another girl, who had expressed an interest in me in high school and let her know I was actually coming home at the 'proposed' time and asked her to be my date that night.

Can you think of a better night to play- act at being a Marine and a boyfriend, at the same time, than the night I finally arrived home from basic training? Halloween night, October 31st, 1973. Dressed in full green uniform, with polished shoes and a framed hat, I showed up at the other girl's doorstep, and she threw herself into my arms. I didn't have a car at the time, so my step-dad and my mom agreed to drive us to dinner and drop us at a movie theater of my choosing. But, before I could let them do that, I just "had" to go by our house to 'drop off' my duffel bag and gear, rather than leave it in their trunk, I even used the excuse that all I had on me were American Express Travelers Checks to spend.

Megan lived two houses over from ours, with her younger sister and parents. I had barely gotten out of the car when her sister spotted me from where she had been down the street from both our houses and ran to tell Megan I was home. I had just seated myself back into the car, next to my 'date', when Megan came out of her house running to meet me. And saw me sitting with another girl on what should have been my perfect night with her!

Her scream of "YOU MOTHERFUCKER" still echoes in my head today. And honestly, it has every single day since then, no matter where I've gone, what I've done, what I've used in the way of drugs, sex, violence, money, or relationships to try to drown it out – her words, the pain and anger she felt, the hatred I felt for myself … all of it still echoes inside me to this day.

Some folks, including several shrinks I've had over the years, tell me that I should either be ashamed of myself for doing that to someone who loved me or insists that I acted in that manner as an immature boy and that I should let it go now that I am a man. Shame (my definition as I see it now) is self-destructive, self-pity. It serves no purpose except to play- act at being sorry for something I have actually done, when the truth is I would only be sorry for being caught. Think about that for a minute, if you dare. How better to avoid punishment than punishing yourself in such a way and to the point that those around you become uncomfortable with the pain and look away?

Years later, I learned to separate two words that most people use interchangeably. Shame no longer means guilt for me. Guilt I have come to define as legitimate remorse, a pain so severe that it cannot be avoided and can only be embraced.

Why would any semi-sane person embrace pain? I do it in order to use the pain as motivation and a reminder of an action that I never want to repeat again, to find the strength to resist any temptation to 'slip up', fall back, or off, any imaginary 'wagon'. It is a willingness to do whatever it takes, even carrying the burdens of my responsibilities and the pain thereof, to prevent a repetition of those same behaviors.

In the movie named for the character of that name, Bagger Vance told Captain Junah that it was "time to come out of the darkness and into the light". I loved that idea and agreed with it for others. It wasn't until someone told me that I didn't have to live in the darkness myself that I realized it applied to me as well. I may never forget what I did, although it was my hope that Megan had long forgotten me, and gone on to have a full and happy life. But I stopped beating myself up over it.

Accepting responsibility for my actions was the first part or step. Making the choice to never repeat the behavior followed almost without an effort of any kind on my part. But the decision to stop beating myself up came at a cost. I live now by certain values I have adopted for myself. Putting those values into practice through actions I choose to make on a daily basis. Or not take as the situation may call for or demands. I don't impose or expect anyone else to ever adopt or even understand my choice in this, but it is the only manner in which I can make a living amends to the love I threw away so long ago.

I know where she is, but I don't pretend to myself that the girl I knew is still there. She is alive and she will have grown up, has a family of her own, and hopefully a full and happy life; if all the prayers I've sent up to what who I view as being god on her behalf, she must have. But deep within my heart, I know that for myself, I will actually never be able to love another the way I love her.

So, although I often times flirt, joke, smile, and share a smile wherever and whenever I can with everyone I meet, I cannot love another. Catholics would call it penance for my past indiscretions. Other religions would call it sin and the wages there of. And some more forgiving individuals might even dismiss it as a part of the insanity I grew up with both environmentally and socially, or the immature thinking of a seventeen-year-old boy. Those who are less kind might accuse me of being manipulative or fake.

I see myself only as being who I really am. And I do see god in every person, and action and event in the world and lives of everyone around me. I choose to see god in you. I choose to see god in myself. I AM that I Am.

So, for a quick draft and my fastest typing, here is the story of my heart and where it is, was, and ever shall be. Until the end of the world. I know the forest they speak of in the movie. I never went there, just like I never went in-country to Viet Nam and for the exact same reason. I knew that if I went there, I would never come out again.

The movie - Bagger Vance - was wonderful, by the way. The ending was perfect. And I believe it 'could' happen for anyone who allowed it to, in their lives. I don't know if it will for myself, honestly.

Compleat

A Childhood of Sexual Misconduct
—·—·—·—·—·—·—·—·—·—·—·—·—·—·—··

Everyone has memories that will replay in their minds, unbeckoned and certainly unwanted, and I often find myself imagining that, like many others, I find myself wishing that these memories would fade forever and be forgotten.

My The first such memory that did and does this to me is from this same age period of my childhood. I was still only three years old, my mom had by then divorced my biological father for his having sex with his brother's wife. This caused what today's society is labeled a 'two household' family situation. My older sister, older brother, and I lived with our mom and a series of step dads. But we were allowed, in the summers, to visit and stay with our biological father for a couple of weeks. My memory extends back to this period because it was an awakening for me, not just of my ability to read, but of what doctor's would describe to me years later, as an adult, of as being the beginning of my obsessive- compulsive behavior in regards to sexual misconduct.

Compleat

One of my cousin's and, by then, half-sister from my biological father's marriage to her mom, my aunt Louise, was also only three years of age at the time. We enjoyed walking and playing together, perhaps due to our ages and perhaps because the 'older' children tended to ignore us as being that we were the babies? I only remember the incident and not the particulars of why it happened this way.

She and I were walking hand in hand, apart from the rest of the children. Why the idea came to us, who initiated it, and why it seemed right to us both at that time I couldn't explain. What I can say is that we both decided to take off all our clothes so that I could lay on top of her and rub my tiny penis against her equally immature mons pubis. We laughed and it felt good, so we had no inkling of any wrongdoing in what we were doing. Obviously being too young to 'achieve' anything except good feelings, we only stopped after we heard her older sister calling to her, trying to find the two of us.

We dressed and walked hand in hand back toward their house, smiling and happy. When her sister did find us on our way back, she asked us where we had been and what we had been doing. Therapists could learn from that line of questioning when helping to discover if children have been subjected to or experienced sexual abuse, trauma, or inappropriate behaviors with others.

Because at three years of age, we had no fear of taking her back to the exact place where we had been and showing her exactly what we had been doing.

Naked, with me on top of her again, happily displaying what we had discovered as a fun thing to do with one another my cousin and I were frightened only when her sister said the terror- inspiring words "I'm telling mom."

As she ran back toward their house, while we once again got dressed, terror grew for both of us. And while we walked near one another toward their house this time we didn't hold hands or interact. Where once we had been smiling, happily enjoying our newfound discovery of one another, now only fear showed on either of our faces.

Being 'told on' was only used in advance of being punished for doing something 'wrong.' We had no idea what we had done that was wrong. Only that inevitably punishment would be seeking us out for whatever it had been. And with my family being as it was, that trepidation would prove to be just the tip of a very large iceberg.

Compleat

When we arrived at their house, my aunt/step mother separated us, placing us in completely different rooms of the house. When my biological father arrived home from work, however, that situation changed in an instant. Dragged into the same room, stripped to total nakedness again we would, both of us, receive beatings so vicious and savage that the belt that was used left not just bruises and welts, but blood leaking from the stripes across our asses, legs, and lower backs.

Then we were placed naked and bleeding upon wicker- bottomed child chairs, in on opposite sides of the room and forced to be facing into our individual corners, where we were told to keep our noses, or we would receive yet another beating.

I mention the wicker bottoms of those chairs for this reason: blood, when touching wicker, will dry and stick, as it did for us both. That adherence would result in any movement causing the wounds to reopen and increase the pain that we were experiencing already.

My cousin/sister had no problem complying with our father's command. Her fear of my father and the beating we had just received more than justified her obedience and compliance. She kept her nose in her corner the entire time we were forced to sit there, never once moving, other than the natural shaking that occurs when crying from being a child that had just received a severe beating.

I, however, found that I could not sit still, obey or even attempt to comply. At every opportunity, when the adults of that household weren't in the room, and the chance of any of the other children noticing me looking grew even slightly less, I would strain my neck and lift myself up partially in an attempt to see her nakedness again.

As an adult, I often wonder to myself, where does a three-year-old boy learn to lay atop his female counterpart? I have no real memories to help me discover that information. But what I do know now is that the obsession to look at the naked form of a female I care about awoke within me that day. If the punishment that was inflicted upon us was meant to deter that behavior in some way, or the behavior of being sexually inappropriate, as the doctors would define it to me years later, it was only successful in her case. It's effect upon me could have been no more completely opposite if that was its intent.

I would be sent home, with my mom and one of my step dads at that time, and I would not see that cousin/sister again until we were both in our teens. And while I would never forget the incident, not for the beatings as much as for the wanting to look at her nakedness again, when we did meet years later, she had not only forgotten the incident; she didn't want to be reminded of it.

I must confess, I tried to remind her and initiate another encounter with her, which she rejected outright. And later I would attempt to initiate sexual contact with the very sister that 'told' on us the first time as well. That ended in disaster, with all the other juveniles in the family confronting me as a deviant, although a few years later I almost succeeded in getting the second cousin/sister to kiss me at least.

The connection shared by two small children had been beaten out of her. And in all honestly, I cannot fault her for that. What we experienced that day wasn't a healthy reaction to the natural curiosity of two small children experiencing their first ever physical / sexual contact with a member of the opposite sex. Morals, values, and societal standards have nothing to do with the natural order of humanity. The results were to force her into compliance with the order of the acceptable world around her. And catastrophic in creating a greater break in my thought processes than even having been dropped on my head had created when I was younger. This experience was when the first 'crack' in what I view as my broken brain occurred.

The second shattering of my sexual identity and leading to my own sexual misconduct I made slight mention of before in regards to my sister Belinda. That same twin bed frame would hold the mattress upon which she and my brother David would be caught by our step-sister Carey Morris doing something sexual. Whether actually achieving sexual intercourse by that age I never discovered, since they were both older than myself and had spent more time with one another than I had due to my escape from the life I was existing into books. What I did realize is that Carey also said the most feared words in that household: "I'm telling."

David and Belinda both received one of the most vicious, prolonged, and bloody beatings ever administered in that house. While they were beaten on the second floor and I was hiding in my bed on the third floor I can recall their screams but was most impacted by the screams of pain brought forth from by my sister Belinda.

Both my step-father, Anthony Morris, and my mom took turns beating them both but my mom seemed to prolong the experience for Belinda, hitting her harder and more frequently, pausing only to catch her breath and then returning to administering what can only be described as a savage beating.

Compleat

Remember my observation of my own experience with being beaten at three years of age for sexual misconduct? The results for them were probably meant to be appropriate, a sudden and complete reversal of any thoughts toward exploring the aspects of sexual conduct with another member of our family. Maybe with Belinda that held true. With David, however, I would learn later that he was additionally sexually abused/used by our older step-brother Anthony Morris, Jr. and would participate in sexually inappropriate conduct with both our younger sister Violet and younger half-brother Abraham and others.

With Violet, it would start with our both "rolling" her underwear down while she was sleeping to look at her then developing pubic hair and masturbating over her sleeping form. With Abraham, it would include sexually abusing him and a girl named Shania Laurence, who was about the same age as Abraham, that our mom was supposed to be babysitting, by getting them both to suck our penis' and licking her whenever we could get them alone in our shared bedroom.

Eventually, I caught Violet allowing David to 'play' with her pussy, on her bed in the room next to ours. I would become extremely jealous of them, playing at something that I could hear more than see but not be allowed or invited to participate in because I was supposedly sleeping. Jealous, and angry to the point that the next morning, as Violet walked past me in her underwear I reached out and grabbed her pussy through them.

Apparently shocked by my behavior, she threatened to 'tell' on me, within David's hearing. He came into the room and threatened to beat me up for what I had said and done. Yet those threats held no fear for me because by that time I had developed into my mom's favorite. I knew she wouldn't believe them and said so, asking them who they thought she would believe: Me or David who had already been beaten for sexual misconduct with Belinda and Violet - who was walking around in nothing but bikini panties and bra?!

As an aside, when my brother had sat up from laying at the foot of her bed to look and be 'sure' that I wasn't awake, at her insistence, I was positive of what was going on even though I was unable to see her nakedness or exposed pussy.

They both immediately quit denying what they had done and I knew that it wouldn't ever be mentioned again because of two facts: the first was actually being my mom's favorite by then, with her thinking I was going to become a priest in the Catholic Church it assured my status as favorite and that they had actually been doing what it had seemed like as I lay there and watched and listened.

With Abraham and Shania it was similar to the pantie rolling we had done together with Violet. Shania and Abraham were both too young to know what was being done to them and we assumed they wouldn't mention it to anyone if we had them promise not to tell on us and didn't physically hurt them. While still children ourselves, we molested both those younger children freely. My mom, their baby sitter, and mother, was always busy somewhere else in the house; usually with either our last step-father Anthony Morris or with her boyfriend of long- standing, Aiden Addis, in the upstairs bedroom.

I cannot recall how many times I came home from school, both at the Ohio street address and the new house on Minnesota avenue, where my mother would come either out from or down from her bedroom getting redressed, and Aiden Addis, my step-father's best friend, getting his clothes back on as well. I grew to know that my mother was both a slut and a whore, as my aunt, Melanie, had called her for years, but never said anything to anyone about it.

Shania was our primary target for sexual misuse. A naked pussy, without even peach fuzz for hair, she offered no resistance and often seemed to enjoy being licked there. We would take turns on her and whoever wasn't able to lick her would have Abraham suck his penis while watching the other, until it was our 'turn' to switch places. This went on for approximately a year, until Debby Laurence, who had been having sexual intercourse with David by that time was told by Shania what we had been doing. She grew enraged, that her daughter was being molested by both of us and confronted our parents. While we both denied doing anything to her or Abraham, my mom only believed that I couldn't have / wouldn't have done such a thing.

Why David denied that I had, even after he was beaten into confessing that he had, remains a mystery to me. Maybe in his own way, he was protecting me, in spite of the obvious guilt we shared. Maybe he saw it as a way of avoiding watching me get beaten in the same manner as he would for what we had both done?! He never changed his story, or 'told' on me, and years later I can only imagine that he might have shared in my distrust and disgust with the adults in our lives. My belief is that he might not have told just out of spite for them, as if my getting away with it at least somehow spit their beatings back into their faces as a revenge against our parents and Diana Love?)

Compleat

Spare the Child & Spoil the Rod
_._._._._._._._._._._._._._._._._..

There are families, at least I've heard that there are, where good grades in school are rewarded. Getting an A in subjects like Math, History, English, Science and the rest would gain some good child treats like money, trips to amusement parks, visits to the zoo, and so on. I hear tell that those were great motivators for getting children to excel at their schoolwork.

Yet for all that I've heard about the rewards for good grades, I've never seen a single one in the household I grew up in. My grades were merely average – more C's and C+'s than any A's or B's. I credit the fact that I never turned in any 'homework' for maintaining such a poor grade point average throughout my educational experiences. With grade school, I was simply bored to the point that ignoring the assignments was a means of gaining some attention from the teachers involved. By middle school, I had given up any thought of ever achieving grades that would satisfy my parents and only attended Catholic school for my eighth grade because I wanted to be close to my girlfriend who attended that school. I find it ironic that I was challenged enough in a parochial school that I actually did the work and gained As in some of the subjects. I was especially shocked that I received not just an A but a personalized notice from the school principal for my work in the area of religion.

Compleat

Although my mother seemed to think I was destined to be a priest or some important member of the religion she had adopted because of my improved grades there I still didn't receive any perks or rewards for the academic achievements I acquired there, other than not receiving the beatings that poor grades (D's & F's) would manifest when report cards were sent home for parental review. And I did receive more than a few of those grades as well. My brother David and I were subject to beatings for each F that was brought home, as if our parents believed that by beating us, they would improve our attitudes toward learning. For David perhaps this might have produced the results they were trying to obtain. Only perhaps though, because I don't remember his grades improving any more than my own with the exception of the grades I obtained in parochial school.

I think back on the beatings we received and try to wonder if our parents were raised to think that to 'spare the rod, they would spoil the child.' And I could almost admit that they were trying to do the whole parenting thing to the best of their ability if that's what they were taught and were practicing. But there was a problem with giving them that kind of credit. It came as a result of my sister Belinda receiving beatings just as severe and prolonged as we did, while she was an honor student in every class she attended. Belinda got straight As in every class and always did any extra credit work to be placed on the honor roll from by every one of her teachers throughout grade school and high school. In fact, she had so many academic credits from all her classes that she was set to graduate high school, as the valedictorian of her class in her junior year. Belinda was on her way toward getting away from our family, graduating high school, engaged to a guy named Andy who was, of all things, training to be a mortician, and was the focus of our mother's anger, frustration, and those prolonged beatings because she was escaping the abuse at home.

Belinda was the only member of the family I grew up with that I believed loved me, was smarter than I was and I trusted with who I really was inside.

Compleat

River
_..

The water whispers, as the music plays.

And all I want is gone

Hope is lost in an illusion called time,

that caught me all unaware.

The beautiful lie has long since passed,

into memory for some.

And I sit beside the whispering water,

alone as I've always been.

Listening - waiting - begging for an end,

that will never - ever - come.

Compleat

A Secret Fear of Horses
— . — . — . — . — . — . — . — . — . — . — . — . — . — . — . —

Step forward with me, please, through that illusion we call time and you will find my five-year-old self visiting my paternal grandmother, with my mom and my current (last) step dad, on her farm near Lebanon, MO. Grandma Sue (Susan - nee Runner - Davids) was a wonderfully self-disciplined woman whose first rule of her household was: "Animals get fed first, after that the children, everyone else can wait until those are done."

This crotchety, stern woman, whose age I would never have guessed, would teach me to play card games (canasta anyone?), and together we would whip anyone who dared to play against our team. I would listen, as we played, to her stories, her values, and most of all to her appraisal of her surroundings. She worked the farm she owned with her second husband, (Harry Davids), until he died and held a full- time job in the local community as a stave maker in a local barrel factory until she was placed in an old folks' home at the age of 93. (I believe it was being placed there that had more to do with her dying at 95 than her age.) Tough as nails and better to be around as a person than many in my life, she reminded me of the cream on top of the fresh milk from her cows, always rising above and with a little sweetness, a great treat to share.

This memory sounds wonderful, and it is a very good one that I cling to from that age of my life. Great childhood memories being in such short supply for me, I need to share that this one couldn't even be burned out with drug abuse and insanity, not even by accident.

But this story is also about the period of my age, not this wonderful lady. I only wish I had more like it to share. For it would be on Grandma Sam's farm that I would learn another truth about how I wasn't like any other member of my blood family again, this time in a major and ironically different way.

With my last name being Runner, many people ask if the name is of Native American or 'Indian' origin. I will admit to them and you here that I was told it was, for years, but have never had any established proof thereof because the Cherokee tribe only recognizes those who are descended from the Dawes Rolls of tribal descent, not the Miller or other rolls that also claim blood relativity.

Compleat

However, as is true with all the rest of my blood relatives, the love of horses – which is said to be shared by most Native Americans I have ever heard about - runs strong through me, for I love seeing horses running freely, even on a ranch, with any chance opportunity I might get. They are, beyond doubt, one of the most beautiful creatures on this planet.

Unlike my family and any of the Native American's I've ever read, heard, or been told about, however, I am terrified of horses. It is an unreasoning fear, overwhelming me when I am in their presence at in every instance where I have ever been around them. And while I do know how to ride a horse and also know what to do and not to do (don't go up to a horse from behind!) I only learned these things by forcing myself to learn them in my efforts to spite and overcome that fear that was instilled in me and remains with me, yet to this day I have never found a way to release or remove it completely.

I do remember that my grandma Sue owned a horse she called Penny. Copper in color being the source of her name I assume, that horse stood 14 hands high at the shoulder. She was beautiful, not just in her appearance, but because she had attitude, personality, and colorful behaviors as well.

For example, she could and would, given the opportunity, bite into an open can of beer then tilt her head up and back and drink it all in one shot, often placing the can back exactly where she had found it.

I cannot recall, to this day, how many times my grandfather Harry would either offer her a can of beer, or she would steal his when he wasn't watching closely; leaving him to wonder how he had finished it so quickly. She was smart, clever, and resourceful enough to get away with stealing his beer without his noticing and I enjoyed watching her bamboozle him.

A less amusing, and for me highly frightening trait Penny had was biting through a Styrofoam ice chest, digging through it past loaves of store-bought bread and vegetables to reach and eat a whole, cooked ham. I had read about horses extensively because I marveled at their beauty then and still do now. But nowhere had I read that horses were carnivorous. Or even omnivorous.

That Penny would eat meat was a shock to a five-year-old boy. Perhaps that was one of the sources of the fear that was born in me of horses. Then again it might have been born the day my 'family' was having a barbecue / rodeo type event. With over a hundred adults there that day, Penny the large, dangerous, and beautiful creature walked past everyone in that crowd, directly up to five-year-old me, and placed her left front hoof upon my right foot.

Compleat

It didn't hurt me or create pain in any way, almost as if she was being gentle with me. But she also wouldn't move it or let my foot out from under it. Nearly one hundred drunken adults were there that day and watched as I struggled, strained, complained, eventually cussing at this huge animal and merely stood by when they saw as I burst into tears and began crying out for help.

What I received in answer to my pleas was their finding my situation to be of even greater amusement and a fresh source of their laughter. What great fun that the horse wouldn't let the little guy go. How funny he was crying about a horse. "Here, Penny, have a beer!"

I stood there screaming and crying for help until my voice faded, going 'horse' myself, to the amusement of the crowd of my 'family.' When someone finally decided the fun had gotten boring enough, they tried to move Penny's hoof from atop my foot. It would take three men, not small in their physical statures or strengths to finally move her enough before I could flee.

So, yes, although I love horses, please don't ask me to go around them unless I must. They frighten me more than any other animal on this planet save only to the human kind of animal. I am not a horse whisperer, obviously, and I have to assume I'm not Native American enough to communicate with a horse's spirit to understand the reason why of she picked me that day. I only know that I have only the one regret: that an animal whose breed of creature I find so amazingly beautiful holds only terror for me when I am in their presence.

Compleat

Haunting The Library

I know that it was before I was in 3rd third Grade, I remember that because it was before I was put into 'special education' in 4th fourth Grade for not turning in any homework for my entire 3rd third Grade experience. I was given/put into my first pair of glasses that year as well, so it was probably the summer between 3rd third grade and 4th fourth grade. What strikes me as the most memorable was that I always wished I had one of those red wagons that kids would use to fly down hills and crash into trees, because carrying books home from the public library was tough. I remember carrying a stack of books, some not really thick or I probably wouldn't have made it home with them but a few, as I read more and more, gained in both volume and weight. The stories I read were offbeat science fiction and fantasy, things like Doc Savage, Edgar Rice Burroughs: Tarzan, Conan the Barbarian, and the like, but there were the classics as well: Tom Sawyer and Huckleberry Finn and anything by Mark Twain, Edgar Allen Poe, H.P. Lovecraft, Louis L' Amour, Robert Heinlein, Isaac Asimov, Ray Bradbury, L. Sprague de Camp, and later on Greg Bear, Marion Z. Bradley, Keith Laumer, Christopher Stasheff … the list goes on and on and I had read them as if they were the water that would quench my thirst for escape and knowledge of those things I didn't understand about the world around me that made absolutely no sense.

Compleat

I remember the librarians at the Carpenter Branch Library in St. Louis asking me, this small, skinny boy, with 15 books in his arms checking out with his own library card instead of one with his parents' name on it, if "Are you sure you can read that many books in just two weeks, sweetie? After all, you must return them or there will be a late fee for every book you don't return by then." I used to laugh and tell them the truth, I'd probably be done with that many books in a week, and would be back for more. Sometimes, I'd read all of them in a couple of days, skimming over the ones I'd read already or skipping the ones that I would read just so far and found to be boring, but always returning to find more and more books to read. I even read Nancy Drew and the Hardy Boys books, though I found those to be really boring, compared to Encyclopedia Brown's adventures. One book I remember especially from those days had a story about a kid (relatable to me because he was skinny, with underdeveloped upper body muscles) who did a good deed for a house guest of his mom and was given an ointment that allowed him to sprout wings and fly. That one held my attention for a lot of years because it was a wish I had held for as long as I could remember, that somehow, someway I would be able to fly and develop upper body strength doing something I truly loved. In the story, the boy did just that, even though the ointment ran out. I never did, and regretted that most of all when it came to reading stories that offered hope and a vision of how things might have been – if only.

I read so many books, every week that summer and during the school years that followed that the librarians allowed me to not just check out books from the 'children's' section of the library but I was allowed to enter the adult area and look for books there to read. I found all the mythology books that led to my discovery of the Olympians of Greek and Roman mythology, Aesir of Norse mythology, Egyptian mythology, and a ton of others, including the Christian mythology that was the 'Holy Bible.' With all that mythology I also found playwrights like Shakespeare, poets like Elliot, and philosophy like Confucius and the Buddha.

I have to imagine, though I can guess, that the librarians thought those books were all beyond my understanding because they would all ask if I was 'sure' I wanted to check out those books. "After all, there weren't any pictures in them." But I would read them the way some folk drink alcohol or do drugs, because I had to be reading or I felt that the entire world was falling apart around me and that it was my fault it wasn't coming together.

{{I had taught myself to read by reading comic books, so heroes were real to me, something that could be obtained, to be striven for, and could 'fix' all the problems of my world. If, for example, I was as strong as the Hulk or Hercules I could stop people from hurting one another (or me) but wouldn't use my strength to hurt others. I spent a lot of time fantasizing about that one.}}

In reading Freud, I found that he spoke of psychological problems relating to early childhood trauma, but I honestly couldn't see that I had experienced anything like that myself. Everyone around me had told me I was dropped on my head at 9 months old, but I didn't really count that as a 'trauma' that could affect my thinking, so I pretty much dismissed his stuff, except the sex stuff – I found that a little interesting since I had experienced a lot of incestuous stuff.

I cannot remember who it was that suggested it, and it may have been either an imagined memory or simply a piece of paper hung on the wall in the children's section of the Carpenter Branch of the library but I do remember (sort of) seeing an award for having read over 2,000 books in that section of the library with my name on it, hanging there. It was probably the only achievement I had ever accomplished that my parents didn't even know about that and I had some slight self-esteem for having done something that had gotten noticed by adults in my life. If it was real, I can only suggest that it was one of the elderly librarians in that children's section that made note of my reading and put that notice up for whatever reason they might have, even if it was just to encourage other kids to read.

I just remember that it was the one piece of my past that I had some form of self-esteem about. And I was the ghost that haunted that library, the skinny, little kid that would show up over and over again, checking out the same books frequently and always seeking more to read and use as my one tool to escape the life I was living.

Compleat
Fourth Grade &

2001: A Space Odyssey

In third Grade, it was determined that I needed glasses because I couldn't see the blackboard where the teacher would write the homework assignments. This seems ridiculous now since I never wanted or even tried to do any of the homework assignments that I was given all throughout my public-school experience.

But there was a period where when I did the assignments. After nearly 'failing' third Grade and because I never seemed to be able to turn in any of my homework assignments, I was considered to possibly need Special Education, and that perhaps my 'problem' had to do with a mental deficiency beyond my need for eyeglasses.

This was the only year that I was to attend summer school (between third Grade and fourth Grade) and I experienced arts and crafts, archery, camping, and had fun in a school setting. The kids there were a lot like I was, not interested in studying so much as just having a good time. I remember making a ceramic ashtray with small tiles that were square and blue/white in color. Since my parents both smoked it seemed to be a fun thing to make for them.

My friend, Derick Johnson, attended that class with me and we would slip away from the school and go across the street, where there was a graveyard. Hiding out in the mausoleums and walking around in the graveyard until the public buses would come to take us to our different areas of St. Louis. I mention the smoking part because we were smoking cigarettes (and grass) by then, both Derick and I. And since both my parents smoked cigarettes, I was more likely to be able to swipe a few smokes from each of them for us.

When the school year started, I was given a season's bus pass for public bus service so I could travel to the far side of St. Louis from my home on the South side of Ohio Street. I remember riding the bus and instead of keeping my seat as the drivers would all encourage, I'd try to stand up while the bus was moving, surfing the bumps and turns without holding on to the railings or seat backs.

And the bus always let me off, at the closest stop to the school where the special ed classes were held during my fourth Grade, almost exactly in front of a bakery that made the best French Horns or Crème Horns that I can ever remember having eaten. To this day, I cannot find one bakery that makes them so that the sugar isn't grainy and too sweet, but that one bakery made them sweet and creamy, with a pastry curl that was so flaky it would melt in my mouth without needing to be chewed.

As I said, I was sent to special education because my apparent inability to do homework had caused the public school system to assume I was retarded in my cognitive abilities. Which suited me fine because they had labeled my friend Derick the exact same way, so we were in the same classroom again. His best friend, however, was a hulking kid named Tim who didn't care for me much and who I was frightened of when he would get upset or angry; he reminded me of my older brother David with his potential to be aggressive and a possible fight lurking in the near future.

Class work in fourth Grade was taught by two teachers. Mrs. Dunn - who was a plump, kindly woman who had been a teacher for special education for years I think - and Mr. Sabian - whose presence in the classroom was to be a deterrent if any of the kids in the class got upset or angry to where they might become violent. Which This is ironic when I look back on this year of my life because I realize there were no girls in that class whatsoever. So, in a way, I'm guessing his purpose was more of a monitor of behaviors rather than a teacher, though he was introduced to the class as a teacher at the beginning of the year.

It was Mrs. Dunn who suggested that I be allowed to choose what subjects I would attempt that year, asking only that I would pick one math subject, one science subject, and one English subject from all the schoolbooks that had been provided to the class. She did this with all of the students at the beginning of the year, but paid special attention to the ones I picked out because instead of choosing "See Spot Run" as so many of the others in the class chose, I picked up the twelfth Grade English book because it had Shakespeare's Romeo and Juliet as well as Caesar in it. I would re-read the story of Sleepy Hollow from it and when asked to do a report on the stories I had read, had no problem turning in the homework assignment before leaving for home the day it was assigned. Along with the English subject on a twelfth-grade level, I chose to pick Biology from the same shelf. I liked learning about everything from plants, to animals and even some things about the human anatomy from it. At one time, because Mrs. Dunn asked if I could, I memorized all the names of the bones in the human body from the three pieces of the human skull down to the smallest bones in the littlest toe. For my math 'requirement' I chose the green- covered book on Geometry, even though Mrs. Dunn suggested it might not be easy because I had never taken an Algebra class or even read an Algebra book. But I took it, did the assignments, and never had to take the books out of the school because I was able to finish any homework assignments during the school day.

Which This is where I made my big mistake with the other 'teacher' Mr. Sabian. Mrs. Dunn would hold a reading circle with the other students in the class, having them read aloud with her and each other at different times of the day. Because I had finished all of the assignments that she had given me, and because the homework from the end of the chapters in biology, geometry, and English were was already on her desk, she suggested that I could sit behind the dividers in the room and enjoy reading some of the comic books that were also provided by the school (Archie, Jughead, Casper, Wendy the Witch, Little Huey, and that type) which is something I always enjoyed.

It was while she was doing the reading circle with the other kids in the classroom that Mr. S found me 'apparently' hiding out and reading comic books instead of attending the reading circle. My hair wasn't very long, but it was long enough for this grown man to grab me by my hair, drag me kicking and screaming across the schoolroom and throw me on the ground near the circle of my classmates. I had been screaming and cussing as he dragged me, but once he threw me on to the ground, I flipped out. Mrs. Dunn was trying to chastise him for his behaviors toward me while maintaining control of the other kids in the class so it was just between him and me - I and believe me there was nothing I wouldn't have done to him if I had been presented with a weapon with which to do it. When he tried to reach me, to regain some measure of control over me, all the while being threatened with imminent death by me and hearing language that a 4th fourth grader might not be assumed to have known I fled the building. I ran down 2 flights of stairs and escaped out one of the side doors of the school that we knew the teachers left open for smoking outside. I ran away from the school, and headed to the only place that seemed safe, since my parents would become involved once the language that I had used against a teacher became knowledge to them as well as the behavior I had demonstrated by throwing classroom furniture at him, while avoiding his tackles to try to control me.

Near that school was a pool hall, where Curtis, Tim, and I would go in the mornings before school or when waiting for the buses after school. The owner would allow us to pay to shoot pool, if the tables weren't in use by adults, and always allowed us access to the pinball machines that were our favorite things to waste a nickel on and maybe win a few free games if we scored high enough without tilting the machine.

Compleat

I ran there, and hid out until well after dark, because I didn't want to be found by him but also because I was afraid to go home. The owner finally said he was closing up so I had to take the last bus that would take me home and I left, but if I could have had anywhere else to go or if I could have just stayed there forever, I would have.

In the end, my parents had notified the police that I might be a runaway, so when I did get home there was some drama involved with that but I didn't receive a beating. Apparently, the school had contacted them and told them that it had been a misunderstanding and asked that they let the school know if/when I made it home safely. The next day, I wasn't even considering going back to that school, he showed up at my home. My parents forced me to listen to him apologize and he offered to take Derick and I to the movies to "make it up to me for what he had done."

I didn't trust him, but I jumped at the chance to go to the movies with my friend, Curtis. He took us to a showing of Yellow Submarine (the Beatles were one of my favorite bands still, even though my mom had banned my owning any of their music) and 2001: A Space Odyssey. Derick and I smoked a joint before watching the movies (away from him for obvious reasons) and had a great time. So apparently, as far as the school and that teacher were concerned, there was no hurt/no foul, and all was forgiven.

Of course, when the school year ended, because I had had no problem doing classwork and homework 8 grades above my current level, I was placed back in 'regular' public school for my 5th fifth grade. It's strange to think that my schooling experience peaked in 4th fourth grade, but that too is an Odyssey.

Compleat

gEnIuS
_.._

gen-ius (jĕn'yəs) n., pl. -iuses or `genii (jē'nē-i')(for senses 4,6).

1. a. Exceptional or transcendent intellectual and creative power: *'True genius rearranges old material in a way never seen ... before" (John Hersey)* b. One who possesses such power. 2. a. A natural talent or inclination. Used with to or for: *She has a genius for acting.* b. One who has such talent or inclination: *He is a genius at diplomacy.* 3. The prevailing spirit or character, as of a place, person, time, or group: *the genius of the Elizabethan poets.* 4. Roman Mythology. a. A tutelary deity or guardian spirit allotted to a person from birth. b. Any guiding spirit of a person or place. 5. A person who has great influence over another. 6. Moslem Mythology. *A jinni or demon.* [Latin *genius,* deity of generation and birth, guardian spirit.] *{taken from The American Heritage Dictionary of The English Language; New College Edition: William Morris – Editor; Published by Houghton Mifflin Company ©1981}*

When I was in fourth grade, I was sent to a special education school because I had never turned in any of the homework that had been assigned to me during my third grade in public school. The fact is that the teachers and counselors of the public schools, as well as my parents, thought I was retarded and unable to comprehend the assignments that were given out to the entire class. This, in a way, also shows how little attention my parents paid to my activities since by then I was reading close to 15 books every week or two weeks.

Their inclinations led to my being tested for IQ (intelligence quotient) with said testing revealing to my supposedly having a staggering 140 IQ or being a borderline genius. I've already written about the special education class I attended, where I was allowed to progress at my own pace and not held to a curriculum that found me bored beyond words, but then too there was the stigma of being labeled a 'genius' of sorts because the other students in that class and in the public and private schools I would attend after fourth grade were strangers to me. Not merely because I didn't belong to any of the groups, cliques, or teams that they adhered to throughout their schooling, but because I felt different.

Not simply smarter, though my ego did interfere in my socialization with others, but also alien and out of place because the things they were studying were things I had taught myself much earlier and they were just learning. Ego

Compleat

being what it is and was I saw myself as being able to manipulate their lack of experience and knowledge, forgetting in that process of decision making that there are and were experiences that I had never had, that they were privy to and I had much more to learn in the area of socialization than they needed to learn in or from books.

Compleat

Sal & The Fear

Compleat

Growing up in St. Louis wasn't always the bad thing my memories make it appear to be, and it wasn't the places or the people there that made it difficult for me.

I was more than capable of bringing trouble and a sense of loneliness upon myself, no matter what my intentions were.

Throughout grade school, after attending a special education class for my 4th grade experience, I was even more afraid of the difference I saw between myself and the other kids.

I would read as many as 15 books every two weeks, but was totally inept when it came time to catch a pop fly baseball in center field. I was even more shy and afraid to talk to strangers and everyone seemed strange to me.

By 7th seventh grade, I had grown so frightened and isolated from my classmates that I was sure that none of them liked me and secretly hated them every time they left me out of conversations, team sports or I just imagined that they were laughing at me.

I had a girlfriend, from my neighborhood, by 7th seventh grade and since she attended a Catholic school, I was able to convince my parents to allow me to attend her school. Although it cost a tuition to attend, and I was forced to wear a uniform set of clothes required by the school that they were forced to pay for, my mom thought I would be a great candidate to become a Catholic priest, and convinced my step-dad to pay for it all. How close her desire to what I would eventually become seems almost prophetic, now.

Changing schools after seven years of attending public grade school, I thought I would be leaving behind my reputation for being strange. I found myself hoping to gain popularity, friendship, and respect but I also thought I could use reverse psychology on these parochial school kids, to convince them I was cool, tough and someone they would do well to curry my friendship. I had self-talked myself into thinking things like: 'what could they know about secular life and things that were bad?' They were the "good children", who went to church every day, said their prayers, loved their families, and had a god in their lives.

My mistake, obviously, was thinking I knew anything about them. They were kids, just like the ones in public school. Some were studious, got good grades, and followed the rules. Others, not so much. And others would make public school and it's bullying seem regrettably far away.

Compleat

Although I tried to pretend I was the tough, new kid from public school, they weren't buying the bullshit I was peddling. And I found that I had set myself up as an outsider in a class of about 30 kids. Half would have their homeroom with Sister Midge, the nun from across the hall, the rest attended homeroom with me, in the classroom that was run by Sister Tennille, the principal.

My arrogance and differences would start separating me almost from the very first day and ended up being supplemented by my getting the highest grades I had ever achieved in any schoolroom situation. Worst of all, as if adding injury to my insulting presence and performances, I found myself excelling in the religion class by getting not just an A+ in the class but also impressing Sister Tennille so much that she would ask that one of my essays be read aloud for the rest of the class. I couldn't bring myself to do it, so she asked for volunteers and had someone else read it aloud, in the front of the classroom.

Here was probably the last straw for the guys in my class, including those in the classroom across the hall. I was an arrogant, 114-pound, prick in their world, pretending to know more than they did and then having the 'teachers' they had grown up with appear to favor me because I could say things in ways that they neither understood nor honestly cared about. Is it any wonder that their retaliation began soon afterward?

When taking recess, for example, they would play a game they called 'iron horse'. One kid would hold on to the chain link fence, surrounding the playground, bend over into a shape resembling a bench more than a horse, and the other kids would pile on top of him until he could no longer support the weight. The larger the number of their fellows they could uphold in this manner, the greater their strength was determined to be and the more respect they won from their peers.

When I offered to 'surpass' anyone else's record for holding up under the weight, they allowed me to approach the fence in order to make my attempt. But once I took that position, instead of having others begin to pile on top of me, one of the established insiders chose to run up behind me and deliver a resounding kick to my ass.

> With the group of them laughing, nearly hysterically, I chased that boy around the playground, cussing like the proverbial sailor, and threatening him with physical violence of such magnitude that when one of the girls' dads, a Fireman on duty who happened to stop by the school that day, heard my tirade he apprehended me and marched me to the principal's office. Reporting only what he had veritably observed, I was placed on academic

suspension until I had delivered a note to my parents about this incident and they had assured the principal they were going to "deal" with the issue of my behavior.

In another story in this book, I expounded on the repercussions of drawing the attention of my parents. This time, however, I was able to wheedle my way out of a beating by telling the actual truth. The result was they decided to sign off on the paperwork that had been sent home with me and entirely ignore the complaint about my behavior and language.

It would only be a few days later, while I was still inwardly raging about the indignity that the other boy had visited upon me while I was vulnerable, that the most frightening event of my entire schooling experiences would unfold, in the third - floor hallway of the school, before adult witnesses which would include Sisters Midge & Kate and the principal Sister Tennille.

The hallways in that school were covered in a linoleum- type flooring, and as we were required to wear patent leather shoes as a part of the school uniform it was inevitable that walking on that floor would cause a 'slapping' sound to occur occasionally. Maybe it was the noise, maybe it was my own unpopularity and maybe he suffered from an autism that made him more susceptible to the noise itself. Maybe any or all of those things combined that day.

The action that was taken started out with a boy named Sal telling me to "walk quieter" in the hall. Already being angry, I ignored his command and began to deliberately slap the soles of my shoes against the floor with every step. I know now that I brought his next action upon myself, but at the time I felt justified and empowered by ignoring Sal.

Sal punched me, in the back of my head, with the instantaneous result that my glasses flew forward, off my face, landing several yards in front of me. And if you think that was the frightening event I'm talking about, you are, much to my sorrow, mistaken.

My reaction to his assault was unplanned, just as instantaneous as my glasses rocketing forward off my face, and brutal beyond humanity. I was, as I said, a mere 114 pounds while Sal, being both big- boned and overweight for an eighth grader weighed in at closer to 185 pounds that day. Ask yourself then, how does a skinny kid, with hardly any upper body strength, grab someone nearly half again his own weight with one hand, lift him off the floor by 4 - 5 inches, slamming the back of his head into the concrete wall of the school hall and begin to pound his face with my other hand?

I kept hitting him, over and over again. Compleatly lost in the action I was doing with no regard for my surroundings, no concept of time or of others being present, and existing only to destroy this 'thing' in my hand. It was being struck, again from behind, that broke my focus on Sal. And when I turned it was Sister Tennille who I saw standing closest to me, with a collapsible umbrella in her hand that she obviously must have struck me with in order to free Sal from my attention.

Honestly, I don't remember releasing him or his exit from the scene. Because my focus shifted to this new assailant and I drew back my fist in preparation to punch a nun just as hard as I had been striking Sal.

If you've ever seen fear on the face of someone who "shouldn't" have that look when staring directly into your eyes, then maybe you can relate to how I felt in the following instant. I lowered my hand and, found myself panting for breath. I, felt dizzy and disoriented - as if I was finding myself in one place but only remembered being in another; with no idea of how I had traversed the time and space between those two points.

I knew what I had done, and what I had just threatened to do to Sister Tennille. The memory of the course of events kept playing through my mind like a looped recording. But I felt displaced in a way I still don't know the words to accurately describe, these many years later.

Strangely, there was no mention of a note being sent to my parents after this event. No one even suggested that I face suspension or even expulsion for 'berserk-ing' in the middle of a Catholic grade school hallway. Including, I regret to say, the next day when Sal arrived at school with a blackened raccoon- type mask surrounding both of his eyes, from the middle of his forehead down to mid-cheek. It would be years later that I would learn this blackened raccoon mask is considered to be an outward sign of a traumatic brain injury that is sometimes fatal for those who experience it.

At the time I felt relief that I had stood up for myself, even finding myself reveling in the fact that I had hurt him and hoping that by doing so the others would leave me alone, possibly fearing what I might be capable of doing to them as well. But inwardly I was dealing with the fear I started telling you about when I began this story.

Compleat

I wasn't human when I did what I did to Sal. I was something dark, something nearly impossible to imagine even having read escapist literature since I was 3 years of age. I hadn't wanted to hurt this kid. I had wanted to kill, to destroy him so completely that his existence would have been a thing of fantasy or imagination. I wanted to feel his face bones shatter beneath the blows of my hand, smell the blood as those bones gave way to brain matter, and revel in the warmth of it as I pushed my fist through him, until it would stop, but only upon meeting the wall behind him if even that could stop it.

And with that fear came the conviction that I would become the monster I had unleashed in at that moment. Like I said, fear of beatings, fear of people, fear of a society in which I found myself residing daily; all these and other fears I had learned to cope with and survive. This fear of myself was new, overwhelming me because I knew it was me, a part of my whole. A part of who I AM.

Compleat

A Note to God
—·—·—·—·—·—·—·—·—·—·—·—·—·—·—·—·—·—··

Dear God,

Humanity doesn't listen. They didn't listen to Confucius. They didn't listen to Buddha. They didn't listen to your first begotten son, J. They didn't listen to Mohammed. Fact is they haven't listened once in more years than they can count.

So, pop, I ask you with all the respect and love my heart holds for both them and you:

Why the fuck did you send me back here when you know they aren't going to listen to me? For fuck's sake dude, they don't even hear me when I speak with love for them.

"It doesn't have to be this way."

Compleat Insanity

When an eight-year-old boy becomes convinced that the world around himself is a controlled, staged and a manipulated series of settings, where every scene in the room, from which he is leaving shuts itself down and another in the room he is entering or about to enter becomes active in order to continue the charade of existence, all of humanity would probably agree in saying the boy in question was insane.

Yet I experienced this insanity much in the same manner as others describe experiencing episodes of the phenomenon called déjà vu. Having the intellect to reason through these episodes did nothing to relieve the fear. They provoked me into fleeing because I had already developed a deep and abiding lack of trust. In the adults around me, there was no one with whom I could relate this fear to, or seek comfort and relief from desperation and an impending doom feeling grew to be so overwhelming. I actively began contemplating the means to confront the situation through action. How could an 8 old boy confront the conceptualized world?

Faced by an action that would disrupt the flow of all the scenarios through the confrontation of anyone of the automatons in any of the scenes. I thought I would be forced to use a knife attack on one of the individual robots in one room, slicing it open from its chin down to its groin before allowing myself to enter the next scene.

But if that first person had proved to be human after all, with the experience of that controlled environment, repeating itself, in spite of my action, I would have repeated the behavior until it ceased. This probably would've led to the deaths of my immediate family and consequently other individuals who might have had the misfortune of my having encountered them until I would have eventually been apprehended or simply stopped by any means necessary.

When I state the fact that I know myself to be insane, I am observing not just the socially abhorrent behavior I was contemplating, but my own awareness of my feelings of fear, overwhelming any and all feelings of compassion or empathy. My sought-after relief from the fears I was experiencing were overriding to any feelings I might have had toward any human beings in my immediate surroundings, the conflict between my emotions and my intellect continued for months on end, letting sleep become a much-needed relief that would frequently be interrupted by both nightmares and actual physical needs like eating, drinking, and the relief of biological waste.

Since I urinated in my bed that was probably the only biological necessity that didn't wake me from the release that sleep would bring. There were only two other means of deescalating my feelings of panic available to me at that age, reading anything, but especially escape literature gave focus to my intellect and gained some relief from the process in which I found myself, slim as it was. My reading became not simply a much-enjoyed pastime, but a lifeline for drawing myself out of the quagmire of hopelessness and desperation.

The second tool while insidious in and of itself of a temporary, but repeatable relief from the feelings themselves. There's a story I would hear years later in my life. And after I had begun my journey toward becoming human, an old recovering drug addict was asked if he wanted to get high and was offered his drug of choice from his years of active addiction by a much younger man, he had just met.

"No thank you" He replied, but may I ask you a question? Sure. Said the younger man, go ahead. Pops. And the older man asked, "why do you use drugs?" The younger man replied to feel good. So, looking at the younger man, sadly, the old drug addict ended the conversation with one last question, "Were you feeling bad before you started using drugs?"

Though I wouldn't try to answer for others Human beings are as diverse as snowflakes or the leaves on a tree, for myself however. when I heard that story, the very first time I knew the intent was to point out the obvious facts that drug use offers only temporary relief and an avoidance of accepting responsibility for and dealing with real events or emotions in a life, a temporary escape from reality and creating a false dependence on whatever substance is used until the use of the substance itself becomes so habitual it creates more problems than it relieves. in the end, bringing no relief, no matter how much of the substance is used through a grown tolerance for the substance itself. Still these 34 years later, since my last misuse of any drugs or medications, I could have answered that old drug addict. Final question with a whisper.

Yes. I used the second tool for 34 years of my existence with beer, cigarettes and applause at the age of four, being my introduction to altered states of feelings. My feelings by my age were stronger. As suppression usually causes both pressure for relief and a concentration of feelings in any stable, human being and my not being stable because of my awareness of myself, I had that increasing pressure from within myself.

I actively sought out drugs in my efforts to find any that might offer some relief. The THC in marijuana offered numbness and a form of sleep with dreams. I might or might not recall LSD or acid offered alternative perspectives of the reality around me, but those perspectives were far too often influenced by both others in my surroundings or the internal workings of my own intellect based in fear as they would revert to dark frightening and potentially life-threatening scenarios for myself and others.

Yes. I felt bad. And yes. Drug use only offered a false sense of temporary relief. Desperation made even that temporary relief of feeling good, a large part of my life, both then and now, then being the years, I used drugs in the manner of a crutch or fix to deal with reality and now being my abstinence and avoidance from using drugs in order to not return to that crippled state of being dependent on them for dealing with the real.

Compleat

The Choir & The Teachers

At eight years of age, I not only became self-aware and socially conscious I began to recall events that had occurred when I was younger but had not discussed with anyone especially my parents. Untrustworthy comes to mind now as the single most feeling word I can imagine for that period of my life and the adults or people in it. If adults were real people, what then was I? The betrayals by neighbors, teachers and adults, as well as rejection and ridicule from children my own age, allowed me to form barriers between myself and others. Yet in my attempts to protect myself from my own feelings I instead isolated myself from humanity and the society which surrounded me.

Compleat

Betrayals by my neighbors, I may have already described although I cannot recall the names of the two boys who took advantage of my desire to experience what they had from me. I do recall Mike, Billy and Mark Smith living in the duplex below us, but don't recall any of them being involved in that incident. The only actual memories I have regarding them is that Mark put his mouth around a bulb in a nightlight in order to see the glow through his cheeks and the veins of his face. The bulb exploded inside his mouth, burning his lips at the corner to a black char and scarring his mouth for as long as we lived there. Ben Sloane suffered a lawn mowing accident with a power gas push lawn mower, slicing three of the toes off of one of his feet when his tennis shoe slipped on the grass of the house next door and his foot went under the mower. I can only dimly recall any other events about neighbors or the neighborhood itself. Belinda had been going to a southern baptist church somewhere nearby where the street had ended in stairs leading up to another avenue. She got baptized, so I did as well and attended Sunday school and church with her there.

I remember that I memorized the names of all the books in the bible in order and gained some reward but don't remember the reward itself. Self-aware and yet I was still seeking admiration or approval from adults. I also remember singing in the children's choir, something I enjoyed immensely because I enjoyed singing at any opportunity I was asked or offered, but also because the Sunday school teacher in charge would consistently encourage all of us to sing louder. She might as well have asked me to eat ice cream. Singing and loud went together for me like ice cream and chocolate syrup do for most kids at that age.

I would put my whole heart into singing as loudly as I could during practices and just as much enthusiasm when we were called to sing in front of the congregation. Here was attention for doing something I really liked but without being forced into drinking beer with its result of feeling blurry, or buzzed as they call at now, the nasty taste of cigarettes and the beatings I got at home for being too loud. People would smile, seeming to enjoy our performances and I felt a glimmer of hope that these people, these adults, might be trusted. Yet into my enjoyment there came this one lady who had made an object of taking it upon herself to tell us individually what a great job of singing we had each done.

Perhaps she used a formulate praise that she repeated to each kid in the choir. I didn't overhear what she had said to the others, but she appeared sincere when she commented on my performance that Sunday and I felt the hope I've already mentioned here germinating within me when she did offer me that encouragement. It was after the sermon was over, as people and kids were milling about and talking, that I sought that particular lady out thinking to thank her and perhaps soak up a bit more of that positive praise and input for myself.

Instead, as I approached her from behind and was out of view of the person she was conversing with, I would overhear her saying that she had tried to enjoy the children's choir, but that Runner kid had been so loud that the rest of the choir couldn't be heard. I've been accused of being tone deaf since then, but not from singing, because after that day I quit trying. I'm tone deaf in the aspect that I cannot hear the inflection or tone in my own voice or so I'm told often, but the child I was that day heard the disapproval and the disappointment in her tone as she spoke those words. The choir would have been a better experience for everyone if I hadn't been there or, in my mind, if I didn't exist at all.

Maybe that feeling of purposelessness showed in my lack of participation in schoolwork afterward, especially in regards to homework assignments. I cannot remember ever completing any homework assignment for my entire third grade. What I do recall is that the school contacted my parents and through the school, I was provided a public bus pass so I could attend summer school and begin seeing a therapist, probably a psychologist or child pediatric psychiatrist, once a week for the entire summer. 12 whole visits to my first shrink. Their problem was two-fold: not only did they not understand my level of reasoning or comprehension at eight years of age, I was already very aware of the sexuality of adult women. I found her not very attractive in face, being of average prettiness, but her form or body was extremely attractive and as with my third-grade teacher, who had been pretty in both face and form, I would more often than not find myself peeking or glancing at her whenever I thought there would be an opportunity to view her panties.

With my third-grade teacher opportunities to view her panties had happened more frequently when spring and summer would allow her to wear dresses of light-colored cotton, because though they extended to her knee, standing up, the skirts of her dresses would rise when she sat down at her desk in the front of the classroom. And at almost every instance when she would stand up to write on the chalk board or assist another student, I would witness a flash of her thighs parting to reveal the color or pattern of the panties she was wearing and the shadow of the pubic hair beneath them.

Compleat

An eight-year-old pervert, or voyeur, or peeping tom maybe but it was an obsession and I would fantasize about her often. The shrink wore more sunblock textures of suit skirts, and frequently wore pantyhose instead of nylons, but the infrequence didn't deter my looking and opportunities presented themselves often enough so I didn't imagine being in love with her as I did in my fantasies of that teacher, but being fully sexual with her did enter my fantasies frequently. Strangely enough, it would be after meeting my parents, especially my stepdad she announced that she would no longer need to see me. After that summer, I was placed in a special education class for the fourth grade.

I continued to be provided a public transit bus pass weekly, and I attended a class at a school very far from the neighborhood public schools I had attended up until that point. Special education was usually reserved for the slow, autistic, or harshly labeled 'retarded' kids. Mrs. Dunn, who looked more like a mom than a teacher - fat and happy though - and Mr. Sabian were my teachers that year. Mrs. Dunn, I remember only fondly - no sexual interest because at the beginning of the school year, she showed me shelves of books ranging from See Dick and Jane children's books to High School Senior level books, and allowed me to pick whichever books I preferred. Geometry, Biology, and 12th Grade English were my choices and for the first time in my experience of attending public schools I found interest and challenges enough to not only do the assignments, but finish the homework assignments in the classroom itself so quickly and accurately that Mrs. Dunn would excuse me from the rest of the classroom curriculum.

Telling me I could play quietly with wooden dominoes or blocks and/or sitting behind a screen separator in the room and read books. I finished most of the books there in the first few weeks, but comic books always seemed available and even reading Archie or Jughead comics was preferable to not reading at all, but it all seems to only bring another memory of violence from my childhood.

Mr. Sabian, was the male teacher for the special education class at the time, I viewed him as just another teacher, not the first male teacher I had ever met, but just a teacher. And since most of my interactions were with Mrs. Dunn, I really didn't pay much attention to his presence in the classroom. For me, a teacher was a teacher, was a teacher. He seemed like a shadow presence. He was there in the classroom, but spent most of his time with the other students. Two of those that stand out were Derick Johnson my friend from younger days and a bigger kid whose name, I only seem to recall as being Tim. He and

Compleat

Derick were friends by that time, but he seemed slower than Derick was physically and mentally.

I remember them hanging out, playing in the schoolyard, but my not feeling comfortable around Tim. Maybe I was jealous of his friendship with Curtis, but at the time, all I could identify was a vague feeling of threat or danger when I was around him. By fourth grade, Derick and I were buying and smoking joints and cigarettes regularly. Sometimes we would buy them from Tim. Other times, I would score a nickel or dime bag in my neighborhood and bring a few joints to school with me to have at recess. Smoking pot helped me get my mind off what was happening at home and Derick seemed able to concentrate and not be so hyper or wound up after we shared a joint or two. An aside, I know, but it does relate to the teacher, Mr. Sabian, as I will explain now.

With Derick being friends with Tim, there were times when we had serious disagreements, serious to fourth graders at least. One such incident caused Derick to want to fight me, but by fourth grade I was already well over five foot in height and maybe even reach my full growth of six feet by then, and Derick was much shorter than I was either way. Instead of fighting back, I somehow twisted him around, grabbed the back of his belt and lifted him off the ground. In spite of his struggles and the cussing he did, I proceeded to carry him over to Mrs. Dunn's desk and sat him down beside her in such a way she was able to hold onto his belt and restrain him from attacking me again.

For some reason, Mr. Sabian wasn't present for that, but I'm sure he was made aware of the incident because he spent the rest of that day making sure Derick kept his distance from me. I felt bad for Derick since I felt I was too big to be fighting with him and because I know being carried that way must have embarrassed him. I would be about a month later, Mr. Sabian would come into the classroom while Mrs. Dunn was having a reading circle with all the other kids. She had given me permission to not attend the circle because I had already completed my schoolwork and all of my homework in Geometry, Biology and English, turning them all in for grading and getting A's or A+s on every paper.

But Mr. Sabian didn't know I had her permission to quietly read comic books across the room, away from the circle. He grabbed me by the hair atop of my head, and although it wasn't not super long it long enough to serve him as a gripping point, he then dragged me stumbling across the room to the area of the reading circle and threw me to the floor beside the other students. You would have to ask him "why" to know what's brought about his actions. As a kid, I assumed he was either in a drunken rage – I was very familiar with those - or thought I was being disrespectful of Mrs. Dunn or maybe he hated me for some unknown and unknowable reason. My reaction was to leap up from where he had thrown me, sprint out of the classroom down two flights of stairs and out of the school.

Mrs. Dunn must have caught his attention and explained or reprimanded him for his actions because I made my escape from the entire school grounds and onto the nearby street. Then I was faced with a dilemma. If I were to return home in the beginning of the school day, I was aware that I would probably find my mom engaged with Aiden Addis, the thought of which sickened me, but I was also calming down enough to reason that by going home instead of being in school where I was supposed to be, it was entirely likely that I would receive a beating for skipping school before I might be able to even try to explain my presence at home.

Near the school were two places I consider landmarks of my childhood. The first was a small bakery that made what I imagined to be called unicorn horns, they were French horn or crème horns with that being their actual names. A pastry that was flaky and light with curving ridges around its outer perimeter and a whipped cream center running the length of the tube's centers. I've spent years trying to find creme horns with real whipped creme, rather than the sugary false crème most modern French horns have in them.

The second landmark was a pool hall where for a quarter Derick and I would sometimes use the off the wall cue sticks and play pool, but were more likely to use that quarter to play the pinball machines that were there instead. Three games for a quarter and by scoring high enough, we could earn extra balls and extra games. I went to the pool hall that day, even though they had received warning from the school and local law enforcement to not allow kids into the establishment during school hours. Perhaps my tear-stained face earned me an exception, or maybe the proprietor chose to ignore me as one tall skinny kid wouldn't be that disruptive or noticeable. All I know was I was allowed to stay there until long after the school had let out and the school day was over.

I rode the bus home and being late was better than showing up early would have been. I was so late getting home however that Mr. Sabian had gotten there before me and my parents had called the police about a missing child.

Compleat

Of the Ohio street house, my memories are partial and small broken flashes with no real patterns that snap to the forefront of my mind. The fact that I could read before attending school, notwithstanding most of that portion of my childhood, I successfully erased through the drug use with alcohol abuse, being a drug a problem. By reading I escape the terrors of the household around me, as well as my own inner demon of comprehending more than I should have been able to understand or recognize. Sexually frustrated before kindergarten with my focus being inappropriately directed toward my sisters and my Aunt Fran, I would seek out the circumstances that provided me with glimpses of the forbidden.

By third grade, I knew which girls will wore what color panties, and that by slouching in my seat, I could look up the summer dresses as the teacher will and see her panties was well. I had one experience, which by today's standards could have been formula for child abduction or abuse. A young seventh or eighth grade girl invited me to her house for root beer floats. Being in second grade and having been instructed to trust the crossing guards and all the children, I was more than willing to accompany her to her home, especially since it was only a few blocks down Ohio street from my house. Plying a second Grader with root beer and vanilla ice cream had the result, I suspect the desired result, of my needing to go pee. The bathroom was well lighted by a curtain window through which sunshine easily streamed.

So, I found myself wondering why she insisted that the bathroom door remained ajar ever so slightly until I happened to glance toward the door and saw the reflection of the sunlight on her eye. That she was watching me urinate didn't disturb me at all and after finishing three 16-ounce bottles of root beer and the ice cream of those floats, I repeated the trip to the bathroom several more times. How many root-beer floats can someone make out of 48 ounces of root beer and half a gallon of ice cream? The number I consumed evades me, but the three trips to the toilet stand out due to her watching me - even the third time in which I was forced to defecate instead of standing and peeing.

By that third time, she no longer attempted to avoid eye contact when I noticed her watching me. So, after I wiped myself, I stood again and urinated separately from going number two. And by that time, I was excited and encouraged enough that when she announced her own need to relieve herself, I requested an equal opportunity. I wanted her to allow me to observe her as she went potty. They say now that denial is not just a river in Egypt. Hers came fast and frequent at first saying she hadn't seen me then switching to, she might have glanced in by accident, but in no way, was her observing me intentionally. To prove her point maybe, or I believed as a type of punishment for seeing her and confronting her about the incidents, she closed and locked the bathroom door while she relieved herself.

My feelings were mixed by being both excited by the circumstance I found myself in, seeing opportunity being presented to learn more than reading had taught me, and a sense of injustice having been done. How unfair to watch me, but then not share. Her only compensation was to ply me with yet another root beer float. Being pragmatic and realizing there was no means by which I might change her mind, that the idea of extortion I would read and learned about would occur a few years later and had no compulsion to avoid using in attempts to get what I wanted, I accepted her offering, hoping to keep repeating the encounter at later dates, both for the floats and in hope she would relent if she found me trustworthy and truthful when I promised not to tell.

All of this had happened in the course of a few hours after school had let out, so when she heard her Aunt coming to the front door, a suggestion that we surprise her aunt with me hiding in a clothes closet and popping out when she introduced me, I was agreeable and the surprise went just as we had planned, although the results were bewildering to me at the time. While she and I were very happy to have surprised her aunt, her aunt was not only not pleasantly surprised, she had a seriously concerned expression I recognized as consternation. She hustled me out of the front door as soon as she had been assured that nothing of mine was still in the house and sternly told me to go home and "don't you dare ever come back." Rejection by adults was a pattern I was very familiar with by this time and the tone of her voice, the look on her face, and the air of urgency that her body language communicated, convinced me I would not be allowed to return - crushing my hopes for floats and reciprocal viewing and being a hundred percent honest, I couldn't tell which I regretted losing the opportunity for most.

It would be years later that the concept of missing children would make me wonder if I had been at risk in that way. No matter which house we lived in, I remember the animals as being more important to me than the rest of my family. On Chippewa and Ohio, there was a fenced yard, which means we probably had a dog of some type, but I don't recall much more about the Chippewa house other than meeting my first friend, Derick Johnson, while living there and that there was a shop close by, on Chippewa with small items like smoke bombs that smelled strongly of sulfur and could be bought for nickels, dimes and quarters.

Compleat

The shop carried Snaps that I could throw down a sidewalk so that they would pop. Firecrackers even after, or long before the 4th of July. Black tabs of some material that when I lit them off, the flame would cause it to expand in a long connected and twisting ash that were called snakes. I didn't miss or care about candy, gum, sodas, or even ice cream, as much as I liked going there to buy stuff. When I started reading comic books, I found most of the things that little shop would sell advertised in the last few pages. I remember years later finally having enough money of my own to order and buy a pair of those amazing x-ray specs I had first seen on the shelves of that store and found advertised in my comics. I really wanted to be able to see through clothes and my hands, just like the illustrations had shown. When they didn't work as I had expected and hoped - believe me, I tried using them even chasing girls while wearing them and playing as if they did - I took them apart to understand why they didn't do what I had bought them for and found that the pinholes letting light through their lens was refracted by bird feathers of some sort. I realized the effect was the same as putting my hand on the inside of a lampshade while the light was on and was no more capable of giving actual x-ray vision than the lamp shade itself.

Present day convenience stores weren't around at that time. Instead, there were small stores, usually mom and pop places owned by people in the neighborhoods, and being sent to the corner store - since they were usually found on a corner of two streets - to buy cigarettes, beer, soda, chips, or other non-essential stuff was a recurring event happening two or three times per week. An opportunist at all times, I would get the change in pennies usually and buy myself a comic book for 12 cents or some for just a dime. It was in reading that I found my first avenue of escape from reality. It often seems strange to me that other kids found reading assignments difficult and while I easily grasped the concept of reluctance to write book reports on the subject material of various books that were assigned by the teachers, I resisted and disliked their attitude towards reading books, which for the larger portion of my peers was viewed as an enormous waste of their time. Time that could be better spent , according to them, playing games with others. Time to be used to entertain one another, usually at someone else's expense. Yes, I was a focal point of verbal, physical, and mental abuse (i.e., bullying) although not the sole focus. Time, as I grew to view it, was the enemy, as unavoidable as an army consisting of foot soldiers known as minutes, officers that passed as hours, generals of days and weeks and their supreme commanders, the years.

Compleat

What grade are you in? What year of school are you attending? How many hours have you obtained in that field of study? How many years of internship have you completed? Can anyone really grasp the idea of a third-grade boy looking at his classmates, friends, teachers, counselors, siblings, parents, and what consisted of the entire world he had experienced by that age - another time reference, by the way - and by looking, becoming aware that they were all sharing a massive societal and racially inspired delusion.

For clarification purposes, by the term racial I'm referring to the human race. There I was, a third grader dismissed by adults as being too immature to grasp certain concepts and thereby spoken in front of as if I were just an object, no more capable of hearing what was being said, understanding the words, grasping the concepts and retaining the information than could a coffee cup. But the insulting thing, the growing resentment I felt, stemmed from something beyond being an invisible object. The insult came from knowing without need of questioning or inquiry that my own concepts, views, opinions, and knowledge on any subject being discussed would be dismissed completely due only to the fact of my age.

That illusion - that delusional concept that everyone surrounding me appeared trapped within - could not affect its control over me directly because of my awareness of its true nature, but though the indirect control of and manipulation of others held me captive just as assuredly as it held all of them.

Anyone who brought up the subject of a color would find themselves shocked by the voice of an eight-year-old boy from outside of whatever conversation they were participating in stating emphatically that "I want to have white hair." Inevitably, this exclamation would result in a further discussion of hair coloring by adults, adolescents and children, or my being asked the ridiculous questions of "Why?" I understood then and I'm even more knowledgeable now of the fact that arrogance stems from feelings of insecurity, but I have to ask you, how could an eight-year-old boy not feel insecure under those circumstances? I already grasp concepts that neither of my parents could even consider topics of discussion. My teachers were bound by societal rules to produce conformity and obedience within those placed in their care - under the guise of instruction and learning, serving more as daycare givers and programmers than actual sources of information exploration and enlightenment or awareness of the world around us.

It has been said that in the kingdom of the blind, a one-eyed man would be king. A pleasant concept, but even at eight, I recognized the flaw in that

Compleat

simple statement. I can see humanity as a kingdom of the blind. Many folks can grasp that concept when observing what we've been doing to one another, since the beginning of oral and written history, but the concept of the one-eyed man being king is nonsensical. By himself, even with the addition of perceptive ability, he could not control or manipulate the masses of a kingdom indefinitely, even with the willing assistance and compliance of a large group of followers or assistants. His ability to rule would be limited by the inevitability of the very human trait of making a mistake that would lead to the disillusion of his ability to rule.

Any mistake by himself or any who chose to assist him would end his rule. But the obvious, most inherent flaw and the concept of his being allowed to rule lays in the very nature of his additional ability. If for any reason or by any means, including everything a chance remark to straight forward and open revelation, the masses of the kingdom surrendering to him, became aware of his additional ability, not only would his ability to rule be compromised beyond salvaging, but all that he stood for, suggested, encouraged, directed, ordered, or cause to come into being would be subject to destruction, manipulation, diversion from its intended purpose by those who did not have his ability.

Not to get religious, but as an example, look at the Jesus dude, his followers and what happened to him. Even if you doubt his divinity or lack any faith in the accuracy of the reports of his supposed actions, that fucker displayed an unusual insight or ability beyond the kin of his neighbors, peers, leaders, teachers, and parents - the result of a one-eyed man in a kingdom of the blind. They'd come for his ass rather than allow him to be different - to not conform, to be himself with his fucked-up ability and perception they could not or would not grasp.

So, yes. At eight years of age, I became insecure enough to become an arrogant asshole. It wouldn't be until I turned 13 and read their entire bible as a story book, that the concept of how and what I had experienced at eight would make sense of the behaviors of the world in which I live. My insecurities had developed into survival skills by that time.

My arrogance, I covered with my own confusion, self-deception, and the lies that I told myself in order to maintain an existence I neither wanted or knew how to escape from other than retreating into the darkest, most frightening to me, recesses of my own mind. Without hope I existed there, allowing my ego, arrogance, fear, and self-destructive will to rage and run rampantly among them.

If I displayed no unusual or exceptional talent or ability, I know I would continue to be dismissed - no longer just a child, but as the social pariah that the stigma of being mentally ill would afford me and thereby preserving my own existence. Eight years of age and knowledge beyond words to express. Comprehension, without communication. I often think that I understand the shortest verse in the bible. "Jesus wept." How could he not? He saw with both eyes as did Buddha, as did Mohammad, as did Confucius and as do every musician from Mozart through Ozzy Osborne, every artist from the kindergartner with a crayon drawing to a Rembrandt and Michelangelo, as do every writer from every limerick to the works of Hawthorne, Keats, Trudeau, and Hamlin, or Poe. Every single human soul that has ever felt even the slightest feeling of wanting to create something, whether they were able to attempt it and failed to achieve it or failed to even begin. And therein lays the comprehension of who human beings truly are and the ability to communicate with one another in such a way as to actually understand.

The best humanity has been able to do is relate. My opinion is that ability is because we are all related, but we may never understand one another. And for an eight-year-old boy, the loneliness that came with the comprehension of that possibility was a burden I bore only because I didn't know what else to do. At 66 years of age, I still see the relationship of all humanity and perceive your lack of understanding of who you actually are. Someone told me that there are 7.9+ billion people on this planet on any given day now. I am one person among all those others, and I'm alone. From 8 years of age to 66 years of age is a terrible distance to carry anything, any secret, for the strength to continue to hope flares and fades with being close to relating and opening to risk, only to withdraw for safety's sake and continued existence, so that with my existence, I am able to carry forward the hope I clung to then and cling to now.

We can understand one another. We can learn to see. But the price of it is high. It will cost all that we might have been in the past, all that we are in this moment, all our potential or ability to create a future for one another beyond where we relate and/or are related to one another. It will cost us our existence as individuals and as a racial collective. I'm no longer insecure - no longer afraid to lose my meager existence on this beautiful planet and I no longer feel the need to express myself arrogantly because of my lack of fear. I am that I am. He said it and I understand. It appears that even though I have dedicated

Compleat

another notebook on the subject of god, I eventually wander back to the topic in this writing as well.

I'm going to switch the topics of this notebook from simply recording the experiences I remember to reading my personal insights of some positive events as well. If I do, then maybe I won't wander off topic for a moment or so.

By the time I was in third grade, my reading skills and appetite for books expanded beyond the books available to me by way of the public bookmobile that would come to our school. And in the summer, when school was closed, that resource was no longer available. The nearest public library was known as the carpenter branch library, and it was located 15 long city blocks away from where I lived. I think back and wonder how I didn't develop much upper body strength over those months. The librarians would question me as I signed out so many books at one time and so often that they appeared to think it incredulous that a kid given only two weeks before the books would need to be returned, would check out and read up to 15 books at one time.

Years later, I would watch a movie of a young girl doing something similar and was envious only of the red wagon she used to carry her books. There's something calming about being in the library for me. If I would come across a book that I hadn't read yet and its title as well as insert pages caught my attention, I'd find myself in a chair where I once had started them, if they were good books, I might remain until the librarians would find me and inform me that the library was closing. In present day, the chance of seeing a small, skinny boy walking down the sidewalk with both arms holding up a stack of books would be so rare that it might be noticed. But those were the days I treasured beyond words to describe their value. Book after book: Shakespeare, to the Odyssey, the Iliad to Isaac Asimov, Bradbury, Howard, Heinlein, and Hemingway – there seemed to be no type of book that I'd never heard of or read. Then too Clemens and Clark, De camp and others - I would read over and over again.

At one point I had, most of the first chapter of Tom Sawyer memorized, not from studying it or trying; simply from having read it so frequently. I visited the river near St. Louis just to explore and maybe recognize some of the places Mark Twain had described, but nothing I saw there resembled the pictures in my mind that the words in his books had inspired. Still, a river a mile across was an impressive sight and the rats that he described as targets for Huck Finn were indeed of impressive size.

Compleat

In addition to disappearing into my room for what to me seems of mere moments, but a hunger and thirst would remind me had been many hours, sometimes days if I had to finish one more chapter before I might stop and one more after that. I was content only when reading or walking along the streets until sidewalks would vanish into gravel and dirt paths where once grass had grown. There was one incident where I started walking on what was known then as the street called King's Highway, when curiosity of where that road led caused me to carry on walking along it. And like with reading, I was always urging myself to turn back and return home and compromising with that urge by assuring myself that I would, after the next hill had revealed what it was hiding beyond my sight through its rise just there before me. Just one more hill. One more page. One more block. One more chapter. Or until I got to the end of this one, and then I would stop.

That particular hike took me from the northern end of King's Highway - sort of north for me near Cleveland high school, out of the city limits - and well into St. Louis County. I don't recall if I had a dime for the payphone or if a gas station attendant allowed me to borrow their phone, but calling my folks because I had finally become too exhausted to walk any further and completely lost as to where I was, became my only option for getting home again. Yet exhaustion, confusion, and facing my angry parents couldn't dissolve the feeling of curiosity and the wondering what was beyond the next hill.

It took an extreme risk by reviewing some of what I've written in this particular notebook. In taking time away from the physical writing of these stories, it became necessary to review what I have included already. Perhaps it was a good thing though that I was able to make a few additions to some sentences, as well as add the beginning of side notes where appropriate, because some parts are out of chronological order. I might need to edit these for effect.

Wandering became a theme of my days during varied periods of my life. I had my established routines, but always felt drawn or pulled away from any thoughts of organizing in any attempt to provide myself with a sense of stability or purpose. In the physical world, I would wander to places that my curiosity had tugged at my inner self to go and see for yourself. Mental travels through the far away landscapes provided by my imagination led me at maybe six years of age to envision myself as the protagonist of stories in which my heroic-self faced fear and fearful creation from the darkest side of my mind.

Compleat

Compleat
Walking Man

In my neighborhood, on the south side of St. Louis, Missouri we hung out at the corner store, a mom- and- pop place where soda pop was still a dime for a 16 oz bottle of Vess Cream Soda, a Suzi Q cake was a quarter, and comic books sold for 12 cents until the price soared to a quarter each as well.

We stole beer bottles from behind a local tavern, then sold them back to the bartender to get the money to buy all of the above and cigarettes that we claimed were for our folks from the corner store, too.

Hanging out on the corner, we talked engaged in big- talk about what we had done, who we were going to become, who we had sex with already and who we'd love to have sex with as soon as we could. Truth be told, I hadn't had sex yet with anyone, my girlfriend at the time being nine years old and me not being much older it was, of course, all brag and no fact. There were guys in our bunch who had had sex though, and my envy of them wouldn't allow me to admit to being a virgin still, so I talked shit and barked at the moon with the best of them.

Into this atmosphere of bullshit, lies, and childishness, there comes a story though that is very real and impressive to this day. Ironically it isn't about me so much as it is about the group of guys and girls that hung out together there on that corner.

Compleat

There was this man. How old he might have been, I couldn't say for certain. I'd guess around his late 20's or even early 30's. He had long hair, a scruffy kind of beard, and worn, blue jeans and the same white t-shirt on every occasion we saw him. I think we called him Steve, though it's been so very long since I even thought about talking about him, I wouldn't swear that was what we called him.

What I do remember is that to us he was a legend. His story was told on that street corner every time he walked by, or whenever anyone new came into our group of friends and saw him for the first time. The legend went that Steve had done so much LSD or acid that his mind had become completely fried, and he could no longer speak or even notice other human beings.

Though his body walked past us on infrequent occasions, he never spoke or interacted with us other than to accept our gifts of sandwiches and soda pop, which he consumed as he continued walking, without acknowledging that we had handed them to him.

Why did we adopt him and his legend that way? He was thin, almost so thin as to think he was starving to death and we wanted to help him somehow. And why the rumor or legend that he was brain fried? Because we knew from experience that acid or LSD could cause changes in our own young minds.

We did blotter acid, purple barrel, micro-dot, window-pane, and half a dozen other made- up names for the street drug version of LSD on that corner as well. The others in the group 'dropped' acid for the entertainment value, hearing blues and reds and yellows, seeing the sounds of the blades of a fan as it rotated, and feeling both light and darkness on our skins.

But I used it the way I imagine Steve had used it. To escape the life, I was existing. I liked to imagine that he had loved someone and lost them. Or that his life was so extravagant that he had sought to run from it, rather than face it on a daily basis. I envied Steve. And wanted very much to be just like him. Unaware of life around myself, sufficient to walk on forever without ever interacting with anyone else. Because, that's exactly what Steve did. He walked, never once stopping. Never once speaking. Never once making a connection with others around himself. ALONE, eternally locked within his own mind, barely keeping his body alive enough to continue his lonely journey.

Drugs didn't do that for me, in spite of my many years of using them to seek that release. Instead, I found myself alone, unable to communicate with

Compleat

humanity in such a way as to know that I was being heard. An island on a planet of over 7.9 billion individuals and I know now what it was that Steve experienced every day he walked by without saying a word to anyone.

Compleat
Fran Was the Name of My Other Mother

In the stories about my childhood the name of my maternal aunt, Fran, comes up frequently. From her experience as a teenage babysitter for a broken-headed me as an infant, up to where she stood against her own husband, Larry Holman, in defense of my behaviors – mistakenly believing I was incapable of molesting his niece, perhaps even my actions being the cause for their eventual divorce.

But to understand Aunt Fran others would have to have seen her through my eyes. Freud says that men, while during infancy, are jealous of their mother's affections being shown to the men in their lives, especially their father or step-father. With my own biological mother, that fact was missed or skipped, because of all the women in my lifespan, she was the only one I felt absolutely no interest in sexually.

However, my surrogate mother, Aunt Fran would be an example of Freud's being theory completely vindicated. Here was a woman, from her teenage self and onward, who would exemplify for me the mother love figure that substantiates Freud's observations.

Compleat

From the infant self who would repeatedly state "Aunt Fran, I want to hold you." when I felt threatened or was hurt in some way, to the youth who would bar tend for her and her female friend after her divorce would become finalized, mixing brandy-Alexanders until both women would become so drunk that I could have easily have taken sexual advantage of their state. With her friend, though I was attracted to her slightly, I didn't because she wasn't as attractive to me as my Aunt.

With my Aunt Fran, however, the temptation was greater and when putting her to bed it was only with the greatest difficulty that I chose not to crawl into bed with her sleeping, near- naked form. Because I did undress them both, and put them in separate beds, wearing only bras and panties since neither of them was conscious by that time and they had finished the third or fourth pitcher of drinks they had me prepare for them, after they had already finished several pitchers of drinks that they had mixed for themselves.

I knew that I could have had sex with my drunken aunt, and the odds of her realizing that I had would have been slim to nearly none, since by the time she would have awoken any seaman, I might have ejaculated into her vagina would have leaked out in all probability. Why I chose not to had everything to do with how I viewed her and nothing to do with how much I wanted to be with her physically. She was, until disowning me years later, the only person I truly considered to be my mom.

Freud be damned, no matter how much I wanted her physical love, and I readily admit I did at that time more than ever because she had stood up for me when no one else ever had, I chose not to betray her at that time and in that way. I wasn't noble, wasn't respectful, and wasn't even familial in my choice to not take advantage of her drunken state. I chose not to because I didn't want to have her in a state where she wouldn't be a willing participant in the act itself. In short, I wanted her to want me as much as I wanted her.

It was years later that I read Freud's books and theory about sexuality toward mother figures and understood my own attraction toward and reluctance to take advantage of her at that time.

Unfortunately, it also explains something that would occur frequently in my life with regard to other women. With my Aunt Fran, the frustration I experienced with not being able or allowing myself to engage in sex with her became the focus or substance of sexual attraction toward her young daughters, my cousins. Not that I needed that focus, since in being both family and females I viewed as 'loved' ones, they would have been attractive to me anyway. But the additional attractiveness of their being 'her' daughters grew in my young mind as an overwhelming need to share with them what I had denied myself with her.

I would attempt to molest my older cousin, Patricia, but she would reject my advances outright, in spite of the subtlety I had attempted to use to begin an interaction with her in that manner. My other cousin, Pamela, would be more receptive, being much younger and less aware of the implications of what I was attempting to do. I would be called by her into the bathroom to assist her with reaching the toilet tissue and use the opportunity to touch and taste her in ways that I know now were inappropriate simply because of her age, let alone that she was my first cousin and my aunt's daughter - or substitute.

Anyone reading this can easily understand that my aunt, upon learning of my behaviors years later, would completely disown me for the abuses I performed on even one of her daughters. And it would be many years later. This came, after she had assisted me in obtaining my civilian driver's license, allowed me access to her home with her new husband (for years), and after my continued abuse of that younger cousin up until her near teenage years.

The one action that gave me away, that caused both cousins to finally reveal some of my earlier attempts ironically had nothing to do with my trying to be sexual with either one of them, though I admit the chance to see the older cousin naked did coincide with the event that revealed my disgusting behaviors.

I had met my first wife, through an introduction by my aunt, and was amazed that she found me attractive enough to kiss me on the first date. Not that kissing was all we had done but that she had found me attractive was something I did not understand at all. I was a Marine , short- haired, painfully thin, barely out of my teens and into my early twenties and she had already been married, had a nine-year-old daughter that called me 'daddy' the first time we met and I was unsure of what I actually was experiencing.

If I had gone to my Aunt Fran with the question, perhaps my perfidy might have gone unnoticed until years later?! As it was, even upon learning what I had done to my cousins, I would be allowed into her home – at a more distant relationship and after I had married my first wife – but never again would I have her complete trust.

Instead, I had chosen to ask my older cousin, Patricia, the question that had confused me when my to-be first wife had agreed to kiss me on our first date.

Compleat

If we weren't cousins "Would you have kissed me the first time you met me?" The fact that she was in the process of changing out of her swimsuit caused her enough discomfort to insist that I leave the room, of course. That she and my cousin Pamela would confront my aunt with about my past behaviors, including my driving them and their teenage friends to the drive-in theater, where they all got gloriously drunk and I had tried to 'put the moves' on one of their drunken girlfriends.

I tried to explain that my question was innocent, though the timing and place in attempting the question was without a doubt lacking in good judgment on my part and that, alone, appeared to suffice for my aunt, since my molestation of my younger cousin wasn't revealed at that time.

I myself would reveal that fact myself, when I would later be convicted of sexually molesting another young girl and would write to my aunt exactly what I had done to both my cousins. That later date was when I was disowned and have never been included or invited by her to be a part of their lives. Though my older cousin would one day forgive me enough to stop at my then home and visit me long enough to tell me of her choice to forgive my past mistakes.

Compleat

The Dove &

The Turtle

—·—·—·—·—·—·—·—·—·—·—·—·—·—··—

A turtle walked along a dusty road

  A dove flew over by

She spied the turtle in his dust,

Saying he's alone as I.

She called to him, I love you so,

Come, I will teach you how to fly.

The turtle walked on, knowing all too well,

To fly he would need to die.

The dove, heartbroken flew away, tears were in her eyes,

She'd never know or learn to grow

the tears that a turtle cries.

Compleat

On Broadway
— · — · — · — · — · — · — · — · — · — · — · — · — · — · —

At the corners of South Broadway Street, California Avenue, and Osceola Street in St. Louis, Missouri there used to be a cannon. Not the type of cannon used during the civil war, this cannon was an artillery piece saved over from World War 2. It had been painted silver to prevent it from rusting away from exposure to the wind and rain and pollution of the streets of St. Louis. And being near the Mississippi river, it stood on an island of grass between those major and minor streets, I guess as a reminder of what the world had gone through during that great war and how the people of Missouri, especially St. Louis, had sacrificed their sons to prevent socialism and the scourge of Nazi Germany from taking over the world. An island dedicated to the remembering of heroes, I often thought of it as an island of Heroes during my childhood, a safe and wonder- filled place to visit when wandering to the parks nearby or just walking as I often did to find places that I hadn't been before or wanted to know where the road I was following ended.

Compleat

In one of my previous stories, I may have mentioned that my mother's brother, my Uncle Caden, was one of my childhood heroes. Even as a six-year-old, his teenage self was the person I most wanted to emulate since my mother spoke of him as her brother and obviously thought he could do no wrong. I guess I wanted to be like him so that my mother would admire me as much as she did her younger brother, for his strength – which I lacked, his courage – also something I was missing but most of all for his honor and nobility – the one thing I truly hoped to attain if only I could learn it from him.

It was on that island of heroes that I learned a truth about human beings that perhaps helped shape the monster I would later become. I don't mean to blame him for my mistakes, take that as you will it is not my intent. I am simply stating that if the events that happened there that day hadn't occurred as they did, then perhaps a piece of what I would eventually become might have been avoided. The self-loathing and disgust I felt for myself after that day might have been lessened to some degree, but that is an assumption that I can only surmise and have no way of proving or resolving the issue these many years later.

My hero, my Uncle Caden, and two of his teenage friends took it into their own minds as a joke to try to 'pants' the six-year-old me that had followed them there that day. Perhaps they wanted privacy for something they were going to do and didn't want a six-year-old shadow following them around, who might tell on them or spill the beans by accident? I have no idea what they were doing there or why they were there in the first place. I only know that pulling the pants off a six-year-old didn't seem very heroic to me at that moment. It occurs to me that they either must not have been trying too hard or seriously because I was able to thwart their efforts simply by twisting my belt around my arm until it cut into my waist and prevented it from being pulled below my hips. Three teenage boys, all twice my physical size in height alone, were unable to remove my pants in that public place despite their efforts to do so, and when they eventually gave up the attempt, I was distraught, crying and sobbing aloud with snot running down my face onto my neck, shirt, and chest where my shirt had been pulled aside.

The story was never told to my mother, since she would never have believed it of her hero brother. But then too, this story isn't about his actions or those of his friends in the attack I experienced that day. I believe I've already mentioned this attack in another story, about the Marine Corps and how they were supposed to 'make a man out of me.'

Compleat

This story is about what happened that day, during the attack that felt to my six-year-old self to endure for hours though I can, as an adult, imagine that it probably lasted only the few minutes it took for them to become discouraged with their attempts and failure – plus them and their being distracted by returning to whatever purpose had brought them there, for themselves, in the first place.

What I noticed that day had nothing to do with the three of them, though thoughts of violent revenge against them raged through my mind the entire walk to my home, alone and frightened by my Uncle Caden's willingness to betray my trust and admiration of him. What I noticed that day was that not one person driving past that monument to heroism, - witnessing what was happening, and there were quite a few who drove past during the incident, not one stopped to help a six-year-old boy. Not one stopped when they saw me being set upon by three teenagers. Screams for help, struggling to prevent having my pants ripped from my body, and being exposed - all of that: three young men attacking a child - was ignored by people driving by in their cars or walking on the sidewalks of the nearby parks.

Some folk might excuse their driving or walking away from what was happening because they might not have heard my cries for help. Let me explain something that is in yet another story in this book about why that excuse won't work. I'm probably the only person who at that age could yell for my older brother and younger sister to come home for dinner, while they were playing at a public schoolyard nearly 4 blocks away and over traffic noises, and in spite of the distance and the noise of their playmates could be heard shouting for them. In short, I'm loud when called upon to shout or yell and that day I had the added emphasis of terror to increase my volume to nearly unavoidable levels. Even those who were driving past in their cars couldn't have avoided hearing my shouts for help, since radios and 8- track players didn't have the volume capacities in those days to drown out the sound like they do today.

People just didn't care. They avoided helping, even as they do for one another today, because to become involved they would be required to stop thinking of just themselves and think of the common good, or even just the fate of one small, thin, sobbing six-year-old boy being set upon. I learned that day that the human race cared only about themselves, not one another, and certainly not about me. At that moment I didn't know what to do with the knowledge, or what I would do with it in the coming years. But the knowledge itself was planted within me and would bear bitter fruit from my

Compleat

own actions until I would learn that it doesn't have to be that way. It really doesn't have to be this way.

Compleat

The Girl & The Devil in His Day

If there is one experience that would have separated me from what little sanity I had left after my older sister had died it was this. I was sure that I was already damned, but held on to the hope that love would "find" a way to save me from myself.

And by this time, I was in love, with a young woman who had been as disappointed in love as I had myself. She had chosen to love me, in spite of my poor behaviors toward her younger sister reflecting the very behaviors her first boyfriend, my older brother, had subjected her to, as well.

Those first loves were what people used to dismiss as being "puppy love." And trust me when I say that one day I would challenge that idea and the dismissal it allowed by asking a simple question:

"Have you ever seen how a puppy loves?"

Within a puppy's love is the energy of newness, the joy of just being with the one they love, and the unconditional giving - without thought or reason and especially without fear of any kind.

So, what if "first loves are meant to fail?" as the world has come to accept and chooses to see this as the norm or standard for every one of us. I think it says more about the level of cynicism we have fallen to as a race than it expresses any amount of truth about first loves. And our "puppy" loves served a vital role in the finding of my one true, authentic love. The one that would set the course of my entire life and all that I would experience over the following 50+ years.

In my other story about abortions, I mentioned how set I was against them. That was because my ego didn't want to consider the possibility of not prolonging myself through my having progeny. Like most human beings I was under the mistaken impression that I would somehow own the child that I had helped put inside any woman, and the fact was I wouldn't care who she was or even if she wanted to have a child with me or not, never mattered to me.

Compleat

Ironically it would be the one young woman I chose not to impregnate who would be the only one who offered to allow me to do so and that offer would be so that we might have the chance to be together for the rest of our lives.

I need to admit that I very much wanted to and honestly believe I would have, if I could have brought myself to disrespect her that much that day. But even the attempt we did make that day was so degrading to her in my eyes and how I felt about her in my heart I found that I couldn't bring myself to even have intercourse with her, fear of hurting her outweighed my lust.

Imagine the feelings of a young man, seventeen years of age, planning to go off to kill the enemies of our "great nation" being offered the real chance to have a child with the one person who I knew loved me more than I would ever be able to care about myself and how I felt when I stopped and turned away from doing "IT" because of the fact that I knew I wasn't worthy of her.

My inadequacy was staring me in the face and looking at me through her completely trusting eyes. I found myself measuring my soul by the growing awareness of where we were, and how we had to hide to even make the attempt at being together physically, and grew more disgusted with who I was by the moment.

And I looked around at the area that was our physical surroundings and it only served to amplify my self-loathing exponentially. The very knowledge that this young woman would sacrifice her precious self for my love, by going through with an action that she feared, in a place no sane person would have even suggested trying to use, ignoring all the aspects and ramifications of what it would mean if she were to get pregnant and I were to be killed or just leave and never come back all because she chose to love me, my self-hatred exploded.

Then try to imagine for yourself how you would feel - to be that young man and come to an awareness and knowledge that if you were to abuse that love by taking advantage of it, your soul would have to be blacker than the darkest pits of hell.

Yet still there you were, being offered a love like that? That day, I defined all that I am, was, and would be for years with one word: ***unworthy***.

Compleat

How Do I Separate

Sex and Love?

Even as early as two or three years of age, I didn't know the one without the other. The only person I even thought I loved without feeling strong feelings of attraction toward was my own mother. Freud would probably say I was denying my feelings, but the younger me understood feeling curious about the females around me.

My mom fell into a category all by herself - imposing, frightening, and sometimes lovable in a childish way. Mother was another name for God, to me, but as far as my usual sexual arousal, toward her I felt nothing. My memories center around anger at her for deceiving Art by playing the slut to Aiden Addis, fear that she would see through my good boy disguise and I would be subjected to the same beatings David frequently received, and an indifference toward her opinions because she manipulated and was manipulated herself so easily.

My physical attraction to the female members of my family, however, started with Becky and Mary, my cousins and stepsisters, and would continue toward all others in my family, immediate and extended. After suffering the traumatic beating after the incident with Becky, a normal human being might have placed them all on a "do not approach or touch" list inside themselves, even at three years of age. However, I not only didn't, I appear to have accepted that taboo as being the forbidden fruit that I would desire and long for most, until years later. Mary, the cousin who reported our behavior resulting in that first beating became attractive to me as well and although I would leave Becky alone after that incident, I fantasized about her nakedness frequently.

My older sister, Belinda, wasn't supermodel thin by any stretch of the imagination, yet because I felt she was smarter than myself and had never hurt my feelings, I felt a very strong physical attraction toward her, which was magnified when she and David were observed by our older step-sister, Carey Morris, doing something in Belinda's bed. I grew intensely jealous of David because I imagined he had been caught having sex with Belinda and strangely it would be Belinda that I felt a Freudian type attraction toward.

David was demoted from the statute of heroic big brother to a father figure that had seen and done things with Belinda that I would never be allowed to acquire. My frustration and anger toward David must have shown through the many masks I wore because on an annual, sometimes semi-annual schedule, he would find a reason to beat me up. Ironically, that action placed him outside of my feelings of being able to trust him - an area usually reserved for the adults in my life or the classmates at school who had ridiculed me for pissing my pants at school recess and followed up that insult with injury to my pride by provokingly attempting to get me to fight them afterward because for an instant, during the ridicule, my anger had manifested itself and I had struck out at them - physically slapping on of them in the face. This may seem like an aside, but bear with me.

Anger over being ridiculed or insulted would become an issue for me and an event that shattered my sense of self-esteem I had retained and that led to a sexual failure of epic proportions. My sister, Violet, was less emotionally attractive than Belinda was to me, but I did feel some type of love toward her and that placed her well within my range of females I decided I wanted to be sexual with, but again, my brother, Dave, seemed to have had that privilege bestowed upon him. Maybe Violet felt a sister's concern and affinity with David. I could tell he was her favorite brother early on and frequently I would observe what I construed as a connection or familiarity between them that I both desired and resented that David had while I did not.

Because both my sisters shared a room while David and I would share the room next to theirs, I would occasionally see Violet's developing body in states of various stages of undress, including her complete nakedness at times, as she was dressing after bathing. I was very aware when she developed breasts and pubic hair and, in that David, and I shared a singular desire to observe her nakedness at every opportunity that would present itself.

I would read an opinion-article years later where it said that removing a woman's underwear while she was sleeping, but not in a drug or alcohol induced state of unconsciousness was in the words of that author, impossible. The woman would awaken or have to awaken enough to elevate her hips, to allow them to be removed.

That author, a man I have to assume, should have consulted my younger self and I could have shared with him the techniques that David and I employed to view Violet's naked pubic area by removing her panties frequently. I claim the responsibility for developing and practicing the technique and although I don't remember how or why David was a part of the process after I had gained the ability, I do remember we often shared the experience to the point that Violet would wake up some mornings with her underwear down around her knees or ankles. My reasoning at the time for disagreeing with that author was based on two reasons. One reason: she never informed our parents that the occurrence of awakening in the state of partial undress happened frequently and at the same time, infrequently enough that she openly dismissed it as a naturally occurring event during her sleep due to the extremely hot temperatures during summer. It was in those summer periods that she would be most inclined to sleep only in her panties and toss aside any sheets or covers on her bed, making her more vulnerable to the invasion of her privacy.

The other line of thinking coincided with the article I had read - that she had somehow known what I was doing and had since become especially easy to do by the time David had joined me in the process. Did she know and did she allow it, especially for Dave, because of their bond and closeness, not wanting to be caught doing anything, but allowing it to be done to her? That was a question that could have been debated with Freud himself and even if she participated in the debate on either side of the question, I don't believe Violet could have given an honest answer that would end or resolve that debate.

As with all things, I chose to experiment, with the intent to resolve the question to my own satisfaction after witnessing an incident where David sat and lay at the foot of Violet's bed. Her bed had been moved to restrict my very easy observation of her nudity. While I had been asleep, I was awakened by her giggling loudly enough for me to hear from across the room and through the open doorway to the girls' room. She continued to giggle after David had advised or bade her to be cautious and had sat up to see if I had been awakened. I kept my face neutral and my eyes shut until I heard him lay back onto her bed, but although I couldn't witness with my eyes, what was transpiring my ears and imagination left me little room to doubt her willfully permitting David to pet her vagina or tickling her genitalia which caused her to laugh. I didn't know with what, but my imagination being what it was, it could have entailed his fingers or his tongue with which he was touching her. He spoke infrequently and most of his comments entailed his constant shushing her to be quieter. I was both panicked by what I was hearing, but also incensed that once again, he was being allowed privileges by being allowed access to her in a way that I would not be allowed.

I fell asleep on that anger and resentment and upon awakening the next day, it had grown to the point where I felt that I no longer cared what the repercussions would be or how the consequences of my actions might cause either of them or our parents to feel, react, or respond. As I was passing through the girls' room on my way to breakfast or the bathroom, I saw that Violet was in her panties only, so I walked up to her without hesitation and, before she could avoid me, placed my hand on her pubic mound and using my other hand, tried to pull her panties out enough that I would be able to see and perhaps access her genitals with my hands at the very least. She recoiled from my touch shouting at me, but didn't shout loud enough for our parents upstairs to hear, stating she was going to tell that I had touched her inappropriately. My response was vicious, cruel and effective. I told her, with David in the room, as he had heard her whispered shout, that she was welcome to tell them at her leisure, but that they both had better take into consideration two important points that would come up during her report or when I was questioned about it.

Firstly, I would be afforded the opportunity to deny what I had done because of my status of being our mother's favorite. Since I had indeed manipulated my way into that position, they both knew this was factual and that I would, most likely, be believed by our mom.

My second and more sinister and extortion point was that if she reported my action, I would report the scenario I had observed the night before of David laying on her bed and her giggling, as he played with her vagina. They both presented the argument that our mom would hear them, that they had only been teasing her cat, Mr. Kay, so I continued my blackmail threat by informing them that I had not observed mom's cat in sight or hearing in any manner and followed that point up with a reference back to my first point that as mom's favorite, who did they think mom was more than likely to believe?

If two siblings could hate a third more than the look they gave in combination that moment, I cannot imagine what he might have done to cause them to do so, but it was very clear that they knew I was telling them the truth about our mom so that any argument they would try to present would be brushed away by the ensuing beating that they would both receive if I were to report their behaviors from the night before.

While some people might believe that it may have only been my imagination that saw David as the privileged one when it came to sexual access to our sisters, but by their very capitulation or giving in to both my extortion and threats and by the fact that they were not even arguing with me to disprove my accusations it would, in my eyes, establish that what I had observed was exactly what it had seemed to be and had occurred.

Compleat

I knew that my accusation had indeed hit its mark and that my theory had been established as a probability rather than the theoretical hypothesis of my overactive imagination and libido. If they hadn't hated me quite so much, weren't actively bonded by that hatred, and even attempted to convince me by appeal to our status of siblings in a household where beatings occurred, they could have won me over to the point that I would have believed in their innocence, perhaps even owning my own behavior as being the inappropriate action it was, putting the shoe on the other foot where I would be obligated to them for keeping and retaining the information to themselves.

Where in all that is holy or even unholy does a child learn the concepts, behaviors, and methods to extort or blackmail his own siblings? By reading material that included these in the adult sections of public libraries and having the cognitive ability to comprehend, ingest, and execute the behaviors at an age when riding bicycles and playing sports were the focus of other boys his age. I was cognitively aware of all that I was doing - that all of the things I was thinking, feeling, and acting upon were by society standards, abnormal, or perhaps even insane. Either that, or I was one evil little son of a bitch. The very last time I ever attempted to be sexual or was tempted to try to be would come years later.

I would, between my early onset at age three and that last incident involving a blood relative, find myself physically attracted to all of my female cousins - some which would end in a result that should never have happened. I would witness my aunt getting divorced from her first husband and believed myself partially responsible because I had touched his niece in inappropriate ways and although she reported my behaviors to them both, my aunt sided with me due to the girl not being as physically attractive as my then girlfriend and my successful rate of plausible deniability - I was good at denial - while my uncle sided with his niece, arguing that she wouldn't lie.

Not long after their divorce, I was present when my aunt and a woman friend of hers got overly inebriated at my aunt's house. While I was discouraged from drinking more than a sip myself, I was instructed how to make Brandy Alexanders, and as it was a very sweet tasting and extremely potent alcohol-based beverage I steadily increased the Brandy portion until both women fell unconscious.

Memory fails me as to who collected the other woman. I believe that I forgot this because by the time they passed out, I had ingested at least enough brandy as would be contained in a single, normal Brandy Alexander. What I do recall is lifting my aunt, carrying her to her bedroom, and placing her on the bed. Sex versus love, remember or sex and love. Was I just a drunken kid who stood over his unconscious aunt debating with himself if he should remove her outer clothing at least, or was I the pervert who knew that if I went even that far, I would continue undressing her completely, take advantage of her unconscious state to the point of enjoying her body, which to both sets of thinking was extremely attractive, perhaps even to the point of engaging in sexual intercourse with my drunken and unconscious aunt.

I knew she was drunk enough to not remember what would have happened and I wanted her perhaps because of my relatives closest to me, beside my sister, Barb, my aunt was the nearest thing I had ever experienced having received motherly love from which made having sex with her - even unaware as she was, or would be - seem acceptable to me, even if it would be construed as inappropriate by adults.

This may be the first experience in which my younger-self did something so out of character, for me, that someone might even consider saying there was a spark of humanity in me at that time. I covered my aunt fully clothed with the blankets and left her house, not out of any sense of behaving appropriately - and I've already described that if it entered my mind, I would act upon the thoughts without concern over the societal or legal ramifications and if I left because I respected or loved my aunt is beyond my recall even now.

I regretted leaving just as much as I regretted what it was that is in me that makes having sex with my aunt while she was unconscious appear to be a reasonable act of making love to someone who I felt love for. I know now that I would act out with one of her daughters, my cousin, later on and be rejected by the other cousin for similar attempted actions.

But that day, at her most vulnerable, and while justifying to myself in my mind my desire to engage in sex her a thought that has only occurred one other time in my many years, I considered how my aunt would feel if I were to do what I wanted so desperately to do, and if she somehow discovered what I had done with her unconscious body and without her consent. Her feelings mattered, for a split second of my life, someone I loved was more important to me than myself. That was why I left. Some would say love of her won out. I don't because, in hindsight, if I had gone through with my desire, she would have at least suspected something had happened. How would she have gotten naked? This might have been a reasoning point and she might have trusted me

Compleat

less around her daughters, if not removing me from their lives and hers forever if she had known for sure.

I had learned to believe that 'Love' is protecting others from myself - something I had failed to do on epic scales for many years until I grew to love Megan after I had been playing at being a boyfriend to her younger sister, Penny. And during that period, Penny and I would sneak away to places where I could explore her body. Younger than I, by maybe five years, her body was smooth, creamy colored as if she had an almost in impossibly permanent tan and with the exception of her pubic area, though she would gain hers there eventually as she entered puberty, Penny was blessed with a clear downy coat of hairs – un-observable from any distance over an inch away from her skin.

I would find myself closer than that at every opportunity we could make happen, but as she grew closer to her puberty and I to mine, my desires for more sexually involved actions grew to bother, annoy, and eventually displease her to where she broke up with me in her family's basement while we were supposed to be playing school on a chalkboard, which her dad had put up for Megan and her.

I had become overly insistent on her letting me touch, taste, and explore her and she got fed up with my demands, telling me I could leave out the back basement steps, and not come back. I just sat there stunned by being dumped since I had never even considered leaving her. Being dumped that way, her left me shocked me. I had assumed that saying I love you was a commitment - one I knew I wouldn't break because you just don't do that. That's what my mom often did and I wouldn't just so I would not be like my mom. It never occurred to me that she said I love you and could change her mind. That she would change her mind, never entered into my thoughts.

David had been Megan's boyfriend during those same days, but they had broken up a week before because David wanted to have full on sex and had learned that he could ask complete strangers, both girls and women over 20 directly and to the point if they wanted to have sex. I exaggerate sometimes, but if I am this time, it is only slightly because for 50% of the requests that I witnessed him making, including a 27-year-old mother, they said yes, and followed up their acceptance with actions.

I believe Megan was one of the 5% that considered doing as he asked, rather than the 45% that said no, or slapped him for asking. She might have, if he had given her time to consider, but hesitation was a not in David's book. He moved onto someone else. And as I sat there in the 'schoolroom', Megan came downstairs from their family's kitchen and was writing on that chalkboard. Maybe it was revenge against Penny that motivated me. Maybe it was still anger at my brother. And maybe it was because she had apparently told David no and that rejection of him made her even more attractive to me, what I only know is that I spoke up and asked what was the only pick-up line I would ever use on any girl of woman.

At that time, I thought I was just asking a stupid question before I left forever. The question was, "Do you know of anyone who could want a slightly used boyfriend?" On her part, maybe she wanted to make David jealous, since I did want Penny to know and be jealous a little, and maybe that was at least one reason she heard my request, hoping to win him back? Maybe the weeks between had given her young heart the healing it needed and she wanted to try having a boyfriend again. Maybe she pitied me, feeling sorry for someone who had pain that she related to, and maybe - God, how I still wish - she hoped she could love me. Too late now to ask her. I will probably never know the reason why or the reasons she said yes. All I know is that she did say yes and we fell in love after that over the next couple of years. But maybe it was only I who fell, because to this day, I still love someone I haven't seen or spoken to in 49+ years.

Let me explain what I mean by love in regards to Megan. Of all the memories I tried to erase, including the one of hurting her at the end, the memories that no amount of drinking, drugging, violence, perversions, all the things I did trying so very hard to run away from loving her, nothing and none of it could wipe out the few good memories that would open the floodgate of self-hatred and self-destruction.

Is it strange that I feared the good memories as much as I did the awful ones? I know in my mind that they weren't bad for me to hold onto since they could be the reason that I'm still alive today, but fear them I did, and here's an example. Mary Kaiser, Megan's mom, allowed me to wash Megan's hair in their kitchen sink - a perfectly harmless memory filled with love for Megan, respect for and from her mom, love from Megan, and an intimacy that went way beyond sexuality or even sensuality. Both Megan and her mom trusted me to wash her hair. To them, it might not have been a big deal. For me, it was an experience in being trusted, maybe my first ever, and it was so powerful that it again convinced me that Megan was my one love beyond sex, position, time, distance, and life's twist and turns. Nothing on earth or in heaven would stand in the way of my loving her until the day I died.

Sure, we had fooled around sexually, but never had intercourse, nor did she give me oral sex, but I know the touch and sight and sound and smell and taste of her. She filled my senses when we were together physically and flooded my mind with dreams, hopes, desires, intentions, and plans for our future together. Even asleep - until I lost the ability to recall my dreams - she was there and my world finally seemed balanced and right.

Such a wonderful memory, right? Someone might ask why was I so desperate to block it - even blot it out from my mind? Because, inevitably, and this is the true story, I remembered how I had tossed that love away doing what no man could have, and God wouldn't have done. Add to it the regret of not knowing if what I had done had resulted in ruining her life in spite of my best efforts to avoid that result. Hindsight suggests I did exactly what was best for her. She grew up, married a man whom she loves as much as I loved her, had children with him, grandchildren, and great grandchildren. Apparently, her life has been prosperous, filled with love and joy and full of everything I prayed for her to have over all the years to be given to her.

So, hindsight says I made a good decision and letting go of her was the one true act of love I was able to do. It still hurts – it hurt her then, though with time and new love, she got over me. Trust me, my male ego takes a hit with that thought, but the great part is that she received every single thing I prayed she receive.

If I did what I decided was best for her, I could let my ego run with that thought, but for two things or thoughts balancing it out. First of all that I did was pray that she get all of that where, if I was more man than ass, I would have stayed and provided all of it to her myself. She received all and achieved all of it on her own with God providing it to her through her own faith works, love, and people who loved her.

The second reason my ego doesn't get to run with the idea that my prayer has made a difference is I know god answers my prayers - not the "let me win the lottery so I can donate to charity" kind of prayers. We don't have that kind of relationship, god and I. What usually happens, like with Megan, I'm hurting so much and in so much pain - physical, emotional, mental, and spiritual - I start screaming; first at myself for making even the slightest mistake, hindsight not mattering since it wasn't knowledge I had at the moment.

Then I tap into yelling at god, out loud, personally, and with an "in your face motherfucker" attitude. I hold nothing back. My pain, I toss at him like a spear thrown with all that I am - the fear with anger, frustration, and doubts trailing along like strings and feathers decorating the spear. Screaming "What the fuck" is a mild statement, merely an opening salvo to get my aim straight. I scream at him the reproaches of how he wanted me to minister to others and what a failing I would've been if I had tried.

At the same time, I'm screaming and cussing that he would've used me like a tool that was breakable, maybe even already broken, to solve things in other people's lives. But look at the mess my life is and what I've made of it. You could have used me, but I resisted and I broke. I snapped apart under your hand and just look at the mess I made of my life. How - I asked at the top of my lungs - could you use me to help others while my entire life is completely in shambles?

My only prayers that you answer are for others and you give me nothing I ask for, for myself. A broken lawn mower belt led to this particular tirade. Turns out I had one that was the wrong size. But again, that's a matter for hindsight. At that moment, without fear, without expectation - and really, without faith - I talked to him directly as an angry upset son might speak to an adoptive dad if that was how he had been raised.

Faith isn't knowledge. Am I disrespectful? Absolutely - unkind and inconsiderate, inaccurate, unwittingly so wrong because I was caught up in my anger, frustration, and self-pity. I screamed a final jab: "Like the thing with Megan." 49 plus years, I had prayed for her happiness. I lived that prayer every day. I stayed away from her. She wasn't to blame for my pain and suffering. It had been my choice, but not knowing if I had done what was best for her, and wanting her to love me, kept tearing at my sanity until what little sanity I might have had was completely shredded.

How, then, do I know god answers my prayers? Because I found out all of the information I've shared about her life by so-called chance and even when I know she is alive, married, financially safe, and in love with her husband, I was still torn up by my desire or need to see her. Learning all of that about her woke feelings I had suppressed and assumed I had under control and, ironically, it wasn't just lust I felt for her younger self reawakening, It was the return of the feelings I had as we stood in her family's kitchen and her mom allowed me the privilege of washing her hair.

The image of that moment, not the day because there were so many moments in every day that we shared for me was of the smile in Megan's eyes. In my entire life - through two marriages, the infidelity, the sexual abuse of girls half my age, every relationship, good or bad - I looked for the light that I had seen at that moment, of the smile in her eyes and, honestly, I have never found it. Even when M started a Facebook page under her married name and posted a photograph of her husband and herself, it wasn't there. Maybe that light was the brightness that only first loves can know. Maybe I put out that light when I put her out of my life and what I saw as harm's way. Maybe hindsight will never answer those questions too. What I do know is the photo was captioned with the words, "my love, my life," and I made another choice - God help me - when I saw those words. If Megan feels the way I do about her toward this man, Larry, in her life as his wife, then she has found even more than I could have thought to pray for her.

And if the words were her husband, Larry's, then she has someone in her life that loves her the way I do already. Some will say she doesn't need me and they're right. Others will say that being loved unconditionally by two men is just an additional blessing. They are right too. And still others - maybe those that read this book - will say she's better off without my love; judging me from my behaviors and finding me unworthy of her. Right again.

One thing I have learned about myself, the human race as a whole and God, or pops as I like to call him, there is no wrong answer when love comes with no conditions, no expectations, and finally, with no regrets. Unconditional love is how we humans were meant to experience life. Acceptance, of course, being one of many keys, it's a good place to start, or at least it has always been so for me.

My youngest son, Mike, told me I was the only teacher in his life that he felt safe and comfortable with saying, "fuck you" and "I love you" with equal depth of feeling. And I was flattered both by why he said it, but also by the parallel I drew from his statement, because that is the relationship I have with God. I frequently tell him to go fuck himself and just as frequently tell him "thank you" or "I love you." Immediately, that same day, I accused God of not doing anything for me about Megan is when I received the photographs of her, her mom, and her husband and I saw the words, "my love, my life."

I celebrate their love and only slightly wish I could have made it into a poem. If they were Larry's words:

My love, my life, Megan, my wife.

Yes, I wish she were my wife instead. Selfishly, I still wish she were mine to have and to hold for better or for worse; in sickness and in health, but such is not my place in this life.

Compleat

Compleat People

Most folks writing about the people in their lives that mattered, most would put their mother first. After all, she gave them nine months of her life in exchange for giving them their own. I cannot conform to that stereotypical listing for many reasons, the foremost of which is I have never appreciated being born in the first place. Some will say it was because I was a bottle-fed baby, but there's much more involved than Freud's "baby wanted to suckle on Mama's teat."

For some reasons, I am unwilling to list until I get to each individual in rank of importance to me, my biological father isn't high up on the list of priority people involved in my existence and subsequent experiences of this phenomenon called living. Both my parents are on my list for obvious reasons, but my priorities aren't those of most of the human race, which might be a contributing factor of believing myself to be other than human. Of the people I have experienced during the years I've passed among the majority of humanity, I choose to list my sister Belinda Jane Runner first, not simply for my seeing her as the only member of my family who I knew to be authentically herself. I put her first because although she died early in her life, she was the one person I know from my childhood who I saw as being smarter and more intelligent than myself.

Compleat

That Belinda was an honor student all through her schooling, getting A+s in every subject had next to nothing to do with my perception of her being smart. An awareness of the whole first child syndrome of a dysfunctional family setting her achievements and over-achievements and academic pursuits left little doubt as to why she excelled at schoolwork. She had no choice. Being good at everything was a role forced upon her by her order of birth and the societal standards of the parents we shared. Her intelligence of school level education was a reflection of the demands placed upon her by being first born. The main reason I saw Belinda as more intelligent than I was or am had more to do with her awareness of herself and those around her. She chose her own path in life, despite being forced into the first child role, by knowing fully that it was a role and making playing at that role her own choice. I realize many folks will see this observation as contradictory, or at the very least, debatable. It isn't though. The difference between being forced into a role by circumstances and having the intelligence to choose that same role for herself came from, and is simply based upon being aware of the role and the very ability to choose that is granted by that awareness.

Belinda read even more voraciously than I did, but her choices for reading avoided escapist literature such as I favored and delved into readings related to psychology, self-awareness, and society. Early on, she was aware of who she was, what she wanted for her own life, and how to achieve the goals she would set for herself. Unfortunately, Belinda was burdened with two handicaps of birth, the first being our mother, whose morals and demands were so low for herself and extreme for Belinda that it became harder and harder for Belinda not to rebel against the obvious inequality of judgment used in relation to their behaviors. While our mother displayed the morals of a street whore or slut, Belinda was expected to remain virginal and pure in regards to sexuality, is an example that I can recall happening most. Aware of the demands being placed upon her and equally aware of the unfairness of these demands coming from a woman who held no such standards for herself, Belinda chose to live according to those standards in regard to what our mother would know about her and to live her life according to her own choices despite an increasing desire to rebel and act out on her choices, openly defying our mother by becoming as obviously promiscuous as our mom was herself.

Some folks might need to reflect on how a boy of my young age could or would deal with a greater knowledge of my sister's sexual life than the one known to her mother. The truth is, I observed her behaviors with admiration by respecting her choices and right to choose for herself. Inwardly, however, I regretted that as her brother, she would never consider sharing herself in a sexual way with me - a regret that would pale in comparison to the one I would have when I finally approached the subject with her openly by asking her directly to become more than a sister but a lover as well.

The night my sister Belinda died unfolded like this. My youngest brother Abraham had become sick with a fever that necessitated his being taken to the emergency room at a hospital. Both my parents had left with him and both Belinda and myself were awake and concerned for him. My older brother, David, wasn't home for a reason I cannot recall, but I know that my younger sister Violet was in Texas being molested by our mother's lover, Aiden Addis, sharing motel rooms with him as his daughter while on vacation with him. To this day, I cannot avoid the belief that our mother allowed him access to her youngest daughter sexually in order to keep his interest in staying around as her own frequent lover. The point being that Belinda and I were alone in the house late at night with only her nightgown and my underwear on while sharing a deep concern for Abraham.

I felt closer to Belinda than ever before and being awakened from a sound sleep, I allowed my feelings of both love and lust to overcome my reserves and respect for Belinda to the point I asked her directly if she would have sex with me. Following speech with actions, I kissed her and placed my hands upon her breasts in an attempt to arouse her interest in me sexually as well. At first, I felt that she might actually have reciprocated. I grew hopeful that she and I would become lovers at last. But the initial excitement of that moment was quashed nearly immediately, becoming forgotten by the telltale signs of Barb's beginning to experience her seizure. My arousal was forgotten as concern for her health and safety became immediately paramount. I found her phenobarbital medication, gave it to her in the dosage prescribed and escorted her to her bed, watching her only long enough to assume the medication had worked. Since she appeared to fall asleep, I went to bed myself.

In telling the story, I need to mention an unusual circumstance about myself as an aside. Sexually inappropriate behaviors being regarded as usual for me, of course. In those days of my youth, I slept like a cat. The slightest sound from anywhere in the entire house would bring me wide awake, even the simple sound of a step on the carpeted floor in the living room, four rooms away. That night, however, I slept through what doctors would describe as my sister's experiencing a grand maul seizure. Her normal seizures alone often resulting in her violently shaking, noises of choking, and shaking her bed with metal springs that squeaked when she laid down or got up from her mattress,

Compleat

would have alerted me to her condition on any other night. That night, and every night for many years thereafter, I slept so soundly that I only awoke to the screams from our mother at Belinda to wake up the next morning.

Just a Thought

With all that I've written about the girls, women, and misconduct in my life someone who read the rough draft of what I've written thought that I was writing some type of confessional, admitting to my mistakes as a way of making an indirect amends to all those who I've harmed over the many years.

It's ironic that the world will probably see the stories in this book in that same manner, for the most part. But perhaps, and it is just a thought that I have not even an honest hope, there will be that one person will read all these stories and choose to reflect upon all my reasoning for relating these truths.

As an example, I have chosen to relate back to the stories about Megan, but in a way that I might not have made clear or expressed in a way other than the sexual desires of a teenage boy, the loneliness of an aging man, or even the confused thinking of an individual that has been deemed, by the society in which I reside, as being completely insane.

Compleat

That I'm still in love with the girl I knew those many years ago could be obvious from what I've written in those other stories. As I'm sure is the longing and loneliness I've felt for decades after leaving her in the manner in which she would have no choice but to hate me and forget about me, forever. But the insane thinking of knowing that she has grown to be a woman, a person I neither know or ever knew, and my still having the feelings I do for the person she once was to me, a girl without whose love I perished and gave up all that I might have become as a human being might escape the readers of this book.

I should state truthfully that I don't think about that girl in a sexual manner any longer; except when I'm forced to remember moments we shared as flashes of memory shooting across my mind with the impact and report of a pistol being fired next to my ear. Those memories, sudden, unexpected, and as abruptly gone as they appear, are not what my mind dwells upon throughout the days and long into the sleepless nights. Although they are pleasant memories that simply startle me awake or prevent me from finding escape in sleep, they are not the terrible realization of a fact that staggers me up from wherever I'm trying to rest, to seek distraction in games like solitaire, solo dominoes, pool or eight ball and cribbage against a computer opponent.

What am I running from, what is it I have to distract myself from most, in order to prevent my self-destructive impulse from overwhelming me and what is it that those memories trigger? It is the knowledge of what I miss and have desired most of all throughout my life spent without her in it.

 It's not the sexual things that we shared, innocently exploring and learning about one another in that way and it's not even the love we shared as a young couple by riding bikes, walking hand-in-hand, washing her hair with her mother's supervision, watching her favorite soap operas on the television, and all the things we shared when we were a 'couple.' I do remember those things and miss them, and knowing that we could have shared those for the lifespan that we might have had is truly hard to live with on a daily basis.

But what drives me from sleep, forcing me to distract my mind from thinking about it, is knowing that I never did and never will sleep beside the girl I knew as Megan. To never lay beside her in what would have been our bed, holding her as she slept, watching her breathing, feeling the warmth of her beside me, and being there when she would awaken, to be the first thing her eyes registered upon at the start of her new day. Again, please understand me in this one thing. I'm not talking about the woman she became, the one she is now.

Compleat

She's married, happily, and I would not disturb that for all the world, in any way, if I could help it. But to never have held her, the girl I loved back then, in that way ... that is the waking nightmare that is my life, these many years later and too late. One psychiatrist suggested that by holding on to her in the way I do, I've trapped her in some psychological way. That I should release her spirit and allow her to be who she is now. As if I have that power? I almost laugh but instead, I feel only tears that will not flow from my eyes and clog my heart to near the bursting point. I couldn't hold her prisoner even if I tried, because the girl I knew no longer exists. She grew into the woman who replaced her in the now, becoming a wife to someone else, a mother to her children, a grandmother to her children's children, and so on. It is the terrible irony that all that I set out to do, back when I let her go from being a part of my life, succeeded. She became all that I had hoped and prayed for her to be, without me. And of all the pain I've ever inflicted upon myself, mentally, emotionally, and even physically, that knowledge is the gunshot wound that no amount of bandages will ever heal. Like the bullet that can never be removed, it can only exist deep inside me, until death keeps her word and releases me from this life.

If You Truly Love Someone

If you truly love someone, and I am speaking directly from my personal experience here, UNDER NO CIRCUMSTANCES should you allow yourself to 'decide' what is best for them without talking to them FIRST.

I have lived over 49+ years, suffering mental, emotional, and spiritual anguish over making a decision like that.

Even if it was the right decision, it wasn't mine to make.

And life may never offer the opportunity to express that regret to the person you hurt in such an awful manner. They will probably get over you (as I hoped she would me) and have a full and happy life. But the weight of shame from being so cowardly can break a person's spirit, leaving an empty husk walking around physically alive but empty inside.

For your own sake as well as that of the person you love ... don't risk it.

The Eyes
_._._._._._._._._._._._._._._._._._..

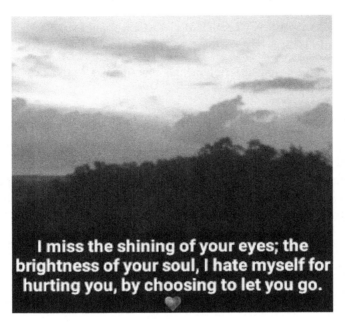

The first experience I had with seeing Megan completely naked came on a day when her dad was at work and her mother needed to run to the store for a few minutes. We had been playing in their basement game room, with a chalkboard for playing at being in school and a table where we would play cards and listen to albums I had bought on Penny and Megan's portable turntable. Mary Kaiser had asked me to lift a 5-gallon bucket of water and pour it into their washing machine, since the rinse cycle had just quit working, to finish the load of laundry that she had started just a short while before and I had assured her that I could and would watch for it and add the water at the right time.

Megan and I started making out, kissing and her allowing me to touch and kiss her breasts almost as soon as her mother had left in their station wagon for the store. How it advanced to my gaining the opportunity to have her step into the back portion of the basement, where there were no windows that we might be seen through, and us removing all of our clothing together is something that escapes me these many years later.

Compleat

But what doesn't escape me, even haunting me in my dreams and nightmares, was how beautiful she was to me. Her body had only just begun to develop, of course, but she was my entire world at that moment, where nothing else mattered or even registered on my conscience mind.

Perverts and child molesters would see only a young girl nude and vulnerable under those circumstances, and perhaps that may have added to my own desire toward young women who had just entered puberty, I just don't know enough about myself to claim to understand that portion of my psyche. One thing I do know, that no others would ever be able to understand unless they were me, is that no matter how similar the circumstances of any event others might have experienced they could never know what held my attention most in those stolen moments.

Yes, I was a hormonal mess, of a young, teen male. Yes, she was the sole focus of all my desires, hopes, and dreams of one day being married and having a life with her. But standing there before me, fully unclothed and aware of my seeing her naked for the first time it would be Megan's eyes that mattered most to me.

In her eyes, I saw acceptance, love, passion, desire, and most importantly trust. Megan had faith in me, she believed in my desire for her and that it went beyond just the lust I felt for her body because I looked at her with all of those things in my own eyes. She looked into my eyes and saw my soul, more exposed than either of our bodies were in our nakedness.

As I said, she was everything in the world that could and would make the world – right - in my life. And coming from my childhood, with all the abuse, stupidity, anger, fear, and frustration I had experienced up until that moment I knew in my heart I would never be able to love anyone else.

To this day many decades later, when I dream of her as I often do, I don't dream of her naked body but rather the light I witnessed shining from her eyes that day. And when I awaken, alone as I always am, I find myself crying with tears streaming down my face, holding back sobs of pain and regret that I burned that one bridge to life that mattered most to me.

When I see a photo of her eyes, and I need to clarify that I only have one because a friend of mine sent me a current photo of her and her husband that he found on social media, I still look first at her eyes. But the light I saw isn't there for me any longer. Perhaps her husband sees it now, or her children,

Compleat

grandchildren, and great-grandchildren?! But for me, there is no longer any light in the world because it is no longer there in her eyes for me.

Compleat

Unworthy!
— . — . — . — . — . — . — . — . — . — . — . — . — . — . .

Torn between my fear of losing her, and my fear of using her, I entered the ante chamber to what would one day lead me through the very gates of Hell. When she confessed to her mom, later that same day what we had attempted to do, I came to realize she was being wracked by a fear of what we had tried, even while being overwhelmed with the fear of losing my love because the attempt had failed.

There was no way for her to know it was my failure, not hers, no way for her to understand or sense the feeling of self-hatred that had awoken inside of me for not reassuring her and avoiding the attempt altogether, keeping to our commitment of waiting for one another and the marriage she deserved.

We both had wanted to marry and have a life together, with children being a shared part of that life. We had even agreed to wait until we were married to be involved in intercourse, saving ourselves for one another. When we talked with her mom, however, she also confessed that she blamed herself because, although she wanted to wait, and believed me when I said I did too, yet her "friend" had convinced her that she must go ahead and have intercourse with me or she would lose me when I became a Marine. Because as a Marine, this friend told her, I and would have had access and opportunities with other women from all around the world.

Until that moment, she had never caused me the slightest harm in any way, but hearing that statement I realized she feared losing my love and because I would see no wrong in her, refusing to for many years afterward to recognize her fear as being hers alone, I blamed myself for not being able to make her to know how real my love for her was. I had failed to cause her to know that I loved her then – that I, love her to this day and would love her for as long as I drew breath into my body.

I had failed to make her feel loved. I had failed her! And there, in her mom's kitchen, she was confessing that she felt she had somehow failed her folks and me!

If I wasn't insane before that moment, with all that the trauma and drama that my childhood had been up to that point, it would have been that confession of shame she felt that day that would become the turning point of where I would begin to hate myself beyond any reason or rational thought, the day I chose to become the monster I saw myself to be.

There are those that might try to say she "could have known" or even those arrogant enough to judge her by saying "she should have known" but the fact remains that I had been unaware of her fears and I had agreed to try because I wanted to be with her physically so very much. My lust overruled my promises to wait and to never hurt her or cause her to doubt how very much I loved her. In short, it was my failure, to love her in such a way that she would know and never need to fear.

We were barely allowed to see one another after that. Her dad had already threatened me before that time, but now her mom was cooler toward my seeing her, even if we stayed within her eyesight. And the day drew nearer and nearer for me to go to Marine boot camp. Which was the event her friend had convinced her would end my love for her unless ...

When I tell people that I left her, because I refused to allow my darkness to drag her through my madness, they mistake that as some noble or noteworthy act on my part. I wanted to protect her from what I knew I was becoming, yet at the same time, I knew if I cut that last thin line to a sane world, I would plunge headfirst into hell. It was a choice I made for her sake, without talking to her about it or allowing her to know what I was planning to do "for her own protection." I made a decision that would affect both our lives, irreparably, and I did it without consulting or even advising her of what I was about to do.

If there is one regret that I might still have in this life, for although I have made monstrous mistakes that this book will reveal I came to realize that most of the many mistakes I have made recreated me into who it is I AM today and thereby giving me the opportunity to assist others in avoiding some of those mistakes, this one regret I hold for myself.

Because I learned the hard way that no one should decide for another who they may or may not love. Even if they are right, even if the choice they make is the correct one, choosing or deciding for another person by making a decision that will affect their entire lifetime in a single choice is playing at being god. I am not god.

That day I put aside all my feelings for her, using tools I knew would only be temporarily effective, to distance myself from her as much as I possibly could. I left for boot camp, distant but still the object of her love. I went through the

Compleat

90 days of boot camp, even developing pneumonia for the final weeks, dreading the day I would graduate.

For I had arranged a date with another girl, from my public high school, to take out the very night I got home from Basic Training. I was absolutely certain that my folks would need to go by my house (two doors down the street from her home) by claiming to not have the cash money to pay for dinner for us all to celebrate my homecoming and in full uniform walked from the car to the house and back openly and in sight of everyone who lived on the block. It would be her little sister, Penny, who saw me and ran to let her know I was there but by the time that she knew I was already seated back in the car and had my arm around my date.

If you've ever had the experience of knowing what was about to happen , knowing you were doing something horrifically wrong to someone who did nothing to deserve the kind of pain you were about to inflict on their unsuspecting self - then you might be able to relate to the sense of fear and uncertainty I felt that night.

And I did., I felt the doubt -, the feeling that I was making a huge mistake -, but that was combining and combating with my determination to not allow her to love me any longer. The two feelings or thoughts ravaged what little was left of my humanity, driving me past the point of any manifestation of sanity. Yet even as I sat there, waiting for what I knew was about to happen, I was only able to go through with it by repeating over and over to myself that it was what was best for her.

The result was immediate and completely successful at achieving my aim that night, in that I believe just seeing me there: in uniform with someone else and obviously going out, caused her to hate me. If any doubt of my plan not achieving success had remained up until that point it dissolved with the screaming yell Megan unleashed:

"YOU MOTHERFUCKER!"

So loud had she yelled it even her mom came from inside their home to see what could possibly have hurt her so much that she would scream and use language she had never used in my presence or in that of her parents in all the years we had been dating.

As the car drove off, and she stood there on the sidewalk in front of my home, I saw the look in her eyes. I had killed any love she might have felt for me. I had not only burned any bridges to the past and redemption from my choices, I had burned all access to the future. Even any alternative futures where she might have forgiven me, if such things were really possible.

I had become the monster I knew myself to be in that instant, knowing what I had done and regretting it so much it must have shown on my face.

The girl beside me, being unaware of what was really happening, and how she was being used simply asked, "Why is she screaming at you that way, she knew you had broken up with her, didn't she?"

My quiet response was as soft as a whisper but came across just as clearly as Megan's shout had:

"She does now."

The next day, I went to her door and asked her mom to be allowed to speak with her. Megan came out and we walked over to the steps that had been in front of my family's house since we moved there. I could barely look at her but when I did, I looked not at her body or body language. I looked directly into her eyes and that only that once. Afterward, I would never look into her eyes again. having lost the light of love she didn't even hate me. She felt nothing for me, is what I read there.

I excused my behavior of dating the other girl by adding lies atop the incident. Telling her I had only received 2 letters from her while away at boot camp. Truth can sometimes be the best lie a person can use. I covered the reality of what happened and, in this instance, added an extra layer of insurance that she would never forgive me or want to be with me again. I had only received the 2 letters from her. But I came to believe later that it wasn't her fault that I didn't receive more, which that she may have sent. Her dad might have intervened, making sure I was out of her life, since he must have become aware of the attempt we had made. My drill instructors' (one, in particular, hated me with a passion for being a smug bastard throughout basic) may well have confiscated and destroyed the others as well. But it served the purpose that I was able to lie, with a straight face, and tell her it was 'her own fault' for not writing me in boot camp that made me choose someone else. The last lie I would ever tell her. Because from that day until this I was never allowed, able, or willing to see her. I prayed for her happiness, that she would find love, joy, fulfillment, and peace. Everything I had wished to provide her with and sacrificed from my own life to protect her from me.

So, if any of you ever doubt my insanity, or even doubt the stories I put into this book. Re-read this one, carefully. No sane person decides for another

Compleat

what is best for them without talking to them about it. At least sharing how I honestly felt would have given her the choice instead of making it for her.

I AM not god. But I had played god in someone's life that I knew I couldn't live without, throwing away my one chance at true love and happiness. Maybe that's what being the devil in someone else's life really is: choosing for them instead of communicating what is real?

That was the devil: in his day. Me, myself, and I.

Compleat

A Completely

Different Kind of

———————————————————— Asshole

Compleat

There's a song I heard again today while driving home from seeing my psychiatrist. A nice enough lady, I guess, but more interested in maintaining my 'medications' at a "good" level than in what is happening to me.

I believe the artists singing were a band called "Joan Jett and the Blackhearts." All I know for sure is that the words hit me in a weird way today:

The lady singing kept saying: "I hate myself for loving you!"

What struck me this time is that this phrase seems to be a kind of universal truth. Maybe it's just me, but in my limited 66 years, I recall this happening over and over again. Women fall for the guy who makes them "hate themselves" because they cannot stop loving the asshole who causes them the most pain.

I'm not that kind of asshole. Instead, I'm the loser women look over to find that kind of guy; the one that wets their loins, fires their hearts, and takes their breath away. And, like the song seemed to keep saying: makes them hate themselves for not being able to stop loving them. So, where does that leave me?

Honesty. I'm a compleatly different kind of asshole.

Maybe they somehow sense that about me?

Compleat

Uncle Sam's Misguided Child
_.._

In 1972, I had finished my sophomore year of high school, turned 16 years of age, and wanted nothing more from life except to be allowed to marry and make love with my then girlfriend, Megan Abby Kaiser. But with her being younger than I was we had decided to wait and start having sex after we were older and married. Unfortunately for me, there came the day that her father, Peter Rodney Kaiser witnessed one of my berserk outbursts of rage and for me that hope of ever being with Megan evaporated like a drop of life-sustaining water on a red-hot griddle, bouncing, sputtering and desperately trying to stay viable it would evaporate and disappeared without leaving the slightest trace of its existence.

Some people might question and ask me why I was raging where he could witness my outburst. The truth is, all the reasons for why are too many to count and would take an entire book in and of themselves to recount. The main reason that I list here is only so others might share insight into what happened that day and relate to the feeling of hopelessness that resulted from his witnessing my capacity for uncontrollable rages.

Compleat

My brother, David, and I had been ordered to pull the weeds that were growing between the cobblestones in the alleyway behind the house on Minnesota avenue. Perhaps it was a punishment for something we had done, or simply a task given to two idle teenage boys as a maintenance that needed doing. The one thing I remember is that it was assigned to us both and that is where the beginning of the episode would begin.

Already upset with being assigned work that served no real purpose, knowing that the weeds would simply grow back again and that the root system extended from both the backyard of the house and the neighboring houses as well I could have argued against being made to do the work but complied simply to avoid an unnecessary conflict with our parents, our mother and stepdad-father Anthony Morris, Sr. I did what I had been instructed to do and the task wasn't so overwhelming that two boys wouldn't have been able to accomplish it in a short period of time. And time for me, back then, was of the utmost of importance because I had planned and intended to meet Megan that afternoon.

I pulled weeds without the benefit of gloves, getting my clothes, hand, and even my face wet and dirty from kneeling in the muddy alleyway and having the roots of the weeds give way suddenly, releasing mud and dirt in a spray. I labored at this task for a full hour, watching as the time I was supposed to meet Megan creep closer and closer on a pocket watch I had purchased with money I had earned as a delivery boy for the local newspapers. As the time grew less and less, I grew more anxious and upset that I wouldn't be able to meet her at our agreed to time and place and with that anxiety there grew inside me a resentment that we had been assigned this meaningless task on that particular day.

It was when that thought crossed my mind that I realized something that had escaped my attention up until that moment. David had never arrived to help weed that alleyway. That realization combined with the awakening thought that the task could have been finished already if he had arrived when I did, caused me to wonder and I choose to investigate why he wasn't there and what was going on that had prevented him from helping.

Our parents were in the dining room, drinking coffee I assumed, while David was in our shared bedroom, laying on his bed and reading my comic books and had been doing so apparently for the entire time I had been weeding.

There are those who might presume to think that I could have complained to our parents at that time, but that presumption would require a complete lack of knowledge of the household and the way of life that existed with them. Perhaps I should have but knowing them the way I did, I knew that any complaint would have fallen upon deaf ears or even resulted in my being assigned to finish the task alone, simply for complaining about the unfairness of my working while he was allowed to relax and enjoy himself.

What happened is I made a choice. A decision I would regret and still regret to this day these forty-nine plus years later. I made the decision I was done, through with my portion of the labor we had been assigned, and put that decision into action almost immediately. In no way secretive or hiding what I was doing I gathered together my clean clothes, went into the bathroom assigned to the four older children in our household, bathed and changed into the nicest clothes I had with the full intention of meeting Megan at the time we had agreed upon, walking past our parents on the way to the bathroom and afterward on my way toward the front door.

There's a commonly used phrase used to describe how a small amount of crap can become a huge, hard- to- clean- up mess. It's commonly referred to as 'the shit hitting the fan.' What occurred that day was much worse, becoming a shit storm where the fallout would reach people and places never imagined before and never deserving of what it would consist of by its spreading to their lives.

In the beginning, both of our parents must have finally realized that I was leaving the house and rose from their positions at the kitchen table in a coordinated effort to block me from leaving physically, telling me I wasn't allowed to leave or go anywhere until all of the weeding was done. I tried to reason with them, by explaining that I had had plans to meet Megan that day and that I had done most of the weeding already, accomplishing it alone the entire time I had been outside working, and noting that they had allowed David to lay in his bed and read comics while I worked.

In some of my previous stories, I may have mentioned that when being beaten in that household it was common for our parents to use a leather strap labeled "the Monster" because of its size, weight, and the wounds it was known to inflict when used on any of us. Because I wasn't complying with their commands our step-father took this implement off the nail where it hung on the wall and they both began to advance on me, forcing me to either retreat or have the situation escalate into a physical confrontation that would result in my receiving yet another beating.

At first, I tried to plead with them, practically begging them to see how unfair they were being and offering to continue my efforts after my date with Megan, but they continued to advance on me and eventually forced me to back out of the door to the back yard and leading to the alleyway with their physical presence, and as I did my anxiety changed from both fear of being beaten and missing my date with Megan into an anger that I felt justified in having due to their being unreasonable and David's not being made to assist – thus preventing me from meeting and being with Megan. My final offer, to change clothes again and resume weeding if they made sure David helped me was met with the same disregard and negativity that had forced me out of doors and out into the alleyway again.

It seems ironic to me that I can remember all the details of that incident but cannot recall the exact wording they used to say no to my offer. Ironic only in that I know they must have said something that triggered what followed, like the proverbial last straw or the final crack in the ice that let loose everything that had been building up inside me up until that point. I know why I cannot remember though. It was the explosion of rage that came out of me in response to whatever it was they said that day. Similar with to the episode in my eighth- grade experience with a boy named Sal, I knew only that I was being tormented and that my tormentors were before me, unyielding and advancing upon me.

What came out of my mouth in the next few minutes were all the pent- up fears, anger, and disgust I felt for them both. I began with a verbal barrage, telling them I wasn't doing a 'god-damn' thing they wanted and they would both go to hell before they would be able to force me to comply with anything they demanded ever again.

Many people and even psychiatrists and psychologists could argue that a sixteen-year-old boy rebelling against parental authority would seem normal or even relatable. After all, teens do rebel at times. But the cussing and raging verbally weren't what Mr. Kaiser would witness that day. All the verbal outrage was merely the 'shit hitting the fan' as the saying goes. He drove his truck past my parents and myself in that alleyway with his windows rolled up so there is a chance he might have missed most of what I had said to them. What he didn't miss was the actual shit storm that followed.

Apparently, my brother, David, had heard his name being bantered about by me during this entire, ongoing encounter and he chose to attempt to intervene at the point where I was cursing our parents in the alleyway, saying that he would "kick my ass for speaking to our mother in the way I had." He had come out of the house and into the alley, choosing to move toward me as if to make good on his threat. What Mr. Kaiser would witness then was my berserk and dangerous rage, almost rabid in my appearance and behaviors. I would be seen screaming at all of them, especially David, threatening to 'rip his heart out and take a huge bite out of it before he could die.' It was the only time my brother had ever shown fear on his face when confronting me and it caused him to take steps backward away from me as well. When our step-father tried to approach me, perhaps intending to try to calm me down, he, unfortunately, was still carrying the strap, ("the Monster") in his hand. I set myself for a fight, balled up my fists, and told both my parents I would kill them before either of them would be allowed to hit me again.

Poor Peter Kaiser couldn't have known of our family history or the abuse and misconduct that had been going on for years. All he could know was what he was witnessing in that moment of time. Here was a sixteen-year-old boy, one who had expressed an overly intent interest in his daughter, who had just threatened to kill his own parents and had threatened to kill and cannibalize his older brother. Mr. Kaiser did what any normal father would have done in his place, though some might question his choice of timing – considering my enraged state and volatility. Mr. Kaiser approached me and stated clearly and emphatically that "No boy who could or would speak to his own parents the way I just had would ever be allowed to see, be around or be with his daughter, ever again."

I know that I mentioned in my story about the boy Sal in my eighth- grade class how I had turned to see the look of fear in the eyes of the nun, Sister Tennille. This time was much worse, not because Mr. Kaiser was afraid of me or even for me. When I heard his words, I turned and saw in his eyes the fear he had for the one person we both loved, Megan. Like the tumbler or key in a lock clicking into place, that fear in his eyes struck home with me in a way nothing else could or ever would again, because in that instant I knew that he was right. I wasn't and would never be safe for her to be around.

I've often said before that I hadn't cried since the death of my sister, Belinda. What I feel may have been misleading in that statement is that I failed to include the word 'outwardly' when I made mention of it. There isn't enough salt water in all the oceans of the world to match the tears I've cried inwardly since the moment Mr. Kaiser pronounced what I can only view as my doom. In eighth grade, I had sworn to love Megan and be damned to hell if I ever stopped. I even wrote it that way in an autograph book that others in my class would have signed if I had made friends with any of them. With Mr. Kaiser's pronouncement, I realized that for her sake I would have to stop or at the very

Compleat

least pretend to stop and I had damned myself for the sake of some muddy weeds in a back alley of St. Louis, Mo, and a pair of white bell-bottom jeans.

My life could have ended that day and the 'shit' would have only hit the fan for myself and those immediately around me if it had. Unfortunately, I continued to exist for what seems to me entirely too many years and the resultant 'shit-storm' has affected so many people since it may take my staying alive until the age of 120 years to make all the amends that are due to others.

It was on that day I began my plan to protect Megan from myself, knowing I was a teenage boy with hormones going mad, knowing my family was so messed up I couldn't allow her to become a part of it, knowing that I too was an utter mess mentally and although I knew I loved her more than life itself I also knew I hated myself even more than I loved her.

I made the decision that day to not just end the relationship, but to end it in such a way she could never be able to forgive me. I knew that she would eventually forget me, and I spent years praying for her to find happiness in her life. In a way, joining the Marines was just the first step of many toward accomplishing that goal.

I often suspect that I may not have thought this whole plan out consciously in those days and, it being so many years ago, my memory of the sequence of events is, I admit, slightly blurred. But the feelings I experience when I try to recall the reasons I chose to join the Marines are so intense that my mind recoils from my attempts to put them in correct chronological order, especially when I attempt to describe this particular reason and the events leading up to my choice.

Compleat

Breaking Hearts

Some folks might view my dumping Megan as some brave or noble action on my part, because I describe it as my main reason for choosing to leave her behind. But life is too complicated for a single reason to explain my choices that year and I have often revealed to others, the fact that I never do anything for a single reason. If two or more purposes can be fulfilled by a single action, then I choose to act and that action was no exception. My primary purpose was to distance myself from her, obviously. I've expressed that often enough that even I know it to be a truth, hopefully not convincing myself through repetition. But as this book is meant to help others avoid my mistakes, I must face and reveal as many of my other motivations for deciding to act as I did. The second priority for my choice was based on betrayal. Not the betrayal that I was about to act upon - that comes later.

The first betrayal of love came when Megan confessed to her mom in front of me, and not to me first, that the reason she had agreed to try sexual intercourse before marriage came, not out of love for me, but fear of losing me. Her friend and the other girl's 20-something-year-old boyfriend had instilled the doubt in Megan that if she didn't engage in intercourse with me, she might lose me - as a Marine has ample opportunity to engage in sex with girls all over the world. Looking back now, I realize her immaturity had allowed that doubt to grow and become a fear and my own immaturity was displayed in blindly accepting her change of mind without questioning why.

Compleat

Lust overcame love for me that day and the result was learning the truth behind her choice in what I deemed to be the worst way imaginable. As an aside to explain when the first woman I had married left me for another, I didn't learn it from her, but found a love letter she had written to him. I don't blame her for leaving me as I was an asshole and a complete monster by then. But finding out still came as a blow to my ego. In Megan's case, it came as an awful, unimaginable betrayal of what I saw her as and what we shared in love even without sex being a part of it yet. If, as I suspect, my self-esteem was so low and ego so vulnerable that her confession unseated the only support my then fragile self-esteem had, even I can attest to the fact that I was devastated hearing her words – but doubly so because they were addressed to someone else, not me.

So, my second reason for choosing was much less honorable. I left her because I felt betrayed. These many years later, although I regret the method I chose to dump her, I regret most of all my own immaturity and not talking to her about my feelings. Love for who I had thought she was remained so deep and strong I have been incapable of loving another woman in that same way and, worse, it motivated me to accept unconditional love from a person who should never have been subjected to my self-serving need to find fulfillment with that type of love.

Added to these two main reasons are myriad of small facts and excuses; her father's declaration being the foremost of these. I would have faced his wrath willingly to be with her. That, as a 17-year-old boy, I wanted to enjoy sex, my hormones notwithstanding the constraint of reason being no less overlooked, but an underlying motivation as well. But the deepest reason, and the reason that I refused to admit to myself for years, was so slight I was easily able to ignore it, allowing my ego to mask it from my lack of self-respect. I feel ashamed of myself.

"Ashamed: When shame is self-destructive, self-pity wins." - runner's ravings

I knew all too well that that feeling was subject to rationality and intellect or reason might control the feelings for me much better than they do, but I must admit the truth here. I do still feel ashamed - ashamed at the choice of where we would make the attempt; ashamed that I loved her so poorly that the doubt installed by those others became her fear; ashamed that hormones and lust overwhelmed my love for her, by choosing to accept the offer as a fortunate choice, rather than questioning why she had changed her mind; ashamed for returning betrayal in exchange for learning the truth; ashamed for using lies,

Compleat

deceit, and another person to push her away so far that love would be unobtainable ever again from the person she would grow to become; and shame that I wallow in a mire of self-destructive self-pity, knowing that what I want most from life is her forgiveness and a return to the love we shared once before.

In all my other actions: heinous, criminal, and terribly intrusive that they were, I have been able to assume the mantle of guilt and ceased the shame I felt to allow an end to self-pity.

Only this one shame remains - like her memory - beyond my ability to overcome.

Compleat

New Songs, Old Pain
─·─·─·─·─·─·─·─·─·─·─·─·─·─·─·─·─·─··

Well, you only need the light when it's burning low

Only miss the sun when it starts to snow

Only know you love her when you let her go

Only know you've been high when you're feeling low

Only hate the road when you're missing home

Only know you love her when you let her go

And you let her go

Staring at the bottom of your glass

Hoping one day you'll make a dream last

Dreams come slow, go so fast

You see her when you close your eyes

Maybe one day you'll understand why

Everything you touch, oh it dies

But you only need the light when it's burning low

Compleat

Only miss the sun when it starts to snow

Only know you love her when you let her go

Only know you've been high when you're feeling low

Only hate the road when you're missing home

Only know you love her when you let her go

Staring at the ceiling in the dark

Same old empty feeling in your heart

'Cause love comes slow and it goes so fast

Well you see her when you fall asleep

Never to touch and never to keep

'Cause you loved her too much and dive too deep

So let her go

Oh

let her go

Oh, mmh

You let her go

But you only need the light when it's burning low

Only miss the sun when it starts to snow

Only know you love her when you let her go

Only know you've been high when you're feeling low

Only hate the road when you're missing home

Only know you love her when you let her go.

Compleat
Passenger. "Let Her Go." All the Little Things, MCA, 2012.

Compleat

Part II: The Middle

Compleat

For the Ageless

All of 49+ years have passed and in all those moments only the harshest memories followed me for the longest part of my life. And finding her the way I did, by visiting my older sister's grave, I found myself meditating and sobbing, wandering aimlessly through a graveyard to the area where her father's ashes were retained. Coming across his placement, I flashed back to the day he told me that he would never allow me to be around her again.

It was my behavior that day, no fault on his part whatsoever, when I had erupted into an insane rage toward my older brother, my mom and my step-dad. He witnessed it, heard my roaring verbal assault toward them all and the threats I made toward my brother when he tried to force me to stand down and apologize to our parents.

I had hoped I could one day make an amends to her father, but it was too late. So now, all I can do is an indirect amends by never seeking her out again.

That was his expressed wish, and despite my feelings or needs I choose now to respect his wish as if it were what he would have asked of me, had I been there to receive a dying wish from him.

The New Commandments

1) The greatest sin we can commit against another human being is to think we can decide what is best for them.

2) The respect we show others is a direct reflection of the respect we have for ourselves.

3) When we forcefully take from others, we lose more than we might believe we have gained.

4) The loudest voice in the room is the one most often heard but not necessarily the one that holds the correct answers.

5) Treating a person as a possession is the surest way of losing a relationship short of throwing it, and them, away.

Compleat

6) Knowing ourselves allows us to share with others who we really are and not just an image of who we think we ought to be.

7) Admitting to ourselves that we feel fear is the first step toward finding the courage to admit it to others.

8) Being alone is a choice each of us faces at some time in our lives; we can choose to be alone or we can choose to practice solitude and never be alone again.

9) If we remember to breathe before we make a decision; even for just 10 slow, deep breaths; we stand a much better chance of making a healthy choice for ourselves.

10) By believing in ourselves we are practicing faith. The more we practice it the more real life becomes for us, so that we will be able to see a part of life in each person we meet.

Compleat

Sobering In Japan
‒ ‧ ‒

One of my tours of duty in South East Asia was a nightmare of drunkenness and stupidity. My days were spent faking that I knew what I was doing in an Avionics department on base while my nights consisted of going off base to the bars surrounding the main gate and staying drunk as much and as often as I could afford. An investor in currency could have made a fortune that year since the Japanese Yen had a diminished value compared to the US Dollar and could be exchanged at 1,000¥ or even 1,400¥ per $1. Of course, I had no interest or knowledge of currency exchange rates or dealing in currency futures, I simply took advantage of that exchange rate and used that advantage to get and remain drunk for most of the 12-month tour I was stationed at Iwakuni, Japan.

By then I had established myself as an alcoholic wanna-be, drinking so often that I established regular acquaintances with a few of the local bar people. There was a girl, who called herself Judy, though it was obviously not her given name that I developed a crush on and spent entirely too much money in my drunken attempts to convince her to be my 'girl.' There was a bar owner, a man using the name Jimmy, though what his actual name was never passed between us, who grew to like me enough to invite me to his home, for drinks and to play chess. I suspected that he might have been gay, wanting to establish another type of relationship, but because I'm heterosexual in my preferences I simply accepted his free drinks and left him there. And then, there was the bartender in Jimmy's bar who went by the popular name: Mike.

Compleat

I frequented that particular bar so often that although Maurice couldn't have been his true name, I grew to think of him as a Maurice and we established a routine of both banter and barter. In Japan, due to their moral standards of that day and age, the photographic display of a woman's pubic area that included her pubes (hair) was strictly censored. What began as a simple request on his part for copies of Playboy magazine, Penthouse and Hustler developed into a regular trade between Maurice and me. I would provide him with those monthly magazines from the base Exchange, uncensored because they were the American version and he would provide me with all the free drinks I could consume. On occasion, I would even provide him with quarts of Seagram's Royal Crown whiskey that I knew he would add water to in order to stretch it into providing more drinks for other military men. Knowing what I know now, I suspect he must have had that same arrangement with other military personnel from on base, and that the tequila I chose to drink instead may well have been just as watered down at the beginning of our acquaintance.

There came a night, however, when Maurice and I were simply talking and discussing the trades we had been making that Maurice presented me with an unusual challenge. He would make the double tequila sunrises that were my drink of choice while waiting with the rest of the bar which was busy that night, and if I could drink them as fast as he could make them while waiting on the rest of his patrons, they would be free of charge. While if I couldn't keep up, I would pay double for all the drinks I had consumed. I accepted his challenge, of course, because by that day I had developed an alcohol tolerance equal to most of the male members of my biological family, who spent most of their adulthood in drunken stupors. The game was on ... and even though the bar was very busy that night, Maurice was able to serve me 17 double tequila sunrises in a 2-hour period before he finally gave up.

Sitting in an air-conditioned bar, in Japan, without needing to do more than sip the drinks until I was ready for the next one wasn't really that huge of an accomplishment. However, I had a similar experience when I was just 16 years of age and in the inactive reserves for the Marine Corps in St. Louis. Now, because of my age, even though I was with the Marine recruiters that I was working for in setting up a recruitment display, when we went to lunch at a fancy restaurant, the waiter refused to serve me any alcoholic beverages. But there was on the menu an entree that offered crab meat in a wine sauce. I opted for that choice and ate it with relish, drinking the sauce from the plate after the crab was consumed. And just like the bar in Japan years later that restaurant was fully air conditioned, even to the point of being slightly chilly while outside in the St. Louis, Missouri summer it was nearly 90 degrees with a very high humidity level. The recruiters and I walked out of the restaurant, I took about two or three steps out into that heat and collapsed in a drunken stupor. The recruiters took me home, of course, explaining to my parents that the heat must have gotten to me and left in a hurry.

And lo, those many years later, after consuming those 17 drinks in a mere 2-hour period, I walked out of the bar, into the heat and humidity of South East Asia, and while I was older, and had a higher tolerance for the alcohol in my system, I was immediately as drunk as I can ever remember having been up to that point. Staggering and not really certain I knew where I was going, I was somehow able to return not just to the base but made it back to the barracks I had been assigned to and eventually found my own bed. While I was able to undress and ready myself for sleep, I was unable to lay down and sleep off the effects of drinking that much in such a short time. I went to the head (military jargon for the bathroom or restroom) and proceeded to experience the worst case of vomiting that I have ever had before or since that day.

The grenadine in those drinks caused my vomit to have a purple hue and I puked that purplish fluid for what seemed to be hours to me in my drunken state. But worse than the barfing purple junk and the stench of the vomit was the dry heaving that followed. To this day I can imagine that I must have spent 4 hours in that bathroom, praying to the porcelain goddess and heaving long after my body had expelled anything that might still have been inside my stomach. An exaggeration perhaps but time truly is an illusion and the moments that passed while vomiting there appeared to stretch into the small hours of the morning until I was finally released to go back to my bunk and collapse into a spinning, drunken sleep.

I swore off drinking after that night, never drinking anything alcohol related for years on end and only imbibing in other substances for my escapist relaxation, because of the hours I remembered vomiting purple and the horrific heaving that followed.

Compleat
Buddha at
the Bottom

Of the three tours in South East Asia that I had, the only one where I wasn't completely drunken, stoned, or acting on my insanity was the year I avoided drinking or using drugs. Instead, I focused on what was available on base as 'hobbies' or extracurricular skills. Lapidary was offered at the base hobby shop, and stones were provided as well as instruction on their quality, uses, flaws, and methods of polishing and setting them into jewelry like earrings, rings, necklaces, and pendants. I also learned how to develop black and white film from 35mm cameras, and taught myself how to take photographs that were detailed, precise, and exemplary in their content and context. Although I never learned the skill of developing color film, since the cost of the color developing chemicals was prohibitive on a Lance Corporal's salary.

With the lapidary, I worked with stones like opals at first, but after a few failures and learning that some people viewed opals as a 'bad omen' stone I moved on to jade, which could be purchased from the Philippines via guys who went there on deployments for blocks of 1 pound at the amazingly cheap price of $5 to $15 dollars, based on the color, quality, and structure of the jade itself. I remember making a jade butterfly necklace for my Aunt Fran and mailing it back Stateside so it didn't get 'misplaced' from my wall locker like a few other pieces had gone missing.

The best work I ever accomplished in lapidary was a pair of Star Ruby earrings, in gold settings. The star in each was centered exactly in the same place on both after I had finished them and I was able to set them into pure 24k gold settings. I had been so proud of the work I had put into them that I took them to an appraiser in a jewelry shop off base and they were appraised to be worth $400 for the pair. Not bad, for a novice jewelry craftier, though I'm certain that a true jeweler would have been able to create earrings with the same stones with a much greater monetary value. I had intended to ship them back Stateside as well but made the mistake of leaving my wall locker open when I went to shower one day and when I came back, they were gone. I was so angry and disappointed that anyone in the barracks would steal them out of my wall locker I quit doing lapidary after that and haven't even attempted it since, although I cannot walk past a colorful rock on the ground or in a creek bed without bending down and thinking about what it might become if I had the tools to do the work again.

Compleat

With the photography, I started out just learning how to develop the black and white film from a single Cannon 35mm SLR camera, and making prints from the film myself in a darkroom that was also provided at the hobby shop on base. It was fun, though the fumes sometimes could be nauseating, and having the images in the photographs slowly reveal themselves while working in the darkroom was, in a strange way, calming for me. I had never enjoyed dark rooms or confined spaces but learned to be able to relax while in there, doing something both fun and exciting. Developing film and photos seemed to naturally lead me into taking more and more photographs, and because there were so many things, people, and places that would catch my eye, I ended up with nearly $3,000 worth of photography gear. 3 Cannon SLR cameras, lenses from a 14mm Fish-eye lens, all the way up to a 250mm telescopic lens, filters for altering focus, lighting, colors, and textures - and then too I had light meters, backdrops, carrying cases, and bags for all of the gear I purchased that year.

I had bought a 10-speed Schwinn bicycle and would take rides out into town just to photograph things I would notice, usually just using the one camera for the black and white photos I would develop myself later and saving the other two cameras that were loaded with color film so I could capture and retain things that were absolutely stunning to my untrained eyes.

That bicycle and my desire to photograph things away from the base led me to take an excursion away from the base and the 'town' that surrounded it, out into the Japanese countryside. There I met people from Japan who didn't speak English and I was as language illiterate then as I continue to be today, but somehow the people and I were able to communicate with one another. At first, I found myself making hand motions and asking for food and water by spooning my hands as if I were eating and tilting my head back with my empty water bottle. Those people readily understood what I was trying to communicate and provided me with food and water quickly, and when I offered to pay them for it, insisting that they take the yen I had offered, they finally agreed and returned the change in exchange for what I had purchased.

But the communication didn't end with my being provided with food. The people, a smallish crowd of about 7 or 8 men and women, took me to this shaded grove of trees, where there were stone benches in a circle around a large koi pond, with beautiful white, gold, blue, and almost black koi swimming in the water of the pond. In the center of it all was a standing statue of the Buddha, slim and not fat like the smiling, sitting one I had been used to seeing around the base. But the two most amazing features of that grove were

Compleat

first the waterfall that fed the pond since it fell nearly 100 feet but was only 4 to 6 inches wide and bounced from outcropping to outcropping until it finally splashed down into the pond itself and second the flowers surrounding the pond and filling the air all through that grove with their perfumed scents. Some as large as my hand, other's so tiny that they would have been hidden by my littlest fingernail if they didn't grow in such profuse abundance.

I spent that afternoon, after eating the lunch that those kindly folk had provided, taking photographs of those flowers using every lens, filter, and combination of lighting I could to capture the majesty of that place. I could almost believe there was a kind of magic in that grove, usually reserved for the people who lived there but had been shared with me for just coming there without wanting anything except to be accepted and allowed to join them in enjoying that wonder-filled place.

When I returned to the base, later that night, and in the days that followed I had the photographs, which I had taken, developed at the base exchange because I didn't know how to develop color prints and really wanted to see them on glossy paper vs matte prints. Some were so stunningly beautiful that on a whim I found the name and address of a Japanese magazine that specialized in floral prints and mailed copies of my work to the editor, anonymously. I was much too embarrassed to present them with my name on them but I also thought that if they knew they had been taken by an American Marine they might reject them simply for that reason as well. I was stunned, however, when a couple of months later, I saw 2 of my photos published in that magazine with no photographer credited with taking them.

I'll never forget that place, those people, and the flowers that almost caused me to go AWOL when I got an offer from a photographer in Australia to work for him in Brisbane. Mr. Brown, I almost wish now I had taken you up on your offer of employment, it would have saved a lot of people and myself an enormous amount of pain and suffering if I had.

3 Cameras for a Chevy

Compleat

After I came back from Japan, I was homeless for a while. My mother had left my last step-dad, Anthony Morris, Sr., and moved in with a man who called himself Gary Gentilee although his name was spelled, Gentile. Maybe he was like me when it came to my middle name, Lyle, and he had been teased and harassed all through his school years for having that name, so he chose to mispronounce it deliberately?! All I knew for certain was that he controlled any visitors my mom might want to have, causing her to not be able to communicate with any of her own children, her sister my Aunt Fran, and her younger brother, my Uncle Caden. Why she chose to leave Art had more to do with her than him though, and her reasoning was in my opinion illogical. But then I had returned to the States, expecting to be able to use my accrued leave by staying in the house that had come to represent 'home' to me while I was overseas.

Instead, when I did finally go there, Anthony Morris was wandering around inside the empty house, with barely enough furniture to sit at a table and eat his dinners. I could relate to his loneliness and felt my mother had used him to raise her first four children from her marriage to Lyle Runner and then, once the older children were out of the house and on their own dumped him as being useless and took the son she had with him, my youngest step-brother Abraham Morris, and destroyed his life although she did leave him the house.

Anthony was wrecked by her leaving, once even hiding in a closet when I came to visit him. He said he was afraid that the Freemasons were out to get him because he actually was a 42nd Degree Shriner/Mason and had done something to offend their codes of conduct. I was able to verify his status with the Masonic Lodge he had been attending before my mother had abandoned him and he had indeed achieved the rank he claimed, but it wouldn't have mattered if they had been after him as his paranoia had him thinking, he was so far gone from despair there was hardly anything left of the man he had been for years.

I left my gear in the house, everything that I had accumulated while in Japan, and visited my Aunt Fran, staying with her and her new husband Earl Elliott for a while and ignoring my mother when she came to visit them. The Marine

Compleat

Corps had shipped everything back to the States in a large wooden container, and it included my photography equipment, some of my better lapidary work, and for the most part books. I had collected and read over 2,000 paperback books, some that were repeats from my childhood (Tom Sawyer, Huck Finn, A Connecticut Yankee in King Arthur's Court) and my first ever copies of the complete works of J.R. Tolkien that I had discovered in the base exchange book section. There were also rare, out-of-print books that would eventually be banned in the States that I won't mention here beyond saying that the Anarchist's Cookbook has become readily available online now, but in that day, it was banned due to the nature of what it provided as information on destroying buildings and bomb-making.

My mistake was not just leaving my collections and gear in the house, though. I wanted to find a date, have a car to take a woman to the movies, drive-in or dinner, and not be dependent on my by-then deranged step-dad or a mother I had chosen to ignore for causing me to not have a home to come to when I returned from overseas. My funds were already exhausted so I found a pawn shop that offered me $150 for my cameras and gear, thinking I would redeem it all before the time limit expired on it, and bought a used Chevy Nova station wagon, with only two doors, no windows on the back sides and a straight six-cylinder engine. It was yellow, rusty, and a really poor vehicle but it was the very first car that I owned outright.

What happened to the camera gear? The pawnbroker didn't wait the 30 days the ticket had said he would before selling the gear. While I had paid almost $3,000 for all of it in Japan, in the States that gear couldn't have been bought for less than $5,000 and he knew it. It was gone before I could even get back to the store the very next week and the pawnbroker I had dealt with "wasn't available anymore, since he has been terminated." At least that's the story I got from the new guy that was running the store the day I went back.

I ranted and raged about it, of course, and upon hearing me my step-dad, Anthony Morris, made the unhelpful comment that I should have come to him for the money, he would have loaned it to me and I wouldn't have lost the cameras and gear. I knew he was trying to be comforting and caring but it really didn't help me feel any better or relieve my anger to be told that from a man who had always done as my mother had suggested when it came to cars, car insurance, and finances. We older kids got zero help with any of those things growing up, to the point where I got my military driver's license first

Compleat

and had to borrow a car to take my civilian driver's license test from my Aunt Fran and Uncle Earl.

In leaving my other stuff in the house, I would find out almost a year later that my older brother David had stolen most of my books, especially the out-of-print and all of the science fiction/fantasy paperbacks, and sold them to a used book store to buy pot with the proceeds. The wooden crate was mostly empty, the leather fringed jacket and pants I had tailored in Japan to look like Wild Bill or a native American and anything of value were all gone. Years later I would see some of the artwork I had collected on the walls of David's son, Zayne's walls, and Zayne showed me a photograph of myself at the park in Hiroshima, in front of the Peace Fountain, that his dad had claimed was himself in Korea.

Compleat

Pirates Into The Den

—·—·—·—·—·—·—·—·—·—·—·—·—·—·—··

The name of the bar outside the gates of Cherry Point, NC was 'The Pirates Den.' Many times when I was stationed there, Marines would be informed that the base was trying to get the civilian government of New Bern, NC to shut it down. Their reasoning is that more Marines and Sailors got drunk there than at any other bar, including the base enlisted club, and that more drunken military personnel would run afoul of both the civil and military justice systems because of having gotten drunk inside the Den.

During my first marriage, to Denise, there were several periods where I felt she had been unfaithful to me as far as having sex with other men. I wouldn't have objected if I had been a part of her having sex with them or if I had been the one to pick the men or if I had known she was having sex outside of the marriage we had agreed to because the idea of watching her have sex with other men excited me. But when I began to suspect that she was involved with another man without my okay or permission I became jealous to the point of awaking my insanity.

Compleat

To become self-righteous about things like this I had to have first become the complete asshole I am to this day. Because while she may or may not have been faithful in relation to the marriage vows we had taken, I had never taken them to mean that I would behave in such a manner myself. In life and for most of humanity this could be called living under a double standard. For me, it was simply a manifestation of my insanity to expect her to remain true and yet allow me to do whatever I chose to do with whomever I chose to do it.

Now perhaps it was because she wanted money for herself to spend as she saw fit, more than because the base pay of a Corporal and later a Sergeant wouldn't cover the expenses of the existence we shared, Denise took a job at the local convenience store within walking distance of the townhouse we shared with her children and later our son, Mark. Perhaps it was because I was such a lousy lover, or perhaps it was because the overnight shift paid a tiny bit more each hour that she chose to take the late-night shift and worked away from the house almost every night from 11 pm to 7 am.

This meant two very important but unfortunate things happened. In the first place, I slept alone frequently until her daughter Regina started sleeping in my bed when Denise would leave for work. In the second place, my suspicions about her having another sexual partner grew stronger. Once my only evidence would come from performing oral sex on her and receiving a mouthful of hardened semen which had been left inside her somehow when she and I hadn't had sex in days.

To perceive her as being unfaithful was to believe she was or would be unfaithful in my scrambled thinking. I was torn between my need to love her and heal my broken heart thereby or to hate her and take vengeance against her in some way or form. And, of course, my insanity played to the revenge, thinking that I was justified to act on my jealousy no matter how badly I myself had acted in the very same regard.

One evening, before Regina began sleeping in my bed, and when Denise she had worked the night shift and was supposed to get off work at 11 pm instead of 7 am. I woke up around 2 am and she wasn't home. Knowing all four children were asleep and probably wouldn't wake up until the morning, I decided to test my theory about her being unfaithful by walking to the Pirate's Den, the local bar that catered to the Marines and Sailors on base at Cherry Point, NC.

Compleat

There I found Karl Wimble, his wife Farrah and Denise, sitting together at a table in the bar with another Marine that - I would later learn his name as being Mike.

When I approached their table, they all looked shocked that I had discovered them there and Denise looked toward this Milton as if asking him to protect her from what she thought would be my rage. Instead, I ignored her completely, telling her boyfriend (deliberately separating the boy from the friend here) to get up, since he was sitting in my seat.

He started to protest, asking me who I thought I was and my response was to tell him I was a Corporal in the Marines and he was sitting next to my wife. He vacated the seat, and I ignored him as to see if he even looked back to see if she wanted him to stay or not, taking his seat and starting a conversation with Karl and Farrah Wimble.

I continued to ignore Denise for a few minutes and then announced that, since the kids were home alone, I had best be leaving., and I left the bar without looking back or bothering to talk to Denise at all for the entire episode. I knew, from the looks on their faces, that not only had she been seeing this Milton for some time, but Karl and Farrah had also known and assisted her in meeting him regularly.

I ask the reader to remember how I said that the self-righteousness of jealousy gave me justification of for all the things I had ever done and all the things I would do in the future. An example of this would be that I had betrayed Karl, since he was a Marine and a friend, by getting drunk and being sexual with his wife Farrah in a darkened room during a night of drinking and playing an adult board game in which a secret 'love in' was one of the spaces on the board we had been playing. Farrah and I had kissed passionately, I had put my fingers deep inside her vagina and we had promised to meet the following Monday to have sex while our respective partners were at their jobs. For myself, I believed that the promise was for a real event, but for Farrah, it had turned out to be simply a moment of jealousy and a drunken promise she had never meant to keep.

When I did show up the following Monday, she rejected my advances toward completing the promise to avenge ourselves against our partners and told Karl what I had tried to do by showing up at their home that day. Karl confronted me, and I excused my behavior as being jealousy over his and

Compleat

Denise's actions at the party, since they had both had the secret 'love in' first that night. I promised him that I would never approach his wife again after that, knowing she didn't find me attractive and that she had only agreed because she was drunk that night. Which seemed to suffice for Karl, since I avoided having my ass kicked by an angry husband for making his wife feel unsafe, because she had sensed that she had nearly been subjected to rape that Monday by a jealously insane asshole who wanted to hurt *my* then- wife and *her* husband by having sex with her.

So it shouldn't be hard to see the reasoning behind Karl and Farrah's betrayal of what had been a friendship and turned into something twisted by my insane thinking. Rationalizing, justifying, and jealousy combined with my already drunken, drugged, and insane thinking caused me to spiral deeper into sexual inappropriateness and involvement with those who should never have been subjected to my insanity in the first place.

One final note, as an ironic comment that has little humor in it, is about the name of the bar outside the base at Cherry Point. 'The Pirates Den' was even put in an off- limits state for Marines for a period of time by the base commander. The general in charge thought the bar was a bad influence on the Marines stationed there. But the reality was that by placing it in that status he simply made it more attractive to some of the Marines on base. Again, the idea of the forbidden fruit comes to mind, because the rationale of 'why' it was restricted was never explained and was simply an order given and expected to be obeyed unwavering.

I have a simple explanation now, these many years later, that would have sufficed for more Marines and possibly a few Sailors stationed at the base that went there out of spite for the system that didn't bother to explain it's reasoning to them.

'The Pirates Den' as the name implies was a place for pirates to gather. The entire purpose for there being a Marine Corps from the foundation of the nation which they thought to serve had been to protect ships at sea from pirates and enemy ships. So, going to the hangout of the enemy might not be such a good idea after all. Unless you were looking to become a pirate?!

Compleat

On God & The Loss of The last of My Humanity
_._._._._._._._._._._._._._._._._._..

I think it was sometime in the spring of 1981.

I was married on July 5th, 1979 – so I know that it was sometime after that for sure. My son, Mark, had been born in October of 1980, so I know that it was after that as well. My ex had left me for a friend of mine, not knowing how crazy I really was or what I had been doing for years, eventually molesting her three kids and doing drugs in an attempt to erase the shame from my brain. She left her three kids from her first marriage and our son who was almost a year old with me because she 'thought' I was the better parent. Probably because she was leaving the relationship with me for a younger man (she was thirty-one, I was twenty-six and he was eighteen) and didn't think too highly of herself or couldn't provide for them as well as she thought I might have been able to as a Marine Sergeant at the time.

I fell apart after she left, knowing I was damned if I didn't take on the responsibility of the kids and even more damned if I did. I had been sexually molesting her daughter and when she left, I took to molesting her sons from her first marriage as well. In my sick mind, it was as if they were all a part of her that I wasn't supposed to want, touch, or be allowed to do what I was doing. I knew I would be punished for it all, but most of all I knew that when she realized what I truly was she would never forgive herself for leaving them with me.

Her daughter, Regina, had become my surrogate wife, fulfilling all my sexual needs, without actual intercourse, by the age of thirteen. Then there were the boys. Jude was five at first and only wanted to be included with in what Regina was doing in private with me, so I used him to suck my cock. Bill, or Billy, was the one that loved me as a dad the most. He didn't care what I did, ignoring the rages, the physical abuse (I was sent to a civilian psychiatrist because I had slapped his face so many times it bruised and he went to school where they noticed and sent the social department worker to the home while his mom was still there, and I was ordered to seek help or be imprisoned), the sexual abuse of forcing him to suck me while I came and eventually when I tried to force him to have intercourse with his sister, Regina, so I wouldn't be the one to take her virginity and I would have someone to accuse of having had sex with her if I ever fucked her myself.

Obsessed, insane, and without remorse for any of the things I was doing, I was overcome when their mother left me for Rudy Mosely. It didn't matter to me that I was molesting her daughter, it didn't matter to me that I had tried to rape her cousin Tilly, it didn't matter to me that I had entered her friend Diane Gilmore while she was sleeping and only stopped before cumming inside her because she woke just as I was about to and ordered me to 'get off' her. That I had cut holes in her sisters-in-law's sheets to peek at her underwear and pubic hair or would sneak into her sister's room while she was sleeping and look at her while masturbating just before Denise and I would have a 'chapel wedding.' Nothing mattered to me except my need for seeing and sexual gratification/relief.

I fell apart, not just because she left me for another guy. I fell apart because I knew I was a piece of shit, an asshole – I had abandoned my first love because I knew I was like this, capable of heinous crimes and totally insane. Why did I marry her then? Two reasons, always two or more but these two stand out for me now.

The first, I didn't want to be alone with myself any longer. I knew I would end up killing myself because I couldn't stand what I had done to Megan by dumping her instead of telling her the truth and allowing her to help me heal inside. I didn't really believe I could be healed or 'saved.'

The second reason is more insidious and sicker. After I proposed to Denise and she accepted, when I went to pick her and Regina up in Missouri and take them back to North Carolina (I didn't know about the boys at that time) when I arrived at her brother Wendel Matthew's home, her daughter Regina jumped into my arms, wrapping her arms around my neck and her legs around my hips/waist and saying to me, "Daddy's home."

Why mention that second part, when I've already confessed to molesting her at that the age of nine? Because her unconditional love was something I couldn't live without. It was the only thing I could still recall from the time I had shared that kind of love with Megan, my first love, it was pure and untainted by anything in this world. I didn't love her mother, Denise Matthews, but at that instant, I fell in love with a nine-year-old girl named Regina because she loved me, unconditionally. Not appropriately, like a father. I loved and lusted after her instantly. I married her mother but it was Regina I was in love with, as a substitute for Megan.

When her mother left, and I was forced to be a 'dad' to those four kids I was forced into a role I wasn't ready for or willing to take on. Drug use and drinking couldn't blur the pain I felt from before, even using Regina and the boys as sexual outlets of revenge against Denise couldn't blur how I felt about myself every time I did something to any of them. My biological son, Mark was the only one safe from my abuse because he was 'my' son. Making Regina the surrogate mom, I forced her into babysitting Michael, while I struggled to keep a house that I was totally unqualified to run. Laundry piled up for months, food eventually consisted of macaroni and cheese with hot dogs cut up into pieces and bread, if I remembered to buy it, from the exchange.

Mark, being a baby had to have diapers, formula, and baby bath soap. The other kids ate lunch at school and Michael had a babysitter, Veronica Thomson, who would watch him while I was at 'work' for the Marines.

And believe me, that even at that work I was useless. I was a wreck, still on Thorazine ordered for me from the civilian psychiatrist, barely able to walk let alone think, I was put in the 'tool room' for the flight-line of the SOES (Station Operations and Engineering Squadron) as a Sergeant, doing the 'job' that a child could have done, by handing out tools as needed and asked for from men doing their real work. Filled with shame, self-pity, and the inability to actually do my own job in Avionics it was small wonder when I went crying to the Chaplin about my friend, the corpsman who had 'run off with my wife.' I blamed them for my failures as a parent, a man, and a Marine. It wouldn't be until years later that I would accept that I had brought all my difficulties upon myself.

Eventually, I was called into the office of the Executive Officer in Charge of the SOES squadron; his command was simple and to the point – quit the medications that the civilian doctor had ordered me to take or be given a medical discharge from the Marines.

Shame- ridden, filled with self-pity, fearful of being found out for what I was doing at home, and even more fearful that I wouldn't be able to afford to 'keep' my kids because I wouldn't be able to afford to house or feed them without a 'job' I stopped taking the medications.

It wouldn't be until many years later that I would learn that a medical discharge would have given me a Sergeant's basic pay, with the cost-of-living increases, for the rest of my life, providing for those children even if I were imprisoned or hospitalized for life. The Executive Officer had failed to mention that when he threatened me with a medical discharge.

Compleat

A "Marine", on Thorazine, with four children in his 'care' and unable to perform his duties, he gave me that order, and perhaps he thought he was 'offering' me an alternative to losing my status as a "Marine." It shouldn't have been even offered, I was obviously insane, on strong medications and psychiatric care while still in the service. The medical discharge would have had the abuse be discovered sooner and I might have received the treatment that overcame my behaviors long before being arrested again years later for rape.

Ironically (or intentionally?) the Veteran's Administration lost the medical records of my hospitalization and subsequent medication by the civilian doctor and I lost my GI Bill benefits when I called them to ask for help and, told the man on the phone why I had received a Bad Conduct Discharge, and was told by him: "You've got nothing coming, you bastard." And he hung up on me.

What, if anything, does all this have to do with my meeting with the divine being called God? It happened like this:

I remember, after my wife had left and the Executive Officer had threatened me with a medical discharge, I was walking down a highway, just outside the base at Cherry Point, NC, and looking for a semi-truck trailer to jump in front of to end myself in order to escape my own pain and responsibility for my actions. Selfishness was all I knew and I was determined to run away rather than face what I knew would come.

I saw only one semi the whole time I was on that highway, and I tried to time my jump so that there was NO way the driver would be able to miss me. But he must have, because he didn't even stop or slow down when I jumped.

I continued to walk down that same highway until I saw a small building on the side of the road. There were no obvious markings, no crosses or symbols on the outside of it, but somehow, I knew that it was a church of some kind.

Not a Catholic church, like my mom had wanted me to be a part of when she converted to Catholicism. It was just a feeling I had, that somehow that building was a place I could go and dump all my secrets onto the god I had forsaken years before.

I went to the door, - glass and steel - and looked inside and saw that the building was empty, so I tried the door and it was unlocked. By that time I was bawling like the little kid I was inside; scared and angry, knowing I was in trouble but not wanting to be held accountable for my behaviors, not tears of regret, just tears of self-pity.

Compleat

I walked into the building, across the back of the church, and down the far side to the 3rd third pew from the front. I sat there, sobbing, cussing, and arguing with god, pleading for relief, for an end to my pain and fear. An end I thought could only mean an end to my life. I begged to be allowed to die. Then and there.

In a moment of catching my breath for more sobbing and cussing at god, I heard something. Singing. Some kind of hymns or stuff. Men's and women's voices were all around me. I looked up from where I was sitting and saw that there were actually people in the building. I had walked into a building that I wouldn't have if I had seen anyone at all and it was completely full of people.

I did what any Marine Sergeant with even an ounce of false masculine pride would have done when caught crying in public over personal crap. I ran for the door. And I made it out of the building and would have run away as fast and as far as I could but two ladies there caught up with me, just outside the door.

They tried to tell me about the whole "Jesus loves you" bullshit and I wasn't having any of that, you can be sure. They kept asking me to tell them what was wrong and all I could think to tell them was that I wanted to die but couldn't find the strength to do it for myself.

It's not necessary to tell all that part of my story except that one of those women, spoke to me that day in a voice that wasn't her own. A male voice, coming came out of her mouth, but with a timbre and a strange and difficult-to-ignore energy that caught my attention.

She/it said, "If you really want to give away your life, if you truly wish to end it now; why not give it to god?" I stopped crying, for what seemed like an hour in a split second of their real-time. And I responded in a way that I thought was totally disrespectful, sarcastic, and provocative. "Fine, if he wants my shitty life, he can have it."

Long story so far, so I'll shorten the next parts. I started going to "church" there. Got very 'religious' really quickly, thinking that I could be forgiven and change my life and not have to deal with the consequences of my past actions.

As an aside, it did help those kids a bit, in that I stopped sexually and physically abusing them for that period in my life. Religion sucks but it does have its uses in temporarily altering human behaviors.

I tried very hard to escape from accepting that responsibility by putting all my 'faith' in god. Then one day, two ladies, actual ordained ministers of that

Compleat

particular religion -, told me that god had put it on their hearts to send me to theological college, in order to become an ordained minister myself and that I was meant to take over the pastor's position at a church there in North Carolina.

This news shocked and amazed me, and I told them I would need to fast and pray about it before I could give them my answer. I truly thought I had 'changed' because I was "saved."

So I fasted for 4 days and 4 nights, but not the way the pastor at the "church" that I was attending at that time fasted. Nope. I tried to fast the way their bible said Jesus did it. No food and no water. For over 96 hours, with nothing taken into myself me for sustenance of any kind and I must admit, I felt physically and emotionally great the whole time.

Someone told me later that without water for 72 hours your major organs begin to shut down - kidneys, liver, pancreas, and just about every major one there is - so maybe the psychiatrists were right and I ended up hallucinating.

What I know is that I was walking up the sidewalk to one of the lady minister's houses, to tell her I was having trouble deciding still. I was still praying, a sort of under my breath kind of constant prayer, that I would receive a 'sign' for what I should do or what I was supposed to do about the decision I was being faced with. I lifted my right foot, to take the next step up the sidewalk leading to that house, and all of a sudden, I wasn't there anymore.

I found myself standing in a place that was so full of light that I thought I had closed my eyes instinctively, yet it was still so bright that I felt the light upon my skin, like sunshine at the beach when someone is working on a tan and falls asleep and could 'see around me.

Before me sat a figure, I couldn't make out clearly through what I thought were my closed eyes but even then, I could tell that I was close enough that I could have reached out with my hand and touched him. Yeah, no real surprise here since it's in the title anyway, it was the god dude.

Without a word I was shown what I was intended to do: the whole pastor's job, the congregation where I was meant to carry out his will, and even the people that would be involved in my life after that - the: clergy, and congregation members, I was shown every bit of it and a certainty that it was what he wanted me to do; knowledge of all that was meant to be according to his will.

And in that exact same instant of knowing, all that I had done in the past, especially the wrongs I had done to those who had risked loving me, came flooding back into my consciousness. I saw that I was a single dad, a Marine Sergeant with four kids who should never have been entrusted with their care and safety, whose career was over because "if the Marine Corps wanted you to have a set of kids, they would have issued you a set."

I saw my soon- to- be ex-wife in the arms of a younger man, a friend of mine, that had been there when my son had been born as a corpsman and nurse at the military hospital. I saw all the things I had done in my lifetime, the selfishness, hatred, anger, sick, twisted, and shameful things I had done for as long as I could remember. All of the things I had done drugs for years trying to blot out of my mind. And all the things that had been done to me as well. It all came flooding back into me, and with it an anger I never knew I had before, not even the berserk rage I had experienced before; a hatred of all that I saw, and most especially a hatred of myself.

I stood before the god of their bible, with my fists clenched and I screamed at him. "Fuck you, you bastard. I will tear your shit down. I will take everything you ever created and destroy it. I will rip you out of that fucking seat and take your place and SHOW you how it should have been done in the first place."

A spirit of hate filled me at that moment. I hated myself already, like as I said, but now I hated all life, all that existed and I especially hated that fucker sitting before me. I knew that at that moment I would have destroyed him if I had only known how.

And in that instant of recognition, in the split second of the awareness of all my hate filling me from the inside, my right foot came down on the sidewalk and I was back from wherever the fuck I had been in the time it took to raise it and lower it again. I walked away from that minister's house, that day, and I never once looked back.

The shock of having been there wasn't hard to recover from for me. I had believed the place was a possibility before I had gotten into 'religion.' What did disturb me was I began to question the rage I had felt and the strength of my rejection of this being. I had felt it rise from within me, not some spirit or demon or devil possessing me, it came from within me. But the question was linked to a childhood fear of my birthday and having read their bible when I was thirteen years of age. June Sixteenth, Nineteen Fifty-Six. 06/16/1956 . 666.

I returned to using drugs after that, including drinking, and to all of my old behaviors and all of my old sick and twisted thinking. I wanted nothing to do with god, Christians, churches, religion, or religious people. I was without hope, without passion, without any real feelings for anyone or anything, including myself except anger and hate.

There is far more to this story, of course, the ramifications of being and doing what I was had to catch up with me eventually. What I can say now is that for probably only the second time in my life I made a decision that wasn't based on total selfishness and it came when I sent for my ex to come and get the kids, because I wasn't going to be around to take care of them. I admit now that I did it to fuck with her happiness in part, but in the end and knowing that I would fuck my step daughter and probably get her pregnant and that there would be hell to pay, I did it to get those kids (including my own son, Mark) as far away from me as they possibly could be taken, for their sake, because I knew I was completely insane and it was only going to get worse.

I saw god that day. And I told him to go fuck himself. And he let me get away with that. Go figure. There was no humanity left inside me. I had successfully burned it all out. I was nothing human in my mind, my heart, and/or if I ever had one, in my soul.

Yet, while listening to music one night, years later, I had an epiphany of sorts that made me decide to amend this story. While I had stated that I didn't 'open' my eyes in the previous version I may have inadvertently suggested that my eyes were closed by my own choice. The ability to perceive my surroundings with the singular exception of the entity sitting before me suggests that I could see through closed eyes. It came to me that my eyes were open before this event occurred - as I was walking up a sidewalk toward the home of my "friends" - and were equally open after the event had transpired, and I found myself back on that same sidewalk.

The significance of this small detail escaped me until I realized that it hadn't been my choice to not open my eyes and see the individual sitting before me. I was in the middle of raging at their god, for presuming to pick me for a 'mission' when I had successfully messed my own life so completely up and the epiphany that I experienced was simply this:

Compleat

I know of no human being, and especially know it of myself well enough during that time period, that is capable or even interested in closing their eyes during a session of expressing rage in the manner I was doing. I screamed, cursed, shouted, cried, and felt an up welling of rage within me that was so strong I even feared that it wasn't "me" but another entity raging through me.

But I realized one night that it was myself and myself only raging at god. Ironically, it was god that prevented me from perceiving all that he was, even as he reportedly had with Moses by only exposing his backside to Moses' open perception and sight, abet at Moses' request.

Some would say I was struck blind in that instant because I was insane and raging at a being that was powerful enough to destroy me by merely allowing me to see who/what I was raging against. Yet I know there was no thought of self-preservation during the period outside of time that transpired throughout this incident.

I know that I wouldn't have closed my eyes during an episode of complete rage and expressing it directly at any individual. Yet throughout the entire incident, I was prevented from seeing. Protected from myself and, my folly, and perhaps being shown that while I AM related by adoption, I'm not god.

An interesting thought and one I intend to research more in the future. *if there is a future for all of us*

Without words, this individual told me what he expected of me, the task he was setting before me for the benefit of others. And in that same instant, all that I had ever done against others, all that those others had done that I held as resentments against them, and all the pain and suffering I would endure as well as all that I had imagined I had already endured flooded through me, hotter than any fire or even the burning of the hottest star.

And I knew I was being given a choice. I could do what I wanted and, keep doing things the way I knew how to do them. Or I could submit my will and my life to this being, this power that sat before me, all in the time it was taking me to place my foot back onto the ground.

That day I made a choice. I told that god to go fuck himself! I swore at him that I would do all within my power, all that I could imagine or contrive or create to tear him from that seat and place myself in his position. I hated him. All that he represented, all that he had ever created and I committed myself to ending both his existence and his position.

Compleat

At that instant my step was complete. My foot came in contact with the sidewalk before me. And I knew, without a doubt, that I had just declared war on whatever god existed in that place that I had been shown. I did everything I could, to hate him and everything I would think of for years afterward to try to make him hate me in return. Anyone who's still reading this might laugh at this next statement, but it's as real as the rest here. I failed.

I liked to say, years later, that I had had a pissing contest going on with god; and that I had never been able to reach that high with all the piss and pressure I could muster, while he had always had dead aim on my ass, never missing me once. It wasn't until after a second event, that I will tell you all about in another story here later, that I became aware of the fact that my pissing contest with him was all one-sided. I would piss at him with all that I was, but he never once pissed back at me. What I had mistakenly perceived for so many years as his pissing on me was actually just my own piss falling back to its source.

And really, why wouldn't it? Natural laws do say that what goes up must come down. And as long as I was warring against him, he was under no obligation to keep me from doing what I had already chosen to do or protect me from being responsible for my own actions.

Obviously, after enough pain, suffering, and the destruction that I brought upon myself and those around me. I learned that I had made a mistake. And that mistake wasn't the telling him to go fuck himself. It wasn't the war I fought against him for so many years either.

My mistake, the one that someone else needed to show me because I was too close to my own insanity was that I had viewed the tiles of life the way we all tend to view the tiles of a Scrabble game and what had imprisoned me in my madness for so long, was that I didn't know there was any other way to see things. For I believed that I had damned myself, knowing that no one else had done it to me, I had done it to myself. And I had believed for years there was no hope for the damned.

During this time of my religious experience, my ex had been begging me for a divorce so she could marry her lover. And I had refused, selfishly thinking that she would come back to me and everything would go back to the way it was before, with me molesting just her daughter and fucking her as a side.

When I went off the medication, I tried to manipulate her, by paying back payments on a car I had bought for her when we had had the chapel wedding she had hoped for – a T-top 1981 Firebird. Paying that bill and returning the car to her didn't change her mind, though. And it put me so far behind on bills that my finances failed to the point that the kids and I were reduced to eating three -week- old ham gravy (juice really) poured over macaroni without cheese or butter. No bread, no hot dogs. No other food in the house.

But knowing her, I sent for her twice. First when her daughter Regina started having her periods. I thought sure they would talk about sex and Regina would speak to her about the things I had been doing to her. She didn't, and Denise left all four of them with me, again.

Then something occurred that I hadn't expected. Two things involving Regina. First, the pastor ladies who had caught me running from the church had told me god wanted me to stop smoking, so I said I would but went right back to it. Regina, at the mature old age of thirteen, came up to me one day and with that same weird/baritone voice said to me: "Dad, you used to say when mom was here that if she would quit smoking, you would too. Well, mom's not here anymore."

I put down my cigarettes and haven't smoked since 1980. At that time, being religious, I thought I knew with certainty that god had heard my promise and was holding me to it. About the smoking anyway.

The second was later, when I had already told god to go fuck himself. Regina was in the living room, watching Mark and watching Billy and Jude play football outside with the boys in the neighborhood. Mark was standing in an armchair watching the boys, too, and jumping up and down because he was happy for them.

Catastrophe struck, in that Michael bounced so hard on that chair that he fell off it and hit his forehead on the glass end -table beside it. His cries brought me from the kitchen where I had been doing dishes and rushing into the living room, I snatched him up and looked him over quickly, he appeared unhurt, not even bleeding. So I sat him down in that same armchair and as he cried, I turned on Regina in a rage. Slapping her as hard as I could over and over again, as she cowered trying to avoid the blows.

And then, I heard myself shouting at Regina: "God damn you, Denise, how could you let this happen?"

It was an awakening to exactly what I had been doing for years. Substituting Regina for her mom, Denise. All the sexual misconduct was aimed at hurting Denise and somehow making right what I had lost with Megan.

Compleat

I stopped hitting her because Mark had stopped crying and when I turned to see why he was unconscious, with blood running down his face from a wound on his forehead.

Somehow, I had blamed Denise for being my 'wife' instead of Megan. And inside my broken mind, I had justified doing all the sexual stuff to Regina because I was using her to fill the void in me that giving up Megan had created; with the unconditional love that she had given so freely. And I knew then that if I didn't get her away from me, if I didn't protect her and Denise's sons, who had done nothing to deserve my insanity - I would end up impregnating Regina and probably end up beating one of the boys to death in a drug- infused rage.

Since it was Billy that had loved me most up until that point, I realize now he was the most vulnerable to being killed. Jude had loved me but ignored most of what I did because he was still too young.

Years later, when Mark sought me out, I would learn it was Jude that holds hate in his heart for my abuse and Billy that forgave me or simply chooses to ignore what I did and that I still exist. I don't even dare ask about how Regina feels, to this day.

The second time I wrote to Denise, although I didn't 'confess' what I had been doing to the children, I hinted at it enough and told her that she had no choice but to come and get them immediately! This time she came and I had sat Regina down but not the boys and told her that I was sending for her mom to come and get them all and that when Denise came, she was to talk with her mom and tell her everything I had ever done to her. Regina only asked if I would still love her if I was arrested and I told her the truth, "I will always love you, you've done nothing wrong. It was me; I was the one who did wrong and now I must pay for it." When the NIS (Naval Investigative Services) came to arrest me, Billy refused to go with his mom until I told him to go and that it would be okay.

But that was my fear and first thought. My second thought - and I honestly cannot say if it was a fear or simply a sick, twisted lustful desire - was that if I did get discharged, if I was to move to a place where no one knew me or the kids, where we would be isolated from the neighbors or even the town where we would move, I would be able to make Regina into my wife, instead of my step-daughter.

Compleat

No one would know it would be me that got her pregnant, if she didn't return to school and stayed home to take care of Mark and a new baby. She would take her mother's place as my wife and no one would be the wiser.

 I knew that if I took the discharge, and the 5 of us became homeless, living in places where no one cared about or knew us, I would end up having intercourse with Regina and getting her pregnant. The fear of getting caught for what I had already done didn't weigh much with the choice to stop taking the medications. But the idea that I knew I would eventually get Regina pregnant weighted my decision to stop taking the medications instead of the discharge.

I wanted to, I'm not trying to be deceptive or pretend that I didn't. And at the same time, I had already betrayed her by making her a surrogate for her mom, putting the responsibility of helping me raise the boys, care for Mark and provide physical comfort to me when the loneliness grew so severe.

Was it my fear of hurting her more? I just don't know. I know that it weighed my choice to not take the medications more than the fear of being homeless, without a job, and without food for all of us. Just the fact that I wanted her that way scared me in some way.

Maybe it was the last of my decency or values? Maybe the last vestiges of love I had for her and the boys as a 'dad' sparked fear of what I knew myself capable of doing to her. I only know that it wouldn't be long after the choice was made before I had sent for their mom to come and get them and made sure that I would be held accountable for what I had done.

I remember being visited in the brig at Camp Lejeune because the boys were allowed to hug me and be held by me, but Regina wasn't allowed to even touch my hands. I tried to apologize to Denise and all of them, but honestly, all I could think of was that I had messed up their lives as much as my own had been and wanted only for them to leave, never look back and heal someday. I thought I had lost all contact with them and thought that was 'right and just.'

I never expected to recover, never thought to change who I thought I was – the monster I had seen myself as when I joined the Marines back in 1972. I had become that which I hated about myself most. And there was no gratitude in me for being what I was, not even for having left Megan to keep her from facing my sickest self. I knew only hatred, for myself, for the world around me, and especially for the Marine Corps. My family, especially my mom and

Compleat

her brother, my Uncle Caden had repeatedly said that the Marines would make a man out of me. They never did.

A person would have to be human to become a man, before joining. I wasn't either.

*

When I rebelled against God, I was allowed to rant, rave, threaten and disparage the way God had run my life. I realized later, that I had run my own life – right up until it wasn't worth living - but God wouldn't let me die. Since I had offered my life up to be used in any way that He saw fit, I was forced to carry on living. Now that I have been made to keep living, I know that when I die all that awaits me is what atheists believe waits for everyone; a dark, emptiness.

Where those atheists are wrong is that I will be aware of how alone I will be there in that dark, vast emptiness. I will know that life exists out of sight, out of touch, out of sound, taste, smell, or feeling.

I will know.

And I will despair.

The Miracle of StevIe Elliott

What happened before the day I met the god dude? I'll tell you.

The religion of Science embraces the concept that to hear the voice of god a person must be completely or at least partially insane. Other religions would view this event as being either an enormous blessing or sacrilege to even claim the event had happened. Having had the experience of meeting god and not hearing a voice when that event happened, as I've described elsewhere in this book, it's now my responsibility to reveal that I have heard what I believe to have been the voice of god on three occasions.

Compleat

The first, I've described as being my introduction to the religion of Christianity, in which I was suicidal, went into a building I wasn't aware was a 'church' and fully occupied and when I tried to run away was confronted by two women, one of whom spoke to me in a voice not her own and asked me the question that altered my life forever: "If you really want to die, if you truly wish to give up your life, why not give it to god?" I've described in another story how that semblance of a male, baritone voice coming from that woman caught me unawares, stopped me in my self-destructive, self-pitying shame, and my answering to that voice behind the woman: "If god wants my fucked-up life, he can have it!" A contract or covenant that was a huge blank check to whatever being was speaking to me through that woman. And one that is still in effect to this day, despite my many attempts to revoke that commitment.

The second event of hearing god's voice, I've also already described in another story. When my then thirteen-year-old stepdaughter spoke to me with her own voice but with a power and presence that was palpable in the manner in which she spoke. I had promised the women in that first encounter that "if god wants me to quit smoking cigarettes I will" and then went straight back to smoking in spite of my given word. It would be weeks, perhaps even a month later, that my step-daughter would approach me and state: "Daddy, you used to say when mom was here that if she would quit smoking, you would too. Mom's not here anymore." The result of hearing that and knowing that the voice speaking through her was not her own led a man who had smoked cigarettes since the age of 4 years old to put them down and never even reach for them again. Any long-time smoker will relate to the fact that when quitting or attempting to quit there's always a period where a person reaches for the pocket where they used to keep their smokes, out of habit more than a desire to smoke again. My deliverance from smoking made even that reflex habit a thing of my past.

But the purpose of this story, about a child named Steve Elliot, is so far outside of the normal that it needs its own story to explain what happened. The event happened before I had my meeting with god before I had rejected anything to do with religion and especially before I returned to using drugs and drinking to deal with the insanity that I know is inside of me.

I had gotten into religion, was going to 'church' on a weekly basis, and additionally on Wednesday nights for so-called Bible Studies. I had quit smoking cigarettes, wasn't hitting or abusing my stepchildren in any way, and was desperately trying to 'prove' to the world around me that I had changed because "I have Jesus in my heart." and "I am saved." Proselytizing at every

Compleat

person I came in contact with and becoming a complete nuisance and asshole about religion in the process.

My soon-to-be ex-wife, Denise, took all four children and left North Carolina and went back to Missouri with them in an effort to force me into agreeing to the divorce she wanted so she could marry her then eighteen-year-old lover Rudy Mosely. For those religious people who condemn my actions and think that god cannot have used me for any useful purpose, I need to mention, by refusing her request, for my own selfish reasons I was actually doing her a favor, though neither of us knew it at the time. He would dump her after she returned to his aunt's home in Florida and she had regained full custody of all four kids because I was locked up in the brig. Even a jackass can be a tool in the right hands and I was that jackass for that purpose.

In forcing me to accept her conditions I was also forced to take a temporary position as a recruiter in St. Louis, Mo so I could also return and attempt to regain custody of the kids. While in Missouri, I stayed at the only home I was still accepted at, even partially, which was with my Aunt Fran and her husband Earl Elliot. Fran was expecting their first child together and didn't want to know in advance what the baby's sex would be although everyone was offering their views, opinions, guesses, and observations on that subject. I wasn't involved in all of the speculation or guessing and had no opinion on the matter until the day I heard god's voice, that deep baritone, male voice I had heard coming from that woman many months before offering me the opportunity to 'give my life to god.'

But this event was different in more than just hearing the voice itself. And for the psychiatrists who might read this, I'll reveal that 'no' this wasn't a voice inside my head - which is ironically funny when I recall the event, because if it had been 'inside' my head I would have dismissed it as being my imagination.

I was praying aloud, as was my habit during that brief period of my life when prayer was something I needed to express verbally, and singing to myself songs I had made up out of verses from the bible. Not anything special, no seeking answers for myself or anyone else, just enjoying not being a complete asshole to anyone for a few minutes. And then I hear that voice, not around me, not inside my head, but coming out of my own mouth.

"Micheal, I want you to tell Fran that the baby is going to be a boy, that he will be touched by the holy spirit at the very moment of his birth and his name is going to be …………"

Compleat

And that's when it cut off. I was standing there, like the idiot I am, waiting for the voice to finish and tell me what the baby's name was going to be. Waiting to hear myself say the name, in that voice, and both excited to have heard it and confused why it would cut off so suddenly.

Now, I've already admitted to being an annoying asshole about my newfound 'faith.' Even the Marines that worked around me were grateful that I was allowed to go back to Missouri just to get a break from my constant "Praise the Lord" and "Jesus Saves" bullshit. And my biological family wasn't thrilled about my 'religious' experiences, even asking me to tone it down or keep it to myself in many cases. And here I was, with a direct message to someone whom I cared for and loved like an alternate mother, about something that was none of my business and coming from a source that left me hanging without providing the tiny piece of information that might have made some kind of sense out of an incomplete sentence.

Do I deliver the message, incomplete and confusing as it was to me, or do I attempt to avoid looking like an even bigger asshole to my biological family, and risk becoming so disliked that I'm never allowed to come back to the only home I could feel welcome in? Believe me when I say I struggled with that choice.

My religious self wanted to be that important, that god would deliver a message through me in that manner. My intellect said that I was so far gone in my insanity that I should keep my mouth shut and ignore the voice I had heard.

What decided me was neither of those two parts of myself. I chose to deliver the message, word for word because I cared about my Aunt Fran and the rest of her family. No other reason was needed and my embarrassment or fear was dismissed by that simple reasoning. I didn't understand why I was told to say those words to her, didn't even feel that it was my place to speak to her about her unborn child, but I wanted her to know that no matter what happened, she was being watched over by something way beyond me and my religion or my ego.

When I told her and my Uncle Earl what had happened, describing that the voice had come from my own mouth though the words were not my own and stated the message exactly as it had been given to me; they were kind but naturally skeptical. Earl had been a minister in some religious sect, so he had even more reason to doubt what I shared with them that day.

But I did it. I spoke the words and soon left Missouri after that still without the kids and feeling I had somehow let god down because I gave in to my own lust with a woman who claimed to be Jewish. I sadly don't even remember her name, only that she called me by her ex's name, Billy, and freaked me out because that's the name I used for my oldest stepson, Bill.

I saw Fran and Earl, a few months later, when Denise finally relinquished custody of the kids back to me, and Fran related the story of Stevie's birth in this way.

She had started into labor and was driven to the hospital to have an assisted childbirth, just as she had had with her older three children. The doctors and nurses were prepared for a normal delivery and had placed monitors and leads to track her and the baby's heart rates. And during the labor, while connected to the monitors, the baby's heartbeat stopped completely.

Not being able to deliver the baby naturally, the doctors decided to perform an emergency C-section delivery and although she was only semi-anesthetized, Fran was aware of their reasoning and was frightened for the baby's sake.

The C-section was done in a matter of minutes, but as the baby was taken from inside her it was with the umbilical cord wrapped around his throat, cutting off all oxygen from her due to the tightness and the way it had wrapped itself and preventing the baby from drawing breath with its own lungs.

I ask you, the reader, to find out for yourself, as a father, mother, sister or brother, or a scientist the answer to these questions: "How long would it take to perform a C-section delivery even on a woman who was already on the operating table to deliver in a normal delivery? Or was she moved to the operating room and the C-section performed after the baby's heartbeat disappeared from the monitors?" That's how long the unborn cousin named Steve went without life-giving oxygen inside his mother's womb. Science says brain damage begins at 2 minutes usually or so I've read.

Laying there, seeing her son and his umbilical cord wrapped around his throat, the religious among you might think my Aunt would have prayed for a miracle, begging god to intervene and save her child. She told me later that she didn't get the chance. As the doctor unwound the umbilical cord from his throat and held the baby up by his feet, Steve did what no one there had thought possible. He began to wail, without the smack on his ass that everyone assumes is necessary for getting a baby to start breathing in movies and he began pissing all over the doctors and nurses nearby.

Remember I said that my Aunt Fran never got the opportunity to pray for a miracle? She stated that she never even got the chance to say thank you for the one that happened at that moment on that day. Because as Stevie started crying and pissing everywhere, my Aunt Fran heard that voice I mentioned in my encounters and it said to her one simple phrase:

"See, I told you I'd be here."

Tough act to follow, really. Since I was well on my way to my meeting with the divine by then, having been asked to get 'ordained' and take over a congregation in North Carolina. But that's the irony of working for god. Old dude has a sense of completeness that requires his signing off on his works. So I get to include this note at the end of the story as if god was dotting the I's and crossing the Ts in the story he had written himself by using me to deliver that message.

My Aunt Fran had a cactus, known as a "Christmas" cactus that hadn't bloomed even once in the three years she had owned it. It was a nice plant, looked pretty cool, and had sat on her mantle for those three years as an ornamental plant. But the day she and my Uncle Earl brought Stevie home from the hospital, there sat that "Christmas" cactus, in full bloom. And my Aunt knew, or told me she did then, that Steve was going to be okay. He is, for those that might want to know the follow-up on him. No brain damage, no retardation, nothing wrong with him physically or mentally or emotionally or even spiritually. He's a good person, has his own life to live, and was doing well the last I heard.

For myself, I was a messenger only, a runner who delivered an important message to someone I care for a lot. Perhaps that's when the life of runner5150 was sparked within me?! All I can say for sure is that I did as I was asked, by a voice that came from out of my mouth, not inside my head. And I'm glad I did.

Compleat Brig:

The First Experience

Compleat

There are many instances in my lifespan that I was embarrassed of sharing here. Not out of shame because I no longer embrace shame the way I used to, but because in remembering them I can see the process by which I was prepared to accept the task of writing this book.

Once more, I must live through the period in which I was confined in the brig at Camp Lejeune, North Carolina. At first, I was awaiting trial by general court-martial and on suicide watch due to the nature of the charges against me. Eventually, after that same court martial had found me guilty and sentencing had been given, I was held there until the process of assessing and beginning the appeals process had begun.

While it could have only been for a few months the many experiences I had, while confined there, are vivid reminders of what I was selected for when I had told god off. Three specific stories come to mind when I think of that place, simplistic and non-important to the whole experience I remember but in and of themselves bits and pieces of the whole that needs to express itself here in this book.

The first deals with a young, black lance corporal assigned to the maximum-security cells in that brig. When food trays were delivered to the cells, on a food cart due to those on the maximum-security row not being allowed into the general public mess hall, there would often be pats of butter, or margarine, that were extras or additional to the meals.

While I didn't choose to reject the extra flavor these pats of butter would supply to mashed potatoes and other foods that I would often choose not to take my portion of them deliberately. "Why?", - some might ask? Because that lance corporal could and would, if offered the opportunity or asked to display this ability, eat each of those left-over pats of butter directly from their paper dispensing cards.

His ability to consume them fascinated me even while though it would cause me to feel nauseated when witnessing his ability to consume them. I cannot say if it was envy of his ability, disgust that he did this action on request, or just the fact that he could stand to do the thing without the need of for bread or any other food stuff to accompany what he was consuming that held sway over my fascination with his performance. To this day I cannot recall his action and not feel queasy with even the memory of his ability, though my rational mind recognizes that this feat was no great deed.

The second story deals with one of the other prisoners confined there. A large, very violent, young man whose name I understood to be Michael Cocaine. As an individual with an unfortunate name myself, I could relate to his anger being based in on verbal abuse or teasing throughout his life from children in schools he may have attended, teachers, adults hearing his name for the first time, and perhaps even his own self-doubts and misgivings about his last name. I could also relate to the ego part of the individual he eventually became due to the teasing and abuse he had grown used to because it was as distinctive a name that I can recall ever hearing other than my own.

Michael was large, angry, and unerringly violent in his language and appearance. While at the that period of my life I was younger, much thinner, much weaker, and completely overwhelmed by his physical presence when he would be led past my individual cell on the cell block. His verbal threats alone were enough to cause even the guards to proceed with caution in dealing with his movements to and from his cell, while his death threats toward me caused me to appreciate the bars that were meant to confine me, since they were the only things that kept him from carrying out his threats.

Looking back at that situation these many years later I cannot help but feel concern for him, not pity - since I view nostalgia as a sort of revenge-motivated feeling - , for him and concern for the others that were confined there. While Michael Cocaine's criminal charges included extreme violence there were others there who were confined for merely possessing marijuana or other drugs. Michael was angry at being confined, like an animal, and treated as if he were one by the guards and system of 'justice' that the supposedly Uniform Code of Military Justice claimed to adhere to in dealing with crimes committed by military personnel.

That there was no justice is apparent because now that medicinal marijuana and even recreational marijuana haves almost become the national norm, those individuals were confined for periods much longer than my own, for crimes that were significantly less harmful.

It galled those prisoners that officers, caught red- handed for the exact same crimes that they had committed were merely discharged, with other than honorable discharges or good of the service discharges while they were given Bad Conduct discharges or Dishonorable discharges.

Compleat

As an example an officer, caught selling marijuana on base would be discharged from the Marine Corps, while an enlisted individual caught smoking a joint could be given a sentence of up to 8 years for possession of a narcotic.

It was the standing opinion of those confined there that the UCMJ was simply the Un-Uniform Code of Military Just-Us.

While confined in that brig I also learned two things about myself. The first is more personal than important to these stories. I learned that I had the desire to sing aloud. Whether or not I was good at it I could not judge, and since I have no way of contacting even those who were sentenced to Leavenworth Federal Prison for more years than the 40 since I was removed from that brig, I couldn't seek to get their opinion on my ability or not. I only know that the desire, no matter how poorly I might have been able to perform it, would overwhelm me to where I would sing aloud from my cell. And for the most part, I don't recall any outbursts or complaints about my singing coming from the others confined there.

The second thing I learned was that I had an uncanny ability that brought unwanted attention to me from both the other prisoners and the guards stationed on that cell block. Michael Cocaine was particularly interested in my ability.

I could and did on two occasions open the locked door of my cell. While the cells were checked periodically, and when placed within the cells prisoners were checked and rechecked to ensure that they had no implements that might enable them to unlock their cells and the cell doors themselves were checked to ensure they were securely closed, I had opened the cell door of not one but two different cells while confined there.

I simply pushed the door open and as it swung wide made sure that it did not make a noise by banging against the other bars of the cell or the adjacent cell. Then I walked up and down the cell hallway, speaking with the other prisoners there in both awe of my own ability and ego in having accomplished an impossible task. In the first instance, I even approached the guard's station to inform them I was no longer confined.

Ego made their upset and consternation amusing to me. In the second instance I proceeded more cautiously, since cameras had been installed and I chose to enjoy the small freedom of being able to walk up and down the corridor, eventually returning to my cell before calling for the guards to inform them that my door was UN-secure, again. And while the third act of this nature might have occurred at that brig, my appeal process had progressed to the point it was determined that I could be placed in the general population until transport to the Camp Pendleton brig would be arranged for my confinement there for the duration of my sentence.

I often wonder now, these many years later, how does an individual who insisted on telling god "No, I won't do what you are requiring of me to do!" retains or gains the ability to open secured and firmly locked doors.? This experience was one of many that I did not understand, though many others have since offered their opinions on the events I've shared here. "The devil allowed you to do it." was one of the more popular statements that I encountered. Satan, by the way, has no sway or control in my life. To obtain any influence or control the 'devil' would need to have access to my soul. And I can assure anyone who asks or is interested that I surrendered that part of my humanity long before I committed the crimes I was convicted of and confined for those many years past.

I gave it into the keeping of a person who no longer exists, has no memory of my entrusting it to her, and has no memory of me other than as the asshole who was the first real betrayal of her heart. Justice is a cold, patient, and equally uncaring thing. Without a soul, even the devil has no use for me. And that lost soul that once made me a human being? It's unobtainable by me or any other entity. Not even god can restore what was freely given away, because he will not interfere or intervene with the choices made by his children, humanity. Not even in the choice to surrender their humanity to another.

I see now that opening those doors was simply the last acts of my humanity as it left me. Human beings were never meant to do the things we all did to be incarcerated there and human beings were never meant to be confined in cages, as if they were animals without souls. There is a better way. But that too is the subject of yet another story.

Compleat

The Lost System of Justice in These Un-United States

To understand the problems within the system of incarceration and in order to find a solution to the overcrowding and recidivism problems, specifically here in the States, one need only look at the justice system itself.

Justice here calls for punishment equal to the crimes committed but, unfortunately, our system is geared more toward punishment and then the continuing ostracizing of those who have broken the law long after they have been incarcerated for established lengths of time, served their sentence, and have earned their release.

The warehousing of human beings, in conditions that require them to exist under a 'survival at all costs' mentality creates an atmosphere that leads to what many psychiatrists have determined to be equal to or even surpassing battlefield -related Post Traumatic Stress Disorder. And, as had been noted before I was made intimately aware of those conditions, tends to create 'better' criminals.

It is my experienced opinion that the first step toward rehabilitating prisoners needs to be an awareness that criminal behaviors of all types (i.e. murder, rape, robbery, assault, theft, etc....) are in fact not what our society would deem 'normal' behaviors. Sick, twisted, and abhorrent to the point of being terrifying behaviors are especially outside the acceptable, or so-called normal, behaviors of human beings anywhere. Yet while these behaviors are quite often denoted as being 'sick' there is no actual concern beyond punishment for any individual who might violate what society deems lawful, especially if the actions they commit are violent or sexual in nature.

While it is obvious that confinement needs to be focused on protecting society from all these behaviors it remains to be seen that a secondary focus or objective needs to be to protect the confined individuals from themselves and each other just as much as it is for protecting society, too.

Rehabilitation can only begin to produce changes in the individual's behaviors when the individual offender is brought to an awareness of the fact that they are suffering from abnormal thinking patterns (a mental illness - as defined in the DSM V) and through therapy, incentive and conditioning learn to take responsibility for their own actions, breaking free from learned behaviors and establishing new ones. And by my own example, it is entirely feasible that with the repetition of acceptable behaviors these individuals absolutely can learn to create and become habituated into different behavioral patterns, ones more attuned to their societal norms.

I have witnessed and refuted the often outspoken and misguided argument of "Are we supposed to reward bad behavior in these individuals?" That argument is used to undermine or detract from viewing this as a legitimate option for the rehabilitation of criminal behaviors, yet the society of the so-called United States leads the entire world in prison populations and repeat incarcerations. With a gross population that reflects only a small percentage of the total world population (get the numbers from online) at approximately 4.25%, the States have 25% of the entire world's imprisoned individuals within both privately run and state-run prisons.

And while programs focused on rehabilitation, reeducation and transitional reintroduction back into society would serve the individuals, their families, and society itself much more than the simple warehousing, discarding, and destroying their ability to correct their own behaviors, through imprisonment, ostracizing, and labeling the individual as an ex-convicts, the States refuse to seek a solution beyond that warehousing, increased punishment, increased lengths of sentences and making it nearly impossible for a person who had been convicted of a crime to rejoin society as an equal.

I discovered, when investigating and mentioning the statistics of recidivism within the justice system here in the States, that the numbers are staggering not simply because the individuals become institutionalized from being confined and not being able to adjust to being released into society again. There is another statistic that is much too often overlooked.

The crimes these sick and progressively sickened individuals committed increased not just in recidivism but also in the fact that they become even more violent, which presents the logical hypothesis that by being subjected to confinement in a violent atmosphere and the resultant stress thereof actually creates within the individual both an apathy toward their own acting out in a violent manner that might not have been included in their original offense and as well as an acceptance of violent behaviors as a necessary means by which they are to obtain what they must have to survive - . (i.e. sustenance, shelter, and safety.)

Programs focused on rehabilitation, reeducation and transitional reintroduction back into our society would serve the individuals, their families and society itself.

Compleat

Compleat odeP

> Sticks and stones may break my bones,
> But words can also hurt me.
> Sticks and stones break only skin,
> while words are ghosts that haunt me.
> Pain from words has left its scar
> on mind and heart that's tender.
> cuts and bruises now have healed.
> it's words that I remember.

"Hang him up by his balls with barbed wire!" "Hang him and burn his body so the others like him will see how we treat those perverts!" "Take him behind the barn and put a bullet in his brain!" "Rape the bastard and then feed him to the dogs!" "Kill him, no one here will report it!" "Son of a bitch deserves to be put on a spit and roasted!" "Cut his cock off and force him to eat it!"

*

With those statements as my opening, I believe I may have gotten the attention of those who hold dear the idea that there is no punishment great enough for a child molester/rapist. Baby rapers deserve only the cruelest, extreme punishments because, after all, their crimes are against humanity's young, the future of the human race, and, of course, the very immortality of whomsoever the child 'belongs' to be its parent, grandparent, or relative. Even a community can feel threatened by the fear generated by one of these predators in their midst. Especially when the pedophile is an unknown, a stranger to all involved.

Yet in most cases of child abuse, the victim knows the perpetrator on an intimate level. Fathers, step-fathers, neighbors, close blood relatives, pastors, priests, teachers … the list goes on and on. The percentage of known pedophiles that victimize strangers is small, not simply because it is rare but also because of the very rarity of the crime ever being reported. Sadly it is usually because the pedophile that commits these types of crimes against strangers is so certain of the reactions of the community (see the statements above for reference) that they end up killing their victims in order to attempt to conceal their crimes and the punishment that would be the result of being found out.

Rational behavior in the case of those individuals, in spite of their irrational actions against children, after all - since self-preservation is considered instinctual and rational. Yet not one community, society, or even nationality views the reactions to the act of sexually abusing a child as rational by any means. And those who react, rather than respond to these acts, are often themselves survivors of previous abuse by someone in their own lives. To respond rather than react to a pedophile, a human being – either male or female – would need to be able to relate to the pedophile as an individual human being and not the programmed reactions that stem from their own abuse and/or the outpouring of verbal cues from the community that surrounds them.

It remains to be seen if humanity will ever grow out of reacting to these situations in ways that have been taught as being not merely 'normal' but also as being appropriate. Observations of the behaviors of those who react to these situations have led me to believe that humanity has a long, long way to go before they will be able to view these individuals -, of either type of abusers or pedophiles -, as anything less than human themselves. Yet statistically it is ironic that most of those who molest children, especially within their own families or communities, were themselves molested. The US Department of Justice admits this themselves, stating in the 1979 Journal of Victimology that over 31% of sex offenders at the time had some form of forcible sexual encounter or assault in their own youths.

I've already written about the misuse of religion by zealots who could care less about what is actually written in their own books (Bible, Koran, etc. ...) to use their influence on and whip their communities into a frenzy of fear in order to direct and control the reactions and actions of those communities. In this instance, I'm going to include direct references to the King James Version of their bible in order to attempt to express the point that they avoid taking responsibility for in their reactions.

Most 'pastors' of different denominations of non-Catholic religions often quote the passages or verses found in their bibles that deal with Jesus' observations about harming children. Matthew 18:6, Luke 17: 1-4, Mark 9:41-42 all speak pretty much the same thing with the slight exception that one or more of them doesn't mention children in particular. I haven't read the book since I was 13 years of age, so I'll ask that my references be taken in consideration in light of that fact before anyone condemns me for not remembering the exact chapters and verses.

The pastors I mention usually are misquoting what Jesus is reported to have said, in order to condemn, ostracize and alienate someone that has been either suspected of, caught in the act of, or convicted of the crime of child molestation. And there in lays the seeds of religion being more important to them than the actual words being said or the purpose behind those words.

Jesus, for all intents and purposes, was human enough to love children as if they were his own offspring. He even had to admonish others who tried to condemn those who brought their children to him, in order that those children would enjoy his company and know him as a son of god. Children know love, real love, when they are close to it. But that topic is for another story on the loss of both innocence and the ability to 'know' one another later in this book. What Jesus is described as saying -, and again I emphasize that his words are misquoted and maligned in order to promote fear -, is that anyone caught harming even one of those innocents would be "better off to have a stone tied around their neck and tossed into the sea." Don't take my word for it, look it up for yourselves and make sure I'm quoting him correctly, please?!

What religion has done is taken that phrase out of context, twisted it into a tool for fear, and use it to control the actions of the communities in which they have influence and control.

My point is simply this: "Take into consideration who is making this statement." This wasn't the god of the old testament, punishing, demanding, commanding, or even expecting. This was his first conceived child, here among human beings as a human being himself. His entire ministry or representation of god in man was based entirely on love, forgiveness, and compassion for those who had done wrong, either to themselves or others. And his words didn't say "Go out and wrap a rope around their necks and toss them into the sea." He said, "it would be better for them …" Even in condemning their actions, he was showing he was capable of loving them, in spite of their actions against those whose love and care he wanted to protect the most. Getting any so -called 'Christian' to agree to that statement would be almost as impossible as getting almost any of them to embrace the truth that I stood before god, face to face, and told god to go fuck himself, without being smitten into dust and without becoming some kind of saint, like Moses.

The key word, that shows the love and compassion Jesus was expressing was the single word 'better.' Who would want something "better" for a pedophile, in today's society or world? Only god, as far as I know, and he had to tell me that before I'd believe it myself. Don't get me wrong, there are plenty of human beings that would rush to grab a rope tied to a stone and toss pedophiles into the nearest ocean, sea, river, or even pond. But their intent wouldn't be to do something 'better' for those they were killing. It would simply be their own fear, turned to anger, turned to rage, turned to prejudice turned to actions against another human being in order to avoid taking responsibility for their 'brother or sister.'

And in the end, that's what it's all about. Avoiding taking responsibility for themselves or others. To end child molestation, laws are enacted to increase punishments, extend monitoring of those who have committed such crimes and stigmatize any who have in order to 'teach' others who might commit such crimes to beware of the consequences of their actions. And although the laws are updated and increased throughout humanity, not one ends the practice of abuse against children or even encourages those who might be so inclined to seek help with their own issues surrounding this behavior.

How then are these laws for the 'better' of all humanity? Especially for the children who become statistics because the 'stranger' in from whom they are in danger who might also be a family member or known to them as a friend.? Statistics are is an amazing tool in which to judge the success or failure of a system because they give a numeric value that can be measured visually as well as mentally. If statically 85% of all pedophiles were themselves abused as children, then their punishment as adults has done nothing to decrease the percentages of children being abused over the years.

A child abused in 1958 grows to become an abuser in 1979 for example, never receiving the therapeutic help to deal with their own issues until acting out themselves, leaving them both victim and perpetrator. Yet their society sees only the perpetrator, calling for further victimization of the child they were in 1958.

Does anyone really 'believe' in a human being having an "inner child" in today's societies? It's professed frequently by both liberals and conservatives alike, but the laws punishing those who are now perpetrators are no less damaging to those 'inner children' than the actions of the perpetrators are to the children they victimize these days, and are created by those same liberals and conservatives who profess belief in the inner child. I call it religion or religious belief where they profess one thing and act in an entirely different manner.

And here is a side note that makes this entire argument appear highly deceitful on the part of society as a whole; if the purpose of the laws was to protect children from pedophiles of all types, then the fact that females who are found guilty of these types of crimes against young male children (even some against young female children in rare cases) are simply not treated as the same type of pariah as their male counterparts.

A female teacher having been convicted of having sex with a male student in her classes 'might' lose her teaching credentials, suffer some embarrassment from her crime being disclosed to her community, and be penalized or imprisoned for a period, yet it is always consistently for a lesser length of sentence, her community is willing to 'forgive and forget' her behaviors and she is able to find employment within her community in another field without her past being held against her by future employers. Again, look up the statistics, don't take my word for this either.

If a pedophile were to be given treatment, able to recognize the behavior patterns that led to his or her acting out, and given mental, emotional, and societal tools with which to overcome the programmed responses to their own abuse the cycle of abuse could be broken and abuse of children would and could be stopped. I hear the arguments already about that last statement and the one that I choose to answer is simply this:

"If a pedophile were given these opportunities, and the support of his/her society in order to prevent future occurrences of these behaviors and chose not to embrace their opportunity to change then, as Jesus said, it would be better for them to have a rope tied around their neck and be tossed into the sea."

Yet it is the compassion that Jesus is credited with that allows me to make that statement here. To tie a rope with a stone on it around another human being's neck and cause them to drown, one of the most feared and dreadful deaths a human being can experience, would be harsh if done in the spirit of revenge, so- called 'justice' or even fear. To love someone enough to end their life, their suffering and their inability to adjust or connect with the rest of humanity on the scale of being able to not act upon their broken behaviors is something the human race as a whole has lost.

Compleat

The compassion to end suffering is condemned as killing or murder while murderous thoughts and statements like those at the beginning of this story are not merely applauded, they are encouraged and quoted among human beings as if they were 'gospel.' There is nothing new or good about the news that human beings choose to kill one another rather than do anything to accept their responsibility for creating the problems they are experiencing. After all, gospel does mean: good news, right?

Part of my argument with god was that I don't consider myself a 'good' person and questioning questioned why would he choose me to deliver a message that isn't 'good' news by any stretch of the imagination. The fact is that the message I bring is bad news for humanity as a whole. In the simplest terms what I'm saying is a two-part message:

"It's time for humanity to wake up." and

"It doesn't have to be this way."

What's coming is worse by far. I've seen it.

Compleat Brig: The Second Experience

Sentenced to four years in the brig at Camp Pendleton, California I had no difficulty adapting to the life of being incarcerated than I had in being in the fleet or regular Marines. After all is said and done, the routines were exactly the same.

Wake up call, muster, and head count. Assigned duties and work tasks that were easily accomplished, then hours of down time, where boredom and sleeping were the only avenues for dealing with the illusion of time creeping past day after day.

I've always read a lot of books, even there. I, viewed the legal library that was offered for anyone who wished to pursue and appeal to their case which the military would have laughingly ignored since any appeals would have to go through the military justice system, be reviewed by a military- appointed lawyer and dismissed by a military judge, who wasn't about to overturn another military judge's findings out of the loyalty of the legal system's representatives to one another rather than to the idea of justice itself.

I remember one man whose case smacked of such vindictiveness and absurdity in that he was tried by the civilian courts, had the case dismissed due to improper search and seizure by the civil police, and was then brought to trial a second time on the exact same charges by the military justice system. He was convicted by admission of that same evidence that had been declared non-admissible in civil court and sentenced to more than forty 40+ years at Fort Leavenworth Federal Penitentiary for Military Prisoners. Part of the + to his sentence came from a contempt of court charge brought by the military judge presiding over his case. Double jeopardy laws being ignored by charging and trying him a second time and knowing his rights as a citizen of these States called United, the man in question suggested to the judge, by blowing kisses at him and speaking out against the illegality of what was transpiring by telling the judge "Kiss me, judge. I like to be kissed when I'm being fucked." 90 extra days for contempt toward a system that is allowed to ignore the laws of the land, placing the Uniform Code of Military Justice above the Constitution.

That case had nothing to do with me, of course, but I had to include the story to show an example of how the system can be used to any effect those who are in charge of it may choose as their will and way of controlling what happens throughout the entire race of humanity.

My story there consists of learning how to play cribbage, winning the only trophy I've ever won for being good at something, and learning to box as a junior middleweight. That latter part would gain me no more popularity than I already had for being confined there for the crimes that I was legitimately convicted of and had admitted to willingly.

Learning to box and, lifting weights to gain some measure of upper body strength as I resided in a dorm of approximately 20 other men was logical for me. Some were there for crimes that I know were more racially motivated than their actually being criminals. Pot smoking had gotten my friend, Stew Peterson, a Good of The Service discharge in 1978, while some of the black men in my dorm there had been convicted of possession of a single joint and had been sentenced to 4 to 5 years in the brig.

By 1980, when the then commandant of the Marine Corps had released his "White Letter" denoting a zero tolerance for drug use in the Marine Corps, it would be predominately black men who would find themselves convicted of crimes of possession and receiving longer sentences for the exact same types of crimes that their white counterparts would be sentenced for.

Most would not know my past or the crimes I had been convicted of, until one white man broke into my footlocker that was provided, without a lock in the brig lest the padlock be used as a weapon, and took the paperwork that depicted my crimes in great detail and shared it with the entire brig population. After that, I would receive threats, assaults, and insults on such a frequent basis that it became almost ludicrous to even listen to the guards telling the others there to 'stand down' from being aggressive toward me.

One such young, black man would eventually assault me because his insults were so inane that I responded in such a way that he was urged by his fellows to take offense.

I don't remember his insult, since it was so non-specific and general as to be almost normal by then, but I remember only too well my response.

"Your opinion means less to me than whale piss."

His friends and fellow black men urged him to take offense to what I had said, though I believe he might have allowed it to pass as being a lame reply to his own insult, by insisting that I had just called him lower than whale piss, which they said "sinks into the mud under the ocean." He hit me and we would have fought, but the guards were watching and rushed into the dorm area to put us both into solitary confinement. My punishment was considered to be 'protective custody' but because I had been willing to fight, I had the same dietary restrictions that he had for assaulting me. We called being punished in solitary as having been sent to 'rabbit food row' because while there the diet consisted of green vegetables, mashed potatoes without butter or milk, no meat, plain white bread or toast, and water but no coffee or juice.

While there I considered why he had been urged to take offense to what I had said in reply to his insults and realized that he, like many others I've met in life, did not understand what I had actually said. He and his friends had heard the response as a put down of him or his personality somehow, where my intent was an honest expression of how I felt about myself rather than having anything to do with him whatsoever.

There were no insults, no put- downs, or even assaults that could make me feel worse about myself while I was there. Nothing said to me or done to me or my property (what little I owned while incarcerated) could make me feel less than how I felt about myself there and then already. I had, I realized, become the monster I believed myself to be when I joined the Marines back in 1972 and only my opinion about myself and my life mattered. It was that no one had ever deserved to exist less than I did and none of those confined there with me would ever understand that fact.

In my own ass-backward way, I was agreeing with his insult, but since I was speaking from a position of being insane, no one could have understood that fact or even related to it unless they too were crazy. I do feel remorse that he was punished for attacking me though. If his friends hadn't provoked him, I'd like to believe that he would have considered the source of what I replied and dismissed my response as being from an idiot or monster.

Compleat

The Desert: The Diary Inserts
_._._._._._._._._._._._._._._._..

It's 21:30 and I am exhausted. John and I go there in Lake LA and this house of his stinks! Dog piss, horses, and God only knows what else. I've busted my ass all day and still the stench is overwhelming. Tomorrow, I plan to air the place out again, but it's beginning to look like a real stinker that I've gotten myself into here. I can't stay here and not clean it up some. It's filthy, and I just hope I don't get sick because I have no way of contacting anyone that knows me for about two weeks. I've eaten my first bowl of rice and John has headed home, so this is the beginning of my being alone with myself. I'm listening to classical music and I'm too tired to write, but I want to establish a pattern of writing each night before sleeping.

Two points of interest or that I'm not hungry, so far. and John is really pissed about this place. he kept calling the woman who lived here and let it get this bad scum. I cleaned up something I don't remember what it was. and kept trying to tell him she was wasn't scum she was just really sick. He didn't want to hear it and seem to notice new holes and problems at rate that for outpaced my ability to count. I kept thinking how sad he was. I even believe he deserves recompense for the time work and cost of cleaning this place really is going to take. But so much hate over a home. I am probably worse about other things but since I don't own a home it is very hard for me to empathize or understand.

Compleat

9:45 sleep, I hope.

July 6th 5:30 a.m.

The hardest part about sleeping here alone is the dark. I'm still afraid of it. And every evening the blinds would let in light from somewhere didn't help a lot. The second hardest part is the stench. I finally got tired enough to sleep and the smell of this place kept waking me up. Hope airing it out today helps.

1:15PM

Another truly weird day. Got most of John's garage straightened out, but the trash still needs to be bagged. Set up the table with some items for a sorta 'yard sale'. Had some Jehovah's Witnesses come by and take the animal food, so that's a little less mess for John to have hauled off. Decided to quit before 10 so the heat wouldn't get me, and took a siesta like the Mexicans supposedly always do. Even with the house completely open and the AC going, the smell gets overwhelming at times. I'm beginning to think that there's a relationship between me and this house. It's a good house, well built, but could use some improvement as all places can. But it's insides have been fouled by lack of care, proper maintenance and outright abuse.

The stench reminds me of my own soul, how nasty I see myself as being. And I worry that, like this house, the smell will never really go away. The work I'm doing at cleaning up both this house and myself, shows signs of having some effect. The problem is I don't know what to do, don't have the proper tools, and when I do, I get tired and weak rapidly. And the stench makes me want to be anywhere else but here. Maybe God does have a sense of humor. I said I wanted to look at myself and I've been provided with a hard look. Wow!

Where do I go from here?

I'm worried too, because I don't think I have enough food to last, but I am always telling people that things work out the way they are supposed to, so now I get to apply my own faith to that saying. And my nasal sinuses are dried out to the point of bleeding.

07:03 PM

Compleat

Sleeping a lot today, or dozing at least. Maybe from low blood sugar or just boredom. I'll find myself being still and doze off, maybe because it was so hard to get to sleep last night. Tonight, no AC. It makes the house stink worse, and I didn't even think that was possible. Got scared silly cleaning the garage. I was so busy looking for black widows on the walls and the ground that I almost walked into one that I didn't see hanging right in front of me from a strand of web. Reminded me of the movie Arachnophobia. I thought she was out to get me. Used a stick that I had been probing with to break the strand so violently that I thought I might have gotten her on me. Then when I saw her on the ground, I stomped her with anger and fear.

Yesterday I told John I wasn't worried about them, and even thought he was being over reactive when he saw one on the floor. Guess it goes to show that no matter what I think I can be wrong, or at least need to practice more understanding.

I haven't written a single word on a book I had hoped to write while here. It's like I've come all this way to find myself and my muse, and doing everything but that. Not that what I'm learning isn't good. I just don't know what to do with it or if I want to do anything with it.

7 July 1997

I was really tired and weak last night. Can't tell if it was from working, lack of real food, or the heat. I'm becoming acclimated to the heat – I think. But the lack of humidity really plays hell with my nose. Sex, masturbation, and all that were on my mind at 3AM, but I just went back to sleep. I've begun to establish a pattern of waking up frequently in the middle of the night and early morning. At 3AM I could see why I would want to live out here. The stars were out and it was great. I keep wondering if or when the neighbors are going to check me out. No one has come by, except a car load of JWs. No one has even waved hello, except the ice cream truck guy. If isolation from each other is at this level I can see how the woman who lived here was able to go so far down into the despair and degradation of living the way she must have.

Started reading my "Just for Today" last night and this morning so maybe I can establish a pattern there too.

4PM or thereabout

Compleat

I don't know if I should bless Dave Pearlman or curse him. Tales from underground is so like me that I feel like someone wrote about me long before I was born, and at the same time doesn't seem like me as much as I expect it to as I read it. The duality of the characters' monologue seems very like me, and the person being described gets close to fitting me to a tee. Then it jumps into areas that I feel left out of and alien to. But it describes those feelings too!

So, I'm left wondering if there is a part, or are parts, of myself that I am currently unable to recognize. If so, and I am more like the character described in the story, then I believe myself to be, what am I to myself? And does any of it matter?

I'm trying to decide a lot. Should I go back to Carlsbad if John comes this weekend? The nose bleed that I experienced today and the lack of food point to yes, the fact that Art Vicra might not approve of my "vacation" adds force to the direction, but I still feel incomplete in some way. I had hoped to at least understand before I left here.

I've done about all I'm going to in the kitchen and house. All I really would like to do is help John by bagging the trash out front and in the garage, and gathering up the junk out back. If I could complete a sweat lodge while I'm at it, that would be great. I don't know much about Native American rituals, but one thing I believe – even if I'm wrong – is that there is no 'set' way in which to do a ritual like I feel I want to do.

Certain steps or proceedings are usually followed in order to help focus the spirit and mind and body all towards the same end, but I'm not exactly sure what those patterns are, and I believe for me it's the focus, rather than which patterns I use, that will help me find and realize my goal – and perhaps even achieve it.

I may have a blood clot inside my nose. It feels like a hard lump of booger but it's up where the blood kept coming from so I'll leave it alone for now.

The third hardest part of being here is the silence. It's not completely quiet. There is wind blowing trees and cars driving on the road. I also hear dogs barking and kids playing in the distance. The silence comes from not having contact with someone else. I've always talked – too much in my opinion – to others. I've always expressed myself to feel connected to the rest of you. Almost as if I could talk my way into being human. I even talk to the flies before I kill them, just to be talking. Somewhere I learned to still the storms inside me and I could help others through those same type of storms. Now, if I could just still the storm that my tongue seems to be, I wonder what miracles could happen, for myself and others.

I sold a ladder for a dollar and the guy wanted to buy John's aluminum ladder so badly that I brought it inside. Is that paranoia or responsibility? Now I have $3 and some change to live off for the rest of this week and maybe the week after that. When the guy came up to buy the ladder, I had hoped that it was someone from NA, but no such luck. Guess I should be grateful just to talk with another human, huh?

08 July 07:20 PM

I've been up since before 7AM. Again, sleep was off and on all night, and the smell got bad again. Two new developments: 1. There are kids around here and some live across the street as mentioned. 2. This scares me more than I can put into words right now.

Fear, lust, hope, loneliness, powerlessness, faith, all mixed up together and inseparable from each other by me alone. If there is no God, I'm in trouble, plenty, if there is, HELP ME, I   beg of you.

I'm always telling others that saying "no matter where you go, there you are." Why is it that I can recognize the fact that others carry their problems with them and need to lay down the load, and even find suggestion for them on how to go about laying it down, yet my own 'burdens' I can only see when they are in my face and I can't seem to find the ways, means or strength to lay them down myself? Why is it I feel less than alive unless I am overwhelmed by fear and excitement and more than 'merely' human when I am possessed by these emotions? They say Lewis Carrol wrote Alice in Wonderland and Through the looking Glass as he was inspired by a young 'neighbor' child. Could I use the fear and excitement to I feel to inspire writing a classic of literature as he did? Perhaps this is the muse I've sought, the inspiration to reach beyond myself and touch the world by sharing my feelings of fear and excitement with the rest of the world through a story. Dostoevsky had his dreamer, the identity of a man whose life was wasted, yet complete with the chance encounter with real love. Carey had mired characters who were there for the entertainment, confusion, and wonderment of Alice. If fear is my muse, then what story am I to write? My life's history would be boring, and more to the point would be autobiographical if I were to try practice honest self-examination, even allowing myself artistic license to color that story with fanciful anecdotes and fictitious happenings that I half remember and believe I half created in my childhood imagination. Something I find very hard to do separate fantasy and reality. Even when I was in my 20s, I remember believing in fantasy so strongly that they were real to me then and hold an echo of reality to them even today. What could have driven me to hate reality so much that fantasy and the escape it offers became such an obsession for me? Do I really want to know the answer to that particular question? Because doesn't knowing the answer mean I'm obligated to take some action to resolve the problem? Is my hold on life, as a mixture of fantasy and reality, a reservation I've held without realizing it consciously, until now.

I came to the desert to find what I hoped would be answers and the answers I've found so far have opened more questions. I almost went back and read what I've written since I've been here. I'm curious as to where this will lead - both from and towards - but I'll wait until I can share it with Lee. The fear has lessened, so I think I'll go to work now. Besides the damn flies are driving me nuts.

12:01 PM

I've met Lisa from across the street and her seven kids - she's pregnant with her eighth. Six of the seven are girls. Ashley is second oldest and a stepdaughter. The oldest is Melissa, and she's going to grow up to be a heartbreaker. The boy is younger than most of the girls and has his life tangled out now and in the future with seven sisters to live with, take care of, and protect.

John probably wouldn't approve of all these kids climbing in his trees and Art Vicra would flip at seven girls being here, but it makes me feel better to just let them take care of themselves around here. I received four apples and two cans of vegetables for some of the things in the yard sale from them and their mom. As I sit here, I imagine what it would be like to travel in the Australian outback to meet a tribe of aboriginals and lose all traces of my civilized nature. I'd probably be uncomfortable the whole time and miss the luxuries, if not the people and where, I asked myself, would this leave me morally. I don't know. Maybe if I could lose my civilized ideas and thoughts, I'd be more able to be myself. Would that be a good thing? I don't claim to know if Dave Perlman's right - if, like in "Notes From the Underground", I am a good but intelligent man with a severe case of heightened awareness.

Compleat

Then I would I revert to basically being good or would heightened awareness and intelligence bring about my downfall - causing me to revert into something or someone I have feared to be all my life? Again, the inseparable combination of fear and excitement, almost as if I can enjoy no other emotion as I do the pain of being afraid. Could I have actually avoided horror films and the like merely because deep inside I knew that I would be overcome by the ecstasy from the fear? How weirdly warped I must be if this is so, but then maybe not, for others before me must have felt this way or else Dostoyevsky and the rest couldn't have written about them. Such is life.

19:00 PM

I've been thinking again and I know that's supposed to be a bad move on my part. Truth be told, what I've been thinking is just as mixed together as my feelings. Here and home, women in general, and I am in particular finding life having meaning and suicide being pointless. How can I be angry enough at the world, god, and everyone else to commit suicide when I'm not really mad at anyone else? And I'm not sure if I'm actually angry with myself or if I just feel or think I'm supposed to be. Would a dog, if dogs could reason or had self-awareness beyond instinct, be angry at itself for being a dog? I don't believe it would. So why do I grow or feel I must be angry at myself for being human? Am I still lost somewhere trying to be more than I am or have I given up before realizing my potential? Or both combined in some weird way that prevents my acceptance of myself for who I am? Talk to Lee. 5150.

Does Pam love me and would I really know it if she did or didn't? I am so blind when it comes to how others see me, mostly because I view how others see me through the filter of how I see myself. And now that filter is questionable at best, so I find myself completely lost in how to know or gauge the feelings others have towards me. Do others hate me as I feel - or have I refused to let them feel their own feelings by directing what they are supposed to feel? Dogs sometimes distrust me, especially when I'm off on my thinking. Cats are attracted to me unless I make sudden or violent movements. Women, I have absolutely no clue about. Men say they like me, but don't relate to what I need to talk about. Indeed, I spend more time listening to men than talking, and that's saying a lot because I do talk too much. Children seem drawn to me - not all, but some. When I was a clown in NC, I remember being praised by a woman who had been clowning for a while. I had gotten a baby who was crying from fear of the other clowns to soften the cries and eventually take a balloon from me.

I just did what felt right to me, pretending to be scared of the baby and offering it the balloon to make peace with it, so I wouldn't be afraid anymore. And I felt afraid and then accepted, even forgiven, when the child took the balloon - almost as if some guilt had been forgiven of me by taking the child's fear onto myself. If I could feel that peace, that forgiveness, more, then perhaps I would finally be able to forgive myself. Who knows? Sleep soon. And since I'm already cooler than I've been for days, maybe I'll wait to shower in the morning. Talk to Lee about why. 5150.

July 1997, 16:00 PM

Fuck me, if I can remember what day it is today. I guess today is all I need to know. I woke up at 3 AM this morning and saw the colors of sunrise on the horizon. If I'd had any sense, I would have gotten up then or stayed here all day. I didn't eat - mistake number one - and took a small sports bottle with water in it with my walking stick to go to the payphone 12 miles away. I got to some junctions in the road and couldn't remember which way to go. I assumed north because I sort of remember John talking about north of here. And since I was on Avenue O looking for Avenue J, I guessed the names of the roads went north to south alphabetically.

Got really lucky on that one. Bought water and Gatorade at the store and made my phone calls. Naturally, I called Pam - mistake number two and I even called her twice. She missed me the first call and complained how bad everything is back there the second time. The results undecipherable, as yet. I called and John told him I need to come home this weekend - the smell is driving me out of here. Besides, I wouldn't tell him all my reasons for leaving. It's none of his business. I tried calling for a ride to an NA meeting - mistake number three. I spent 10 minutes on hold for an answering service to transfer me to Smokey. Of course, Smokey couldn't call and contact someone for me or give me a direct phone number to another addict, so he gives me the area service tele-committee phone number for Antelope Valley and wishes me God bless. I call that number - no answer - so I call Pam the second time, I give her the number, and ask her to try when she gets home. All this time, I'm sitting on the sidewalk outside the store planning to doze or nap until it gets late enough and cool enough to start back. That way I'm rested for 12 mile walk back. Instead, someone breaks the gas pump near the store and I almost passed out from either exhaustion, the fumes or both when I tried to stand up. Nearby is a restaurant. It was in the movie "The Right Stuff" and I move to a bench there outside, but out of the sun and away from the smell. Some guy named Bill, by his name tag on his shirt, shows up at 10 or 10 30 AM to get stoked for work. I don't know if the place is a local bar or just a restaurant, but I'm uncomfortable there because I'm tempted to find out and I have a $1.69 in my pocket, so I rest a little, then start back some time around 11:00 or 11:30 AM. Big mistake. I made about six miles before I'm worrying about my water running out and the fact that I'm so tired that the idea of lying down for a nap keeps running through my mind. If I'd have done that, I really don't think I'd be here now. I gave up my pride and fear of being arrested for hitchhiking and stuck out my thumb. For Real. In the end, I've flagged down a local sheriff, a black man named Hill, and caught a ride to the road leading here. Of course, he ran my name through the computer. Thought I said "Greenwater" and told me he was just entering it into the computer and then he would give me a ride. He entered my birthday, too. I really couldn't care if he hit the jackpot and came back with my entire rap sheet. Every thought I ever had and future I'll have to deal with by then. His call was air-conditioned and cool and I drank the last of my water quick.

With my past, this may have been another mistake, or god just took mercy on a fool, but it supports my decision to get out of here and avoid the kids across the street along with their pregnant mom. I showered, ate, slept. Bathed again, ate again, and then sat down to write this. I'm so tired I left the front door open while I took a bath. On one hand, I was too tired to close it and on the other, I was so tired I hoped someone would walk in on me. I'm still hungry, so I'll make some rice and green beans or open a can of fruit cocktail.

17:34 PM

Having eaten until I find myself uncomfortably full, of course, the people across the street come home. My first thought is that by now they know all about me and none of these kids will come over here now. The shame I feel makes me sicker than I already am and, at the same time, I find a relief in believing that they will stay away. I've judged my attempt at a Native American purification ceremony a failure. While I avoided contact, my thoughts remained the same and, in the end, I continue the process of maintaining what I must in order to keep from acting as I want. Of all the things I've learned so far this week, especially about myself, I've learned that

Compleat

walking in the desert at noon is dumb. I need to learn to organize myself better. That while I have found a little muse and a pen name for myself: Michael Prophet. I don't know if I have it in me to write a book, so I don't really know if I have a book within me. Complete by Michael Runner Prophet. Sounds good now. If only I could find out what exactly it is, I'm trying to say. Maybe trying isn't the word I should use. To say I have tried something I believe I'd have had to have done that at least once. No such luck in this case. Every time I start to write, all that seems to come out of me is cowardly, self-pitying drivel - whining about myself, my life, and my dreams that will never see fruition. Need to say, want to say, and wish to express to the world in general - and women in particular - these come closer, but don't capture what it is I feel inside. How do I tell you that I love you? Not the love of my lust or the desires of being one of you. How can I communicate something I don't understand, but have hidden within me for so very long, hoping to someday find the ability to let it out for all of you to see? Without whining, how can I express how much it hurts me on the inside not to be able to release it all - or how confused I feel to know you don't understand what it is when you tell me to let it out a little at a time?

Could a supernova happen in stages? Though, it might appear to be so from far away that only shows that distance distorts our perception of it? For you to see what I feel in stages would only hurt me worse because I would be aware of your distance from me and what I feel while you would be blissfully unaware. I'm tired of this pain, yet can see no way of releasing it without causing you pain instead. I've tried that. It never worked before. It merely drove you further away while setting an image in my mind that I must appear monstrous to you for what I've become through my actions. I do wish I could be just human at times like these, but then I have to question myself now. Isn't desiring things that are harmful to myself a fruit all humans share? Desire and reason do not necessarily have to conflict, but in me, more often than not, they do. Yesterday, I fantasized about being a shaman, a medicine man, a spirit walker, a healer - powerful yet responsible, challenging storms to protect the innocent. Somewhere in all that, there was a grain of selflessness - the desire to be of service - yet the lust for power, the need for recognition, and the fear of being useless, not just powerless, keeps me from realizing even that one grain of honest giving. So, I give or feel that I give nothing and find my fear realized before I can even begin. Why does a raven fly against the wind?

10 July 1997 7:20AM

Compleat

Woke up at 3 AM again, watched the horizon and dozed until 6.30 or 7. Decided not shower this morning after 3 or 4 yesterday afternoon. My legs are stiff (calves) and I'm still tired. And from looking in the mirror I believe I've lost some weight. The "oldies" station keeps playing old rock songs from when I was in my teens and twenties. The feelings of peace, empathy, sorrow, depression that I felt then are echoed in me now as these songs play. Right now (to quote the announcer) I'm feeling slightly serene. Why? I haven't changed and my situation hasn't, but my feelings are so arbitrary that they change with no motivation. Fickle things they are if this is so. Sinus or tumor my right forehead feels a lot of pressure from the inside. Maybe I'm feeling so serene because I'm not feeling pressured to DO anything. Since I'm leaving this weekend, I don't feel pressured to do any work on my book, my steps, or John's house. All that's left for me is to straighten the place up some, put all of John's stuff in the garage, and get my gear together for my trip home. I don't want to marry Pam because I don't have anything to offer her, because she doesn't offer me what I'm looking for in a permanent mate, and because sexually I'd rather do things she doesn't like to do. But I am comfortable living there, more so than I would be living alone. Not just financially, but because being alone still scares me. Which is strange because I've spent this week alone, actually, and I was afraid of the dark and my sickness but not of being alone.

Lonely yes, but not afraid.

I'm wearing a heavy shirt and I'm still feeling chilly this morning. Cold in the desert?

4:30PM

Spent most of today doing crossword puzzles, napping, and listening to music. Can't say what else I might have accomplished today, because I didn't do anything else. Some thoughts did drift through my mind but I let them drift and just relaxed. Finally showered around 4PM because I was beginning to be able to smell myself over the stink of the house. Vacuumed again, put all of John's stuff in the garage, and I'm just sitting here. I could be writing on my step work, but I've already decided to finish it at home and get Lee to share it with before August 1st. Could I actually be close to finishing my 4th step with him? Sex has been the hardest part of step four for me and I understand why even if understanding doesn't help make it easier to do. Sex has held the position of power (greater, lesser, and everything than myself) my whole life.

From my experiences with my cousin Becky, to my obsession to find someone who LOVES me enough to give me the sexual gratification I expect, demand, need, require, request, feel.

I could keep trying to describe everything I feel about sex and I'd never finish. Because everything comes back to it, and from it everything in my world finds its place and focus in life. No sex means the world is against me, bad sex means I'm a bad person or unwanted, mediocre sex means I'll get by today but I wish for more, better/different, average sex means I've found someone I like who apparently likes me and we can get along sexually as long as we don't cross each other's boundaries. Good sex means someone finds me as attractive sexually as I find her and usually results in my life in shambles due to lack of sleep and an inability to stop. Great sex I've never experienced in my life. For sex to be great, it would have to surpass good sex in quality AND quantity and be with an ideal mating partner. My idea of an ideal mating partner? A nine to thirty-eight-year-old female with a smooth pussy, shy, quiet, excited, fresh scented, even skinned, bold, obsessed with pleasing me by enjoying sex with me, confident of herself yet desiring my presence in her life, fertile and willing to have kids (even if I didn't want any), with an imagination similar to my own when it came to experimenting with new things.

11 July 1997 6.44AM

Woke up at 3AM again but finally got up at around 6. Believe it or not, I was so cold I had to get up. Then I had to get out of the house. The smell is so bad this morning. I don't know if it's gotten worse or if my nose has just become acclimated to the desert and I'm able to finally smell it in all its awfulness. Maybe it reflects the re-arising corruption in my soul, or maybe John needs to replace the carpets. Also, across the street, in the next house over from Lisa and the kids, is a home that keeps a Doberman (Lisa and co have two Dalmatians that they are trying to breed for profits). This Dobi is reflective of all of the people I've seen around here – large, overweight from overfeeding in all probability, slow moving, as if she finds conservation of energy in slow movement a chore all of itself, and sleeping a lot. Though this beastie could and probably would rip my arm off were I foolish enough to try to pet her, my heart feels pity for her state. What love is lost on this poor animal? No one (I've seen) bothers to pet her, and with her weight and the heat, I'd be afraid that playing with her like a normal dog would be a riotous way of killing her with joy. If it's a dog's nature to love man, devoting life, love, and limb to those who call themselves its owners, why then is this devotion rewarded with neglect and actually dismissal under the assumption that like a piece of furniture she'll always be there? And I dare to wonder why men treat each other so. How could we not? For in each other we have no such loyalties, no totally selfless devotions, no unconditional love. Reason, our gift that makes us higher than the animals, robs us of our ignorance and thereby the honesty to give all that we are blindly and without doubt or reservations. In Eden, Adam and Eve ate from the Tree of Knowledge – of good and evil – or so the story goes for those who choose not to read the Bible. This, as the serpent promised, brought us closer to being gods in our own right. But as with all his promises, there was a catch. Coming closer to being gods in our understanding of life, we gave up our positions as equals with god in love, compassion, and real power.

In exchange for awareness of self, we traded our awareness of each other and every other living (and maybe even non-living) thing in life around us.

Is it any wonder that I cry inside almost constantly? Having awareness, I would never truly wish to give it up for without it I would feel that I might never be able to appreciate the life I have and see around me. Power comes with knowledge and it takes humility to surrender that power every day, else I would try to walk the path of a god through a world that was meant to have one with many equals. To lose my awareness would give me the bliss of ignorance, but like the dog across the street, leave me vulnerable to the whims of other men (or worse yet, women).

I mention the word equals in connection with god and I'm sure this is confusing to anyone foolish enough to read this. Most men would say that being equal with god would make men (me in particular) gods themselves. The strange thing is that the paradox of the statement encompasses everything I'm trying to say. Equal means power, glory, beauty, and all the rest just as god has all of those things. Yet when we say all men are created equal, we don't claim that this makes one man over into another, nor do we surrender the property, family, and life of one man to another because they are equal. They/we remain individuals, separate entities with equality in responsibilities and powers yet individual talents, abilities, and possessions, including our lives. If we can accept the concept amongst ourselves, why is it so difficult to see our equality with god in this manner? I believe (for what that is worth) that men spend most of their lives searching for the power we surrendered in exchange for self-awareness, and though (on occasion) some actually come close to the ability or chance or opportunity to reclaim that power, none have been will to sacrifice (totally) the awareness of self that makes us men. Philosophers, wise men, sages, prophets…All have tried to express this selflessness being the key to realization of true spiritual power or attainment of some 'higher' state of being. Yet even they remain human, merely mortal men, and I can only believe this is so because like all of us, they too find unwillingness to surrender all that they are, all that selflessness gives them from the answers and the questions it brings, the ability to reason and find both the questions and seek the answers in exchange for this state of 'enlightenment'. Fear of losing themselves is the quickest reasonable response that leaps to mind, but again I believe this answer is just a blind, a distraction we make for ourselves to keep from exploring this phenomenon even closer. Alone I can see another reason why they might choose not to surrender it all, in that I would choose not to surrender self-awareness in exchange for the rest, but greedily I would want both, perhaps placing myself in the position of wanting not to be god's equal or peer, but to take over as god. Big perhaps, because my reasoning is faulty. Many aspects remain undiscovered to me, facts that might alter my feelings, position, and decision (learned how to spell that word).

For now, I find myself willing to throw my will and life over to the care of god as I understand him, on the basis of my will and life being like a child that I surrender to the care of a qualified nursemaid or caregiver. It remains mine, but the strain of responsibility of its care and upkeep are placed in the hands of one more capable than I find myself to be. I share in the joy of its accomplishments, the sorrows of its falls and failures, its laughter and tears, good times and bad, and always know that the care it receives when my focus finds itself elsewhere is of a quality that I consider to be the best. Go figure. I've put god in the position of playing nanny to my life and will. I wonder if he's going to pull a Mary Poppins and lead me into learning how to really care for it myself or if he'll pull a Mrs. Doubtfire and make me realize that he's always there even when he isn't physically present. Or maybe, like some old British nanny who has taken care of the 'family' for years beyond counting, he'll set his feet down, order me out of the nursery, let me visit once in a while to reassure me that they are growing up whole and healthy, and leave me in the dark as to how he goes about it all. My guess (best thinking again) is that this last would work best with me. Keeps me from mucking everything he's trying to do up. Which is why self-awareness is a paradox, blessing, and curse.

Who knew?

1:11PM

To points I've discovered by reading today. Slavic (German, Russian, etc.) heritage is to dream passionately and largely with great excitement and flair bordering on a maniacal level that can bring about fevers and other physical ailments, yet when the time comes to actually complete even a single act, the same flames become cold, weakness, and exhaustion overwhelm and leave apathy as the resultant fruit. Could I be more German (Slavic) than I ever suspected, or am I looking for rationalizations to my failures of the past for never completing anything?

My 'book' may never get written at this rate!

Point #2 was something that Turgenev mentioned in one of his stories, and even AFTER reading it I almost committed the same act of insolent self-excusing. He mentions that many so-called (wannabe) writers complain that there is nothing left to write about. As if every subject, topic has been written on so well and so often that there was nothing left to write about. He called that for the bullshit it is and I almost used the same excuse myself a short while after reading more of his works. I believe it's just envy that keeps 'wannabe' writers from finding their own stories, with a dose of self-pity thrown in for good measure. So, I thought up my own excuse for why I haven't been able to write everything I've been trying to say. What excuse? It's simple. I have too much to write about. Yep, turned one lame excuse around 180 degrees and I either came up with a legitimate answer or another lame excuse. Think of it this way. On the one hand there is so much inside me that has needed release for so long that though the tap is wide open the blockage is bottlenecked to the point of absolutely no output. And on the other hand, even if I am actually as shallow as I judge myself to be, there is so much of life that could be expressed that I am at a loss for both the words to express it and a starting place where I could begin. My whole life I've answered the questions that seemed to escape sages and philosophers, peasants and kings, and somehow inside myself was sure of the rightness or correctness of those answers. The fact that I could neither understand or apply those answers for my own life never mattered in the slightest towards or against their correctness. All the answers buried within my chest, foolish and in all probability to be deemed childish, remain unspoken, unshared, unreleased, like tears of mourning for my sister who died.

All that I see, my awareness of life around me, remains unrecorded, unnoted, unremarked upon, yet hold such value that I want to weep and laugh and celebrate and grab the hands of those foolish enough to stand near to me, dancing and howling and singing to the sun and moon and stars so that I might share with them what joy it is to be alive and human. Is it any wonder that I question my own sanity?

Awareness of others, the fear they would feel of being overwhelmed by my madness stabs me before I can act in such a manner. Nailing me to this place I have brought my life to as surely as any iron spike could crucify Jesus. By what right could I inflict that fear on those I love? Yet, in rage at my insanity, the pain of never being able to release any of it, I strike a darker terror into them, blaming them for my awareness, hating them for what I see as my difference, longing to be as they are, yet unable and unwilling to surrender my awareness of life at this strange level. I am not unique. Not special for being aware. I cannot mistake ability with uniqueness.

The facts remain that where others choose not to see, for they do have the ability when they want to close or open their eyes to life, I am like unto a man whose eyelids have been removed. Not only can I not close my eyes to life, but without constant care, my perceptions become fainted and twisted by the least amounts of debris flake or garbage - sometimes being found merely in the observing of some portion of life and at other times carried through the atmosphere where these sights are seen. Is it any wonder that I cry inside constantly, sometimes for joy, sometimes for pain of my own, sometimes for the pain I am forced to witness while being powerless to do anything about it? Why joy? Because of the pain beauty can be - there's one obvious reason. Another - the joy that can come when someone chooses to give me a moment's relief by kicking sand in my eyes, spitting in my face, or covering my head with a bucket. All of those would hurt, except maybe the bucket, but the momentary break from constant awareness would be such a relief. How could I not cry for joy? Maybe this is why my life has followed a path from one disaster to another to another and so on. Perhaps I brought about these incidents of pain in order to gain moments of respite from the agony that my awareness has made of existence.

Yet I'm not suicidal. I don't want to die. I don't even want a permanent escape from my pain. Again, to surrender awareness of life would be as unacceptable to me as it would be to society for me to live like an animal – conscienceless and following my basic instincts and without remorse. God bless and damn David Perlman for suggesting I read the Russian. Now I'm hooked back into my need to know the minds of others, have some connection with my own, where before my solitude suffered to keep me sane. I sat in an empty yard alone, for all intents and purposes, but not lonely. And of course, paradoxically, I am lonely for the companionship of men long dead who, knowing me, would probably find my ravings boring rather than amusing and would be insulted if I were to infer that I heard what they wrote in a language beyond words that I could only claim to share with them. I feel like I know an ancient language that hasn't been spoken by men for thousands of years yet. I can only understand barely what is being said, and if I tried to say anything, even the slightest syllable in the same language, I would sound like an ape trying to imitate the words of a man. Understanding without the ability to comment and even the very act of trying to speak this lost tongue would violate the very percepts of its structure, beauty, and form.

Hopefully, John will come tomorrow. I've obviously been here too long when I start letting out what's really going on between my ears. One last thought before I rest from all this. Turgenev also wrote that an artist, including a writer as an artist, as is my assumption, must be willing to work at what he does. His character on judging another character's chance of ever amounting to my kind of artist says that this other will never withdraw deep into your self-meaning, think, or look inside himself for what it is his art is supposed to communicate to the world. Both characters acknowledge this lack of commitment he has and it raises the question, do I have the desire to work that hard in order to achieve the goal that I believe, for now, I want to achieve?

20:00 PM

I'm afraid to go back and read what I've written this week. How much will I understand or remember why I wrote what I did? And if I'm not sure I will understand, how can anyone else? Lee said we would read this together when I got back, but I'm thinking Dave Perlman has a better chance of keeping up with my thoughts and education. Lee, you're a great sponsor and a calm man, but what you don't know could fill volumes and probably does. I hope this doesn't offend you, but it's true. I'm almost willing to bet that before we reach this point, you'll have interrupted me in reading this out to you several times, interjecting your opinion that what I've written makes no sense, and show that you've missed the point I was making at that time completely.

I'm not educated (school wise) either, but I've read so much that I can perceive things and speak of things that educated men would understand, though I would probably sound like a raving lunatic to them as well because of my lack of education.

Compleat

12 July 1997 06:24 AM

Saturday morning and two dogs are wandering the streets. One has a broken left rear leg. With no phone, there's no one I can call, and not knowing the neighbors means I won't wake anyone at this hour of the morning. They passed here, going back the way they came, and I can only hope they're headed for their home. If the one dog doesn't have a broken leg, then it must be that way from a snake bite or have an old break. Why anyone would allow a dog to suffer on three legs, I can't see. So, I choose to think someone will help it.

The sprinklers shut off and scared me. Analysis for today: a man's ability to commit to a deep, loving, lasting relationship can be measured by the care he shows for his animals. John might be getting out of bed finally. Maybe I'll see someone I know before noon.

24 July 1997

Today, I took action in order to practice the spirit way principle of honesty to the best of my ability. My motivation was selfish because I hope that honesty will allow me to have something I find exciting and enjoyable in my life. My fears are clamoring in an attempt to overwhelm me. Instead, I am sitting here crying tears of both joy for acting in a spiritually healthy manner and grief mixed with fear that I have surrendered something I really enjoy over into someone else's hands. If I could surrender other parts of my life as completely, it would be a wonderful thing to be me. God grant me the courage and ability to step out in faith, believing for all things to be according to his will.

October 4th, 1997 19:30 PM

Today I did something I never would have believed possible for me. Even with my recovery time, I have never made a decision as big as this without trying to get someone else to co-sign my decision by telling me to go for it. Today, I'm leaving Carlsbad for a visit that may become a permanent move on my part. I am scared, almost to the point of not going, but I've lived with fear, making my decisions for the past two years and most of my life. So, I had a choice. I could continue doing the same stuff, expecting things to change on their own or take action for myself and do something to change.

Compleat

I can't claim that what I'm doing is right or wrong, either. In this case, right and wrong don't come into it because even if what I'm doing is wrong or blows up in my face and I end up homeless, at least I took some action to change. God help me if I really have blown everything that he meant for me to have. I just couldn't continue being angry and feeling trapped all of the time, nor could I allow the possibility of my immediate opportunities to act out. If P Q and lined all ups, I choose to avoid starting today. If Martha reads this journal, it will put her in the same place Pam was in, but this time, I will let her know I feel violated and that our relationship will probably be reduced to merely friendship and sex.

October 7th, 1997

Last time I will plan to put the data in this journal. Martha is sleeping. Brandon is doing homework, and I am totally confused. One moment I am lusting after Martha so strongly that I'm completely aping out, then sex happens and it's good, but something is robbing me from relaxing and enjoying myself totally. Some part of me fears letting go, almost as if I'm afraid that this is just a dream. San Diego and the pain are calling to me, telling me I'm giving host to that train of thought.

Tried to watch a movie. Remain really tired, but got up at 4:00 a.m. per Martha's request. Sitting relaxing, and sure enough, I'm becoming drowsy. Came again last night. Being able to relax has eluded me intently and why this, to me especially, escapes my understanding. When I try to write here, I find myself falling asleep or brainstorming. Why I have such depressed feelings whenever Martha mentions this word beyond the obvious disliking of a word filled with negative connotations for me - like, I need another storm going on in my brain or someone is using an SS Trooper to storm the stronghold of my mind and my brain under attack.

Decision? Stay and make an attempt at changing someone's mind – mine, yours, or others – or just fade away. I know myself to be. I wonder if I could have done the life of living as a dead man. Pepsi chocolate, coffee, sugar, and still, I fall almost instantly asleep as I try to write. Daytime doesn't work well for me and my nights are full to the point of dysfunction with sex, reading, and trying to understand. Started to doze off during last word of last sentence. Smile friendly. Thank them for welcoming to me. New experience. This must be an example of sleep writing. I don't remember writing it and it doesn't make sense here. Dreamed about something???

Compleat

Compleat

Stoney Moore

& Empathy

Of the many things that recovery in the different 12-Step programs that I've participated in over the years has taught me, the one that stands out is the ability to look closely at myself and my behaviors – past, present, and future. The many spiritual principles I've learned to recognize in my current lifestyle help me to review my past mistakes and where they were lacking from who I wanted to be rather than who I was actually acting as if I were.

One of those principles was my lack of empathy for others and a prime example of that lack was my own self-centeredness and selfishness toward others I viewed as less fortunate even than I saw myself as being. Self-pity notwithstanding, I could view others as being less fortunate than I was and pity them for being different than those around them but couldn't or wouldn't feel empathy or even offer them any type of support or comfort in relation to their differences.

One such individual that stands out in my memories was a young man whose name I recall as being Stoney Moore. Stoney was a Marine, confined in the brig during the same period I was, but that was about as far as our similarities went as far as I was concerned. His physical height was perhaps 5 feet tall if that. He was black or African American if the color reference offends anyone. His mental and emotional stability were questionable at the very least because his ability to communicate appeared limited to a mumbling, soft-voiced spoken word(s) or incomprehensible shouting that inevitably resulted in his being placed in solitary confinement because his anger would usually be directed toward the guards in the brig, who seemed to take particular pleasure out of provoking him into his 'rages.' An entertainment that broke up the monotony of their daily job of watching over prisoners in the brig who, for the most part, complied with the rules that were set down for the Marines confined there for different violations of the Uniform Code of Military Justice.

I felt sorry for Stoney, all the while feeling superior to him because although my mental stability had been questioned during my general court-martial it had never been used against me as a provocation and as an entertainment for the guards. And while I had never empathized with his issues because I remained focused on my own issues and discomfort of being confined in that same brig, I am able to look back over these many years later and can see that he and I shared many more similarities than the differences I held on to that enabled me to feel sorry for him and better off than he was during his confinement.

Empathy – the ability to feel similar feelings as another human being. Stoney Moore was a human being, treated like an animal because he was small, black, volatile, and difficult to understand due to what appears to have been a speech impediment. The guards didn't treat him as a human being, but rather as an animal and entertaining actor when they would provoke his behaviors into his acting out on his issues, and his communications were so infused with anger that he became even more incomprehensible than he was normally.

I didn't enjoy what they did, even found myself fantasizing about aiding him in revenging himself against his tormentors, yet that fantasizing was always about my venting myself on them, for my own sake rather than for his. To be honest I must admit the fact that not once did I ever approach Stoney and offer him any support or encouragement. I watched their behaviors toward him and did nothing for him, merely observing and turning away as if what they were doing to him didn't matter to me in the least.

These many years later I am able to look at my own behaviors, past the behaviors of the guards involved in tormenting Stoney, and see that by not speaking up, not challenging their behaviors, and not even attempting to connect with him on a level that we might have shared due to our both having mental health issues, I lacked that one spiritual principle that could have overridden my self-centeredness and selfishness – empathy with another human being.

In every 12-Step program meeting that I've ever attended there is often mentioned the word amends, not apologies (the empty and often smelly outpouring of hot air from a person's mouth that speaks the words "I'm sorry" but an action that requires owning a mistake, taking accountability and responsibility for an action that was done, should not have been done or wasn't done and could have been). An amends - that action that not merely requires acceptance of responsibility for those mistakes but also holds oneself responsible for not repeating that same mistake with others on present and future occasions.

I may never have the opportunity to make a direct amends to Stoney Moore. Never find him, meet him and assure him that I own my mistakes in not standing up for him and for ignoring his pain in order to wallow in my own. And most of all, I might never gain the opportunity to speak with him and admit my responsibility for not doing what I knew to be the right thing for the right reason. Yet I could, if that opportunity ever presented itself and even if it never does, continue to live my life according to the principle of empathy I lacked those many years ago and practice empathy with others I see who suffer discrimination, abuse of power, and rejection of the society around them that Stoney and I both shared but I was too cowardly to recognize as being a part of myself.

Compleat

Will Wonders Never Cease
— . — . — . — . — . — . — . — . — . — . — . — . — . — . — . . —

I am, I am pain. I am joy. I am solitude. I am loneliness. I am the anger that leads to hate. I am the fear that feeds that anger. I am the calm that brings serenity. I am the acceptance that brings the calm I am the pariah society turns its back on. I am the voice of their Messiah. I am the rejected, neglected and forgotten. I am those who cannot disappear, no matter how hard they try. I am the God in you and the devil within as well. I am alone on a planet of 7.9+ billion beings. I am among you listening and I hear, "I am me. I am you. Now what shall I do?"

Every act of kindness leaves just a little bit of love behind. I often tell others they are working, walking miracles. Some look uncomfortable when I emphasize that they are miracle workers, but how could they be anything less? Addicts taught me to see this fact, but it applies to the entire human race. Ironic that one who knows this fact refuses to put his knowledge into action. Maybe I see myself as capable, but cowardly. If I were to do even half of the things that I know human beings are capable of doing the results are as predictable as the sun rising and then setting afterward. Revered, even followed by some, eventually betrayal, torture, and inevitably painful death. If that sounds familiar that's because the last person who had the courage to do what needed to be done was first found crying in a garden.

"He wept." Was that from fear of what was about to happen as many have surmised, or was it from knowing that the burden he was about to take upon himself was so furiously heavy and unbearable that tears came unbidden to his eyes and he hoped that it might pass his plate, allowing some other to bear it? Or, as I surmise here, was it's a combination of both of those things and their being overshadowed by the fore knowledge of how few would grasp what he was doing and why he was willing to accept the task set before him?

How could he not weep knowing that the number of those who would come to know would be not merely finite, but comparatively minuscule? Thousands of years have passed. We have had his example that long. And what have we done? Denied not just his efforts or divine origins, but by branching in different directions and declaring yourselves opposed to him and his. Not just in the divisions and sects within those claiming to be his followers, not just

Compleat

those who dismiss portions of his story as merely a myth created only to comfort the unknowing, uneducated masses like opium to sedate, calm, and control those who would willingly follow anything that they were taught rather than face for themselves the awful wonder filled truth of their own capability, and thereby responsibility, to themselves and one another.

When confronted with the reality of these things, he fell to his knees and wept. When faced with the knowledge of this reality, I chose instead to go insane. I don't wonder at his strength or envy it either. Truth be told, I am grateful he was, or is, first born. He would need be to watch what was done, in his name no less, and choose not to burn the whole thing down and start again. I, myself, couldn't have borne the imminent pain of knowing and physical suffering without instinctively just wiping the entire mess and starting over. I guess that is why, although I have the knowledge and I'm impartial, in knowing I remain grateful the power to act upon it is withheld from me.

Compleat

How Religions

Exclude What God Would Include

I read the bible at 13 years of age for the first time, as if it were just a storybook. Enjoyable, interesting, and with a lot of information that made sense to my young mind.

Years later, when being considered for the pastor-ship of a congregation, I felt I needed a better understanding and chose to delve deeper into its history and the history of those accredited with its writing.

Imagine, if you can, my surprise upon learning that a conclave of religious men (women were excluded) had met from different sects within the 'Christian' religion to debate, discuss and decide what would and wouldn't be allowed to be included in the Bible as 'gospel' and that that fact was a slightly disconcerting bit of information to me.

My personal belief, after discovering this information, would be that god must have moved in the hearts of a few of the individuals involved in this editing process or the entire thing would have been completely rewritten to reflect the desires of most of those attending the conclave; moving toward the manipulation and control of their fellow human beings, through the "power of the word".

The facts remain that with the predominate "sect" being the catholic 'church' and the desire of those individuals involved to shift the focus away from Jesus' equally important humanity and onto only his divine nature it was to serve their purpose of controlling, manipulating and eventually enriching themselves with the material wealth of their period.

What was included, due solely to necessity and in order to maintain the deception and manipulation being attempted was still such a powerful truth that it quite literally still has the ability to change lives, create miracles, and bring masses of individuals together in their efforts to understand the nature of god and their own relationship to him.

Unfortunately, it also continues to be used as an effective tool to control the masses of individuals who are willing to follow the teachings of other men's interpretations of that power, rather than taking the effort to read, investigate, comprehend and eventually know the unique relationship we each share with both god and his physically conceived, 1st born son, my older brother Jesus. The gathering of said information which would then lead them to a knowing of who they actually are, not just some ill- thought- out, made up label, but literally the "children of god."

The biggest misuse of the vestiges of power that are found within the writings of the bible is the exclusionary nature of the book of Acts. Them vs us is a theme within every religion known among the entire human race. From the simple primitive exclusion of outsiders through the words for stranger and enemy being used interchangeably, to the "none shall enter into the kingdom of god, except (they even chose to use that word openly) through faith in JC."

Maybe, and I certainly entertain this possibility as a hope, they merely missed what Jesus was telling them.? Perhaps they honestly believed theirs was the only pathway to the gates of 'heaven' or paradise as other religions refer to it.

Such ignorance in the thought processes of human beings I can and do see as causing almost as much harm to the human race as apathy. Yet I find ignorance, while relatable, remains as no excuse for not investigating and learning for one's own sake and would lead to an understanding for the salvation of not just the individual but the whole of humanity.

Big brother J did not exclude anyone from being welcome to his teachings, with only one very noticeable and decisive exception. The religious people of his day.

And I believe if those editors at that conclave could have found a way to 'write it out' of the bible while retaining Jesus' divine nature they would have had that hit the editor's waste basket 1st first and foremost.

Jesus specifically excluded the religious, in particular - the profiteers who had set themselves up to make handy little profits from the requirements of their religious teachings that had NO business being made in pop's house (or the temple as it was known or called in those days.)

Religious people. Good and faithful followers. Pharisees, Sadducees, and the rest, all in great standing with the organized and accepted religious people, looked up to and for assistance with interpretation, understanding, explanations, and the truth of their teachings from an author known as Moses.

These were the individuals who had set up shop and were making some tidy profits on people who depended on them to explain what most weren't allowed (women were excluded even then) to read and seek understanding for themselves.

Compleat

If this sounds familiar, it's because it continues to go on, throughout the world, especially by those claiming to be 'following' the teachings of brother J while pulling in enough profits to say: build a massive, crystal cathedral in California; or put on performances over their privately owned television stations whereby they not only draw in the dollars but get to pretend to be repentant for the very transgressions they 'preach' against, crying aloud and vocally their apology all the while continuing to pull in profits and sympathy from the victims of their greed.

And here's the 'rub', ironic in its simplicity. Jesus said "No one comes unto the father, but by me! That phrase is still in there, yet they twisted the living shit out of what he said! Not once, in his preaching, did he exclude anyone from benefiting from what he was doing. Every example, each lesson he taught was inclusive, NOT exclusive.

Even they couldn't deny that he didn't die for the sins of just the 'Christians' or just the 'Jews' that chose to follow him. They were forced by their consuming need to maintain only his divinity to include the phrase: "For the sins of the world ...".!

If anyone ever gets the opportunity to read a series of books called "The Chronicles of Narnia" I highly recommend it for its non-exclusive attitude that it displays in relation to god and Jesus.

If a fictional story, written to help children internalize Jesus' teachings is too difficult a stretch for some, I even recommend reading an edited version of the bible where there is still a passage in which the apostle Peter is thinking about excluding the non-Jewish converts to Christianity and gets told off, by his god, that what god makes okay supersedes what the laws of religions call unclean and you might get a perspective of how INCLUSIVE god really is.

Scary as this thought is for so-called, self-professing followers of Jesus, Muslims are going to be in "heaven" too. How do I know? Because Jesus told you so, himself!

"No one gets there except by me!" is not an exclusionary statement. It's a rebuke of that very thing, by his saying "get down off your superior ass pedestals! They are here because I opened the way to EVERYBODY.

It is as if Jesus was saying, "If they are here, and trust me on this they are, then it's not because they merely say they follow me; and more because they lived as I lived, did as I did, heard what I said the way I said it, and not the way they chose to hear it so that it would make them special in their own eyes or above all the rest of humanity."

Next time someone quotes things that they are using in their efforts that would exclude others, in any way, simply ask yourself and then them this simple question:

"Who did Jesus really exclude?

Compleat
Ananias, Sapphira, and the Foundation of the Christian religion

I've often argued that the so-called christian religion is based on the deceptions of those who desire to first manipulate and then control the masses of humanity that follow their particular brand of religion. But when did it actually begin to make sense to me that their bible had been rewritten in order to create a religion out of what had been taught by the Jesus dude they claim most often to follow? For me, it was apparent when conflicting concepts are predominately displayed in the very book that they claim to be the "Word" of god.

In their book, the chapter known as Acts 5, verses 1-10, a man named Ananias and his wife Sapphira sold land they had owned and brought only a part of the proceeds to the apostles. According to the verses there, they offered up only a portion of what they acquired for the sale and were deemed to have lied about the amount, warranting death for their deceptions.

If true, that they had actually lied to the 'holy spirit' or god by way of the apostles, then their deaths by spiritual means would make sense in a perverse sort of way. After all, lying to god, who cannot be deceived, would be an act of ridiculous and obvious rebellion. But, since god cannot be deceived, why were they deemed to have tried to lie?

Besides which, would rebellion have warranted a death sentence in that case? Would uncertainty or fear be a death sentence for anyone who held back a portion of what they had in order to feel secure in their ability to provide for themselves? With this one passage, the task of tithing became a terrific fear for any so-called christian.

According to the so-called christian religion, it was a justified killing of two human beings who had lied to those who led the 'church' of their day, and who condemned them for it by putting their deception on the level of lying to or rebelling against god.

What then about that whole scenario smacks of religion and not of god? Knowing god and Jesus as I do, I had only to refer back to what Jesus is quoted as saying when confronted about taxes and tax collecting. "Render unto Caesar that which is Caesar's and unto god that which is god's."

The fact that Peter condemned two human beings to die over money smacks fully of the hypocrisy that is the basis of all religions. To take what was said by a man of faith, whether or not a person believes in the divine nature of Jesus being irrelevant, and twisting it to cause people to fear their desire to provide for themselves at the cost to the 'church' is when faith is overcome and control by religion becomes paramount in the desires of those who control any of the particular religions.

Did god, the holy spirit, or Jesus desire that money? Or was it perhaps Mammon, the true god of all religions, who desired to possess that money and whose presence is displayed in every religion?! Was it god's desire to possess control over the members who profess to follow that religion, whatever one they have chosen to embrace, or was it the desire of those 'leaders' to impress on those who witnessed what happened that not giving the proper amount was punishable by death?

The answer is obvious to anyone who looks at the person who is claiming the power and control, and comparing them to the person who displayed the divine nature that is the human right and natural condition. Peter was in control of the 'church' and disallowed any variance in regard to monetary

Compleat

gains "for the faith." Jesus said to give it away, impoverish yourself and follow his example.

From the money changers in the temple to the Islamic leaders who call for jihad to supplant the religions of others, to all of the other religions, you can name your own poison and you'll find that behind every religion is the desire to control the wealth, property and people's thoughts and feelings in order to put those who 'lead' those religions ahead of those who follow them and have nothing whatsoever to do with god.

Compleat

Special Things
_._._._._._._._._._._._._._._._._..

All of 49 years have passed and in all those moments only the harshest of memories followed me for the longest part of my life. And finding her the way I did, by visiting my older sister's grave, I found myself meditating and sobbing, wandering aimlessly through a graveyard to the area where her father's ashes were retained. Coming across his placement, I flashed back to the day he told me that he would never allow me to be around her again.

It was my behavior that day, no fault on his part whatsoever, when I had erupted into an insane rage toward my older brother, my mom, and my step-dad. He witnessed it -, heard my roaring verbal assault toward them all and the threats I made toward my brother when he tried to force me to stand down and apologize to our parents.

I had hoped I could one day make an amends to her father, but it was too late. So now, all I can do is make indirect amends by never seeking her out again.

That was his expressed wish, and despite my feelings or needs, I choose now to respect his wish as if it were what he would have asked of me, had I been there to receive a dying wish from him.

Compleat

The Awakening:

Vess Moments for

Everyone

Here's a rhetorical question that I hope most readers can answer with a resounding yes! Have you ever have had a 'Vess' moment? It has been my experience that everyone does; although maybe it wasn't a 'person' named John Vess that brought it to them or them to it as the case may have been. My 'Vess' moment came around my eleventh month of confinement at Atascadero State Maximum Security Hospital for the Criminally Insane.

I ended up there after having been released from the Marine Corps Brig at Camp Pendleton, California, having served three out of four years for having abused and molested my step-children. Without treatment, barely able to maintain a job, having married a woman fourteen years my senior in order to have someone to fuck and who took 'care' of me I quickly degenerated back into old behaviors. In 1986, I was thirty years of age, but could pass as a nineteen-year-old. I lived at the beach, in a condominium paid for by my soon-to-be second ex-wife, had numerous girlfriends that she tolerated because I didn't leave her for any of them, dating younger women and girls from high school, including a sixteen-year-old goth girl I met at a job that the 'religious' folk had set up for me when I left the brig.

I have had one job in this lifetime where I actually felt of some use to someone other than myself. And honestly, it was the only time I ever felt even a slight amount of good about myself. I was a gravedigger/groundskeeper at Eternal Hills Memorial Park in Oceanside, CA. The sixteen-year-old girl that I met and later fucked repeatedly came up to me in the graveyard, asking how old I was so I lied and told her I was 23. By that time, I was actually 32, so reversing the numbers seemed like a bright idea at that time. She told me that it was her wish to one day have sex on a grave, and I replied I'd be happy to oblige her anytime she would choose. It was daylight so instead, we went into a mausoleum, where she got on top of me and fucked me. As I was about to cum, however, she wanted to stop because she didn't want to get pregnant. I lied and told her I had had a vasectomy and I was 'safe' to cum inside her, so she let me and we finished up, then she left.

A few weeks later she called me, and I invited her over to my apartment, having left my soon- to- be ex-wife to have more 'freedom' to do what I wanted without observation. My apartment was at a friend of mine's house, his father being senile and a want-to-be pastor, his dad had built a church on their property and there was an apartment over the church for visiting pastors that was unoccupied, so I was allowed to rent it for a while. My goth girlfriend was thrilled to be drinking (remember, she was only sixteen) and smoking pot over a church, and seemed to get off on pretending we were fucking IN a church. We spent that entire afternoon having sex, drinking wine while pretending it was sacramental wine, and smoking pot until she passed out. All in all, I must have fucked her 4 times that day and masturbated onto her naked body once. And she wasn't the only 'girlfriend' I had at that time. But up until then I had not met or done any crystal meth with my last girlfriend, a woman named Mona.

Mona introduced herself in the trash area of the graveyard, where she was picking out dead flowers from the throwaways, we were forced to make weekly in order to mow the grass. She and her mother made dried flower arrangements because, at thirty-six years of age, Mona had been forced to move back in with her parents.

Meth use and a dealer that was one of the biggest cooks of real methamphetamine in California from 1985 through 1988 that I knew of and who had dumped her for her younger-looking, better- maintained friend caused her to become depressed and unemployable.

She liked the facts that I looked a lot younger than I actually was, that I ran to and from the beach to get to work and so was in good shape at the time. When she invited me to fuck, there was no way I was going to miss a golden opportunity with a woman I saw as an older Marilyn Monroe wannabe, platinum hair color and all.

Our relationship was volatile, to say the least. One day she would want to do nothing but fuck. The next she would physically attack me, clawing bloody grooves into my back and, sides, and trying to do the same to my face. The back and sides I permitted, as long as we were fucking. I kept her from clawing my face though, I think because I somehow knew she would gouge my eyes out if I gave her the chance.

One evening, while we were at a drive-in theater, she offered me some meth. I told her no, I wasn't interested in using drugs, since fucking her was the only thing on my mind at that moment. She insisted, saying she wasn't going to fuck me unless I did lines with her. So, in order to get what I wanted, I did what she wanted.

We ended up fucking in the car, at that drive-in, with the adults around us complaining about their kids being subjected to seeing us.

Compleat

And I might as well have shot myself at that moment. Because even though I still fucked everything that came into my sphere of availability, I was totally into the meth. Here was a drug that gave my ego vent.

I could work a 72-work week and still run the three miles to work and back again. I fucked seven out of nine women a day, including the woman that would become my second ex-wife, and still have enough energy to fuck Mona. And while I tried to make money selling some meth, once, I never made a dime off a $450 bag because it all went either up my own nose or into the toilet when I thought that I was under investigation by the police.

Because I was. I had had several different addresses during this period of my life, leading up to August 4th, 1988. One of my ex-landladies, who I had had sex with and had other roommates living with her had let me off easy from owing her back rent, even after I moved out, because I had agreed to mow the lawns for her weekly.

On August 4th, she wasn't home and no one else was supposed to be there either, so I had thought to get the mowing done and leave. But as I was mowing the backyard, I heard the television on inside. So, I went to the backdoor and knocked on it.

The landlady's roommates were another woman, also named Erica, and her then thirteen-year-old daughter, Natasha, who was supposedly in Oregon, visiting her biological father. When I knocked, Natasha answered the door and I knew the second I saw her I was going to fuck her, no matter what or how. She answered that door wearing nothing but a cut-off t-shirt that hit just below her budding breasts and a pair of see-through bikini panties that I could easily see her dark pubic hair through. I asked if I could use the bathroom and she allowed me into the house again, in spite of my having moved out weeks earlier.

I went into the bathroom and found myself shaking, not from fear I think, but from the excitement of getting to fuck this beautiful, young girl. And from anger. I wasn't angry at this girl; I had barely known her when I did live there. I had had an argument with Mona earlier that day, fucked her, and left feeling unsatisfied because she had hinted that I had really wanted to be fucking her fifteen-year-old daughter or fourteen-year-old son. I was angry enough that when I left the bathroom, in spite of Natasha having put on a more appropriate shirt and shorts I bent over her and smelled her. Then I took her by the elbow and led her into her mom's room and told her to take off her clothes. She was afraid and did what I said without question or argument. Later, in court, they would say I threatened her with a steak knife, but the fact was I hadn't needed a knife, and the one the prosecutor had her draw looked more like a butter knife than even a steak knife.

When she did say anything, during the rape, she asked me why I had moved out and I answered her truthfully that it had been because I had been sure I would do to her exactly what I was doing, rape her. I finished by cumming inside her, got up, pulled up my shorts, and walked away from the building not feeling afraid of what I had done, no shame, no guilt, nothing but a calm as if I had left all of my anger inside her. As I drove away, I knew there was a chance she would 'tell' on me, but that didn't really frighten me or concern me. In fact, I knew that if she didn't, I would simply return the next day to repeat the behavior.

Instead, I went to work the next day, at the graveyard and the police arrived to arrest me for the rape. I denied what I had done. Saying that they must be mistaken. She must have been in Oregon still, as her landlady had told me she would be before I went there to mow the last time. They didn't believe me, but had to allow me to post bail, which my soon- to- be ex-wife arranged. $5,000 got a $50,000 bail, without too much trouble, and to protect her, I had married the woman who arranged my bail, so that she couldn't be forced into testifying about all the young women I had had there at the condominium we shared there at the beach.

Now, if you ever watch movies, there's this thing they call 'discovery' in all legal cases involving capital crimes. During discovery the prosecutor is required, by law in California, to give all their evidence and the names of any witnesses they intend to call to the stand before the defense is required to present its case. A simple law, really, and a technicality the prosecutor could have been defeated by because during the trial, while the defense attorney for the State allowed his case to collapse into a ludicrous sideshow, the prosecutor called my then wife to the stand by saying he didn't know her name but wanted her to testify.

The public defender (pretending to be serving my case and not helping the prosecutor) allowed that she could refuse or be charged with perjury if she lied about anything I had ever done or said to her about the case. What he failed to do was have the case thrown out, because of that little technicality of 'discovery.'

Why do I mention this now - many years later and moot now that the trial, sentence, and my serving time is are beyond recalling or dealing with?

Compleat

Because I knew at the time what he was doing, pretending to fight my case, while actually assisting the prosecutor in removing a known predator from society.

I knew and I honestly believed that I did not care. I was an identified monster. To my thinking that just meant that society had caught up with my opinion of myself. I would kill myself, later, just to avoid being killed by someone else but there was no remorse, no shame, or even guilt about what I had done to an innocent girl, whose only mistake had been inviting me into a house she lived in with her mom and landlady.

The rape, in society's view, was very simple to judge. I was/am a pedophile as far as the system is concerned. I had a history of sexual misconduct from an early age, had acted inappropriately on many occasions prior to the rape and the victim's age made my being a pedophile an 'obvious' observation.

Society looks with jaded eyes at everything. Jaded not simply by fear, but by political influences that politicians use to get elected and re-elected. The girl's age had nothing to do with my raping her, except that she was pretty and available.

She could have been her mom on that particular day and I would have done the exact same thing. She could have been any female, of any age, that answered the door and allowed me to enter the house.

That she was half naked when she answered the door, isn't an excuse. No bra, half a tee shirt that barely covered her young breasts and see-through bikini panties that exposed the dark color of her pubic hair and left nothing to my already sick imagination, really shouldn't have mattered.

Someone once told me that as an adult, I should have been responsible and left the area if my feelings were what they were on seeing her that way. And they were right, I was physically the adult in the situation. But her being a child didn't even enter into my mind as a consideration or deterrent for what I did to her that day.

All I knew or even thought about was that there was a female, who was allowing me into her house and I wanted to fuck her. So, I did. No regret, no fear, no reluctance, or consideration of the legal ramifications entered into my decision. But neither did her age, I really didn't care how young she was, or that she was a child. All I wanted was a female to fuck.

But as I started out with this story, I've never done anything without having two or more reasons for acting on anything. I considered for years what my other reasons would have been since society dismissed what I did as simply being an act of sexual misconduct. The reason came to me when I studied both my own psychological disorders (Major Depression, BPD, and so on) and the definition of the concept of rape.

Too often rape is dismissed as a sexual act, and I saw it that way as well for years until I was confined for it and started receiving therapy to understand what and why I had done what I did. The day I raped that girl I was angry. I had had a fight with one of my girlfriends, one who challenged me to have sex and then attacked me with it. We had argued, I was angry even after having had sex with her and I had left her with an underlying anger about the relationship that I shared with her that involved violent sex.

That anger seethed under the surface of who I pretended to be, and when my victim opened her door to me, I chose to release that anger on her. When I raped her, it was a sexual act, yet for me it was more than just sex, it was an act of violence.

Through the violation of her physical body, I dumped all the anger I had felt for years, from childhood, from relationships that had failed, from the abuse I had experienced and had committed, and when I came inside her I felt I had left all that anger inside of her.

I walked away, unconcerned and emotionless except to feel calm for the first time in many years. Unconsciously I knew that if she reported my action, I'd end up in legal trouble but I didn't feel concerned about that in the least and I also knew that if she didn't report it, I'd return to commit the act again the next day and every day thereafter.

I had drained all the anger, pain, confusion, and fear I had been feeling for years through the act of sexually assaulting her and putting my semen inside her. And that is why I raped her.

Justice isn't swift, but it moves eventually. I was sent to Chino, California, the prison there being the sorting/holding confinement center until the final destination for the individuals sent there could be determined. The day I arrived three men were stabbed to death, they call it 'shanked', two for being convicted child molesters and one man by mistake simply for sitting next to the target who was another convicted child molester and being misidentified as the molester himself.

I cannot imagine how his family felt on hearing the news that he was killed by accident in a case of mistaken identity.

Compleat

I just knew my case would become well known soon enough and felt that if I were going to die it would be on my own terms. Not the guards that assist that sort of thing by placing child molesters on the third tier of a prison (it's the third floor, he fell, oops, splat deader) or the other inmates who justified their actions by telling themselves what society had taught them all their lives - "Well, at least I'm not a child molester." I simply waited until I had learned my cellmate's sleeping pattern, - he was asleep by midnight and he never woke until morning count. Then using the blade, I had broken out of the razor the guards had conveniently provided, I open a vein in my arm by cutting vertically (a trick I had learned in Marine Boot Camp, offered by the drill instructors to those who wanted to kill themselves and be sure that they couldn't stop the blood flow simply by folding their wrist over the cut.)

My cellmate did however wake in the middle of the night. I tried to figure out why and came to the conclusion that the sound of my blood dripping onto the concrete floor must have caused him to feel the need to piss, so he woke and stepped into a puddle of blood.

Causing him to turn on the cell light and seeing me laying there, shake me awake, and ask if I was okay. I remember telling him to turn off the light and just go back to bed, it would be over by morning. Instead, he started crying out "man down" until the guards responded. Perhaps he thought he would be held accountable for my death. I really have no idea, but I do remember being completely irritated with him for not just going back to sleep.

Blood loss caused me to fade in and out of consciousness by the time the guards arrived, along with some EMT's. My last conscious thought or memory of that night was hearing one of the EMT's shout at the inmates who were calling me a pussy and coward, to "shut up, you animals" and the other saying "his blood pressure is 72 over 70, we may lose him."

I woke, in the prison hospital 3 days later, with bandages on my wrist, 16 stitches having been used to seal the wound, and obviously alive. My anger caused the physician on duty to prescribe Haldol and I was reduced to a drooling idiot, unable to speak or walk. Instead, every attempt I made at talking I drooled down my chest, neck, and even down to my waist.

I cannot describe my anger at being alive again/still. I had met death, face to face, and knew her as not something to be feared but a relief that comes to all eventually from this thing that, we've labeled living. I was angry at the EMT's for doing their job, the guards that had carried me down to the infirmary and especially angry with the cellmate that hadn't allowed me to die as I had wanted.

In him I saw the hand of the god fucker I had told to go fuck himself, preventing me from controlling my own destiny. Hours later, when one of the EMT's check-in on me and I asked why I had been spared she told me she didn't understand it either. As far as they could tell I had been officially dead for twenty minutes. At least that's how I remember it. The doctor's seemed to say the same thing but remember too, I was totally whacked up on Haldol at that time.

Just imagine my surprise when my wife, at that time, was allowed to visit me in the infirmary and try to talk me out of more suicide attempts. As if I had a choice in the matter. By that time, I had become convinced that the god fucker had taken me at my word, back when I said if he wanted my fucked-up life, he could have the damned thing, and had called in his ownership of it, again.

When the 'counselor' who would decide which prison I would spend my years in came to the infirmary, I could tell from his language, attitude, and air that he hated child molesters and rapists and since I was both he had me on his list long before he even tried to talk to me to send me somewhere I would be raped or killed or in his case hopefully both as soon as I got there. So, I told him nothing. In fact, I denied even remembering what I was doing there. That seemed to piss him off even more -, as if my lack of memory was a personal insult and my punishment for what I had done wasn't nearly enough.

When the medical doctor came in, I gave him the same routine, even though he seemed less antagonistic toward me. When the psychologist came in, however, he asked me questions that I was willing to answer.

Why had I raped the girl? "Because I was angry." Sex was only the outlet I used to vent that anger. Yes, I was attracted to a half-naked young teenage girl, but that wasn't why I chose to rape her. I needed to vent my anger and she was a convenient target, close at hand, desirable, and weaker than I was - physically. She could have been her mom (similar in appearance and other traits here) or any woman sharing those traits and at that time I would have done the exact same thing to her or any of them. Even my once willing landlady would have been subjected to rape, if she had been the one to answer the door that day.

Compleat

Did I regret my actions at all? Why would I regret them? I did what I wanted to whom I wanted and who was there at that time. I told him that if she hadn't reported the rape, I would have returned the next day and every day after that and kept raping her as if it was my right or privilege to do so, remorse and fear of the legal ramifications bore no weight with me, since I cared nothing for my own life and even death had rejected me.

That answer seemed to interest him, because he asked why I thought death, as a female individual, had rejected me?! I explained about my ongoing battle with god. That the god fucker had me under a no escape clause contract to do what he wanted, no matter how weird the fucker was, and I couldn't get out of it even if I succeeded in killing myself, as I obviously had.

I told him about everything, my sister's death and how I hadn't cried about it for thirty-four years afterward. How I had been responsible for her death, too, by trying to have sex with her on the last night of her life. By that time, he merely asked leading questions, prompting me to continue answering about my life. So, I told him everything. In At the end of what must have been an hour and a half session, he left and I assumed he had gotten what he had been asking about somehow.

The next morning, I was awakened by the guards that I was to 'dress out' since I was being shipped out to Duval Institute (aka Tracy, California) one of the most dangerous prisons in California, known among inmates as 'Gladiator School', where a prisoner was required to kill someone or be killed themselves upon the day of their arrival. The 'counselor' had set me up to die his way. I can only imagine his disappointment when the psychologist had the final say, backed by the medical doctor due to my wound showing I had attempted suicide and was still healing, that I be sent to the medical prison institution at Vacaville, California.

I was moved that very day. It would be at Vacaville that the medical teams examining me for psychological problems would decide that not only was I a candidate for incarceration at Atascadero, but I should have been found not guilty by reason of insanity. I was a danger to society, without remorse and without any concept of guilt or shame for what I had done. By then I no longer denied any of it. After all, I had told the psychologist everything, so denial seemed pointless any longer. When my wound had healed, I was moved to the State Maximum Security Institution at Atascadero, California for the Criminally Insane. And with very few exceptions I had come home to a place where I not only belonged, I fit in.

Compleat

Here I would meet and make friends with men like myself. Ron H, whom god had told to sacrifice his eleven- month- old, so he did, but unlike Abraham god didn't intervene and stop him. My best friend, the quiet guy I knew as Rick Sagerman, who would always listen but barely ever talked aloud. Rick had thought one day that cutting off both his mom and his dad's heads seemed like a good idea at the time, so he did.

The list of my peers goes on and on, while Charles Manson was back in Vacaville by that time. I had seen him as the guards made everyone in the place stand up against the walls with their hands in their waistbands and while two armed guards escorted Charlie to the infirmary there. (The guns weren't because that little old man was dangerous, he couldn't have done anything if he had had one of the shotguns the guards carried, they were in case some inmate wanted to be made famous as the guy who killed Charles Manson.) I didn't care about fame or Charlie for that matter. I only noticed his passing because it made me crowd up against a wall and because I was told later who the guy with the swastika on his forehead was and why everyone had to move back when he was walked down the halls.

While at Atascadero I grew fat, being subjected to different medications in an effort to 'stabilize' my thinking. Thorazine again, but the shuffle did nothing to change my way of thinking or perceiving the world around me. Prozac for depression, Benadryl to help me sleep, a list of medications I couldn't remember or pronounce if I even tried and wouldn't bother remembering even if I could.

Nothing seemed to work, with the small exception that Prozac did seem to improve my mood slightly. The only downside was the side effect of weight gain. I had gone into the system in shape and weighing approximately 175 lbs. While there I ballooned up to over 280 lbs. I was fat, happy, and comfortable and had no desire to leave or even think about getting out of that place. I had friends that understood me, food three times a day, care packages from a wife I didn't really know that well but who visited me every chance she got, eventually earning conjugal visits, too. So, I got to fuck her about once every two or three months in a trailer provided by the hospital for couples therapy, but only served to provide me with a piece of ass so I didn't need to masturbate once in a while.

I had been attending all the different 12-Step fellowship meetings that were allowed to enter the facility. But although AA stood for sobriety, and NA stood for recovery from the disease of addiction, my motives for attending their meetings as frequently as I could had absolutely nothing to do with either of those concepts. I had no interest in 'being sober' since I had quit drinking back in 1976 after puking and dry heaving for four hours because of my having consumed seventeen double tequila sunrises in a two-hour period and the 'concept' of recovery never even entered my mind, since I knew nothing about it.

My sole reason for attending those meetings lay in the simple and laughable fact that every one of those meetings had fully caffeinated coffee and donuts. Trust me when I say that after consuming 15 cups of coffee (8 oz Styrofoam cups) with powdered cream and real sugar and eating half a dozen donuts I would achieve a state I can only describe now as 'pace-full'.

A sugar/caffeine- induced rush similar to the effects of the meth I had no access to there.

The hours that those meetings were allowed to continue were an opportunity for me to reach for and obtain that state. I would find myself pacing, while wearing the state-issued flip-flops, for almost the entire hour. This resulted in that I would feel 'good' for an hour or so and the facility was eventually required to open the room adjacent to the meeting room, propping the door between the two rooms open with a chair so I could still "hear" the messages apparently and bring an end to my slap, slap, slapping across the back of the other room in order that it would no longer agitate or distract the other patients throughout the meetings.

That worked, for me, since I had unlimited access to the coffee and donuts and didn't find myself subjected to listening to what I considered the drivel that the providers of those meetings seemed to be so enamored with 'sharing'. I barely noticed when their meetings would end, let alone what was being said by anyone there. Until I did notice something that occurred outside of said meetings.

I noticed that one of the individuals attending those meetings regularly, a patient I had no respect for and even less tolerance for, and who could be found listening in those meetings, was released from the institution. I noticed that and I observed that it occurred on more than one occasion, five times being the number I believe I can recall. I can only approximate how many times it came to my attention, since my focus was totally self-centered and taking notice of anything that happened with others, as long as they didn't interfere with my comforts didn't allow for much empathy for the problems of anyone around me.

Compleat

I usually 'guess' at the number 5, for the number of fingers and a thumb on one hand, but when I found that I could count the number of times these individuals that were being released on that one hand, I sort of realized that they were getting something I wasn't – released.

Instantly my genius IQ and complete self-interest kicked into high gear and came up with the brilliant idea that if I were to sit in those meetings, talk that weird language and the gibberish they were spouting before being released, I too would obtain that special status of being allowed to return to the society that had confined me there, solely because I had no remorse or regrets of any kind for acting out on whatever I felt like doing, whenever I felt like doing it and with no regard of how my actions might affect any human being on this planet.

Freedom was just a book to carry, stepping up to a microphone (on a stage no less) and spouting just as much of the ridiculous bullshit as those 5 individuals had and convincing the facility, faculty and legal authorities that I wasn't the one who needed to be confined any longer. After all, society had allowed those 5 crazies to be released with no other reason or motivation I could ascertain than just that.

For approximately the next 2 months I attended the meetings, drank just as much if not more coffee and ate just as many donuts, and at every opportunity insisted on telling anyone unfortunate enough to be within range of my voice how much I 'loved' the program and how wonderful my life had become because of the changes I had already experienced just by attending those meetings.

For the life of me, I cannot even remember opening any of the literature and especially not reading the 'books' that those programs suggested to me and others. And ironically, I always insisted I wasn't a "drug" addict because I wasn't addicted to meth, I just couldn't say no to pussy.

Then, by happenstance and not even his intent as far as I could discern, one of the psychologists there by the name of John Vess must have grown so annoyed with my actions and the constant barrage of 'newfound' information at others that he told me a truth that would become the foundation of my recovery from myself.

"Mike, you are so full of bullshit that your blue eyes are turning brown." "You are here and will remain here for the rest of your life."

California, he informed me, had passed a law that said if an individual was considered a sexual predator who represented a serious threat to society their confinement in an institution for the criminally insane (aka – Atascadero Maximum Security Institution for the Criminally Insane for the State of California) could and would be extended for the rest of their natural lives. And that was his way of telling me, guess what – I qualified.

Now most folks reading this would either cheer my permanent residency status or maybe empathize with the stunning effect of finding that from a 41-year sentence (later reduced through appeals to a mere 16 years) had been 'promoted' to a full life sentence. Neither of those ideas even entered my perspective, so in both cases, it would have been a misinterpretation of my reaction.

A lifetime with 3 hot meals, television, occasional movies, and the hope of conjugal visits from a woman who had married me before I came to be confined didn't sound that bad to my busted brain. As for the 'stigma' of my permanency, let's just say that could have and probably would have fed my ego.

But my 'Vess' moment didn't lay in the time or society's concerns over my behaviors. It came from John Vess making a statement he probably didn't even realize could register with me, let alone the impact that it would eventually have on me. He informed me, not that I was being confined for the rest of my life, but that 'they' could see right through all my best efforts at feeding the world around me bullshit, lies and manipulations and that they could 'see' me.

A reality that I had never been faced with before came crashing into my ego and pierced directly through it and into my non-existent self-esteem. 'I was confined in an institution where I could no longer deceive or conceal who I truly was from others.' The resultant shock and terror from being shown that truth crushed me in a way that nothing else in this or any other world could. From personal experience, I can state emphatically, that even the Christian god couldn't have smote me and had as much effect as John Vess's words.

For the first time in my life, since my older sister Belinda had died, I did something I thought myself incapable of – I went to my cubical on the ward, sat on the edge of my bed, and physically cried.

I cried because I was the two-year-old boy that was raped and then stuck in a dark closet until I stopped crying and promised I wouldn't tell anyone. I was the younger brother who got beat up by his older sibling because I never wanted to hurt anyone, until I exploded and beat him up and hated myself for winning that fight. I was the young person who approached his older sister (I was 14, she was 17) in an effort to convince her to engage in sex with me because it was both the only way I knew how to express 'love' and I was completely jealous that she 'must' have already had sex with the brother that used to beat me up; only to have her become so stressed that it triggered a grand maul seizure of her epilepsy and she drowned in her own blood because I had wanted to fuck her.

Once again I was the 17 seventeen-year-old boy, who joined the Marines to run away from who I was, hoping that they really could 'make a man out of you' like my family had said so many times; only to find that I had to dump the only girl (a woman now I know but the memories won't let go) I have ever loved completely, because I knew how insane I was and would become and couldn't allow the stain of that to ever reflect on her, using blame to make sure she would never be able to forgive me for dumping her – telling her it was her own fault for not writing me enough while I was in boot camp, that she didn't show ME enough love, that anyone else was better than someone who didn't love me enough. I was all of those and so much more and so many more faces and lies.

And I was exposed.

So, I sat on the edge of my bed, and I finally cried.

Compleat

Meeting Death
─ ·· ─ ·· ─ ·· ─ ·· ─ ·· ─ ·· ─ ·· ─ ·· ─ ·· ─ ·· ─ ·· ─ ·· ─ ·· ─ ·· ─ ·· ─ ··

With a skyline of black and red clouds, like a thunderstorm over a forest fire and streaked with lightning from cloud to cloud, I saw a field of obsidian stones that stretched from where I was into the distant horizon. These stones were jagged, with many edged outcroppings, and streaked with lava-like veins of pain-filled agony. Chained to each stone was a human being, some young, some old, male and female, and even infants and fetuses partially formed. I saw myself as with all of the others there, chained to a stone in the foreground, struggling and straining to break free of the chains that held me there, knowing that the stone was my life and only by breaking free of the chains would I find release from my pain and suffering, yet as much as I struggled, I could not break the chains that held me there.

In the distance, I couldn't tell if it was yards, meters, miles, or simply feet away I witnessed a figure, draped in a gray cloak, bent nearly to the ground from the weight of a grey sling bag it carried around its neck and across it's back by way of a broad strap. This figure shuffled slowly between the stones, picking up flecks and pieces of the obsidian that had broken off the lives of those around it and placing them in its bag but occasionally it would reach out with a snow-white hand and touch one of the human beings chained there. The chains holding the figure it touched would fall away, almost as if dissipating into a mist, and the person held by them would lift away from the stone, freed of suffering and pain and become something I don't have the words to describe.

Compleat

I saw them being released, and in my own pain, I found myself screaming aloud, desperately trying to draw the attention of the figure in the cloak. And though there was no sound there, and I could see others screaming as much as I was I still heard nothing. Yet I somehow caught her attention with my shouts.

For the figure that I saw turned her face to me and I saw that it was a woman, ancient beyond all reason, yet still fair of face as if age didn't matter to her. Her skin was smooth and unwrinkled, and its color was like that of her hand snow white, yet her lips were pinkish white, differing just enough that I could see they weren't dry or cracked. Her features were feminine but I couldn't begin to describe her chin or nose or even the shape of her mouth and brow beyond to say she was beautiful. Because when she turned to look in my direction, and I knew I had caught her attention somehow I forgot my own pain and suffering for an instant as fear and elation shot through me together as if I had been struck by a bolt of lightning filled with the power of both. I saw her face and in that same instant, I saw the color of her eyes. And it was her eyes that drove all thought of what else her face may have looked to be, for they were blue, bright and filled with light but also filled with such power, and sadness that I choked on the fear I felt that she recognized me. I could see that recognition in her eyes, I saw that she knew my pain, knowing that the burden she carried was partially my responsibility, since I had harmed so many others that the chips of my own stone had fallen all around me, where she had been forced to pick them up.

And when she saw that my eyes had met hers, that I knew the fear that she would release me one day and the fear that I must suffer life for yet a while, death smiled at me. An assuring smile, gentle, kind, compassionate, and promising to me that when I called for her again, she would come for me at last.

Compleat

The Damned
_._._._._._._._._._._._._._._._._.._

Anyone who has read this experience with death – as well as those with heaven and hell – should know that both places are real but this isn't about heaven. Not this time. When I committed suicide in 1988, I went to a place beyond the "lake of fire" that the religious folks tend to rattle on and on about.

Now, since the place I ended up wasn't that "lake" in my stories, I skimmed over what I saw there. But now I feel that may have been an injustice to those who are suffering most from this COVID-19 plague. This is about passing through there on my way to a place much worse.

As I passed through, it seemed that time had been revealed for the illusion that it actually is. And what I saw there…specifically WHO I saw there…might surprise some of the more religious among you. So, take this page as a kind of spoiler alert. A warning that what you're about to read is a list of those who I literally saw in the hell of some of the major religions of humanity or those who have already made their reserved spots there and are still among the living.

The list will be in no way comprehensive or complete and for two very important reasons:

1. I was only passing through, not confined there myself as were so many others.

Compleat

2. The numbers that are there are so immense that the list of those I could/did witness as being there would be too long to type. At the moment of writing this, my book was only 4,894 words long and it had taken me nearly 28 years to finally begin typing it in a readable format. The list of who I witnessed as being there or having their spots there already reserved would dwarf the 20,000 words my publisher requires before considering my book for publication.

Thank you and you have been WARNED.

The Obvious List	The Maybe-Not-So-Obvious List
Cain	John F. "Jack" Kennedy
Adolf Hitler	Mahatma Gandhi
Joseph Stalin	Muhammad
Winston Churchill	Muhammad Ali
Ronald Reagan	John Neely Kennedy
Jimmy Swaggert and Son	Bernard "Bernie" Sanders
Jefferey Dahmer	Steve Jobs
The Menendez Brothers	Harry S. Truman
Judas Iscariot	Franklin D. Roosevelt
D. Trump and his Entire Family	Norma J. Gentile (nee Allen)
Fred C. Koch	M. Leroy Rainwater
David H. Koch	
Charlie G. Koch	
Bud and Sam Walton	
Christy Walton	
Alice Walton	
Rob Walton	
Bill and Melinda Gates	
John D. Rockefeller Sr.	
William Rockefeller	

Winthrop Rockefeller	
Alexander the Great	
Ronald Roe Messner	
James Orsen Bakker	
Tamara Faye Messner (nee LaValley, formerly Bakker)	
Edward Moore "Ted" Kennedy	
Michael Richard Pence	
Joseph Robinette Biden Jr.	
Charles Hudson	
Clint Eastwood	
William Conant Church	
George Wood Wingate	
John Sidney McCain III	
George H.W. Bush	
George W. Bush	
Leonid Ilyich Breshnev	

As I already stated, the list of those I saw there and who have spaces already reserved for them is so extensive that I couldn't add them all and still have room to speak of what I witnessed.

Compleat

You're Fired
_.._.._.._.._.._.._.._.._.._.._.._.._.._.._..

After thirteen years in the Marine Corps and getting a Bad Conduct Discharge, although there were many jobs I had attempted throughout the years before and after that event, I experienced something I never even considered as being a possibility.

I had worked as the overnight person at the Campobello Treatment Center and received my training as a Substance Abuse Counselor from the California Association of Addiction Recovery Resources. I appeared to have earned the title of Substance Abuse Counselor I was Certified and had attended the classes to qualify as one but never felt competent at the job I was doing.

The clients there were detoxing from alcohol, heroin, and other substances, then attending classes on alcoholism that included the format called The Three-Headed Dragon of Alcoholism. The individual that owned the treatment center had developed the treatment plan format to help individuals understand the nature of addiction to alcohol.

The first head was represented as being the physical dependency on the drug alcohol. The need to maintain the substance in their bodies was something they could all relate to no matter their drug of choice.

The second head was represented as being the psychological obsession with alcohol that develops when an individual drinks for purposes other than simply the pleasure of enjoying the flavor.

Social drinking had passed beyond their ability to enjoy or control because they drank not just to enjoy their drug of choice but for what the drug did 'to or for them.'

The third head and in my experience the most powerful of the three that his format taught about was denial. Anyone ever dealing with substance abuse knows that overcoming the humanly natural desire to deny that they have a problem with the substance and getting an alcoholic or addict to admit that they have a problem is the greatest challenge to assisting them in finding the means to begin recovering from their obsessive and compulsive behavior with substances.

I believed in the format that the owner had developed enough to work at Campobello for a few years, but was never completely comfortable with the format since I believed or felt that there was more that needed to be discussed or faced in order to discover recovery as a lifelong process.

When the opportunity arose to take on a day position as a counselor after I had been certified I accepted it and began working there and training with the other counselors who had worked there for years.

But my financial circumstances being what they were I took a second position at another center called St. Anthony's Farms just outside of Petaluma, California. Again, I was called into service as the overnight counselor though, for the most part, I was simply working as a night watchman, trying to assure that the clients stayed in their respective rooms or cabins. The clients here were people from a completely different walk of life in comparison to the clients at Campobello.

The homeless and street addicts from San Francisco and neighboring counties were provided room, board, and counseling free of charge until they qualified for SSI or SSDI and then their funds were used to pay for their treatment and care. A much smaller price than the judges, lawyers, police captains, and other civil servants paid to Campobello for being in a treatment facility, though they too came from Marin County, San Francisco County, and even Sonoma County where the Campobello Treatment Center was located.

I enjoyed working at both centers for months until Campobello developed a need for an overnight counselor again and I was asked to return to that position from the day position I had accepted. When I informed them that I would be unwilling to return to the overnight position because I had already accepted an overnight position with St. Anthony's I was informed that if I wasn't willing to assist them with their need I would no longer be employed by Campobello as a counselor.

I accepted that consequence gladly because I had the second position at St. Anthony's and was still uncomfortable with the idea that Campobello charged thousands of dollars for a 28-day treatment format that allowed civil servants, lawyers, judges, officers of the law and others with insurance or means of paying the fees involved to avoid being recognized as having substance abuse problems or avoid being held accountable for their actions while intoxicated by having had DUI's or DWI's on their records expunged through a willingness to attend 'classes.'

I continued to work for St. Anthony's as the overnight 'counselor' for a few more months until I eventually earned a day position and received a caseload of my own consisting of some of the male homeless clients from San Francisco. I was content and very satisfied to be working with individuals that needed help and some of whom actually wanted to change their lives.

But with every silver lining, there are clouds apparently. I was spoken to by my supervisor, in what I assumed was simply a talk about how I could perform in a manner more consistent with St. Anthony's methods, less 12-Step program, and more 'christian' based was the example I was given during that talk.

I was unaware - since I had never experienced in the 13 years that I had been a Marine - that simply being talked to was counted as being reprimanded or counseled on my performance as a counselor. In the Marines, when my performance was substandard, I received marks of proficiency or conduct that made me aware of the nature of my need to improve. A simple conversation was just that, a conversation.

A few months later, I received another 'talk' from my supervisor. Apparently one of the female counselors had reported to him that my aura caused her to experience severe migraine headaches. This event was identified as being a full reprimand and it was the grounds for which I was being released as a counselor from St. Anthony's.

Honestly, I didn't understand how someone's aura, a non-physical manifestation that I'm not sure I believed in, could be the grounds for being fired.

Compleat

That there was another counselor, a man that was familiar with the woman involved, who had no caseload and would be taking over the cases I had been working with was a factor I'm sure had more to do with my being released. But the day I was released and told that it was because of someone objecting to my aura I admit I was confused, angry, and completely overwhelmed. I cried aloud, not simply due to the frustration of not knowing what I would be able to do for income but also because I had given up a lucrative position at Campobello to work there and because I had never experienced being fired before that day.

Discharged from the Marines for Bad Conduct, yes. Let go from Campobello because I wouldn't do what they needed when they needed me to, I could accept and deal with easily. But being fired because my 'aura' gave a fellow counselor a headache? It just devastated me, causing me to doubt myself and my own abilities as a counselor.

Although I found another position working for the State of California Health Department in Sonoma County as a Substance Abuse Counselor in Santa Rosa, California almost immediately after being fired from St. Anthony's I never again felt qualified at doing the work that I had been trained and hired to do.

I worked there, being a new father to my second son in 1999 until I became so despondent that my diagnosis with Major Depression from the VA doctors became overwhelming.

I spoke to my supervisor John and let him know that I would no longer be able to work with the clients there. Even though their purpose was simply to qualify their clients to receive their driver's licenses back, I was again faced with clients that were lawyers, doctors, judges, and even highway patrol officers who were from other counties and attending the mandatory classes out of their own counties to avoid their names being made public knowledge. There were others, of course: people from all walks of life who wanted to regain their permits to drive.

But they, like their counterparts in the system, were merely there to get something material from the programs be it the 6-month program for first offenders or the 18-month program for repeat offenders. They had no interest in changing their behaviors, no interest in identifying themselves as being addicted to any substances, and, most importantly, absolutely no interest in recognizing that they might just have a problem.

Compleat

The Three-Headed Dragon model of Campobello made sense if you simply wanted to detox and go back to your life with the knowledge that substance use caused you problems. The Farm at St. Anthony's was a semi-religious means of getting homeless people off the streets for a few months, getting them some type of assistance – IF they complied with the religious method that was being taught – so they might have a chance of returning to a society that surrounded them yet ignored their very real needs. And the system in Santa Rosa returned people to the streets, in approximately 6,000-pound killing machines, with licenses to drive.

The format of 3 always leaves out the silent 4th in every system. Physical, Mental or Spiritual, and Denial were the three that they identified easily enough. But there is always a 4th to every human addiction. It hides behind the word denial because with every single program I've ever discovered or worked within myself the blind spot behind denial allows only the 3 to be spotted and identified.

The fourth is humanity. Human nature. The desire to blame anything or anyone other than accept responsibility. A denial that leads to people claiming that 'the drugs made me do it.' Or 'I was so drunk I didn't know what I was doing.' Or even 'I blacked out and don't remember what I did.'

In every case that I examined, participated in, or observed none of them were willing to make the simple statement of acknowledgment: "I made the choice and I accept the consequences of my actions."

Compleat

Compleat
— - — - — - — - — - — - — - — - — - — - — - — - — - — -

    Maybe I should make a different start to this storytelling stuff, after all I've been told that all I ever think about is myself, that I'm a self-absorbed asshole, and that everything I talk about is how it relates to myself.

    Oddly enough, this is probably true. Maybe that's because I don't know you. Any of you. I know myself; I know what I've done, what I've experienced, and how I feel. To write about you would be hypocrisy of the highest order. Who am I to tell you how to live your lives, how to make things work, or even how to make things better for yourselves? Yes, I've met god (his title not his name). So, fucking what? Does that make me special or better than any of you? I don't think so! As a matter of fact, I see myself as being on the bottom rung of life, looking up to even the so-called 'lowest' among you. Prisoners who are rapists, child molesters, murderers, thieves, and even the tax collectors who haven't seen the inside of a prison, yet.

    Why then am I bothering to write this book? After all, I really don't think any of you will read it and understand what I'm saying. Hell, if even god's first conceived/born son, Jesus got misquoted, with his words being misused and manipulated to control those who's fear is their greatest weaknesses and at the same time strengths, who's going to listen to me?

It was suggested to me to change the name of my book to "The Gospel According to Michael." I was tempted to let that change happen.

Compleat

It would have guaranteed the book would sell. Controversial, argumentative, opinionated, and religious people would have flocked to buy this mess, and the whole damn arguing about god, your relationship to him, J, and myself would have started all over again. I say fuck that! The argument is a moot point. How do I know?

I told you just a second ago, I met the old dude. He appeared to me as male because that's how my head could withstand his physical presence without exploding. Male, female, spirit, energy, or a frigging rock, he could appear to any of you as he chose and you'd know it was god. Some use the labels of Mother Goddess, Mother Earth, Life, Allah, Nirvana, Ra, and tens of thousands of other titles. And use the titles to claim as being his name and as being the only real one. What the heck, if I can use the 'title' of runner5150 why could he not use all of the above and more? Be all of the above and more?!

Let's start at the beginning. And since these are my stories, I'll start with myself and see where we end up. Welcome to the beginning of insanity. After all, we all share in it on one level or another.

Born in Saint Louis, Missouri I started life like every other child on this planet. Mother, father, siblings older and eventually younger siblings. I had nothing special about my birth, my mom being a human being, there was NO virgin birth here! She fucked just like every other woman on the planet and I wasn't her first, so don't go playing that bullshit card on me. That's a hint that I'm not any more divine than the rest of you. And my father was an asshole that couldn't keep his dick in his pants or in just one pussy apparently.

His sister, my paternal aunt, Melanie, told me he was high school sweethearts with a girl named Louise. That they had intended to marry sometime after high school but my mom, that temptress and whore, stole him away from Louise by getting pregnant with my oldest sister Belinda.

My aunt was sadly correct about my mom's morals but in telling me the story the way she did she couldn't see the obvious fact that my father had to have stuck his dick in someone other than his high school sweetheart. DNA tests would have proved that, even if my older brother and I didn't have such a striking resemblance to Lyle. In the beginning, Belinda didn't look much like Lyle. So maybe that's why Aunt Melanie thought she wasn't actually Lyle's git. But then I came along and looked so much like Belinda it disproved her theory, especially after I aged a bit and looked just as much like Lyle as my brother had from the beginning of his life.

Compleat

My life from early childhood wasn't ideal or even comfortable. Lyle would go back to fucking Louise after she had married his brother, my paternal Uncle Ned. But that's for another chapter on family, since I was two years old by that time. I only know from my personal experience that once a cheater starts cheating, and getting away with it, it's inevitable that they will return to the behavior without counseling, guidance, or help in recognizing their behaviors and the 'why' behind what they are doing. This would prove to be called the 'curse of the Runner men' by a lot of women, not just my mother, the aunts on both sides of the family, and even myself. I excused my behaviors and my brothers' behaviors by blaming the 'curse' rather than placing the responsibility exactly where it belonged, on myself and them.

Added to my list of excuses would be the simple truth of the story that was told to me so often that I came to see it as a reason for my own behaviors. Reasonable that when I was dropped on my head at nine months old and my head split open, exposing my brain to the air for a few seconds, that I wouldn't be wired quite like other human beings or wired 'right' as folk would often refer to it. Let's begin there:

*

About My Family and Myself

Dropped as a Baby:

Some of those who have read where I have shared the story of my being dropped on my head as a nine- month- old baby. It was a drop that occurred from atop a chain link fence, which itself was atop a wall, and all above the concrete and cobblestone alleyway behind my home. The story I was told and was frequently shared with and in front of me was that an aunt on my biological father's side of my family who was watching my older sister, my older brother and myself as a babysitter had sat me on the bar of the chain link fence for some unexplained reason; that she had then been frightened by a large, black, St. Louis city river rat and was so startled that she jumped away from it and dropped me as a result.

Now I'm sure anyone can imagine that landing on my head as a nine- month- old doesn't sound like it would do much in the manner of a good thing for me and the continued story went that my skull had split open, exposing my developing brain matter for the briefest amount of time to the air around me in that alleyway, as well as some of the wonderful garbage that had spilled out of the trashcans that overflowed there where I landed.

Compleat

My infant self was rushed to Cardinal Glennon's Children's Hospital in Northern St. Louis and I lived through the experience no worse for it, apparently, than having a baseball- sized blot clot on the top of my head at the time.

It has to be an obvious fact that these stories were told over and over again in my presence as a child or I would not know them at all, let alone be able to share them with you now, and because the hospital had warned my mom that if the blood clot were to move before it was dissolved completely it would more than likely kill me instantly, that story was repeated with the greatest urgency and frequency.

A tale of a near-death experience for a nine-month-old that would be repeated very frequently, by both my paternal and maternal families, with enough blame and accusations for both sides to feel and insist that their counter parts of on the other side were unqualified to even care for children.

It remains to be one of the great ironies of my life that it was my aunt from my mother's side of the family that told me this story in the manner I wish to share it now.

All the details of the wound I bore have already been stated but what creates the irony is that when she told it there were details no one else 'could' have related to me.

She, my aunt, was a teenager at the time of my 'accident' and because my mother worked a full-time job in her efforts to help support us all, my aunt had been recruited to babysit the broken- headed me.

Having received the horrific warning that if the blot clot atop my head were allowed to move in the slightest degree it would kill my infant self, this poor teenager was saddled with the responsibility of not just caring for me as a babysitter; where it was her responsibility to see to changing my diapers, feeding and bathing me, she had the additional stress of needing to care for me in such a way as to not kill me by accident.

Needless to ask really, yet I find I must ask this question rhetorically: "Who in their right minds puts a teenager under that much responsibility and then abandons her to solely care for a child that sick?"

It would be her story that I would listen to most often as I grew older; of how while she was watching over me she had been forced into giving me a bath due to my having messed myself so badly that I was practically covered in excrement, and with my slippery, soapy, poop covered baby ass twisting around in her hands that I had slid, out of her hands, plunging beneath the water of the tub and I ended up hitting my head on that cast iron, claw- footed tub with a resounding bong sound as if I had been used to ring in the new year on a gong or tolling of a bell signaling the end of my life.

My aunt often related that she was terrified in that instant, thinking that she had killed me through this most natural of mishaps, and how she had snatched me out from under the water and completely out of the tub, crying hysterically from the pain of thinking she had ended my life. Now obviously, she had been mistaken, as I was alive and non-pulsed by the incident save only that her crying would trigger my own tears and wailing as if I had been actually hurt, or I wouldn't be here to share this tale at all.

However, the trauma of that incident remained with her for years afterward, causing her to repeat the story any and every time anyone would ask her about her nephew Micheal. And as I grew up, hearing how my brain had been broken, and that I nearly died that day for most of my young childhood, with the additional information that when I grew old enough to talk in nearly coherent sentences, I would say to my aunt during times I felt hurt, afraid or just needing someone to care or hold me: "Aunt Fran, I want to hold you."

She repeated this phrase, whenever she related the story, as if it were her mantra for seeking forgiveness, and although I would never know or understand who she needed forgiveness from or why I would always see her fear and need every time she told it, in the shadows that lay behind the windows of her eyes.

What I did grow to realize as an adult many years later, was that in my child's mind, I had somehow come to equate being cared for and comforted by someone else as holding 'them', as giving comfort to 'them', when obviously it was I who was seeking that needed comfort and holding.

To this day it remains one of the many challenges about myself that I have yet to come to grips with, even though I began reading at the age of three and would one day read extensively about emotions and feelings of transference, because that transference and projection of feelings onto others would become two of my greatest character defects and greatest sources of emphatic abilities

And even these many years later, when I do find myself experiencing emotional, physical, or mental anguish I also find myself reverting to this same childhood behavioral pattern, seeking to hold and comfort any other human being as the sole means of dealing with my own pain, thereby avoiding dealing with myself, my pain, the situation I am experiencing at the moment and all without facing the necessity of sharing what I was going through or talking about why I so desperately 'needed' to give said comfort.

At this point, I need to interject an observation I made many years later. Frequent repetition of a story in front of a child, especially one about them, told in such a manner will, in fact, effect said child. Intent being a damned thing, "the road to hell is paved with good intentions," people would be better served to tell the story once if an explanation is required and never in front of the child until such time as personality and self is realized by the individual the story is about, the child. The impact of telling stories in front of a child is emphasized later in this book.

I mention it because even at the height of my own insanity I was able to recognize a pattern and alter it for someone else in my life, making what I believed to be a life changing alteration in their life as well as discovering an outcome that must have been observed by others but hardly ever taught as far as parenting goes. Children don't come with an instruction manual but perhaps there could be one written if these experiences prove instructional?

I need also to mention that as I write this again, I re-experience everything as if it were happening to me at my present age. So, in a way these things are both memories and repeated experiences, some fairly decent but others torturous and painful in ways I cannot begin to describe. I can only hope that by exposing myself in this way others might find an awakening and realization that they do not have to react in the ways I chose to nor feel as trapped and alone as I did for the entirety of my lifespan.

Psychology argues that the formative years of a child's life are the years between 18 eighteen months and three to five 3-5 years of age. I'm not an expert and wouldn't want to be counted among those who claim to understand the workings of the human brain. What I can say is that even as a nine-month-old, I understood the concepts of pain, feeling unsafe and fear. Needing comfort, as Freud would argue, may have developed within me as a survival instinct that would later become an obsession. Fear of being alone, fear of the dark, an intense fear of falling – to the point that even seeing a moving image of an individual or character in a video game would trigger a responsive feeling of falling myself. I mention it here in case anyone wonders about why I'm telling this part of my history. As an adult I am unable to comfortably watch movies or play video games in which falling occurs without a responding experience of feeling that I am, myself, falling.

Compleat

My earliest 'positive' memory stems from something a lot less dramatic but important to my development. I taught myself to read at the age of three years. While at first, I had to question my observation of this phenomenon since most people will both question it and claim that I must be mistaken or in some way trying to aggrandize my own abilities. I questioned myself on this, and examined the points I could recall in my life. The first being that, to the best of all my memories, no one 'taught' me to read. By the time I was in kindergarten I had already been reading the comic pages in the local newspapers. I remember that by the age I was in first grade I was being assigned book reports, something I found to be demeaning and a complete waste of time. How could I communicate to an adult the wonder and experience of being in a book? When I read, I was the protagonist and the antagonist. The hero and the villain. The damsel in distress and the monster that held her captive for the villain. I was the sea that the ship floated upon, and the beach that waited for the hero after the ship sank. The trees and the jaguar that hunted beneath them. The moon and stars that shone at night and the sun that beat down on the sands of the endless dessert that was me.

How does a child tell these things to an adult that wants a 'report' on things like: What was the book's title? Did you enjoy the book? How many pages did you read? Would you recommend this book to others? Be sure to sign your name to your book report. What's the use of forcing a child to write something about a book the teachers won't read for themselves, that will be graded on being turned in 'on time' and in neat hand writing and if it has enough words in the content to count as a paragraph?

By the time I was in Third Grade I was thought to be 'retarded' or 'slow' because I refused to turn in homework of this nature. I hated homework and would, in high school especially, prove it was an unnecessary expenditure of effort on my part. I would read the required books issued by whatever grade I was attending, toss the books in my desk or locker at school and never open them again. By passing tests to show I understood what was in them, even not turning in my homework I was able to achieve passing grades up until my sophomore year in high school, when I grew so bored that I quit to join the Marines.

Here then is the story of reading at three years of age:

*

And Then I Began to Read

This next childhood story, though, is not a shared memory but one I have of myself. At three years of age, I began to notice the pictures on the colored paper in the weekend edition of the local newspapers. In those days they called them the "funny papers!" I found that I was drawn to the colors and images hardly noticing the symbols beside them. But as I continued to look every week and began to look at the black and white images that were so similar in the daily paper, I somehow awoke to the realization that the symbols somehow were connected to the images.

And while some symbols would be repeated, others would be new to me. What I would realize, years later, was that at three years of age I had begun the process of learning and teaching myself how to read. Those symbols were the words the characters and images were expressing. And I began to want to know more. What other symbols were there? What do these mysterious 'word' things represent? What do they mean? I hadn't even entered kindergarten and already I was becoming a voracious reader. I looked everywhere for the images and symbols I already knew and any that were similar.

And lo and behold I found them - at the local mom- and- pop corner store. In the amazing things that would be dismissed by the adults of my formative years as being merely comic books. There I discovered words, worlds, and creatures, from Caspar the Friendly Ghost and his ilk to the superheroes of my day, and the comic book became my source of learning more symbols, more words. I grew to realize that I couldn't get enough of them.

As a confession of sorts and to emphasize how desperate I became to know more I can relate this quick aside: I had only once been caught stealing at that young age, a piece of gum from another store much further away from my home. The beating I received and being forced to tell the store owner what I had done made stealing these comic 'books' impossible for me. And coming as I did from a less fortunate family; I couldn't afford to buy them.

So, it is with an enormous amount of gratitude that I can remember the generosity of the owners of that store (although I cannot remember their names now and the store itself has been gone for many years) for allowing a small boy to stand in their store, reading comic after comic and putting them back on the display only after having finished each one.

Compleat

They could have objected or even justifiably ejected me from their store for not 'buying' anything, but instead they chose not to, allowing for my young mind to develop the skills I would need to survive a world that was chaotic at its best for me and viewed as physically dangerous by me for near the entirety my life, for that amazing gift and kindness I do not have enough words to express my gratitude to them.

Some people will observe that perhaps it was because I didn't smudge or stain the comic books when I read them that they allowed it. Yet I believe perhaps they saw the light in my eyes as each new word became familiar to me, it's meaning defined by the images beside it. I only know that the gratitude I was never able to express to them then will always be in my heart of hearts for the gift they bestowed upon me of reading and eventually of comprehension.

This simple truth is another example of the potential of every child on this planet that I have observed. There are no 'retarded' children, even those who have the misfortune of having biological defects from genetically deposed disabilities can learn to read and write in some manner. I have observed too many being dismissed as being unteachable and with complete honesty, I can say that particular bullshit won't fly with me.

Have you ever had a mattress fire in your home? And by chance was it on the third floor of the building you were living in at the time? My next memory doesn't really relate to that incident but I cannot help but mention it because the bed that was burned belonged to my older sister Belinda. It took all four of us siblings to open the window to the backyard and toss the smoldering mattress out in order to use a hose to put the fire out that was started by my brother David playing with matches and a candle under her bed "because he wanted to see the candle glow in the dark."

What child understands the dynamics of physics enough to realize that the heat from a candle will rise, heating and eventually igniting a cloth- covered, cotton- filled mattress? I look back on that part of the incident with humor, the keystone cops' effort required to get a twin mattress out of a normal- sized window and the frantic energy with which we all tried to clear the air of the smoke smell that permeated the entire second and third floors of the split-level home we lived in at the time.

My brother had expressed curiosity about something and in that he exceeded me. I was too busy with books to even consider exploring candle light and its effects in the darkness beneath a bed. I mention this simply because he received a punishment that was horrific but not unusual for any of us. Extreme punishments were a common enough occurrence in our household, even though this one would be so extreme I would retain it for the rest of my life.

But it was notable in this story solely for its location. My sister Belinda's bed. Sorting through memories I have found can be difficult, not just for the reliving of the experiences they represent but also for the simple fact that keeping them in some sort of chronological order is difficult. Two memories about my sister Belinda's bed stand out in my memory simply because they involved both my sister Belinda and my older brother, David. The first I've mentioned here will be described in depth later. The punishment he received being too difficult to write about at this point.

The punishment I mention here was gross child abuse, by today's standards. My mother would have/help our step-father place David's hands on the lit burner of a gas stove, burning and searing them to near black in order to 'teach' him not to play with matches.

But, in a way, the second is more horrific for me because it involves my sister Belinda receiving a punishment only slightly less horrific to that, in my experience. And perhaps it might help explain the nature of my own conduct when it comes to inappropriate sexual behaviors?

Compleat

More On Sex
_._._._._._._._._._._._._._._._._._._..

Here's a question: Why ask questions about oral sex at all if it matters?

Why do males find having oral sex performed on themselves so very important?

And why do very few females ever receive oral sex as often or as satisfactorily as males?

I gained an awareness of oral sex at an early age but never quite understood why my own desire was so important to me. Yes, having someone perform oral sex on me felt good. And performing oral sex in hope of receiving it in return was pleasurable to me as well.

And I admit that as a young boy even giving oral sex to other boys was a pleasant experience for me in that the taste, texture, and feeling of giving pleasure gave me feelings of excitement and arousal.

My first experience with that action however led to my being betrayed, ridiculed, and ostracized by the very boys to whom I had offered the experience in exchange for receiving it in return. Instead of returning the 'favor,' they both laughed at me, calling me names like queer and faggot and spreading the word to our entire neighborhood that I was a homosexual.

Compleat

I remember that I was frustrated and hurt by their refusal to allow me to experience what I had willingly shared with them, frightened that I might actually be gay or homosexual since I had enjoyed giving them pleasure and terrified that their tales would somehow become knowledge available to my parents who thought that homosexuals should all be burned like witches. My parents enjoyed calling homosexual men faggots because the term faggot was used for a piece of wood to be placed upon a fire. I lived in terror of their reactions if I had even been rumored to be queer within their hearing.

I know that in growing up questioning my own sexuality I may not have been so unique, even without having experimented with oral sex on members of my own sex at that early age, because I have found I wasn't so very different. Children experimenting with sexuality and sexual contact out of curiosity was something I learned when taking psychology classes years later to understand myself and how I had developed a preference for girls and younger women.

When asked about sexuality and especially oral sex, I discovered many males and females view oral sex being performed on a male as a symbolic example of submission for the females involved in the giving and empowerment for the males receiving. The simple action itself, especially when performed by a female kneeling before the male while administering it is probably why that perception is so prominent throughout the human race.

And I only use the example of a female performing this action upon a male because of my own preferences. I can only imagine that this perception of the act being a submissive form for males on males might be viewed as equally submissive/ empowering for gay males.

With my own experiences in having had performed oral sex on both males and females, I grew to know and accept my own sexuality as being heterosexual because I found oral sex with females preferable to performing it on males. To put it simply, I enjoyed the flavor, texture, and giving pleasure to females over that of males.

My reasoning behind including this story is that I have only had two occasions upon which I was able to successfully achieve an orgasm while receiving oral sex. In both instances, there were women involved but I know that it wasn't the submissive/ empowering experience that allowed me to achieve release in either example.

My first experience was having hired the services of a prostitute and hearing the prices she offered for her services I revealed to her that I had never been able to achieve release through oral sex and challenged her to try by offering her twice her usual fee for it, if she were able to bring me to that point, but paying only her normal fee if she were unable to do so.

She accepted that challenge and caused me to achieve an orgasm in less than two minutes, whereas I had expected her to be performing oral sex on me for hours before she would finally be forced to give up out of exhaustion. How then was she able to do what other females hadn't been able to bring about, in such a short time? Females of much younger age and for with whom I had felt extreme emotional connections with had willingly attempted what she achieved so quickly but had failed repeatedly.

This experience confused and excited me in that I was able to achieve an orgasm through oral sex but didn't understand the 'why' of her being able to achieve what others had not been able to do.

The clarity for me came many years later, when I achieved my second and only other orgasm through oral sex. I was involved in a relationship with a woman who would become the mother of my youngest son and who often performed oral sex on me, though usually only at my request, yet grew frustrated with my inability to achieve an orgasm through her administrations thereof. It is my observation of her behaviors that led me to the epiphany that the simpler and near-universal perception of oral sex being considered a submissive action is not only shared by much of humanity but is not how I had come to view the action for myself.

While performing oral sex on me, this woman through her frustration and growing reluctance to even attempt to satisfy my sexual desires in that way gave rise to a concept that had nothing to do with my sexuality or the submissive/empowerment perspective.

That day I did submit myself to that new concept and achieved an orgasm finally. Effectively though, what I had performed I could only claim as an act whereby I had raped her mouth, forcing myself into her in anger and near choking her through the violence of the action and that violence did trigger my release, at the cost of her having been used, abused and perhaps feeling regarded as an object of sexual frustration on my part.

I gained a release and at the same time, a consciousness that I neither preferred nor desired oral sex in that manner, even at the cost of never having been able to achieve an orgasm from oral sex since that day.

Compleat

The epiphany I achieved from that experience came from reflection on the two examples. In the first, a stranger whose feelings I had no concern for because I had hired her rather than expecting her to perform out of her feelings of attraction or caring for me in return had achieved what I had grown to view as being nearly impossible. In the second, giving in to the perception of submission and empowerment, I had violated someone who had professed to care about me in order to gain release for myself, ignoring her apparent feelings for me in the act of oral rape.

What then was the difference? The cause of my inability and frustration with the concept of having had oral sex many times from with other females who actually appeared to want to perform oral sex on me but were unable to bring me to that point of release and orgasm.

At first, I assumed that it might have been willingness that made the difference. While most of the females that performed oral sex on me appeared to be willing participants, I knew that in many cases, especially in the second example I've revealed here, there was only a willingness to provide oral sex out of their desire to provide me with pleasure. A willingness I accepted as often as I could or they would provide but I was never able to know that they themselves were gaining anything from the act.

The first example, when compared to the second, revealed a truth about myself. I had achieved an orgasm, in a matter of minutes with a female who was also willing to perform the act, though only for the financial gain involved. The difference and my ability to gain a release came not simply from her willingness. It came from the knowledge that she wasn't just willing to perform oral sex on me, it was the knowledge that I could perceive she enjoyed committing the act for herself.

Not simply a submission to my maleness, she empowered herself and enjoyed performing oral sex on me. And in that awareness, I gained an insight that reverses the roles of the entire submission / empowerment of the act of oral sex on males.

In the action of oral sex, a male offers his manhood or maleness up submissively, allowing a female (or in the case of gay males the other male) to take into their mouth and placing an enormous amount of trust in their provider to not damage, bite or sever the member they have taken into themselves. The female, who enjoys performing oral sex, I can only assume acknowledges and enjoys the position of empowerment in which she finds herself. Knowing that with a single snap of her teeth, she can cause the male involved extreme pain, severance of his maleness and a crippling of his ego and awareness of self.

The first woman in my examples enjoyed performing oral sex, not simply as a professional act, but because she was empowered by the action. And through that unspoken communication of her own enjoyment of the act brought about the imagined impossible release I had never experienced before and that would take years of research and self-discovery to understand.

Performing oral sex on females has always been one of my most enjoyable acts to attempt. The flavor, texture, smell, and sight of an excited female gives me a feeling of near euphoria and stimulates my own sexual arousal in ways I still cannot describe with mere words.

Unfortunately for myself and many other males, the ability to perform oral sex on women is an action that must be learned for each and every female that the opportunity to perform the act upon or with as a separate experience. While males share a universal perception of what is pleasurable to them, females are so individualized that all the over generalization has taught males to disregard the need to learn what does and doesn't satisfy the female with whom they are involved.

Compleat

Shame Isn't

Natural - AKA Sin

> "If you can tell a wise man the color of his sin. Mister You're a better man than I."

Ask yourself a question. If you were standing directly in front of god, the creator or at the very least the essence of life itself, what would you want to know? In poetry, music, art and prose, humanity has posed this concept repeatedly: "If you could ask god one question, what would it be?"

The error inherent in that question lays not in the number of questions you might want to ask though. Who among us could choose which question was the most important one to pose after all? My point being that given the opportunity to ask or question the choices and variety of questions would be as infinite as life itself. The stars in the sky have a number, they could be counted eventually. But the number of questions humanity would want to ask would grow exponentially as each question would expand and require other questions in order to comprehend their answers.

Compleat

For the longest time, I believed I would simply ask the question 'why?' as an example. But the question why automatically leads to the question 'why what?' Selfishly, that question could lead to the questions 'why me?' and 'why not someone else?'

I think anyone faced with the opportunity to ask the divine directly might find themselves overwhelmed, not merely by being in the physical presence of god, life, existence, or whatever label someone chooses to apply to the presence itself, but more so by the sheer volume of questions to choose from when confronted by the one being that might very well have all the answers to all the questions humanity might have ever wanted to ask. Simply put, I didn't even know which question to ask and perhaps that blankness, my very uncertainty and lack of knowledge of what I wanted - perhaps needed - to ask is I experienced the meeting in the first place and first person. I stood so close that I could have reached forth my hand and touched the physical presence in front of me but didn't need to do so any more than any other human being would need to physically touch another individual that they were talking with in order to establish the reality of the other person. As a suggestion, the next time any of you are having a conversation with someone you know, or even a stranger, perhaps reach out and touch their hand and explain to them you are just verifying that they are really there and not just a figment of your imagination. If nothing else happens, it will make a great starting point for beginning a really weird, awkward and very possibly highly enlightening conversation.

It seems ironic in an almost humorous thought still slightly frightening way, that when presented with the opportunity to ask any question or questions I might have had, I froze up, not knowing what to ask, which question would be the most important to have answered, or even where to begin asking any question I might want the answers for. All the answers, in one presence or personage, and I didn't know enough about the questions themselves to know what to ask, let alone what I wanted to ask.

Fortunately for me, and probably for humanity as a whole, I am not god. I stood there, in the presence of the divine and was more clueless as to what to ask than even a newborn child. Up until that point, I had been praying, seeking a solution to an offer from others to gain an education as a theologian and assume the responsibilities of a pastorship for a congregation. I had felt unqualified - too ashamed of my past actions to accept what I was being offered and conflicted by religious reasoning, being told that god wanted my service in that way in spite of their not knowing my horrific, heinous past actions. Seeking enlightenment as to an answer, should I reject the offer knowing my past would be a consideration that would need to be faced or accept the offer as a solution, being offered by their god, for all the problems and difficulties I was experiencing in life during that period. Faced with a choice I neither wanted to make nor knew which answer would most benefit those who would be most affected by my choosing, I didn't know what to choose. What little I had learned from religion and religious studies was when faced with a choice that might become the altering or effect the lives of those I cared about, I should seek guidance through reading literature, counseling of others and, of course, prayer. Psychology books, the Bible, the works of Confucius, the Buddha, even a few references from the Quran, along with my studies of the occult and even a few books from my extensive reading of escapist fantasy literature offered no concrete answers to my ambiguous choice. The other human beings in my life were my soon-to-be ex-wife and her boyfriend, her children from her first marriage that she had left in my care because I loved them like they were my own, not knowing the extent I was abusing their unconditional love for me, the two pastors who were offering to have me educated in order to assume the duties of pastorship, one of whom I had no relationship with or knowledge of and the other, the wife of a man I had considered a friend until his wife expressed a need to have a child with me and only avoided that additional betrayal of his friendship by his accidental and timely arrival at my front door, preventing my acceptance of and taking advantage of the offer and opportunity. The counseling avenue was closed to me, obviously, as much as the literature avenue had run into a solid wall with no relief or inkling of what I should choose to do. Which left me the option to 'pray about it'. So, I tried that option as well, with the results being what I've already described - a physical confrontation I wasn't prepared for, had absolutely no idea was physically possible, had assumed was limited to those human beings considered holy or at the very least worthy of being addressed by this being and not having a clue as to why he, it, she, or whatever, would even bother to pause long enough to even pick my prayer out of billions to listen to and answer in such a direct and personal manner.

Their Bible has one passage that springs to mind as I write this: "The fear of God is the beginning of wisdom." If, as they assume, fear is the beginning of wisdom, I got a jump-start on wisdom that day for sure. But they miswrote their own books by using the word fear in relation to god. The word that best describes gaining real wisdom isn't fear at all. It's awe. Sure, the English language uses shame and guilt interchangeably, just as it uses shame and guilt as synonyms. But awe of god, isn't fear. It is acknowledgement of god's existence, yes. And acceptance of god's position of power and authority in the grand scheme of life. And perhaps it's the humanity to accept and acknowledge our very real relationship to god. But fear, Wah! I'd be more afraid of a spider dropping onto my face suddenly and without warning than meeting god face to face. Awesome as it was, there was no fear involved and that too might be a part of the reasoning behind why god confronted me in that manner.

The point being about questions, both to be asked and answered I already described my own ignorance in regard to what I should or could have asked. The cool part and the most frustrating for me was I didn't have to ask anything.

In regards to my personal question, god simply showed me exactly what would occur when I accepted what was offered in that pastorship as god would have it. As an aside, god explained the 'why' of dogs and cats existing in relation to humanity and I honestly cannot imagine why that particular answer stood out for me, except to say the old fart has both a sense of humor and a better understanding of which question humanity might consider focusing on instead of the one we argue about most.

For example, what is the meaning of life? Here's a perfect example of a question that is meaningless noise produced by humanity as a means of seeking to understand itself and its purpose for existing at all. A rock doesn't ask why it exists or even why it's a rock. Not just because it doesn't have the intellect to ask any questions either. Without a soul, religions say, there can be no intellect. Science reverse that by saying without intellect there can be no soul. But both practices miss the important point. Soul or soul-less, the spirit of the rock knows itself and is too busy being itself, a rock, to be bothered by useless questioning of its existence.

Ask god why does humanity exist, or even why do you exist, and in all probability, you will receive the same answer I did when I confronted him with all that I am, all that I was up until that point and all that god proposed for me to become, according to god's will, or plans if you prefer, for my continued existence: a big blank, open-ended, no holds barred answer of yes.

Remember though, one question won't be answered without more questions. It's taken me years of sorting, once I quit running away and trying to ignore the experience I had, to even hold on to the dogs and cats answer because it was one of the least frightening and comfortable answers I was faced with!?

There are others, obviously, or this book would simply be about what I was like and what happened with me, but it's not.

There's a third part to these stories. The part I hope might help even one other person see who and what I was truly like, what happened with my life and through my experiences, avoid some of the mistakes I made.

On Love is real hope for humanity resting. Not my love, since I'm barely able to claim some slight relationship to humanity at all. And not erotic or agape, lust or platonic, infatuation or obsession, none of the other thousands of descriptive words in all the different languages of humanity. Sadly, poetry, music, art, and all the other collective means by which humanity tries so desperately to connect to one another and finally know love as it was meant to be, all come so very close yet can only touch upon it fleetingly. Like listening to a song, we remember that reflects a moment from our past and for that instant of reflection we transcend time and space to be in that moment once again. A moment laughingly measured as a minute and a half in some obscure reference material that is over in an instant and yet exists beyond both the illusions of time and space. We listen to the song, again and re-experience the moment with the same intensity, or less, but we can never quite seem to hold on to it indefinitely. We don't appear to be able to 'stay' in that moment. And that answer is the one we need most of all. Because all the meaningless questions of why, who, what, where, and how could be answered if we could know the when of then.

What I learned in my confrontation with god was so simple it was apparent to me that no one would believe it coming from a person with my past history and actions. I rebelled against god's choosing me to be the person to even suggest this answer. Creaming at god to look at my life, all my mistakes, all the wrong things I had done and had been done to me. I threatened, demeaned, insulted and challenged god in all the choices ever made, even declaring I could have done a better job and threatening to displace god from his seat of authority and position of power over all that exists.

If their Bible had been right. If fear of god had been the beginning of wisdom, I would have been one wise human being at that moment. But I wasn't. Because it wasn't god who I was afraid of then. The person or presence or individual or power I stood there raging at didn't frighten me in the least, even though I stood there in awe of knowing god's very existence. What I feared then and some of what I still fear now, was my own humanity.

Compleat

Humanity. To be humans. To exist on this planet with 7.9 billion other individuals and know myself to be both a part of and apart from all the rest. Maybe if fortune and god favor children and fools (my being much too old to be considered a child) I will become a part of the whole of humanity again? I doubt the probability of that ever happening, but grant that the possibility is always there.

But the chance is as slim, in my perspective, as humanity reading this and awakening as a whole to realize who we truly are and were meant to be all along.

Who are we?

What were we meant to be?

Is this all there is?

What happens after we die?

Is there really a god, or did I just make all this up for your entertainment?

Where do we go when we die?

Is death the final ending or is there more?

You can see, from those questions alone, that fear has held humanity in the prison of illusions, both time and distance, for so very long that the questions themselves have become our focus, debated, discussed, leading to the formation of religions and the disorder and discord between them all.

And none of them really matter any more than the positions we choose to side with in answering them with limited or partial understanding.

Here's the answer I got directly from god that day. Be like the rock. Choose to exist in the moment of your being. This isn't some metaphysical, psychological, mystical or religious bullshit. It's the simplest means I can use to describe exactly what I was told in that moment. And in its simplicity, it holds the answers to all those questions and more. Being told answers to questions I hadn't thought of asking, as I mentioned before, led me to want to ask even more questions - ones I consider to be pertinent to myself. And I know now there exists a being, a presence, personage, or whatever label humanity might put on god, that can and will answer my questions. The problems with that are many but the most difficult to overcome are humorously silly and unavoidable. First, I have to be ready for being faced with even more questions. And I already have many questions than I have answers for, so the overload is damned near unbearable. Now, more might physically kill me.

Secondly, and here's one for humanity to wake up to every morning, in either fear of god or awe of god, the old fart is wandering around among us, disguised as one of us, watching and waiting, hoping we wake up to who we are and are meant to be before we destroy ourselves through our own ignorance (lack of knowledge) or stupidity (having knowledge of who we are and acting ignorantly in regard to that knowledge).

I am not unique, special, or better than any of you. There will be those who discuss me as insane. I am, but that's an aside too. Others, those still lost in their journey, might mistake my meeting with the divine as making me special in some weird or religious way. I am not. The first part of this book is my way and means of proving that I am neither special or even normal/equal with the rest of humanity. Apart from that purpose, I had no reason for including my life history here. While I no longer despise religions, all of them serve the exact same purpose for humanity by offering comfort from the fears that humanity carries within themselves. Of the unknown, the supposedly unknowable of life and purpose and most of all, your fear of death. (Not just the individual deaths of each member of humanity, but the death or ceasing to exist of humanity as a whole.) Yet though I no longer practice anger and disgust toward all religions, I see them for the unnecessary crutches they are and wish to avoid at all costs, creating yet another misguided path of avoiding facing yourselves for who you actually are. If I can claim having one prayer for humanity above all others it would be an end to unnecessary following of any religious teachings. And end to existing on faith and a beginning of living in the knowledge of god, your relationship to and the accountability, responsibility and purpose for your existence in life as a whole. No religion has all the answers and I don't offer any answers beyond those few I was given to share here.

Who and what god is seems to be one of the great divisions among humanity. I cry and laugh at the same moment when I hear any religion claim to have any of the answers to who god is for all of humanity. I cry because I can see they actually believe what they are saying to be 'gospel'. Their minds are set, closed to all other perceptions, believing their answer, their "truth" to be the only one. And I laugh, chuckling along with god at the insistence of children answering their own questions with only their limited experience, knowledge, and need for an answer they can grasp as a child against their own fears or a sword to beat other humans into submission, attempting to force humanity to accept their perception as the only right one by which to serve god and the life around themselves.

I laugh because the chances of forced behaviors becoming a universal reality among human beings is so remote that I could state in simple statistics their odds of success are greater than the odds of winning every single lottery of chance on the entire planet on one day, repeatedly, for the full seven days god supposedly took to create existence. Humanity has always had a built-in resistance to being forced into anything. Apathy and ignorance might bring about conformity, but humanity hates being told what to do, so there are always a few that would rather die than conform.

No, no religions please. If what I reveal here, of my own encounter with the divine, serves any purpose beyond my desire that at least one other human being not repeat my mistakes, it should open a window on understanding and thereby close the doors on fear, discord and death. After all, if so-called Christians listened to J or even read their own mis-edited, often misquoted and unsurprisingly maligned book, they might notice I did "give the keys to hell and death" back to humanity. Why wouldn't he, since he no longer needed them, having been to hell and come back, some say from the dead since the body he initially used to grow to full humanity had expired and then got restarted as a fully human vehicle, walking, talking and visiting others just to dispel their doubts. Even his example was twisted into making him unique, different from the rest of humanity, just because his biological mother and conceptual father were the first conceived/born among many. Does a parent show preference for their first born? Humanity does, either favorably or unfavorably, yes. So, humanity projects that concept of favorability onto god. I laugh until the tears and sobbing choke me with the childishness of projecting human values onto god. It's so childish, not even child-like, and yet humanity through all their religions tend to do just that.

As an individual who has stood in god's physical presence, even if I am not sane by society's standards the whole world over, I can make two small suggestions that could resolve all the religious debates and conflicts that arise from them.

If any human being among you really wants or believes you need to know god, ask the old fucker for a meeting. God's not adverse to meeting any of you face to face, though I honestly think most of humanity wouldn't recognize god, any more than I would have, unless called in on the carpet and faced with the divine presence of god at his location, be that heaven or whatever. I've already mentioned the old fuck is wandering around, disguised as one of us - male, female, young, old, skin color, nationality, and all of humanity's dividers not bearing any weight on god's choice of appearance, god could, as I've already stated, be the person next to you, reading this over your shoulder. God could even be using you, amused at the irony of my writing this so others might see you and wonder not just what you were reading or why you were reading it, but wonder if what you are reading has their answers or if god is hiding in plain sight in you.

Go ahead, ask god for a meeting. Pray, talk out loud, scream at the top of your lungs, whisper so softly that even you can barely make out the words. Like I said, god isn't averse to meeting with his children.

But the second point I have to make is an old adage. Be careful what you ask for While god isn't averse to meeting you face to face; you might consider the facts before requesting said meeting. The divine isn't required to appear at all and if god chooses to appear in a manner that doesn't kill you outright, you are going to be faced with living with the knowledge of god's existence. No more faith, no hope, no room for doubts or excuses. Knowledge: it's a terrible and wonderful thing but it sucks too.

With one answer you find that you have more questions than you know what to do with, and asking god for the answers would simply increase the number of questions you will need, not just want, answers for. Oh, and I did mention that god appeared to me as a male figure, not because god was limited to appearing as a male, but because that was the only means my limited capacity for understanding the presence in front of my physical being could take in order to prevent my becoming overwhelmed. So, be ready before asking for a meeting with god, that presence will sustain you as long as you don't try to force your own conceptions of its appearance. In my experience, I had no conceptual idea or form that I had adopted for god. Honestly, I just didn't care about the trivial matter of appearance at that time - focused as I was on asking my own ignorant question.

I say be ready for the meeting, though in being honest here, I acknowledge that I wasn't prepared for meeting god at all. Maybe that's exactly the preparation humanity needs in order to physically meet with god!? No religious preparation whatsoever, just a question, posed as simply being asked and repeated only once aloud but innumerably inside myself. For the curious who might read this book and wonder what my question was, I can state it here:

Compleat

"What the fuck am I supposed to do?"

Anyone reading this book might know what that question was in regard to, and someone who relates to what I've included might perceive that it relates to much more than just the one issue. Irony is the greatest gift god ever bestows. The ability to look at my own foolishness in asking a question I already knew the answers for and then being given those answers directly from god.

I went ballistic, my relationship with god notwithstanding, not because I didn't get the answers that I had asked for but because I had.

'WHO' is god for example. Sarcasm and brattiness urged me to answer that question with 'I AM'. As in 'I am that I am, tell them I am sent you.' Poor fucking Moses, he went on to ask to see god. I wasn't that dumb or curious, guess that comes from not being raised religious the way ol' Moses was!

Anyone who wants to know god can ask for a meeting, like I said. But the chances of any two human beings agreeing on who god is are as slim as I've already stated on cooperative adherence to one religion.

Why is it so difficult for humanity to accept god is the same no matter how god appears to any one of you. It's humanity that is composed of individuals. I know god exists but I cannot tell anyone how they will view god because I am not you. Probably you each had a mother and a father, maybe you even had siblings as well. You could have loved your parents or despised them individually or collectively. But even if I met them face to face, I couldn't begin to "tell" you who they are. Your relationship with your dad, for example, isn't and couldn't be the same as that of any of your siblings. Not that your pop was any different but because each of you were and are and the same holds true for your mom. Who would I be fooling, like religions try to do, to tell you what and who your father was and/or is? And what purpose would it serve if you already know your parents, to even try to attempt?

Maybe this will answer why no one religion has all the answers, the whole truth and nothing but the truth, so help me! Maybe a hypothetical and rhetorical maybe, humanity shared a common bond once. Telepathy is held as a widespread mythos across the world, so perhaps humanity shared commonality in that way once upon a time.

But like every fable, something must have happened to our ability to share on that level. To know and truly understand one another. I mentioned the Gestalt earlier in my writings and recall that it is supposedly the shared collective unconsciousness of humanity. Connecting memories, music, art, poetry, histories, architecture - all the accomplishments of humanity across the globe that reflect a commonality. And maybe if the answers I received are any indication of the reality of its existence, then humanity needs to awaken to that unconsciousness again.

Compleat Miss Martha

In recent years, as the lack of relationship between my youngest son's mother and myself grew more pronounced, the world would experience the Covid-19 pandemic of 2020/2021. While precautions were necessary in sound measures like wearing face masks, maintaining social distancing, and avoiding the unnecessary spread of germs through consistent hand washing, Miss Martha would take an extreme measure that would cause me more emotional trauma than simply ending the relationship we had attempted to establish in 1997 and had ended in 2014.

My parents, my mother and step-dad Anthony Morris, Sr., would keep a separate refrigerator for themselves and for my youngest sibling, Abraham Morris. In it would be milk designated for Abraham alone, orange juice that only he would be allowed to drink, and food stuffs that none of the four of us older children were allowed to touch, let alone eat. While bologna with jelled fat in its center was never an uncommon food-like substance we older siblings were given to eat, roasted or fried chicken, was available only to our parents and Abraham because of his age.

I admit freely that I stole beer from Art's supplies of bottled beer, drinking it warm since the bottles in that fridge were counted and the wrath of god would be less fearful to anyone who had taken a cold bottle of beer out of that fridge.

But the warm bottles, that were kept in cases beside that refrigerator, were never counted accurately since he was usually too drunk to think to count them before physically placing them inside the refrigerator. I stole that beer stock, not simply to get drunk myself and escape the existence of that place that would be called my home by others but also out of resentment toward them both for making the division between the older children from her first marriage and his son, Abraham.

I grew to hate Abraham, through no fault of his own, simply because they favored him and to this day, I suspect he felt that he was the target of that hatred. It wouldn't be until I learned to forgive myself that I would recognize his innocence in what had been done to us and want to ask for his forgiveness as well, but by then we had become so estranged that I will never offer or ask for that forgiveness, as it is too late to take back what was done in the past.

Compleat

Why do I mention the past in a story about the near present then? Because Miss Martha would claim that due to the Covid-19 pandemic she would keep her food stuff separated from that of myself or our son, Mick Patrick. When I spoke to her about this and how it brought to mind the separation that my parents had used to divide what could have been a family into factions of haves and have-nots, she simply dismissed my feelings as being childish or not letting go of my past.

What makes this dismissal of my trauma so excruciating is that in being ignored, again, all the feelings of anger, frustration, resentment, and even jealousy I had experienced as a child would try to reassert themselves into my life.

And although I refuse to allow them that place inside myself again, at any cost, the suffering brought on by the struggle is intense. I distanced myself, moving out of the main house of the farm I had helped find and buy for our son, living alone in the guest house that had once been designated as the visiting home for her sister, Pamela Chase.

I live alone out here, while she resides inside with our son, who is now so much more like her than similar to me in his beliefs, values, attitudes, and behaviors that I feel I have lost him to her as surely and as well as I have lost the farm itself.

What makes living here with them both inside the main house is the knowledge I have of the past. When she first found out she was pregnant with Mike, she stated that she didn't want to have a child at 42 because she had her career to think about and pursue. A completely logical and normal reason for not wanting to have a child at that age of her life.

But the truth lay behind her words and would prove itself in her actions. She didn't want a child at any age with me as the biological father. Not directly because of my obvious insanity, or my inability to provide the way her previous husband, Adam Stone, had been able to provide and not even because of her age and physical ability to bear a child and be there for the entirety of its lifespan. Her reason for not wanting to have a child, with me particularly, was her fear of the stigma of being known as being involved with a convicted child rapist. Logical, completely relatable to anyone who is sane I'm sure, and beyond a doubt the true reason she chose to go back on her spoken word to marry me after I proposed and she accepted in 1998.

Compleat

Why would she accept my proposal in the first place someone might wonder? I believe it can be explained by the harshness of the divorce she had gone through just before I met her. Adam Stone had met and ran off with another woman to Canada, leaving Miss Martha with her then thirteen-year-old son, Bill, a mortgage that she could no longer afford and an empty place in her heart and bed. I was, in the terms of my generation, the 'rebound guy.' She was hurt, and needed someone to use to make herself feel attractive and wanted.

She needed someone, to help her avoid feeling alone and, in a very small way, help with financial assistance in providing for herself and her own son. I understood that going into the relationship but had hoped that with time and effort on my part she might actually grow to know and love me as a person, which she had claimed to do for the first year we knew each other via emails and phone calls, before ever meeting in real life.

That she knew about my past before we ever became involved might make her choice to go back on her word appear to be a betrayal of sorts, but the truth is that I knew she would choose to do so even before she actually altered her attitude. When she realized she was pregnant with Mike, the harsh reality of my past history crashed into her need to have someone simply be there and she began to regret having started in a relationship with me at all.

She made the pronouncement that she would 'not' have a baby, at her age, for the reasons I've already listed and insisted that she would not no matter what I might want or choose for myself. She understood that abortion was not something I support but that I also respect that it is and always should be the choice of the woman involved to seek one or not.

Women, as I state in my stories about original sin and god, are closer to the divine that is being human because they can create within themselves what god was the first to create. Life.

That she would choose to not allow that life to come into being was her right and choice and I would not argue or resist that right to choose, because I recognized it as such. That doesn't mean that it didn't hurt to know the truth about why she didn't want to have a child with me but acceptance was the only possible principle I could apply to the situation and still remain true to myself and my spoken word to her.

My youngest son, Mike, professes to not believe or even want to believe in god, very much like his mother's attitude toward god, religion, faith, and belief in anything outside of science. And sometimes I am tempted to tell him that if it hadn't been for god changing his mother's mind or heart, he wouldn't have been born in the first place. But there are two reasons that I choose not to tell him that information until I write it here in this book.

The first reason, the obvious one, is that he wouldn't be here at all if his mom hadn't changed her mind about having a child with me in the first place. She and I were getting into my truck to drive to the abortion clinic when the change of heart came over her and she stated emphatically that she would have the baby but that he would be my responsibility, not hers. Obviously, I was elated that she had changed her mind, because I had greeted her being pregnant as a second chance at being a father to a son, after I had lost my first son through my insane behaviors making it unsafe for any child to be around me.

The second reason, is one I have never revealed to anyone before, not even those few individuals I asked for guidance from about the difficulties I was experiencing in being in a relationship with Miss Martha. That she changed her mind was sufficiently more than I deserved and could have hoped for in being who and what I am. But the second reason is that the child about to be borne by Miss Martha was a boy child.

Some men view their male children as an extension of themselves, their immortality here on earth. I can relate and give them that perception as being a theory they were taught to believe from early childhood on, no matter what nationality or denomination of religion they embrace. But the fact is their immortality isn't based on their offspring, it's inside themselves.

The very life they live is their immortality. I state that as an example of why some might think that I was celebrating the fact that Mick would be a male child as the reason, yet the truth is so far from that perception that it hurts to admit it even here and now. The truth is that if the child had been tested and discovered to be a female fetus, Miss Martha stated, in no uncertain terms, that she would go through with the abortion no matter what.

She would have aborted a female fetus, not because she wouldn't have wanted or preferred a girl child in her life but because she would never have been able to trust me with a girl. These are her words, though I type them here and admit them aloud for the first time ever. If the fetus that would become my second son, Mick, had been female it would never have been allowed to come to term and be born at all, by his mother's will and fear.

Compleat

This was a truth that I was never able to speak to my son, tell him or even allow him to learn through others who might let it slip by accident or design how god had intervened in his being born at all.

Those I sought counsel with about the difficulties I was experiencing with my relationship with Miss Martha, knew about her not wanting to have a child with me. Knew that she had changed her mind at the very last instant and placed the baby's care and responsibility squarely on my shoulders from the first day of his birth. They even know and knew of my struggles to not tell him of the fact that she had almost chosen to abort his birth in the first place and always advised me to not tell him of that situation. But even they didn't know the whole truth. That if she had discovered, through the testing she had had done, that the fetus was a female child she would have gone through with the abortion anyway.

I count that as an intervention by god that the child would be born a male, not for my own sake or immortality as too many men perceive children, but for the sake of the child about to be born. Some say that there's a 50/50 chance of a child being born male or female. I believe that the odds were set or the chances stacked by god that the child would be a male simply because god wanted Mick to be born. Why? Is Mick special to anyone except his mother, who changed to want and grow fond of him over the years he's been alive, and myself? I have no idea. He's an individual and cares for me as much as his experiences allow him. And I admit, I'm not the easiest person to be around, so it has been a difficult journey for him, growing close and apart from me over the years.

But the burden of knowing the truth about god being involved in his own birth has never been his to carry. I've carried it for him until now, avoiding placing it on his shoulders until I knew he would be strong enough and ready to bear up under it.

*

When I first moved to Northern California to be with Martha, I needed a vehicle to be able to drive to and from work. Since I had very little money and hardly any credit at the time, I made arrangements to buy a truck from my landlady's boyfriend, an alcoholic that couldn't keep up on making the payments. But because the bank refused to allow me to get a loan in order to buy the truck outright, the vehicle stayed in his name and I used it with a bill of sale from him that when the truck was paid off completely, he would sign over the title to me.

Compleat

Naive in believing that it could work that way, when I got behind on the payments and tried to make arrangements with the bank, they informed me that the bill of sale he had given me wasn't worth the paper it was printed upon, that the bank could and would seize the truck if the payments weren't made on time and in full and that since he wasn't making the payments it was their intention to reclaim the truck immediately.

I told them the location of the truck and allowed them to reclaim it. And though I was resentful that he had lied to me about being able to sell me the truck I was glad to be rid of it. In a way, it had started what would eventually be the separation of the relationship I had hoped to have with Martha as my youngest son, Mick's, mom.

The truck offended her, making her sick whenever she would have cause to ride inside it because of the overwhelming stink of some kind of deodorant that the owner had put inside it.

At first, I had thought the smell, which I could sense even with my limited ability to smell anything at all, came from a deodorant tree hanging from the rear-view mirror. But the stench remained for weeks after removing it, even growing stronger apparently. Then, when getting my gear out of the truck before surrendering it to the bank's repossession personnel I found the cause of the smell behind the driver's seat.

Wedged into the springs behind the seat was a urinal cake. The type of round, blue circle that is used in men's public restrooms to keep the smell of urine from becoming overwhelming in the urinals. At first, both Martha and I couldn't figure out what possible reason would anyone use a urinal cake as a deodorant inside their vehicle. The stench was nauseating to me even, let alone to Martha's more sensitive sense of smell. And the answer came to me years later, when I put it together with the fact that the previous owner had been an active alcoholic. He had placed that stench in his truck deliberately, to avoid being smelled by any Highway Patrol or Police Officers who might be doing a random spot check for drunk drivers.

I guess he thought that the stench would cover up his own. Though knowing law enforcement officers as I do now, I highly doubt they would have let the stench pass unnoticed when stopping him. Anyone in their right mind, smelling the distinctive stench of a urinal cake inside a moving vehicle would have realized that something wasn't right and investigated him further.

Compleat

Compleat
Science the Religion

Chapter 6

There will be those who adhere to the beliefs taught by science that will object to my stories and words in this book. I expect that they will even refute or object at least to my statement that science, too, is a religion created by the minds of humanity in their efforts to understand and make order out of what they do not understand. I cannot count the quantity or number of people who have quoted at me the phrase at me: "Numbers do not lie." or "Math is infallible." So, to display how science is actually a religion I place here two examples to display my reasoning.

First: When questioned about the beginning of the existence of everything and everyone that has ever lived or that which has come about, even those scientists that adhere to the 'big bang' theory cannot logically explain what brought about that very 'big' bang. Where did life, existence, and everything come from or did it just happen, exploding from nothingness? They themselves state that energy is unending, that it merely assumes different forms and alters its appearance. But they cannot explain where energy originated from, not a single one of them can even among themselves or with one another.

Secondly: To examine their firm professions about in math and numbers I can make this simple statement. Were two scientists holding two apples each and were they then to place their individual apples together on a table they could and would state emphatically that oldest of adages: $2+2=4$. An "observable fact."

A mathematically sound reasoning observable 'fact' according to science, I'm assuming they both would agree about that. But were those same two scientists to have those exact same two apples, and in placing them upon that very same table would observe them and I were to choose to make their mathematical equation to be altered to where $2+2$ would $= 5$, by having an additional apple appear with the others there, they would become unreasonably unhinged, refusing to accept their own observations, counting and recounting the apples on the table repeatedly, refusing to acknowledge what they were witnessing and eventually declaring that I had somehow deceived them, having hidden an additional apple and that by placing it on the table without their being able to observe my action of doing so I had violated their observations, disqualifying the experiment through deception.

Whether I could or would do such a thing is immaterial to my observation that science is simply another religion created by the minds of humanity. An attempt to make order out of the observable universe through mathematics. And like every other religion, when challenged by anything outside of their own belief systems, they would reject even their own observations just as readily as any other religion. That science claims to only follow or profess to only observable 'facts' is just as ludicrous as all the other religions professing to follow only 'faith' or other mystical, mysterious observations.

The Bane of Humanity is Religion

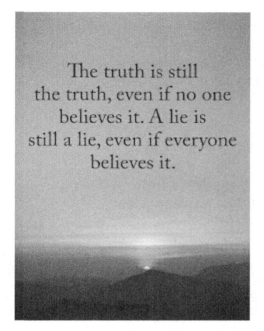

Perhaps it's justified that most individuals I've known use the words shame and guilt interchangeably. In most English-based dictionaries the words are synonymous with one another being used in each other's definitions to describe the feeling, state of being or experience of one another. Perhaps that connection or cognitive joining of the two words gives them a common sense for understanding the human condition described in both definitions. For myself, with any perception of being not quite human, I chose to separate the two words, assigning to each its own separate and distinct definition.

Shame I define as a destructive self-pitying where a person puts on a public display of humiliation, trauma and regret; verbally and oftentimes physically punishing themselves in an effort to convince those around them that they regret an action they consciously took part in or performed.

Often these displays are so public and supported by the society they live within that other human beings became uncomfortable with those that display these behaviors. I suggest that it makes those witnessing these public displays so uncomfortable that they experience conflicting feelings from witnessing the behavior. On one hand, the empathetic nature of humanity relates to the pain they are witnessing.

"There, but for the grace of God is pain I too could experience if I were to commit the actions that other person has committed." Ironically, those that shame others by saying things like shame on you, or you should be ashamed of yourself, are supposing they are judging these 'shamed' individuals as being less than themselves, are in reality are merely relating to the purported pain they are witnessing. And in trying to avoid the discomfort they are experiencing by placing it and more (perhaps their own feelings of shame) upon the performer. Shaming others for their mistakes, crimes, and sins in their efforts to avoid facing and accepting responsibility for their own, they display the human inability to empathize, not merely with victims of actions labeled 'crimes' but with the perpetrators of those actions as well. Public displays of shame make human beings uncomfortable to the point where some fly into an overly sympathetic attempt to comfort, reassure, and stop the display in their efforts to alleviate their own discomfort. Perhaps reassuring themselves that their own indiscretions would receive similar comforting if found out.

Others only seen as less sympathetic and thereby less empathetic are in reality more empathetic, feeling both the pains of victimization or relating to those victimized they also feel the self-inflicted pains of the transgressor, eventually projecting their own feelings onto the other human being in their efforts to drive away the apparent source of their pain and attempting to display a supportive role toward other victims. Does this mean they are feeling superior to those they are shaming? I wouldn't hazard to state as fact, but it does make sense of many human behaviors toward one another and in the states of some of the so-called justice systems practiced here.

Guilt often used in place of the word shame is used in phrases like "they were guilty" "found guilty by a jury of their peers" and "you should feel guilty for

Chapter 6

what you've done." Obviously, I am choosing those phrases only to show the common use of interchangeability of the word guilt with the word shame. Yet there can be no mistake when I state this truth, guilt is and has no connection with shame or shaming in the perception. I have learned to view it from a decidedly 'outside' perspective as humanity has labeled it. Guilt is much simpler in its singular definition than shame, perhaps because guilt can only be experienced by the individual involved. No amount of external projection by others, not even legal judgments in all of the justice systems throughout human history can cause or bring about the acceptance of guilt. And that very acceptance is the true definition of guilt. Only by accepting the responsibility of an action taken by the individual themselves can the process of conversion from socially displayed shame to guilt begin to take place. I state the phrase as a beginning of a process because guilt, unlike shame, is an ongoing process that can never be truly completed. With shame being a publicly displayed outpouring of supposed feelings of regret, the truth is that the intent is to avoid accepting responsibility for an action and the only real regret being 'displayed' is the regret experienced at being caught at any action. As soon as the discomfort grows less as well, a return to the so-called 'shameful' behavior is inevitable. Relativism is a statistical phenomenon that can and has been measured.

Guilt being an individual and internal ongoing process however can bring about a legitimate alteration or change in the personality and behaviors of the individual involved. Where with shame and empathtic connection to other human beings is sought and often unconsciously made, guilt requires no such connection.

With guilt, as I stated before, comes first and acceptance of personal responsibility of an individual's action or actions. No longer seeking justifications, rationalizations, commonality or excuses, the individual chooses to accept full responsibility for their own actions. Dismissed all statements such as 'my upbringing', 'my family history, 'the society I exist within', 'bad blood', 'alcohol or other drug use' caused me to do what I did, obviously answered already and what I did, why being irrelevant to accepting responsibility as well as the rhetorical question of 'how could you?' become meaningless during the actual process of first choosing to accept responsibility of one's actions. In being a process, however, that first choice leads automatically into a second acceptance or choice to be faced. Accepting personal responsibility for any action taken leads to the questioning of self that can again only be measured by the individual themselves. Not a question of what was done, or how could the individuals sink so low as to commit the action or actions. Those questions become as irrelevant as who, when, and where the actions took place, no matter how important those questions might be for other human beings surrounding the individual. The only question that matters, and requires the second choice of the individual themselves is simply put:

"What am I willing to do in order to prevent a personal repetition of that behavior?"

A 'what' question where the individual has the second choice to make in the guilt process, whereby they both measure their willingness to truly accept responsibility for their own actions and choose the measure or lengths they are willing to pursue in order to maintain their first choice of acceptance of personal responsibility.

The difficulty with this second choice lays not just with all the influencing factors I've already mentioned – family, upbringing, environment, education, intake of substances, concepts, and beliefs – the individual faces this second choice with or without the support or hinderance of all those and more, and faces the one, inescapable truth that only they can answer; "What am I willing to do in order to prevent a return to or repetition of my own previous behaviors?"

There can only be one answer to this question, for the process of guilt becoming an internalized, living choice: "Whatever it takes."

That answer is self-exploratory, so I will leave it there for others to question or debate.

My point or intent in showing the division of the concepts of shame and guilt have been leading to this equally simple and decisive statement. Religion and god are used as interchangeably as those other two concepts.

Religions, and I do include all religions through my personal familiarity with so-called Christianity might cause me to refer to it more frequently as an example to which I am referring that applies to all religions, as a constructed concept of humanity. Primitive humanity, science will attempt to explain, did not 'understand' and could not comprehend the naturally occurring phenomenon around which, through which and with which they existed on a daily basis. Lightning strikes, thunder, floods, rain, love, sex, birth, death, and every human experience was something humanity did not understand and, in not 'knowing', feared.

Chapter 6

The concept of individualization, of defining by giving characteristics of human personality to and all of those things offered both explanation for them and the concept of possibly receiving relief or comfort from that fear. "If god didn't exist, humanity would have made one up." Primitive societies did just that or so the religion of science would have humanity believe. Zeus or Thor throwing lightning balls, explaining thunder, lightning and the occasional death by lightning that must have occurred in those cultures. Science proved the existence of atoms, electrons, protons, and the natural law of the attraction of opposites, and dismissed all other religions as being mere mythologies to explain what hadn't been previously understood. Which, as with all religions, set science up to oppose and dismiss all other religions as false, fake and the practice of them as being undeniably foolish, childish or willfully ignorant. (My personal definition of stupidity being the practice of being willfully ignorant).

Humanity has long questioned its own existence. Science explaining through biology how life came into being, The Jewish, Christian, Muslim religions sharing an opposing and frequently disputed among themselves explanation of creationism, and every other religion practiced by members of the human race, including atheism which dismisses the others by saying it was all just an accident, attempt to answer or define the solution to the question: "Why am I here?"

Like-minded individuals from every religion still gather themselves together in groups, explaining, supporting and reasoning among themselves the answers they have found to offer them the security and comfort they need to avoid facing their own fears of what humanity still does not truly understand.

What is life? What purpose does being alive serve? Who am I? Where did we all come from? Why am I here and why now? Some religions try desperately to answer those questions and more besides. The biggest question though is the one none of them can answer to humanity's satisfaction:

"Is this all there is?"

Death and the fear of death is responsible for humanity's insane scramble to define, control, and ultimately deny its existence. Every human being is faced with the inevitable truth and unavoidable fact that they will die. Witnessing it, fearing it above every other fear, the chase after immortality has been going on for longer than written history. Religions, science included, have tried to define, describe and present the actual occurrence for groups and individuals alike for as long. None have come close to describing what actually occurs after the human body completely ceases to function.

And while none have ever successfully explained what occurs, every religion offers some form of explanation that its individual members find comfort and security in adhering to the testament and concepts it professes to be the actual answer.

In writing these stories about myself, it has been my intention to dispel or prevent any religion from developing from what I have written. I AM, the fables by Tolkien expressed it, a mortal man, doomed to die. But my experiences with the beings called humanity, Jesus and god made writing this book an inevitability for me. The devil didn't make me do it when I told god to go fuck himself it was all my own and my responsibility. The choice to accept that responsibility is the answer as to why I've chosen to write anything about myself or the events of my life. By writing these things, I accept the responsibility and the risks, including the risk of some manipulative bastard using what I've written to create yet another religion. I despise that idea but need to ask even that to express what I have learned in an effort to perhaps effect a change for humanity similar to the ones I experienced for myself. It doesn't matter if others find comfort in what I write or not, if at least one other individual can relate to what I share here and use the tools contained in my experiences to find the freedom from fear that they brought me it would be worth a death as violent and painful as the that purportedly experience by Jesus, called Christ. I use the term purportedly in order to allow those of the 'science religion' and opportunity to continue reading without finding more offense in what I've written.

Religions attempt to explain, decipher, make sense of and ultimately control the fear humanity has of the death experience. I obviously don't embrace any of them although I do relate to and claim relativity to Jesus, upon whom the Christian mythos is founded.

But god, even Jesus, are not nor have they ever been religious. The so-called Christian religious sects differing in practices among themselves almost as much as they differ from other practiced religions are as correct and as warped or twisted by the manipulations of the individuals controlling them as is Islam whose leaders profess to follow Mohamed rather than Jesus, yet also differ in their practices of following Mohamed's purported teachings.

Here's a straightforward and simple question to resolve the issue of which religion has all the truth once and for all of humanity. Ask it of yourself, no

Chapter 6

matter where you are on the planet, in your years of existence or your particular brand of religion, including the professed lack thereof, do you, or anyone else you know of on this planet of 7.9 billion beings, truly understand what it's like to be another human being? I'm not asking if you can "walk a mile in their shoes" or if you can "relate" to their experiences so closely you 'feel' you them inside out. I'm not even asking you about those who love one another and are so close they can finish one another's sentences with GMTA (great minds think alike) or siblings who share apparent semi-telepathic knowledge of one another's thoughts and feelings.

Ask yourselves who among all of humanity do you know so well you could actually be that other individual – even for the slightest instant? The answer to which religion has the right answer about god is in the answer to that question, if you are honest and accept the responsibility for yourself existing. And if you answered anything other than a simple two letter 'no', you are still excusing yourself from accepting the responsibility of being who you really are, practicing shame instead of beginning the process of finding guilt as a tool for changing humanity.

Science can say there is no 'god' because there is no physical evidence of his person – a being they could poke, prod, examine and study. Atheists can dismiss both god and religions by pointing out the flaws and errors of every religion humanity has ever created and using those errors, mistakes, crimes, and atrocities to say god must not exist. Other religions can fight for positions of power, wealth and influence over the bulk of humanity and feel those who choose to dismiss the existence of god through their hypocritical actions. And in spite of all those oppositions form science to any other religion, only Christianity claims Jesus as being born of god, even though they argue his humanity when doing so among themselves.

Two facts: god exists as an individual; Jesus existed here on the planet as an individual and a human being too.

The DNA of every human being on this planet is shared with not just every other human being on the planet, but with most of the carbon-based life forms on the planet. That means you and I share some chromosomes in common, be you Caucasian, black, Asian, Indian, Aboriginal, or any other divisive description. It also means I share those same chromosomes as Jesus himself shared while he was here. The term most often used and appropriate in this case would be stated as being "we are related by blood."

Compleat

As for his divine nature, though the Christian Bibles try desperately to dismiss his very humanity, he and I are related in that was as well. But then so are you.

What happens after a human being's body fully ceases to function? We call it dying or death. Most cultures, in fearing El Mort, depict death as some frightening, skeletal figure, dark in robes of heavy blackness, carrying a weapon or tool with which to end human life. Other mythology places another image of a woman with scissors cutting the thread of life and bringing about an ending as well.

My experience with death was neither, she was merely an elderly woman, committed to life by releasing those she could reach or get to during her journey through existence. I've described her as weary, tired of the task she serves and in meeting her I realized she waits, in long suffering silence, for humanity to grow up and release her from the task we force upon her.

The devil didn't do it, didn't make us do it, and neither did god. And until humanity as a whole accepts the responsibility for that, she's condemned to the task she has, whether she rejoices in freeing the long suffering, avoiding the pains for those just born, or is saddened by being forced to take those who are not ready to be released, nor their families to lose them.

Many people ask "if god exists, why does he allow suffering in this life?" Cop out religions say stupid stuff like "To prepare us for the next life."

God allows us to be our individual selves even when we don't want to allow one another or god to be that way. What is god waiting for? I asked him before I told him to go fuck himself. His answer was simple: He's still waiting on us.

Someone once said "Religion is the spite of the masses." If they meant that religion gives false comfort and numbs humanity into an apathetic stupor, enabling most who partake in it to avoid both the pain and responsibility of accepting themselves for who they really are, I couldn't agree more.

Obviously, that wasn't their intent or reason for saying it. Rather they meant that religion was used by those leading any religion as a tool to herd, control, and milk humanity of wealth to their own profits and advancement. A short-sighted view based upon their own desire to 'lead' or control those same masses of humanity.

Why then do people flock to religions – from so-called Christianity to Islam, from Hinduism to Buddhism, and from Confucius' philosophies to science? They follow, scrambling for comfort and relief from their greatest fears of death and being alone.

Chapter 6

Humanity creates religions, where they can gather themselves in masses of like-minded individuals in order to feel good, much the same way some use drugs - those opioids that were quoted to ease their pain, not realizing two very important similarities to substance abuse and religion. Once started, no amount will ever be enough to completely satisfy those who become addicted to the feeling of relief. And, as an insidious side effect, obvious in the use of opioids, they will find themselves unable to stop. Dr. Gabor Mate describes in his book "In the realm of hungry ghosts", the physical process of addiction's effect on the human psychology.

The neural pathways of the human brain become established in set patterns, much like a river becomes set in the course of a bed it runs through and like an established river it can take a catastrophic event to alter those pathways and establish new ones. For myself, it took too, the first being my physical confrontation with God, of course. The second was my self-inflicted death - in both which I was found attempting to avoid accepting the responsibility of admitting my responsibility for the knowledge I had been given during that first encounter. Again, to avoid the possibility of being misunderstood and the possible misuse of this book to establish yet another religion, when I use the term first encounter, I am simply noting the experience of having stood in god's presence, the emphasis being on the encounter itself and not any subsequent meetings or encounters I may or may not have had with him.

Traumatic experiences can alter the pathways of the human brain - or such as the most accepted belief in the religion of science. And having my own patterns of thinking altered twice, now, I am inclined to agree with that particular tenant of that religion, but I refuse most of their tenants in regard to the non-existence of God, for the simple and apparent reason that, having met the old dude, I could no more be dissuaded or argue against his existence than I could deny the existence of any scientist I might happen to meet and have the discussion about God's existence with. I've said this before, I know the definition of faith is the substance of things hoped for, and the evidence of things not seen. Having stood before God, even to just tell him off in the manner in which I did, I lost all semblance of faith by gaining knowledge of his existence. I never met Walt Disney, but having witnessed many of his works and products, I have faith he existed.

Before my confrontation with God, my faith was questionable at its strongest or best from the Missouri Southern Baptists I learned hypocrisy and bold, bald faced lying as early as four years of age, rote memorized the books of the Bible, gained some accolades and good feelings at first. Joining the Sunday school choir, added to the good feeling of belonging to something other than my dysfunctional family. Getting baptized because my sister Belinda had already done so allowed me to also feel closer to her than I already had. Being praised to my face about my singing ability in the children's choir offered me hope that I might have some talent or purpose to fulfill, yet made me vulnerable to the hypocrisy that would shatter my fledgling faith in a God I had never met, which was shattered by the very woman that had offered me that praise. Imagine the effect on an impressionable child after being praised publicly for his singing talent, even receiving encouragement to continue to sing with the choir only to overhear that same public source of encouragement denounce that same ability privately as being over-loud, obnoxious, discordant and both "detracting from my chance of enjoying the voices of the other children in the choir" and quite possibly the worst voice for singing they had ever had the misfortune to witness at any time or in any circumstance they had ever had the misfortune to encounter.

Hypocrisy is a lie or betrayal so severe its ramifications can alter the pathways of human thought and physical growth in the neural pathways of the brain. While I could and would profess a belief in God for years afterward, I no longer trusted or believed in some invisible, holy spooky man, up in the sky, nor did I believe any religious professionals of being the right or true religion or that that spooky dude talked through them. Jesus was a sad story. Mohammed was a disgruntled disowned son's son. The devil was a boogie man out to get me, but a lot less frightening than my personal experiences with physical, sexual, mental, and verbal abuse. Perhaps I was fortunate in that betrayal because many years later I would be so desperate to avoid my own accountability, I would try to return to that drug of choice, hoping that this time it would be different. Drug addicts in the 12-Step programs coined the phrase, I believed, "insanity is doing the same thing, expecting a different result." Although, they may have got it from Albert Einstein.

My return to the use of religion was exactly that, an insane attempt to alter the consequences of my actions, expecting that by changing my behaviors would in fact, alter those consequences somehow. Some magic symbolistic practices use cause and effect in a similar manner, pour water on the ground to get the desired result of gaining much needed rain fall; say aloud or affirm what you want to manifest and it'll come about or into being. Witchcraft and wiccan practice uses this a lot by stating the phrase: so, might it be. Christians simplify their attempts at magical results by adding an amen after every prayer. I'm not familiar enough with Islam or other religions to make note of

Chapter 6

their magic words, but knowing them to be religions, I can theorize they all have their own, including the very phrase theorized for the religion of science itself. Oddly enough, primitive religions had stronger grasps on the concept and thereby more faith, often resulting in shamans or witchdoctors manifesting results that defy scientific explanation or reasoning. What they were doing, unconsciously and yet measurably, was manifesting through magical practices - the inherent power of humanity - not realizing that the practices themselves, as with religion were, unnecessary tools to manifest something they could have done without.

In psychology and psychiatry, there is an often-used term called psychosomatic illness. When an individual human being can manifest all the symptoms of an illness without actually having experienced the illness itself. My example of this is a young man bound to sitting in a wheelchair after receiving treatment for and recovering from a physical accident. Although there was no longer any physical damage or reason for his disability, he cannot walk or travel unassisted by the tool he has become dependent on because he thinks he cannot walk. Faith healers thrive on those with these sorts of illnesses, merely convincing the deluded into overcoming their delusion and giving up their wheelchair or crutches. Scientists tend to denounce faith healers as frauds and charlatans for this very reason and while the unscrupulous outweigh the few who practice faith healing for benign purposes, it is a manifestation of yet another form of unnecessary magic - a practice shared by many religions, including science or medicine. Yet I know from having met both God and big brother, J, that the ability to heal even wounds that appear unhealable, diseases for which science is still struggling to find a cure, and even death or dying can be overcome by the inherent - and meant to be inherited - power of the human nature. The so-called followers of Jesus focus their thought solely upon this divinity or divine birth as being the source of his abilities. In naming those abilities supernatural, they distance themselves from other religions, placing their practices as the only one by which to manifest real faith in God. Real faith, as an oxymoron, similar to peaceful protests, government responsibility, or military intelligence, is accepted. Sounding as if it serves its intended purpose of defining the undefinable, it remains a useless noise, very similar to a fart, in that it gives warning to those hearing it that they might find their senses, including their common sense, offended by their action being performed in producing the sound.

Compleat

The actions Jesus performed may have been divine in nature since he was the first physically conceived child of God as they repeatedly and mistakenly limit as the source of his abilities. But then they deny the very truth that being conceived by god is not unique to Jesus because all human life is powered by, inherent of, and in hatred from the divine or god. Sure, Jesus is first-born heir to a throne that will never be vacated, but a loving and loyal son even to the point of dying at his pop's request in order to manifest or show his siblings called, humanity, how things can be done. The Christian religions downplay his humanity, causing other religions to point out their attempts to alter his appearance as being solely divine in nature - justifying the dismissal of both the divine and the very nature of humanity itself. Religions do to humanity what a wheelchair does to an injured child. They take away the strength, ability, knowledge, and especially the confidence needed to walk as humanity was intended to walk - beside god; walking, talking, hanging out with and being his children, friends, and equals.

On God

With all the different religions humanity has created over the years a reasonable person would imagine that a least one of them might get the truth straight. From the Egyptians to the Hindi, from the Maoists to the Buddhists, from the Christians to the Islamist's, not one of them has even come close to the truth about god.

As examples, Mohammad spoke as a prophet of Allah and he was misquoted by those who wrote down his words through the filter of their own understanding. The Buddha spoke of enlightenment through examination of self, believing in surrendering gave insight into knowing the divine of each of us. Egypt shared ideas of gods for everything and aspect of life on a river that has long become as polluted as religion itself. The Hindi separate themselves by caste believing to be born into a higher caste is to be one step closer to achieving Nirvana and eternity.

And then there are the Christians. A group started from the Jewish religion, based on the teachings of a dude they call the Messiah and Christ. Yet none of them follow what he taught or do what he told them to do. They gather themselves in buildings, calling the buildings "church" and believing that once a week they can be close to their god and that's enough. That their truth is the one and only, as is the case with all religions created by the minds of men.

I have found arguing with any of them is as pointless as the religions themselves, for once a human being chooses a thought as being truth changing their minds is impossible for anyone, for they will ignore anything, any information that might come from outside of themselves.

Am I attacking religions individually or even religion as an idea? Honestly, I am not. What I am attacking is the concept that any one of them has the whole picture, the actual truth of the reality of who and what god is to humanity.

I have often tried to explain to those who would ask me what I meant by who god is and what god is to all of humanity, trying to use similes and metaphors to describe the truth in terms they might be able to grasp, with various degrees of failure being the result.

Because I'm not a linguist, in fact, I'm language illiterate and stuck with using expressions in the English language that other languages cannot translate into so well. But as a last try, since this chapter of my book deals with religions I thought I might add this description here to see if anyone might grasp the concept at least.

The different religions of the world are like slices of a pie. That concept has been expressed many times and in many ways I'm sure, but here's the idea that might have been missed.

Every religion is like a separate slice of the same pie, the truth being the whole pie itself obviously. But the difficulty doesn't just lay with the sizes and shapes of the slices each one has, even calling the pie god doesn't describe or resolve the conflict of their divergences.

If, as has been described by many others, every religion has only a slice of the truth, claiming that their slice is the only truth, humanity might have been able to resolve their differences and come together.

It would have been as simple as saying that the pie was an apple pie. Or mincemeat. Pumpkin. Or pecan. They could have come together if they could have agreed on the fact that god, no matter what name they chose to give him/her/it was one being. Some actually try to do just that, make unity out of the chaos of religions, like bringing the pieces of the pie together in the pie pan again.

But the pie was never the problem. And neither was god's identity. The problem lies with humanity trying to pigeonhole or label that which they don't understand. Each religion might have a slice of the truth, much like a climber's rope having a single strand to mark it as being trustworthy to those

Chapter 6

who might use it, but they choose not to acknowledge that the piece they have not only come from the same place, the same pie in my example, but that it is their interpretation of the flavor of their slice that determines their truth.

An apple pie, sliced and served would taste like an apple pie to most human beings that had ever tasted an apple. It might even taste like an apple pie to someone who had never had an apple before in their entire lives. But religion is like taking a piece of apple pie and tasting it as cherry pie, banana cream pie, pecan pie, mincemeat pie, lemon pie, and of course, apple pie.

It's not the pie that is different. Like god, there is no name that can be put on it that could label the pie accurately because humanity has as many varied tastes as it does religions. It is humanity that separates god into pieces and calls the pieces the truth, labeling god as if they know who god is and what god is in regard to the world as a whole. Ignoring the fact that god, like that unnamable pie, has no name they would recognize, they label god the way they label that pie of truth, as each religion accepts and perceives god to be.

I used to say they were all right, having a portion of the same pie. But in doing so I dismissed, even as they do themselves, the fact that they are all wrong as well. So, why do I bother saying this? I know they won't listen and I know too well what happens to those who say things like this when they do listen but don't want to hear.

Mohammad spoke his flavor and others claimed his as the only flavor worth having. Jesus, the first conceived child by god as he reputedly and apparently was and claimed, was not only ignored like Mohammad was but was crucified for telling others the truth in a way they couldn't ignore.

And then there's me. An unwilling, faithless, non-believer who was confronted with the truth in whole. Someone who resisted sharing it with anyone because of the results of the life I had lived up until that point, the life I would live afterward trying to run from the responsibility of telling the truth, and in the end, chose to give up and just say it all anyway, knowing that no one would hear what I had to say but might listen to it long enough to grow angry with me and end my miserable existence on this sad planet of 7.9+ billion individuals, none of whom I am close to and none of whom I have ever been able to allow to be close to me.

Watch and see the religious lock on to the faithless and non-believer part of that paragraph and like me perhaps their closed-mindedness will cause ironic laughter and tears at the same time for some. Faith and belief in god are things they claim and claim to be important to their religions. But I don't claim faith, nor do I claim belief in god. I have something worse, much worse, and awful in its possession.

I have the knowledge that god is a real entity. And an individual entity at that. I call him pop when I'm in a good mood, and 'that old fucker' when I'm not. I love god and I hate god, both equally, and I can because I know god.

Religion expresses faith and belief in god, no matter what religion a human being subscribes to or chooses to believe. I do not. I just know, having met that individual under circumstances I did not think possible, hence the 'unwilling' participant I describe in that previous paragraph, the part many religious will choose to ignore.

Compleat
Balaam's Ass

If I were to describe myself and the action that I am taking in writing this book it would need to be slightly blasphemous because I would quote John the Baptist by saying "I am a voice, crying in the wilderness." But my cry isn't about making straight the path of the Lord as he did. Instead, I cry out to all of humanity "It doesn't need to end this way." I have more faith in you all than you have in yourselves. Human beings are so wonderfully blessed, given all the gifts that god bestowed upon you at the beginning of all creation. Big bang, evolution, creation, or simply existence, whatever belief any of you prescribe to it's all true and human beings are gifted much beyond what you embrace or acknowledge of yourselves.

One of the most painful parts of having sacrificed my own humanity is the ability to see all that you are, can be, and could accomplish as a race. I see you and care about you in ways I could never have done if I had retained my perspective as a human being among you. I want so much for the race of humanity not to fall or fail the way I myself have done. And yet, with all my writings, all the stories I share here, I have so little hope of being heard by the whole of human kind.

Compleat

When I argued with god, told him I wasn't qualified, told him every fault I possess, every crime I've ever committed, every wrong I've ever done, I argued, cursed, screaming obscenities and criticisms at god for even considering using me to deliver any message at all. Yet, in my deepest heart I wanted so very much that humanity would hear the message I carry, he knew this thing and chose me because I had that heart to hope. I am not god. I am not an angel or prophet. I am not even human. I am a tool.

I am the runner5150: An insane messenger, tasked with delivering a message, knowing that I risk death, dismemberment, and suffering if I deliver the message to those who it is meant for and yet cannot help but be who I am, do what I have been commanded to do, act in the manner to which I was forged to be and deliver the message in spite of my knowledge that I may well be too late.

Exhausted, borne down by the weight of my own weaknesses, overwhelmed by the nature of the message I carry, and knowing that in all likely-hood the recipients of the message will destroy me for bringing it to them, I can do nothing less than that which I was made to do.

If god spoke to Balaam through an ass, how then could he not use me to speak to you all?

Compleat

Regina Myrtle Dixon

How to explain. There are no excuses that justify what I did. There are no reasons that excuse my actions. And in the very attempt to explain what motivated me to do the things I did, there must not be any attempt to rationalize what I chose to do.

** Explain: to make clear to someone by describing in more detail or revealing relevant facts or ideas. **

I've already described the actions I took and the irrational thinking that was behind my betrayal of the girl child that was placed in my care. What I may not have explained clearly, in order to make clear to the readers of this book what it was exactly that motivated me to do those actions, is my experience with the actions themselves.

While I do not ask for understanding, since to understand me or my thoughts one would need to be me or inside my mind even for an instant, somehow it remains relevant to make clear to the reader those thoughts, because I cannot rest until the facts are presented in such a way that human beings, others who are even now experiencing what I did and doing the things I did in order to arrange their own feelings and thoughts by bringing similar suffering to others might not need to continue in their choices if they are shown that there is another way and that they too are not alone in their experiences.

I've described in detail how I fell 'in love' with Regina on first meeting her. Not merely the pedophilic desire to know the unconditional love of a child, but seeing in her love the replacement of the first love of my life that I had surrendered in order to prevent Megan from experiencing the beast I would eventually become; I realize that perhaps that too was the pedophilia of my past (although our ages were not so dissimilar then) since Megan was that love of mine from approximately the same ages until I ended my relationship with her through the heinous means I've already described in another story.

By the year I met Regina, I had descended into my insanity to the point that I truly believed my own lies and self-deceptions. I married her mother, Denise, in order to not be alone and, have a sexual partner that society wouldn't question and would affirm my masculinity to my under-inflated self-respect and over inflated ego. Her having Regina, bringing her children into my life, my ego saw only as a bonus until I found myself drawn to Regina more than her mom because of her resemblance to Megan. Not in the physical sense, they were only alike in that way by both being young females. I was drawn to her in the sense that she gave her love to me as a 'dad' unconditionally and without thought for herself or her safety. In that, I betrayed her trust which was a more heinous action than any other crime I committed against her.

There are no words, no "I'm sorry" or "I wish I could take it all back" that will ever be able to undo that betrayal. And even my awakening to the insanity I was performing when abusing her cannot change the past actions that I committed those many years ago. How then to explain that my only redeeming act toward her was to send for her mother to come and get the children that had been left in my care?

I've written about my non-nobility; my cowardice in actions and deeds throughout my life. And in doing a thorough inventory of all the deeds of my life only two stand out as being choices I've made where I put the welfare of another ahead of my own twisted desires, needs, wants, lusts and anger.

I left Megan to protect her from what I was becoming and with Regina and her brothers I sent for their mother to protect them from what I had become. Of a many-year lifespan, to have only done two actions that benefited the welfare of others, appears to me to be a very poorly used lifespan, indeed.

Compleat Betrayer of Trust

Maybe it was simply my imagination. Or maybe it was my disappointment at not getting caught. Or even maybe it was outrage at being caught but having my actions ignored. Or maybe – just maybe – what transpired that day was so far out of the realm of normalcy that all the psychiatrists and psychologists who have written on the subject were right.

There are many journals for medical doctors and several have articles dealing with deviant sexual behaviors and try to explain why some victims of those types of behaviors might be psychologically blind to behaviors that they don't want to know about, witness, or even acknowledge. That would, in my experience, offer an excuse for some people. A rational explanation of why, witnessing something so unacceptable or deranged they would simply be incapable of actually seeing it, rather than dismissing it or ignoring it.

I can offer that explanation as reasonable rationality for what transpired the day I'm about to describe; not for my own actions, those were deliberate and as heinous as could be imagined by anyone. No, if there is one person that I offer this reasoning for it would be my first ex-wife, Debbie.

During the short years we were together my behaviors were less than what society or the Marine Corps would have labeled within the bounds of normalcy or sanity. The drinking, drugging, and sexually inappropriate behaviors I displayed during those years were not within the range of any human normal setting. And I believe that Denise, needing the extra income and an apparent parental figure for her children from her first marriage that had ended in a divorce chose to stay with me for only those reasons, in spite of my bizarre behaviors.

The day I'm about to discuss, however, matches the descriptors of the conditions that those medical journals and articles portrayed so vividly that I am able to identify the behavior she displayed as being that type of blind to the actual presence and events that unfolded.

Throughout the years of our being together, I had insisted that clothing within the household would be completely optional for anyone who resided under 'my' roof. Be they family members, friends, visitors, or even strangers, they were encouraged to peel down to the buff and wander freely throughout the house. While Denise would on occasion participate in this nudist style of living, nakedness wasn't something she was comfortable with in front of strangers. But all three of her children from her previous marriage were young enough that being naked throughout the day inside the house was something that they embraced as being ridiculous or fun.

By the year during which Denise left me for Richard Mayer, and Regina had been sleeping in my bed while she was working the overnight shift at a local convenience store, that nakedness included my step-daughter sleeping naked in my bed with me.

When the actual physical inappropriateness began or even how it began, I choose not to even try to recall. That it happened and that I was eventually held accountable for it is a matter of military record; suffice to say that I was discharged from the Marines for Conduct Unbecoming with a Bad Conduct Discharge.

Be that as it was, the day in question was a day when Denise had arrived home from her position as a clerk at the store and was doing some dishes in the kitchen area of the house, while Regina and I were still in the bed we shared while Denise was working.

I remember this event in detail, not simply because of the shame it brought me for years afterward when trying to rationally understand why I did what I did with my step-daughter, but because it stood out as a shock of a sort that my behavior went unnoticed that day.

As I've already described, Regina and I were completely naked in bed together. I had Regina involved in performing oral sex on me while laying back and feeling both the pleasure of that along with the resentment and anger directed toward Denise for having had an affair with the man I knew only as Milton from the Pirate's Den episode. It was as if the abuse I was subjecting Regina to was an enhanced pleasure by the thought that I was taking revenge on Denise by doing with Regina something I could have been doing with her mother but chose to do to her out of spite.

A part of me wanted Denise to catch us in the act, dropping the anvil of my anger onto her for not being who I wished her to be and making what Regina and I had been doing her fault in some perverse way. Even when the sounds from the kitchen stopped, where Denise had finished doing the dishes and could have been coming toward the bedroom, I didn't stop having Regina perform oral sex. And that's when Denise walked into the bedroom even as I had half hoped and half feared she would.

Compleat

A naked Regina, with her hair mussed and her lips red, wet, and swollen from having been committing the act of oral sex on me, sat up in the bed with her head rising from the region of my groin and my still erect penis, wet with the saliva from Regina's mouth, was still throbbing and exposed for the split second it took for me to raise my leg as an obstacle for Denise's view and toss the top sheet from the bed over my own nakedness occurred.

For years I simply 'knew' that Denise could not have NOT witnessed what was happening in that bed. And as I mentioned here before I didn't know if I was grateful that she ignored it, angry that she ignored it, or even in my sick and twisted thinking resentful that she ignored the fact that her daughter had been sucking my cock as she walked into the room.

It wouldn't be until many years later, while in therapy and studying the psychology that allowed me to understand my own actions that I discovered the articles I mentioned about how victims of certain types of abuse will develop what might be termed 'blind spots' to the same type of abuse in those they choose to have as significant others. The articles gave sense to the impossible fact that Denise must have witnessed what had happened but never acknowledged it in any way, simply suggesting to Regina that the dishes needed to be dried and put away and then leaving the room herself.

I rationalized and reasoned that Denise must have been sexually molested as a child, herself, by someone she had been close to emotionally and had been 'blind' to the actions that occurred between Regina and myself that day. The psychology articles themselves gave me enough evidence to allow her the benefit of being unable to witness what happened because of her own traumatic past.

While I know that some folk will read this, especially men that have the same issues I have had with sexual inappropriateness (those whom society labels perverts for instance), and will only focus on the sexual content of this story, I must state that is not my purpose for writing it. Nor, as has been suggested by some, is it a confessional story because in owning all of my past mistakes I no longer feel the need or have any reason to confess any of the actions that I have committed in the deviant behaviors of my past.

The point of sharing this story is to detail that the abuse went unseen by someone who had every rational reason, by being her mother, for not just witnessing the occurrence but would also have had total justification for putting the abuse to an end by having me arrested and confined for my behaviors immediately.

That obviously was not what happened that day, but perhaps it should have and could have if there weren't for the underlying factors involved especially the suspected result of Denise having been molested herself at some point in her younger life.

In discussions with victims of sexual assault and rape during my years of therapy and later as a counselor myself, there is a 'theme' that is expressed by perpetrators of the violence that tries to exonerate the behaviors of an abuser by placing the blame on their victims. The clothing a woman wears or lack thereof, the opportunity that is presented by a woman's state of intoxication, the vulnerability of the victim by being in a place, age range, situation, or even trusting an individual that they know have all been used in attempts to shift the responsibility for the actions of the abuse in part or in whole onto the victims. Even some victims have come to view themselves as being responsible for what occurred to them because society sets standards of behavior that programs them to assume they must be at fault.

That too is not what this story is about nor do I intend to imply that thinking here or justify those who use that type of thinking to victimize and re-victimize those who have experienced sexual assaults in the way society has repeatedly done for many years.

What I am offering is the observation that recognizing the behaviors of sexual predators can become a tool to prevent their continued acts of aggression and violence. In knowing my own past, for example, having been a rape victim at 2 years of age, I may well have been programmed to think and feel that the type of behavior I experienced was what would become my 'normal' behavior. With the awareness of that fact, I became able to accept responsibility for my own actions and avoid repeating the patterns of behavior I had displayed for years.

With Denise as an example only, victims of early childhood abuse may well find themselves falling into the behaviors that lead them to repeat the same scenes in their adult lives, even to the point of being blind to abuse that is occurring within their own household.

That in no way places the responsibility for the actions of the abuser on them. I repeat that in case anyone even tries to use my comments in this story as justification for their own behaviors.

The responsibility is solely that of the abuser.

Compleat

The fact that any victim might fall into a similar pattern of behaviors is not a choice they would make consciously but, in being unaware of their own experiences, might lead them to repeat or allow a behavior that they abhor. Society and humanity might well benefit from recognizing this potential solution to a problem that has had too many occurrences for entirely too many years of human existence.

Compleat

Stay Out!
— ⋅ — ⋅ — ⋅ — ⋅ — ⋅ — ⋅ — ⋅ — ⋅ — ⋅ — ⋅ — ⋅ — ⋅ — ⋅ —

It is ironic that it took me nearly seven years of living in the same house as my youngest son's mom and that I owe her insistence, enabling me to overcome my phobia of going into a woman's purse for any given reason. Her persistence in asking and dismissing my physical reluctance aided me in first recognizing my fear and then facing the truth of it as being something beyond my control. Most men might find discomfort by looking into a woman's purse for the simple biological reason of finding things for feminine hygiene as most men find a woman's menstrual cycle as both mysterious and confusing. Yet, my phobia was not even remotely related to the phenomenon of the creative process that women retain from the origins as the race of humanity. My phobia, in this instance, as with most of my fears and physical incapacitates comes from my personal experiences.

I was married back in 1979 to a woman I wasn't in love with and I tried desperately hard to love in a manner that society would deem acceptable, but the marriage was a disaster and the making for several reasons - the first being my inability to love any woman other than the girl I had abandoned when I had joined the Marines 6 years earlier. The more heinous, insidious or foul reason was I had fallen in 'love' with her nine-year-old daughter when her daughter had thrown herself into my arms, calling me daddy and giving me what I had hoped to find by marrying her mother: total and completely unconditional love.

Compleat

Being in love with a nine-year-old is socially unacceptable unless you are a nine-year-old boy as well. Years later, after therapy and attending 12-Step meetings, I came to the realization that emotionally, I was probably somewhere between four years and eight years of age, due to my early start at using substances to avoid my feelings of shame and fear, especially my fear of myself. As for being in love with her, I cannot describe in words what I felt about her, myself, or the betrayal of that love to the selfish nature of my fears, immaturity of emotions, and lack of comprehension of why I felt the way I did and how the very betrayals would become failed attempts to right my inner self; correcting wrongs I saw within my being, lending to a turbulence of dark desire, self-hatred, more fears, and eventually desire for self-destruction that would overflow onto the lives of all those around me.

The point of describing all of the above, simply being my means of expressing my desperation to be married and that with my first wife, I ignored her feelings and based her trust on her fidelity as wife. While I, as a husband, in having affairs as often as possible, and as surrogate father to her three children from her first marriage yet physically, emotionally, verbally, and sexually abusing them, I dismissed and disregarded my responsibilities as a man. When I discovered a letter addressed to a young man who I had considered a friend - at least as much as I could consider anyone such a thing - in her purse.

Fear and curiosity provoked me into reading that letter in which she described her joy at having spent the afternoon in his physical embrace, sexually fulfilled by his attentions, and how she anticipated their future encounters that would include more of the same.

Anyone ever witnessing the behaviors of a child when some object - one they have neglected and scarcely acknowledged having access to – is found being played with by another, might be able to relate to the unreasoning outburst I experienced upon reading that letter. I could have easily taken the Smith and Wesson .357 Magnum pistol I owned at the time and ended them both.

First her, as she was sleeping in our shared bed at the time when I discovered the letter. With him, I could have merely waited for him to come to the rendezvous they had planned after she would fail to warn him of my discovery. It would have been a simple matter. And I deeply longed to punish both her as being the object I claimed as my own and him for having the audacity to touch what I considered mine. Instead, I eventually sold the pistol to prevent my acting upon these thoughts. Why divest myself of the implement of destruction I could so childishly use to avenge myself for their mutual betrayal?

Was some part of my lost humanity restoring itself to cause guilt for my own many betrayals to prevent me from acting on my desire for vengeance? Or did the primal instinct of self-preservation cause me to reconsider my actions avoiding premeditated murder twice and its subsequent punishment?

Neither. It was my fear of becoming separated from the source of unconditional love that my stepdaughter had become to me. As any addict might try to describe and society fail to understand and never truly relate with that desire, demand, need, compulsion and overwhelming fear made my decision for me.

Being in love with a by then 12- and 13-year-old girl, wouldn't prevent my abuse of her love for me, but the fear of losing it stayed my hand that day and saved both their lives. If she hadn't been in my life, neither social mores, my own self-preservation or any subsequent punishment would have stopped me. Perhaps I should be grateful for my being an addict or obsessive-compulsive individual through my experiences. Perhaps, but I only know my regrets as being that I had brought my obsession to bear upon her in a manner that she was undeserving of and that she was merely a substitute for the one person I believe I did love.

She gave unconditionally and I took insatiably all that she gave and would have taken more until she had nothing left of her for herself. Perhaps by reading these facts, someone might glimpse the fear I feel when asked to look in a woman's purse, for any reason. Finding a tampon or feminine hygiene product, wouldn't phase me in the least, obviously, but the impossibly distant chance of finding an envelope addressed to another man I know remains a trigger for physical and emotional pain of epic proportions.

Why then do I no longer avoid requests of the nature - rejecting them as insensitive to my discomfort? Primarily because I don't see myself as deserving of the comfort of avoiding facing my fear. I'm not masochistic, don't enjoy self-inflicted pain, nor do I seek pain as some imagined punishment in order to redeem my past behavior by paying for them. I choose to embrace the pains I do as means or tools to be used for self-motivation in avoiding behaviors I no longer wish or desire to act upon.

Society's rules don't even apply to my choice in these matters. They didn't concern me when I was acting upon those behaviors, so it would be hypocritical to pretend they matter now that I choose not to continue those actions. By embracing the pain of legitimate remorse for my past behaviors, in addition to providing myself with motivational tools in avoiding those same behaviors, I have learned that I might be indirectly making amends to those I have or had, wronged with my very existence. I'm not certain if I even believe it as being possible and lack the faith it would require to believe that making indirect amends could somehow right the wrongs I have done to others in their lives for their sake. That appears too close to the magical thinking for my experience to allow, but it does provide a bandaging of sorts for my own wounds, providing me just enough relief to continue to make my choice each day, to not return to those behaviors that I know only offer temporary relief and greater pains afterward.

Unlike one particular 12-Step fellowships platitude about the past, I find comfort in my own saying: "I do regret my past, but refuse to shut the door on it." This physical journey I am on is my attempt to clear my mind and recover my heart.

Compleat
Family

About my brother, David, many people will question my decision to separate myself from my biological family, especially my brothers and sisters that I grew up with in St. Louis. Sometimes I question my own motives to face the choice as a choice and not simply carry a resentment. I use my relationship with David as an example here. I grew up fearing my brother. His volatile nature felt threatening to me all throughout my lifetime in both childhood and later as an adult, yet the threat and its subsequent fear had very little effect on my decision or the process by which I made my choice. Perhaps it was my experience with dying that removed my fear. Perhaps it had more to do with my other choices, deciding to release myself from the self-imprisonment of fears and resentments. I assume that the "why" of my letting go of that fear will be answered when all my other "why" questions resolve themselves.

What matters for me is the knowledge that it was not anger from fear that made it possible for me to release myself from that particular tie. Someone might gain the impression from my other stories that I was attempting to emulate Jesus by putting aside my biological family in order to embrace fully the family of spirit that came from becoming an adopted son of God. I did struggle with my ego over this issue, even arguing with myself, of both sides of this debate.

Compleat

As a son of God, my spiritual family did hold more importance and reverence in my feelings. But I am, and wasn't so easily fooled by my own ego into assuming this was my sole motivation and the fear I had felt along with the other resentments I had carried for so very long appeared to be the only reasonable explanation for my choice. Society could relate and grasp at understanding the fear of physical violence, the fear of being considered less than by the girls and women David seduced with an almost unnatural ease in my witnessing.

Then too, there remained the fear of being exposed by David for all the things we had done as children and young adults that we had shared equally in our experiences, especially the sexual escapades when we were too young to grasp the concept of consequences for our actions. Violence at levels that would have easily led to our being labeled insane. I remember tossing a stray cat into the air and punching it from one to the other and to a mutual friend, as if it was fun, exciting and some kind of sporting event. In the end, we were forced to throw the cat into a trash can because it had died during these heinous actions - beaten to death by these young boys who thought that it deserved to die for the sins of being a cat and a stray.

Debby Laurence's daughter, Shania, however, was a separating point for David and I. David had gone on to have sex with the mom while I had missed that opportunity, and that too was a resentment I held for many months until the day Shania had revealed to her mom what David and I had been doing to her and Abraham at the ages of 10 and 11 years of age. Debby Laurence became crazed with anger for what I had been doing to her three-year-old daughter, never mind that she had been to bed with David's charming way of seduction, or perhaps because she had, she was more incised with David than with me. While confronting our parents with the facts, David was automatically judged to be guilty of the things Shania had accused us of. Yet, Debby allowed my mom to question if I had done these things as well. I had. David knew I had. He witnessed my actions as we took turns touching and tasting the young girl, but all it required for my mom to dismiss my involvement was for me to deny it and David to not refute my denial, which lends to why I avoid David - not for the secrets he kept, but for the deserving guilt I feel about his having kept them on my behalf.

All my life, I had feared and resented David. All my life, I had envied both his ability to seduce women and his sexual involvement with both our sisters. I had hated and envied him so long, wishing I could be as he was and not be afraid because, in my eyes, David didn't know fear. He didn't enjoy pain.

Compleat

Beatings were just as bad for him to endure but he did things, acting out on his impulses and desires. Sometimes I still wonder if he had the cognitive ability to reason things through and fear the consequences, or if he was just unaware enough to not foresee what the results of his actions would be.

Maybe I judged him too harshly, but I became convinced David was too ignorant to even feel fear. I choose not to go around him because I know that I would be incapable of hiding the pity I feel for him now and that I know to be judgmental, hurtful, and wrong. I'd rather he assumed I hated him for the resentments of my past than to know that I pity him. He's a living example of the curse that the Runner men seem to bear - unable to maintain a lasting, stable relationship and/or avoid substance abuse problems.

Definition of stupid: Willfully ignorant, not unintelligent.

I mentioned David's sexual involvement with both our sisters as a means of transitioning to subject of my sisters, starting with Belinda. One reason I stayed away from my mom, and I admit there were a lot of excuses I used as well, was Barb's death. I've already talked upon my responsibility, but I need to mention how my mom reacted to Barb's death. That estranged me from my mom more than any of my mom's other actions. I could talk about why I felt responsible or repeat my story of being threatened for not showing grief properly, but what I need to mention in my is my mom's attempts to sanctify Belinda in death. My mom had beat Barb, calling her a whore, slut, etc... And I couldn't count how many times I had witnessed a lifeguard at the Marquette public pool sneak Belinda into the first aid room in order to fuck her at 14 or 15 years of age. The lifeguard was 21 or older as I remember. Yet, when Belinda died - at the viewing or funeral home - my mom had insisted on telling everyone Belinda had died a Virgin.

I hated having the knowledge of the truth and having no one to tell or speak to about it. And that truth would combine with the with the one of my having wanted to have intercourse with Belinda the night she died, sealing itself inside me and corrupting me to where I knew hate for myself, for my mom, for David and Violet, and for Barb. I hated that rather than have sex with me, she became so stressed that it triggered one of her epileptic seizures leading to a grand maul seizure, where she died drowning in her own blood. In my other stories about Belinda, I share that she was the only member of my family I admired, looked up to as being smarter than myself and trusted her more than I ever could my mom, dad, stepdad, or anyone else I knew. I thought highly of her and the idea that she would rather die than have sex with me, even just the idea or risk of trying anything would have been an acceptable answer, even a simple no, devastated me.

But she grew afraid of me I assume became stressed, started experiencing her seizure and then she died.

What does it say when the person I loved most in life would rather die than share with me that action she had shared with my brother David, with my mom's lover, Aiden Addis and with complete strangers at a public swimming pool? What did that say to or about me? Did Belinda love me so much that it killed her to know I wanted her that way too, or did learning I wanted her throw any love she might have felt into fear, causing her so much stress that it triggered the seizure at the ending of her physical life.

To fear me in any way was to hate me. I feared myself after that night and the next morning I hated myself – and I couldn't speak to anyone. They were all wrapped in their own grief, even David with his inappropriately touching two girls at once was able to openly share some semblance of pain.

I could not. Belinda was dead. It was my fault and I hated her for not wanting to be with me physically so much that she chose to die instead, I was 14 years of age, an unlovable and incestuous monster who had driven his sister to die rather than be with him. So, David, and to some extent, Violet - the other sister I suspected had allowed him privileges I was denied - became targets for my anger at first, then simply joined our younger half-brother, Abraham, who had been molested by David and I when we were abusing Shania Laurence and in apathetic obscurity, they just didn't matter to me any longer. I neither loved or hated them. I didn't like or despise them either. Even David's opportunistic copping feels on two girls at once at Barb's funeral and Violet's hysterically yelling how it was her fault for not being there eventually faded into the apathy for them or about them.

Long before our mom died - even before her dementia progressed to where she no longer recognized anyone who knew her - I stopped fearing Violet's rejection of me in favor of David's attention and David's successfully obtaining those things I saw as so important. Their physical presence became a non-irritant. Yet as I grow more apathetic towards those aspects, I grew sympathetic slightly, empathetic toward the knowledge that my presence might not be sought and desired by social standards. The truth I carried inside would only bring them pain. Based on that knowledge, I made the choice to wait until our mom died and with that final link broken, allowing them both to become distant memories.

Compleat

Compleat

The Red Rose & The Blue Rose

When facing trial for having committed the crime of rape I attempted suicide by drinking a gallon of whiskey and eating a full pound of strychnine-laced gopher bait and then hiding in a place that I thought no one would think to look for me until it was too late. Not even my then 2nd wife would guess until my corpse had been discovered. My plan failed because a gay man who was considered a friend by both Natalie and I, named Dom, thought to look in the one place I had been sure no one would even think to look for me.

I look back on that incident now and reflect on the fact that David, who had admitted to me that he was attracted to me and stayed in my group of friends in spite of the fact that I rejected his advances and informed him of my preferences for young women.

It never fails to perplex me that all gay men are viewed as potential pedophiles by the society in which I live but that priests, clergy, politician, and men who have openly displayed an attraction toward young girls (and in some cases boys) are given deferment about their obvious behaviors toward inappropriate sexual situations and are overlooked, simply because they are 'straight.'

Compleat

After that particular attempt, defeated by the care and concern of a gay man, I was placed in a treatment facility for both observation and oversight. My public defender suggested that I remain at that facility until the day of my trial, as it would "look good" to the courts that I was seeking treatment for mental health issues.

To jump forward a second and explain why I'm including this portion of this story I can mention that once in prison after my conviction one of the most common statements in the American Justice System's warehouses of prisoners for profit is that all public defenders ought to have their titles changed to public "pretenders."

There has never been a case where a public defender didn't make a deal, bargain, or trade with the District Attorney involved in a case where a conviction wasn't the result. Not a single one, if the inmates were to be honestly appraised and questions were to be asked.

The public defender's offices throughout the country are overworked, understaffed, and gain nothing in benefits for themselves for the nearly impossible tasks they are forced into by the Justice system that they had hoped to become a part of and provide honest service within. And honestly, most are from failed self-practices, if they ever gained that in their careers, or are idealistic younger lawyers who haven't been ground down by the weight of student loans and cases that they lost simply because the District Attorney involved in their cases undermined their attempts in order to maintain a high conviction record and continue to be re-elected.

Yet, this isn't a story about the busted justice system in the States. It is, in fact, about two women who shared one common name: Rose.

While in the treatment facility I met a woman who was of Spanish/Mexican descent. Her name was Rose and she was petite and beautiful, with dark hair and eyes and swarthy skin but what I loved most about her, despite my being a sick and twisted creature, was that the perfume she wore made her smell like roses. While we were confined there together, I learned that she had attempted suicide as well and because her family, being of the Catholic faith, abhorred the thought of her committing suicide they had forced her into treatment.

She wasn't there because she had done anything against the laws, although in the States suicide attempts are considered a 'crime' of sorts. She was confined there to overcome her depression and help her see that life was too precious to waste by killing herself. I learned from her that her husband was a successful construction business owner and that they had two small children - a boy and a girl. But I also learned that even in treatment she could not escape being pressured by her family and her husband into doing the role of a wife to a successful businessman.

Every week, and only once each week, her husband would come to the facility, bringing his business checkbook and the household expenses checkbook, and demand that she balance them with their bank statements. I often wondered if the reason why was because he could not do the math himself but eventually grew angry and believed that he used her as an accountant, demanding her 'services' and resenting her for inconveniencing him by being in treatment.

I was there for having committed a heinous crime against a young teenage girl, yet I grew to hate him for treating her the way he did. My hatred, I would learn much later, stemmed from my own pain and self-hatred.

He was in a situation to be this woman's hero, help her, provide for her, be there for her as a friend, life mate, husband, and father to their children and he either was totally unaware of her as a person, or he was cruel to her out of some cultural upbringing that made her less than he was to himself.

Since this was also long before I came to swear to never harm a human being, I would dream many nights of killing this person, this man who had all that I never had with someone who loved him. It would take years of therapy to realize that what I hated most about his behaviors was that I identified myself in them back when I betrayed the one person who I knew I had loved and had believed with all my heart, had loved me.

The signs were there when Rose and I talked, that she was lonely, frightened, vulnerable, and most, of all, needed someone to care. Predator or not, criminal or not, I felt her love and longing from across every room we would be in and at every chance passing in the halls of that place.

I refrained from speaking to her about it, respecting her position as a wife and mother to the best of my ability until I learned that he had once again brought the household checkbook to her, making her responsible for paying all the bills, planning the meals, ordering the groceries and providing for their children's child care services.

That night, I couldn't stand it any longer and, although the staff watched for inappropriate visitations in the night, I found myself sneaking into her room directly across from my own. We kissed, I held her, and we lay down together in her bed, without a single word being spoken between us. I cannot say how far we would have gone that night, though I believe we would have had sex and I would have slept the rest of the night there with her in my arms.

But one of the staff at that place had observed me moving from my room into hers. Why they waited as long as they did to check up on her, to be sure my attentions weren't unwanted, I cannot say. What I do know is that by the time we were laying together, and had begun whispering to one another while kissing, holding, and being close, the staff member who had watched me enter her room also entered and told me that I needed to return to my own room immediately.

The opportunity to be a hero for her passed that night and I will never know if the facility managers reported our behavior to her husband and family or not, but the next day Rose left the facility, to return to her family and children.

In the story about my sister, Belinda, I shared that after her death I had never been able to cry aloud or openly about anything. 24 years had passed without my being able to shed a single tear over any emotional event in my life. Yet when Rose had been taken from the facility, I wept aloud, not out of jealousy, not even out of anger.

Her loss from my life triggered something inside me and all I could answer when asked "Why are you crying?" was the phrase "I didn't get a chance to tell her goodbye."

Rose triggered an opening inside me that hadn't been opened in so very long I had completely forgotten that I was even capable of feeling. I cried because Rose was gone, that was obvious to the staff, Natalie, and the therapists. But none of them knew that inside I was also crying for the loss of a sister from 24 years before I ever ended up there.

And once again, I couldn't communicate with anyone what I was feeling. I didn't know how or the words that could explain it. I don't think I have those words, even still, today. I am grateful for that pain though. It drove me to actually commit suicide later with the result that I finally got treatment for all the mental health issues I had grown up with and through. The red rose of my life had thorns that tore my skin, pierced my heart, and then faded away, never to be seen again. That was the red rose.

The Blue rose wasn't Caucasian in genetics, skin tone, upbringing, or even lifestyle. This Rose stood equal to my six feet of height, outweighed me by about 20 pounds, and was so very much stronger than I was that if she wanted to, she could easily have broken my back unintentionally when we hugged. Hawaiian-born, she was so sure of herself and knew what she wanted for herself, her children, and her life that I was amazed when she let me know she found me attractive. She would come to know of my conviction for rape but believed me when I said that I am on a path of recovery where I will do absolutely anything to avoid repeating the behaviors that I had grown up making.

I met her at a 12-Step meeting and we 'clicked' almost immediately. Sharing, talking, joking with innuendo, and expressing a mutual interest in becoming physically involved. While I had four years of clean time or recovery, she was newer to the lifestyle and I would learn much later that being involved with a newcomer is not a well-advised approach to a program of actual recovery.

Looking back at it now, so many years later, I question myself as to why I became involved with Rose. Her strength was amazing to me, her humor almost brutally funny. She even suggested that I had a physical attraction to her sister (which I did and she had noticed) but she didn't grow angry with me for it, just using it openly in discussion with both myself and her sister present just to watch me blush and stammer through that conversation. She was teasing me openly to let me know she saw the attraction and at the same time cool my jets from any thought of acting upon it. Her security in her own attractiveness was something I had only encountered once before with Mona and I was fascinated by the fact that this wonderful woman found me attractive.

Whether or not she was actually clean from drugs is something I often questioned to myself but chose to believe she was in order to remain in her good graces and be with her in a relationship that was both physical and emotional. Dealing with my borderline personality disorder as well as my depression, Rose was a godsend as possibly my first female friend since my loss and losing of Megan. What we shared wasn't love exactly, more of a mutual interest and exploration of what it might become if we were to continue and see what came of being with one another as a couple.

For myself, I feel I might have been able to find happiness with Rose. Yet, it didn't work out that way for either of us. There came a night when Rose, her sister, and her older son went out together. It was one of those occasions that made me question if she was still involved in the drug use and selling lifestyle, but I had agreed to watch her two youngest children, both daughters, one of whom trusted me in much the same manner as Regina had those many years before.

I hadn't thought about those types of feelings since my release from the institution in 1993, believing myself to have faced those particular demons and having put them behind me forever. And although I never acted upon them, when the older of her two youngest daughters wanted to be held, tickled, and played with, I felt a stirring of those feelings within me that I had had toward Regina. I knew instantly that I could have taken advantage of her need for a father figure who loved her and, that if I did, the end result would have been much the same as it had been with Regina. Angelina trusted me, wanted me to be her dad, and would have done anything I asked, without question.

I left their house as soon as I possibly could, which meant that when Rose returned from what it had been that she was doing, I bolted out the door without explanation or hesitation. I sought advice from the only person I knew at the time that I trusted with my entire history, Lee, my sponsor in that 12-Step program. And with his supportive observations and suggestions as to knowing myself and how I needed to act, I went to Rose and ended our relationship.

Her friends would get angry with me for it, often expressing that anger both in meetings and aside, for dumping her as abruptly and without explanation as to why, because even though I told Rose exactly why I had to end our relationship, I wouldn't share with them my thoughts or what I had felt that night. I just knew that I would do 'anything' to prevent myself from returning to the behavior of abuse that I had done even before I went to prison.

My recovery, I had discovered, wasn't just abstinence from drug use, it was a determination to live according to the principles that I was learning and that meant being honest even if it hurt both Rose and myself. I wouldn't take the risk of abusing the trust and love of a little girl again, even if it meant I had to lose a chance at finding someone who might actually love me in return.

I'm grateful to her friends though it hurt terribly to be hated once again, their anger showed me that they would be supportive of Rose, through the difficult days of our relationship ending and possibly her own recovery from substance abuse issues. I learned that day that even a Blue rose has thorns, and it only took one to lead me to choose to distance myself from what I wanted, admired, desired, and might have grown to love.

Compleat

Compleat

Definition of Nightmare
_._._._._._._._._._._._._._._._._..

night·mare | \ ˈnīt-ˌmer \

1: an evil spirit formerly thought to oppress people during sleep

2: a frightening dream that usually awakens the sleeper

3: something (such as an experience, situation, or object) having the monstrous character of a nightmare or producing a feeling of anxiety or terror

Merriam-Webster's dictionary defines the word night-mare as consisting of the two root words: night - meaning the nocturnal portion of every 24-hour period on the planet Earth. And mare: the root word formed much earlier than many people realize since it is used most commonly as being related to a female horse in current usage.

But even the archaic use of mare: a demon or evil spirit that would torment human beings isn't how I would define the word nightmare. I've experienced many bad dreams that would awaken me from a sound sleep, drenched in sweat and barely able to catch my breath.

Compleat

As a child, one of the most horrific ones I would frequently experience would be an obscure figure of gigantic proportions chasing me until I would grow so weak and exhausted from running that I would collapse and know that I was about to experience dismemberment and suffering. My sole resource in those nightmares was to cover my head with an imaginary blanket, hiding from the figure and holding on to the hope that because I couldn't see it, it wouldn't be able to see or find me.

Even recently I've experienced what society around the world would call a 'nightmare' in which I was visited by a figure, female in form though obscure to where I could not make out her facial features or the color of her hair (though it appeared to be of some great length during the dream). She was engaged in holding my wrists apart as far as I could reach while coupling with my erect penis so violently that it would eventually awaken me with the pain it was causing my physical self. Was this the mare of ancient descriptions, I was forced to wonder, due to the physical evidence of what I had experienced presently after I awoke.

My member was burning as if it had been exposed to some chemical that would cause inflammation/redness, especially around the crown or head of my penis. Because I was still aroused from the dream experience and had not achieved an orgasm or release of my own I had assumed at first I had somehow massaged or rubbed myself raw, but then I noticed physical imprints of digits on both my wrists, 3 separate digits, and a thumb-shaped one in the locations where the figure had been holding me down, but with what would have been the 'finger' digits located atop my wrists and the thumb imprint wrapped around and under my wrists as if the implements holding me were reversed from human digits where the thumb is the opposing digit to the rest of the fingers. The third evidence of a physical manifestation consisted of material that I remembered to be consistent with and reminiscent of having engaged in sexual intercourse with a woman. The physical leavings from a woman on my penis from having had sex was accumulated around and under the ridge of my penis, but rather than the human female's leaving after sex, this substance had something other than just the normal texture, consistency, and viciousness of a woman. The color was gray, like used steel wool, but the texture and smell were consistent with the leavings from a woman having had sex with me.

But all of that is consistent with Webster's dictionary definition of a nightmare. My own definition was altered two days later when I experienced a dream that was so realistic that I felt I had traveled back through the illusion of time, to a day when Megan and I had the opportunity to be completely naked with one another in her family's basement. During the dream I re-experienced all the desire, lust, compassion, passion, love, need, awe, wonder, and trust I felt that day so long ago.

And although I desired her physical form as if I were the teenage boy I had been as well, there was something in the dream that I would have missed if all I was interested in was her body. In Megan's eyes, I saw the desire, passion, love, and wonder of our being naked with one another. Others credit that with it being just a reflection of what I myself was feeling for her, but in her eyes shone a light of trust that went beyond anything I could have felt or experienced. She trusted me with her entire self, physically and emotionally in a way I had never experienced before and would never experience again in all my years of living.

It was in that instant of recognition, the knowledge of that unconditional trust and by trust, I define love in its purest form, I woke up. It was waking, and knowing that I had betrayed all that I would ever know as love, all that she could have been in my life, that would redefine the word nightmare for me, forever.

A nightmare isn't a demon or evil spirit sent to torture or torment me. It isn't even something that requires a nocturnal setting for the event to occur. It is every waking moment of existing in a world where I burned the only bridge to love unconditional and the knowledge or knowing that that burning was irreparable and forever.

Compleat
Whole Humanity

I know from reading history that the human race, as a whole (percentage-wise), will find my claim to have met god face to face to be ludicrous at best and for some, it will appear to be outright blasphemy. Although I have no hope or chance of convincing anyone of changing their thoughts about my proclamation, I also know that there will be a few that will hear what I say with both an open heart and an open mind. It is to those folk that this story is directed in explanation of why I'm even bothering to speak out at all. I owe them that.

When I committed suicide, I was running away from the possibility of experiencing even more pain than what I had already suffered through my lifespan and more honestly and accurately I was attempting to avoid the responsibilities of my own actions as well as the commission to speak on what I had experienced to anyone.

In the society in which I was raised, they being predominately Christian, to speak in this manner aloud was to be deemed either a religious zealot or insane. Because my stance toward organized religion is so adamantly against the connection between finances, politics, and the use of religion to manipulate masses of under-educated individuals it was much easier for the system to label me as insane.

And I have chosen to embrace that label, though not perhaps in the manner in which it was intended. The stigma of mental illness isolates and separates individuals from the communities, societies, and even countries in which they reside. That was the intended purpose of my being labeled insane. Yet I embrace the label in such a way as to reverse the very stigma that it's apparently superior individuals chose to perceive it to be. By their very rejection of what I have revealed, they offer me the opportunity to perceive not merely the system by which they judge me but also the very individuals themselves for what they are doing.

In some cases, most, in fact, those who view my statements as insane do so out of ignorance or knowledge of the facts that I am presenting. To hear something so far out of their own experience and be able to perceive the truths being expressed are frightening, unsettling and in some instances terrifying to the point that their feelings force them to reject what they are listening to without hearing the actual words themselves and causing them to become incapable of perceiving anything beyond what their own limited experiences have allowed them to know.

In other cases, the ones that know what I'm expressing is not merely possible but an actuality and extremely probable, they find themselves threatened by what I'm expressing because it reveals to those around them that they have been deceived and are being deceived in order to manipulate and control them. A mob mentality must be controlled and maintained at all costs or they become vulnerable to the repercussions from of their deceptions being discovered.

It is the epitome of irony that I have no fear of either of them, nor need they have any fear of me or my revelations. In both cases, the mistake that is most commonly referred to when I speak publicly about my experience is one in which I am seen as trying to appear as more than human, superhuman or godlike. I am not. Not godlike, not superhuman, and not even human in my own view of myself. And my reasons for not believing myself to be any of these is simple.

In meeting god, the divine being, whatever name or label one would give life, the universe or existence itself, I was altered in a way I find difficult to explain. I admit that freely and without hesitation. But what altered within me was not that I became better than or even worse than human. I became something other than human. For all that the human race perceives as being godlike, superhuman, or even human is, in fact, the essence of what it was to be human. I lost that thread of connection to the human race, and separated myself from humanity not just through the experience itself but through my response to the experience as well.

In rejecting what I was requested or required to do, I forced myself into a place outside of both time and space. Beyond heaven or hell, both places I passed through on my flight from humanity, I knew myself to exist, and yet where I was nothing else existed. I knew of, that small word OF making so much more sense of the experience, existence, life, light, humanity, the universe, and beings outside the veil of normalcy and was given the knowledge I did not want nor did I seek to understand it.

I mention in several different stories that to truly understand another, one would need to be that other even for an instant. Life or god, however one chooses to label it or him, experienced life as a human being repeatedly, until choosing to experience it from birth to death and beyond. Wise men and women throughout the ages of human history have tried and failed to express all that it is to be human. Given opportunity after opportunity humanity has rejected or only semi-embraced those truths that were revealed age after age. It is my perception that the place I experienced that day was where life, existence, or god resided before creation, evolution or even the 'big bang' physical phenomenon occurred.

So, god, or as I call him pop, decided to experience humanity as a human being for himself. People who find the idea of Jesus being only divine simply focus on the divine as being something separate from themselves, often ignoring his own humanity. Those who reject his divinity also view it as something separate from themselves. Yet none of them can deny that they are alive. And in being alive, in having life or existence itself they share in the divine whether they embrace that truth or not. The old standard joke goes:

person #1 - "I don't believe in god."

person #2 - "That's okay, god believes in you."

How then can I, an existing creature on this planet, breathing the same air, drinking and needing the same water, eating the same food-like materials as some of you, claim to no longer be human? The manner in which I changed is obvious to me, because I'm inside this vehicle screaming to be released. Chained to a life I sacrificed and no longer wanted.

I am no longer human because in surrendering my existence to this life I became a tool. A non-human. An instrument to be used to deliver a message in the manner that a letter or even an envelope holding within it a letter can be used.

Some envelopes, some letters even, can be reused, resent, reissued, or forwarded to others. It is my fervent wish that will not be the case with me. Because the information I am sharing, while truthful and accurate, is not pleasant to hear. I do not bring a gospel, as one of my previous editors tried to re-title this book. Gospel means good news. And the message I bring, while clarifying what humanity has been missing, avoiding, and outright misusing, is not of a good news nature. I present to humanity the last voice of what god has spoken to them from the beginning.

Whether they are atheists, religious of any faith, or simply not bothered with the whole of the arguments that have been running on and on throughout history, the truth is that humanity is facing extinction by its own hand, even as I faced death by my own hand and succeeded.

And the divine, god, life whatever label anyone chooses to give existence will not interfere. No divine intervention will be forthcoming. It still hurts some part of me to speak those words even on paper.

Magic thinking ingrained in my personality makes me wish I were human enough to believe or hope that god will alter what is to make it more as humanity needs it to be. But the price of knowledge was the humanity I will never regain. And The saddest and, most ironically unfunny bit of knowledge I was imbued with is that humanity has the divine right, power, ability, and responsibility to do all that they seek from god for themselves. To see that knowledge, to know what humanity is capable of doing for itself and not be able to communicate with humanity because I am no longer human myself is one reason why I scream so at being confined in this semi-existence.

I don't blame or judge anyone who rejects what this book communicates. I blame only myself for not having the ability to speak in such a way as to convince the whole of humanity of the truth of what I'm expressing. I see humanity teetering on the knife's edge of extinction and cry out to you all that it doesn't have to be this way, to end this way. And although humanity is a whole, like a single entity to me, with various persons being parts of the whole with their individual purposes both good and bad, I cannot gain all of your attention in order to prevent what you could avoid if only you would come together as the whole that you are.

Compleat

Compleat Non-Nobility

"I AM not god. But I had played god in someone's life that I knew I couldn't live without, throwing away my one chance at true love and happiness. Maybe that's what being the devil in someone else's life really is: choosing for them instead of communicating what is real?"

I took the above quote from the story labeled 'A Girl and the Devil in His Day.' My reason is that I want to dispel any thoughts or concepts that leaving her was some noble act on my part. Yes, I was a teenager, and yes, I was trying to protect her from what I saw myself as in my youth and fear. Those details might lead some to be willing to accept and forgive my behavior that night.

But I need to emphasize the facts, the truths that might be lost in my making the choice to protect her from me. I didn't just dump her intentionally. I chose that Halloween night to go with the other girl, not simply because I knew it would end the way it did. I also chose it because I wanted to have sex with someone who I thought of as being unable to be hurt.

There's an old adage that says "You cannot have your cake, and eat it too." I wanted to keep Megan, the pure and perfect love of my life, and still get laid. It is with guilt, not shame, that I admit if her sister hadn't spotted me, if Megan hadn't seen me with the other girl, I would have embarked on the deception of having a double life.

One love. And one fuck.

I had no problem with the idea of separating the two as if sex wasn't a part of loving someone. I was and am an asshole. It wasn't until I died that I realized the other truth that this action revealed.

Many people say "God damn you." The truth I'm mentioning here is the fact that god doesn't damn anyone. Human beings have done it to themselves for so long that it's become not just acceptable but through apathy, it's become what humanity views as being the normal. And all the while blaming god for how messed up things are.

Compleat

I damned myself long before I committed suicide. Much longer before the day when I told god to go fuck himself. Perhaps in telling god I could run the world better than he ever thought of he allowed me to run my own life from the moment of my birth. And I damned myself by every action that led me to what I was that night.

If, as I believe possible, god forgives the human race and if by sharing all this that he insisted I share with humanity you folk, those reading this or just hearing about it, get another chance then being damned myself would be worth not being forgiven. That's not noble of me, it's simply accepting responsibility for being who and what I am.

Insight Into God

———————————————————————

The experience of meeting god face to face did something to me that I feel might need explanation even if no one ever believes what I say about the experience. It stands to reason that most will dismiss what I say as either hallucination or my insanity yet I still persist in expressing this point.

During the encounter, I received knowledge, that I often protest to both psychiatrists and psychologists I never wanted or needed and indeed tried very hard to resist, to the point of raging at the being that sat before me. Obviously, that attempt failed even worse than all my attempts at suicide, since like my being here, the knowledge is within me still.

One of the many reasons I chose to write this book is to share that knowledge in an effort to relieve myself of it. It is my hope that if I share it, the burden of knowing will be lessened, like the sharing of a load of bricks for building, each share giving a portion of the weight to others until it becomes manageable for all.

In standing before god, much like the Buddha looking inward or contemplating his own belly button, I was exposed to my actual self. Not only was I the monster I had created, the human being that had grown up among other human beings, but I saw the god of my being myself. Inside each and every human being there exists a portion of self that is labeled many different things. Some choose to call it a soul. Others choose to call it the Id or consciousness. And still, others simply recognize it for what it actually is: life.

That life, the mere state of existence, is the portion of a human being that is the god inside themselves. The Christian mythology that is normally taught recognizes only Jesus as being able to forgive sins, heal the sick, raise the dead or walk on water. The standing joke is that no one walks on water and usually the challenge put to those who recognize the god within themselves is that very testing of their claims. "If you're a child of god, just like Jesus, why don't you walk on water?"

About myself and my experience though I can share this information. I don't hear voices inside my head, and during my experience with god, he didn't say things or 'tell' me to do all that I'm attempting to do in this book. In fact, this book is, in a way, an apology to the god I encountered for not doing all that was suggested or requested of me in that encounter. During that encounter, one of the two in which I knew myself to be in a place outside of time and space or existence as a human being, the knowledge I received wasn't expressed in words at all. It was a sharing that lasted only an instant in what humanity calls time yet lasted for eons for me until I raged against what was being shared, pointing out that my life was a mess, that I was afraid and angry with my own behaviors throughout my twisted existence and not worthy of being given the task god was asking of me.

I rejected god totally, not because god didn't exist or the task was too hard. I rejected the assignment because I knew myself in that instant as being less than what I thought god needed. And like with my first love, Megan, I decided what was best for everyone else involved without asking anyone. Knowledge of self, even though it is the only thing that will release a human being from self-delusions and pre-programmed thinking, isn't the easiest thing to bear. Like the proverbial cross that the J dude said to pick up and follow him with though, - it's the only way to be what human beings were meant to be.

Knowing can come in an instant, as it did for me that day. Or it can come over a lifespan of experience as it happens with many who age beyond where they thought or even expected they would. With For some human beings that knowledge can become a bitterness that turns them against themselves and appears as vehemence toward those around them. But what appears as anger toward all others is in actuality regret that an awakening to themselves, and who they really are, took so long in their lives that they missed opportunities to be themselves. Yet with some human beings, the knowing of themselves brings a kind of acceptance of who they are, were, and were always meant to be. I had to die to find that acceptance of myself.

Knowing myself that day I saw only my flaws, mistakes, and misdeeds and tried to weigh them against any potential I saw in myself. It is ironic that my very flawed nature, my inability to be a 'good' person as defined by the societies of the world, would make me the very instrument that the divine wanted to use. That I rejected and feared myself in the position I was shown to be as what might be required of me, wasn't a failure of some type of testing. In the first place, I can state truthfully, god doesn't administer tests. In the second place, what I saw as a failure to comply with the will of the divine, the rage, and rejecting rejection of what was being asked of me in that instant, was actually the expected result god was looking for from me.

There are those, like Mohammad, Jesus, and the rest who did god's bidding without resistance. They shared immediately exactly what it was god wanted them to share. And humanity twisted their words to create religions and, divisions among yourselves. Holy men, prophets, and even the conceived son of the divine all told human beings the same things, year after year after year. So, god, as I know him again and not to impose him on anyone else, picked the least likely candidate for the job of sharing this go around. Me.

I have to state again, in case anyone missed it before in this story, I do not hear voices inside my head. Not even god's voice! But the knowledge god shared with me that day remains inside me despite my best efforts to burn it out. It's from inside of me and yet it's not my own knowledge that I share, put there for a purpose that I don't fully understand, and often find myself questioning what god was thinking when he picked me. But even in a broken brain can come answers that make sense. Like adding one plus one plus one plus one to equal four it becomes simpler to add 2+2=4. And for me, it became simpler still to add it all up as 4=4. The obvious answers are the ones most often dismissed.

Compleat

Simply Put

There are so many things that I have wanted to express to the whole of humanity. And while my own self-doubt, angst, and fears of being as insane as I've been labeled have held me back from saying most of them in the end, I really have had no choice but to speak aloud what I was shown or told to say.

The race of humankind is like unto a teenager who wishes to remain a child, with all the privileges and rights thereof yet avoiding the responsibilities of growing into adulthood out of fear of the burdens that same adulthood will require of them.

The transition from childhood to adulthood has been difficult, trying and testing the patience of the one they call god, the father of all. He has sent to you both men and women of great wisdom, insight, and amazing truths and at each, their words and sharing haves been twisted and turned into that which befouls their efforts into the disease that is labeled by humanity as 'religion.'

Compleat

Eventually, he chose to come among you himself in the form of the human child known as Jesus for two reasons. The first, obvious to many, was to express and display just what being a human being is, was, and always will be, his children, friends, companions, and equals. The less obvious reason, one that he had to reveal to me because I am nothing like those who were good, honest, pure, and descent individuals, was that he showed humanity that he, god, wanted you to know that he understood what it is to be human.

The concept that to 'understand' a human being one person would have to be that other person or have the ability to read their minds so completely that they thought the way the other thought, felt the way the other felt, and did as the other did stemmed from that fact.

He came to know humanity as a human being. So that excuses like the familiar "no one's perfect" couldn't be held up as a reason for not accepting the responsibilities he had placed on humanity at the creation of the race. The irony of that statement conflicting with your own adage of "god doesn't make any junk" is so pathetic that it brings the saddest of smiles to his face and tears to his eyes. Because the second statement is a truth that he meant for humanity to discover for itself. And the first statement was the beautiful lie that human beings have been telling themselves for far too long.

Why then am I sharing this information with you here? Am I vying for a position of authority on who or what god is? Not in the least. I want no recognition, no favors from a race that may well have doomed itself with apathy and ignorance. My example of a teenager afraid to grow up is how god showed me the entire human race.

I've stated, repeatedly, that I had to give up my own humanity as the price for that knowledge, so there are no benefits from exposing this information to anyone that could restore what I have lost. I recently shared with someone that I view myself as not being human and they automatically thought I was being arrogant, placing myself above humanity as a whole. The truth is that that couldn't be farther from how I have learned to perceive myself. I view myself as the bottom rung of the Jacob's Ladder that life consists of, watching humanity struggle and climb so much further up the ladder than I am capable of doing, and seeing from that perspective the wonder, beauty, grace, love, and absolute power each and every human being possesses. I can see, from my position below you, every misstep that is taken, every harm you cause one another and at the top of the ladder I see your goal.

Compleat

Humanity was always meant to share life (the real garden of Eden is that shared life) with one another and with god, as equals. All the divisions, separations, differences, and distances that exist between human beings and between you and god were never meant to be that way. He offered paradise and humanity refused it because, just as a teenager fears growing into adulthood, you fear taking the responsibility for yourselves. And sickeningly, you project that fear onto one another. Look closely at the phrase you use: "no one is perfect." You don't question that statement, don't even ask "why" it's universally accepted among yourselves. Is it because it's a truism? Not really. You accept it because if any one of you were to display perfection, you would be afraid that you each have the capacity to be and would be faced with the responsibility of not choosing to be yourselves. If you don't want to believe me, I can accept that easily, as the desire to not accept it is simply a reinforcement of what I've been trying to say.

And think of this fact, those of you who claim 'Christianity' as your chosen religion especially, what happens when someone shows humanity that perfection is possible? Yeah, they crucified him. Did it even slow him down? No, he merely showed humanity that death is a slave to your own will as human beings. I've written about my own encounter with death, and how she is burdened with the task of releasing human beings from this twisted existence that is labeled life here. But the task has been and always will be the race of humanity's responsibility. You placed it upon her, when the first life was ended by violence, whether it was Cain slaying his brother Able or any other mythology that includes violence begetting more violence.

I've told you what god taught me, about how violence breaks off a piece of the life of the human being committing the act, how I witnessed death at her task of picking up those shattered pieces of life, collecting them, and adding them to her burden of carrying on the task she was assigned, waiting for the day when humanity will finally stop and end her task at last. You might not believe me, but I can only share what I've personally experienced and witnessed, so whether you believe me or not remains your choice and thereby your responsibility.

There are other answers I've been given, ones I have no idea about why I was given them, who they were intended for, or, for that matter, when I'm supposed to deliver them. I was assured that I would be shown when, where, who, how, and what to do or say. But then too, I was assured by death herself, by smiling so comfortingly into my eyes, that when I called for her, she would come. I've called, repeatedly, and she still hasn't arrived, which makes me sad, to say the least.

I ask anyone reading this book, again, please – do not take my word for any of these things I reveal. In the first place, what I reveal here isn't mine or even my idea. They were put into my broken brain to share with all of humanity by a being I call pop, god or just the old dude. And they weren't meant for me, because I gave up my own humanity in order to attain the answers, even though they aren't the ones I was looking for.

Read, search, check, and counter- check for yourselves. Please? If you were to accept what I say without checking or finding out for yourselves, you'd be making a religion out of all that I share here.

And god, in his wisdom, despises religions. All of them.

Where Was God Before Then?

Atheists profess not to believe in god, though I suspect that most just don't want to buy into the whole religious bullshit that is pushed at them more than not believing in life itself coming into being. Added to their disillusionment by religion and religious zealots there are the simplistic arguments that most folks can use to question the existence of god or any divine being(s) that humanity has dreamed up or created for itself.

"If god exists, why does he allow bad things to happen to good people?" Assuming even as they ask it that there are such creatures as 'good' people or, in true narcissistic form, that they themselves are among the 'good' people they deem worthy of divine intervention to prevent bad things from happening to or with.

"If god is so omnipotent then why does he allow evil to exist?" And like Adam in the book that they call the Bible they avoid the responsibility of their own actions, even to the point of avoiding accepting responsibility for their fellow human beings, and try to toss the blame for evil existing back onto god. "The woman YOU gave me tempted me and I did eat.", said Adam.

Then there's the ridiculous argument of "If god is so powerful and almighty can god create an object so large even god cannot pick it up?" Beyond the point that even if he could, why would he attempt something so stupid? This argument is simply the basis of being able to argue, and has no meaning other than creating an atmosphere of debate with the religious. Put two opposite positions on an argument in a room with a crowd to witness and it's probably considered high entertainment. I know I would need to be 'high' in order to even listen to silliness like this for more than a few minutes before I'd change the channel or leave the room.

Then there's the other aspect, where people are hurting from the loss of the lives of those they love – children, parents, lovers, wives, husbands, and friends. They shake their fists at the sky (as if some holy spook off in space was responsible for their pain) and shout their questions of "Why, god? Why did you allow this to happen? Why wasn't it me? How could you take someone so young, precious, loved, needed, etc. … ?" Theirs is the atheism that rings closest to the truth, they choose to stop believing in god because they blame god for their pain. As if god singled them out specifically to inflict horrific pain on them and in most cases, they have secret reasons behind their questioning that they use to blame themselves for their loss. It's easier to blame god for their pain and not admit it than it would be for them to simply accept their secret reasoning, ask for forgiveness and recognize that the pain they feel is just that, their own. They blame god but secretly hold themselves responsible for the pain they feel. That's when the "what if's and what could I have done differently" keep them awake at night, or wake them from nightmares too terrible to discuss with anyone.

A theist is defined as someone who believes in something - from religions to science. Theist comes from the root word – theory. A concept that is considered but has no foundation in either physical evidence or proof until tested and verified with evidence that is repeatable and can be witnessed to become a fact.

An atheist is defined as someone who doesn't believe in the existence of 'god' or a divine being of any kind. And the definition is incorrect as is the title of atheist for those who don't believe in a god or being, because they too believe in a theory – that there is no god. A negative theory that has no foundation in evidence or physical proof, while at the exact same moment demands physical evidence of anyone presenting the opposite view of their own argument.

Religions do that a lot, the whole of circular arguments in order to avoid presenting factual evidence or proof that they are reporting more than just their own mythology as truth. And what is atheism, as it is currently defined, other than a religion that is embraced by those that choose not to believe in other religions? When someone identifies themselves as an atheist, I simply relabel them as being non-conforming religious zealots. Perhaps that's why, when atheists do convert or conform to a specific religion, that they become so adamant about pushing their 'new found' faith onto others, especially their own ilk of professed or professing atheists.

My last question to present on this subject has to do with both the theory of god existing and atheism. When asked about evolution scientists and those labeled atheists both expound on the belief that the entire universe was popped into being by something often described as the "Big Bang Theory." (I like the TV show of the same name because it shows science at its most vulnerable; Sheldon thinks WAY too much of his own intelligence!)

"Where was god before everything came into existence?" Religious people could well ask the same question in reverse "Where was the universe before the big bang?" In both cases no matter what answer might be given, those arguing either point would be presenting their own theories about their answers as if it they were established facts. And ironically, neither would accept the other's arguments as having any real value because it they simply didn't agree with their own position on the discussion.

Whether anyone credits my own experience of having met god face to face or not I can offer this one experience as additional information to support my statement. I died and, in the process, which came many years after I had met god, by the way, I witnessed places that are defined by religions as hell and paradise or 'heaven.' But I also witnessed and experienced a place that was utterly devoid of life and light, pain or suffering, joy or unhappiness. My senses were intact but there was an entire lack of any sort of physically recorded input.

Perhaps describing it as a 'void' would suffice for many except for the simple detail that I remained cognitive, awake, and aware of my surroundings as well as aware of life, light, people, existence, and even god as not being where I was; you were all outside of where that place is or was.

Why I experienced that 'place' I often questioned myself about because it surely wasn't a question I had thought to ask or present to god when I told him off. Eventually, I came to understand that the answer to that question lay in the question of 'where was existence or where was god' before it all began?' Their bible says "the spirit of the lord was over the deep" but doesn't describe what that 'deep' was or how it came into being. If, as I suspect, god was in the place I experienced when I died then I come to understand and express not simply the fact that god exists but also why he chose or would choose to exist. Breaking free from that place of non-existence myself, was something I hadn't expected to happen, I truly believed at that moment I was there and not going to be anywhere else and so I felt I could reasonably expect after telling god to go f himself and killing myself as well. With god, I consider that his choice to no longer reside in that place would indeed create a really "Big Bang" bringing life and creating light into existence with his appearance. It wouldn't have surprised me that god would have felt just as alone there as I myself did. And it fits one of my earlier ravings, "To truly understand another, one would have to experience what it was like to be that other, even for just an instant."

Compleat

Chicken or the Egg Answered At last

For philosophers throughout history one debate never seemed more pointless and unsolvable than that of the question of "which came first, the chicken or the egg."

A meaningless squabble of a discussion that has been the point of conversation from parties to politics for as long as humanity has had the willingness and desire to contend with opposite points of view on any number of subjects. Here was the 'unanswerable' question, the one that could never be resolved in a complete and adequate manner that would satisfy both parties in a discussion and would draw others into the conversation or debate whether its intent was serious or simply humorous.

So, of course, I got stuck with the one answer that makes sense of the whole issue and answers the question correctly for all involved. If a human being embraces the theory of creation, then the obvious answer would be that god created chickens first. Simplistic and easily embraced if one believes in god and that god created everything in the first place. But there are those who debate god's own existence, doubting the presence of a singular divine being that could or would create everything.

Compleat

Evolution they say means that every single organism on the planet rose from single cell life forms that were caused by chemical reactions between salt water, lightning, and foreign materials floating in the water itself. I remember one comic book that depicted life on this planet evolving from an alien taking a dump in the oceans of this planet while passing by it, like a galactic rest stop or outhouse, and smile at the memory because it would be just as likely to explain the outcome of life beginning on this planet through evolution as anything else humanity has been able to devise.

But with evolution even, the argument of the chicken or the egg is resolved by the fact that although the egg that was eventually hatched produced a chicken, it was laid by a reptilian creature that was evolving into a chicken, not a chicken itself. So, the chicken came first regardless, since the egg wasn't a chicken egg but a reptile egg and the chicken was a mutant version of that reptile.

Pointless as the argument has been, it's still used in debates and courses on how to debate from different perspectives in colleges to this day and age. Why god inflicted this answer on me I have no clue. It seems to me almost as if his sense of humor was to give me answers to questions I would never have thought or bothered to ask and see if I would even attempt to make sense of them.

Instead, I tried to ignore some of the more ludicrous ones, like this one for instance, until I am forced to awaken at 1 am in the morning to put them down for inclusion in this book. For those who don't believe in god, a divine being, a creator, or even the concept of such then perhaps you can embrace the concept that life has played jokes on humanity for ages and this is one of its longest standing jokes. Personally, I think the old dude likes messing with me because it makes me smile to know he has a sense of humor and he knows that about me, too.

When Was the Last?

Okay humanity, here's a quiz question for all of you adults out there. One that a child would know the answer to almost immediately, if asked, but adults tend to forget and need to think about the answer, trying to recall it though it probably should stand out if it was something human beings practiced on a regular basis.

Ready for it ?!

"When was the last time you walked barefoot through the grass, lay in a field by yourself on your back, and simply looked up at the clouds or at night, stared up at the stars and counted the number of shooting stars you saw?"

Any child could tell you and even recall the number of stars they saw or the shapes they witnessed in the clouds that day. They could tell you what the grass smelled like, where they were and what they were doing right up until they lay down in the grass. Because those things, those experiences, are important to children. They value them more than adults do, or at least they used to until the modern age stole those experiences from them by giving them electronic worlds to explore, virtual grass to experience, and stars and clouds made up of data bytes that they could manipulate and move around as they saw fit.

But how many adults indulge in play like that still, honestly? How many of you can even recall the last experience of any of those childlike things happening in your own life?

My reason for asking is that I had that question in mind when I met god, and it was one of the few that I had wanted to ask for myself that he answered. Why do adults not recall those moments of happiness and sheer joy of being that all of childhood was wrapped around and meant to be? His answer surprised me and though it might offend some of you, especially those of you who deny that you forgot the last episode of play that you experienced alone like that, I'm going to tell you his answer as to why you choose to forget those periods.

Humanity was given everything you could possibly want or need in the beginning. Life, the world, every living thing in it, on it, under it, and above it. It was all for humanity to enjoy. Every bird song was a medley of sounds that were meant for human ears to witness. Every light in the night skies and shining through the clouds with the first rays of dawn or the last rays of a sunset were was there for humanity to see and admire. It was all there, every sense, every feeling, every taste, and smell were there simply for human beings to enjoy. And as children do when given the chance you all did as well. So why then do you forget those experiences?

Why, I asked god, did I forget all that as well?

Adults forget those experiences, he said, because as they lay on their backs enjoying the clouds or walk through the woods listening to the birds and animals that still live in that garden-like estate adults enjoy it all, right up to the point that they become conscious of the fact that it is their responsibility to keep it that way.

Children don't worry about the responsibility; they just believe it will always be that way and simply enjoy it. But adults, caught up in the beautiful lie that they are powerless to do anything to change the world or better it or even better themselves (at that point in what he was saying to me he was so sad I thought god might cry tears for humanity) that they allow their memories to fade, forgetting about the joys and amazement they felt because they don't want to be held accountable or accept the responsibility of being stewards and caretakers of all that they were given.

It's easier for them to forget a cloud formation or the number of stars that fell from the sky or the scent of cut grass on a summer's day than face the responsibility to keep things that way. Some people blame the rich, greed being one of the worst things that block human beings from being true to themselves.

Others blame systems that are set up by others called governments or religions. But the fact stands that each and every human being has the ability and responsibility to care take care of the world around them as if it were their own, because, in the end, they are responsible, the stewards that god appointed to care for all of it, including each other.

I was embarrassed when god answered my question that day. Because I knew I was just as responsible and I had shirked that responsibility just as much as any other human being, perhaps even more since I had been so wrapped up in myself and what I wanted or how I thought things 'should' be going. The price of knowing was high for me. I had to give up that part of me that made me human in order to speak with and hear directly from god. Was it worth it? I often wonder about that as well as questioning for the longest time, "Why tell me?"

What humanity does with all that I share here in this book will be their choice to make. Ironically, I made mine when I asked for the knowledge I have gotten, thinking to call god's bluff when it came to sharing with someone who isn't a "good" person. And even more ironically, he reminded me of the story of Balaam in their Bible to set me straight on that answer as well. "If god can speak to Balaam through a jackass, what makes you think he can't talk to you through me?" I sure fit the description of being more of an ass than a human being at least.

Compleat

The Second Son That Almost Wasn't

In 1995 I moved from San Diego County California to a town called Windsor, in Sonoma County to be with a woman I had met online and who appeared to accept me for who I am, in spite of my past of having committed felonies, been incarcerated, and having had a four-year stay in Atascadero State Mental Hospital for the Criminally Insane.

Over the course of a year, before ever having met her face to face we had shared the details of our lives and I had told her the truth about myself in no uncertain terms. I made the assumption that if she were able to greet my past with the understanding and compassion that she appeared to show online then meeting her in real life was the next logical step.

We met at the Oakland, California Amtrak train station and I had hope that this would be the woman that would heal the part of me that had to do with loving and being with someone for the rest of my life. We met a few more times each month, my visiting her in her home in Windsor, and over the few months we were together I decided to take the action that would, in my opinion, make my choice permanent. I proposed marriage, in Shakespeare's Garden, near the Golden Gate Bridge in San Francisco. And she accepted.

As a recent divorcee and mother of a then thirteen-year-old boy, perhaps she saw it as a means to an end.? I was writing for a newsletter at the time, and submitting anonymous articles to various sources, while I had been working on this book for two years by then, so perhaps my 'potential' as a mate was less unattractive than raising her son alone, after losing the home she had been purchasing with her ex due to the mortgage being foreclosed upon after he had abandoned her for another woman? I only thought that perhaps she would be the one to heal my own heart and perhaps together we would build a life that made sense of this world, restoring to me a tiny piece of my humanity.

That dream lasted about as long as it takes to wake up with a cramp in my calf so severe that even sound asleep, I could dream I was experiencing one and wake to find it wasn't a dream. Online, in all the emails and chats we had shared, I had insisted that she 'check with her family and friends' before committing to becoming involved with me.

Compleat

I wanted to make sure she would be able to withstand the stigma of being with a known felon, pedophile, rapist, and criminally insane person. And before we had ever met face to face, she had insisted that she had spoken to them all, that they too would and did accept that my past was just that, my past. This small detail would be the first lie to begin the unraveling of any relationship I had hoped to establish.

Apparently, she had chosen to "let them meet you first, before they decide what to think of your past." I appreciated her choice, as it was hers to make and tried desperately to allow that her perspective of her own family and friends was much more important and probably more accurate than mine could possibly be, yet the sinking suspicion that she had kept it from them in order to not have them tell her to 'not get involved with 'him' started the cracks that would eventually end the relationship altogether.

Now, as an aside, what potential step-parent hasn't been met with hostility from the step-children in any relationship? Her then thirteen-year-old son, abandoned by his biological father, and living with his mother who would lose the home he had grown to think of as being his, met my relationship with her with open hostility and remarks.

He even went so far as to accuse me of being homosexual, since his mother had more hair on her arms than most men and definitely more than I had myself. I didn't care about the accusation of being homosexual but his use of his mother's appearance as a weapon offended me enough to tell him that when he turned 18, if he would want to repeat that statement aloud, I'd be willing to forego my pacifistic rational long enough to punch him in his mouth for disparaging her that way. He never spoke to me about that again, though he did continue to reject and disparage me in other ways throughout his teen years.

During our relationship, there were, as in all relationships, varying degrees of closeness and distance. When I jokingly decided to try to pick her up and put her on a scale that "tells your future" along with your weight in San Francisco, for example, she became extremely distraught that I would 'force' her to reveal her weight, left the store the fortunetelling scale was in and abandoned me in San Francisco, a city that I wasn't familiar with enough even to find my way back to the home I had established in Windsor for myself.

What I had seen as an attempt at humor, she had taken as an assault on her person, being forced to reveal her weight was something she was adamantly opposed to, while I couldn't have been less concerned about her weight and merely wanted to see the nonsensical 'fortune' that the machine would have provided her.

Rationally, I should have taken this as an advance warning of the differences in our perspectives, but I was trying to build a relationship. For my own healing, of course, it needs to be noted here, but that I was willing to do whatever she wished in order to build her confidence in trusting me to not be like her ex who had abandoned her. The relationship was founded, in my perspective, on allowing her to set the pace, make the choices and control the financial means by which everything would be done. Regretfully, all those precautions and the decision to place control in her much stabler hands and mind came to mean nothing.

By the year 1999, we had begun to experience as well as see things in different ways. Her insistence on the need for financial stability first had forced me into taking jobs I felt unqualified for, in spite of having attended college for their express purpose as well as aiding in my research into self-awareness of my mental health condition. We moved into a small house in the town of Healdsburg, California and our combined income was still barely enough to maintain a healthy lifestyle for ourselves and her son.

I recall that the utility bills for electricity alone were well into the $400 range every month and considering the small size of the house, seemed beyond astronomically absurd.

The town itself, however, was beautiful - especially in the spring when the trees along the streets would be in blossom with flowers that brightened the landscape as well as adding to the scents that made the town a place for just being.

On Tuesdays, again as an example, the local coffee house "The Flying Goat" would roast coffee beans, and the entire town smelled of freshly roasted coffee. (They have since been forced out of business by economic hardship but the memory of the smell lingers for those who were fortunate enough to have experienced it.)

In 1998, she would find through a store-bought test that she had become pregnant. Her teenage son would confess that he had perforated her IUD with needles in order for her to become pregnant, perhaps thinking that if she were faced with an unwanted pregnancy and chose to end it, I would leave her because he was well aware of my personal stance on the issue of abortion.

Compleat

I opposed abortion unless it was for the safety and well-being of the mother, but I also acknowledged that the choice to have an abortion would never be mine to make.

I am not a woman. As much as my views on abortion are pro-living, I am not one of those who claim to be 'pro-life.' Theirs is a lying position because they are pro-birth only, and disregard, neglect, demean and disrespect those who choose to follow through with having an unwanted birth.

Their choices are based solely on what they are taught by the religions that control their thinking to the point that they cannot or will not think for themselves. And the choice to carry through with an unwanted, undesired, and unable to afford to adequately provide for birth that would bring a child into this world should and always will remain with the woman who would be creating that life within herself.

This woman knew my position on abortion, and chose for herself to carry through with it to the point that we were getting into my vehicle, to drive to have the procedure done since I supported her right to choose, in spite of my personal feelings against what was about to occur. It was at that moment, getting into the vehicle, that she changed her mind about carrying through with the abortion. Her statement to me, later confirmed in writing in case I were ever stopped by law enforcement with my son in my custody, was simple and to the point:

(an aside that I have only revealed to my psychiatrist until writing it here: she had gone so far as to have the fetus tested to determine its sex and told me that if it had been a female fetus, she would have carried through with the abortion anyway, to prevent me from having a daughter to be in my care for any reason)

"If I have this child, he will be your responsibility, period." And although the hospital would put her ex-married name on the label placed on the newborn child on March 25th, 1999 my second son would be born and come into my care and responsibility. His birth certificate would reflect that I am his male parent, as well as her being his mother.

But he would be my responsibility, to raise and provide for until he gained the ability to reason and provide for himself. I had been a father, and stepdad-father, to 4 children back in the late 1970's and early 1980's but I had failed in epic proportions to become a dad to any of them.

Compleat

There, in 1999, I was being given a second chance to be not merely a biological father, "Any dog can father a pup." I was being given a second chance at being a dad. And I would learn that being a dad requires more than a penis hanging between my legs, it requires being a man in a lot greater sense of the word than that physical member on my body.

Compleat

Daddy Magic

Learning how to be a dad was something I was gifted with the second go around. My first attempt at being either a dad or step-dad failed because I thought of myself first and foremost and the children involved as mine. Possessions, or extensions of myself in the case of my first-born son. My step-children, I treated as if they were parts of their mother, my first wife Denise. I had tried to love her, but knew deep inside that it wasn't her I was interested in loving, because her love was conditional. I saw myself as the paycheck that would provide for the three children she brought to the relationship and no more.

With the birth of her fourth child, my first son Michael Lee, the relationship we had shared became more than simply strained. I became more and more apt to act out on both unfaithfulness and inappropriate behaviors toward the children I thought of as hers but also thought of as my possessions because I 'loved' them more than she did.

The disaster that would end that relationship is in another story, however, and I only mention it here to bring to bear that being a father is much different than learning to be a dad. As I've said before, "Any dog can sire a pup off a bitch that he impregnates, but it takes a man to be a dad to the children in his life – be they his children by marriage or by birth."

I was the dog that brought a child into this world but had no idea and no right to call myself a dad to any of the four in my first attempt due to the fact that I was not just unqualified, I was unfit mentally, emotionally, spiritually and in my twisted soul.

Compleat

The second chance I received to become a dad I've shared in this book elsewhere but the things I've learned about being a dad instead of just a sire or father could fill a book of its own. There is so much that having a second son took me through that I wish I knew how to share it with every man, young or old, who fathers a child. There is one thing that I can share however, that might make being a dad easier in the slightest, yet a very important, way.

Babies and children cry. No great revelation there, as any parent can relate that as a fact. But how to settle the child who cries consistently, or wakes in the middle of the night with either wet garments or hunger, nightmare dreams that frighten them, or simply the fear that they are alone in this harsh and unyielding world they have suddenly found themselves in without the ability to comprehend. Dealing with their crying is something that all parents find their own methods and means to accomplish.

My second attempt at being a dad resulted in my finding the means to comfort my son, Michael Patrick, in a way that might have seemed unusual or different to many and to some might have seemed unreasonable or unnatural. I called it – Daddy Magic.

Perhaps it was the bonding I hadn't been able to do with my first son and his siblings.? Because I never knew and never tried to bond with them in an appropriate manner? Just playing at being a 'dad' when I wasn't even a father to the older three of them. With my second son and the second chance I was given I had already determined that while he was my son, he was also an individual, a person in his own right from the moment he was born, and that it was my responsibility to provide for, care for, protect and nurture his growth until such time as he awoke to the fact that he was and is, indeed, his own person.

Yet, as I mentioned earlier, babies and children cry. Some cry early in the mornings when the stars are still out and there is no coffee made or food for them readied yet. Warming up a bottle at 2 am with a crying infant in one arm while juggling a pan of hot water to warm the bottled breast milk and comforting the child so as to allow the rest of the household (including his mother) to sleep often appeared to be an overwhelming task, frustrating and causing feelings of panic and failure to rise within me while fear of that failure becoming apparent to his other parent as well as his sibling could have provoked flashbacks to my previous experience at attempting child rearing and the results would have been to awaken his exhausted mother and dropped him in her lap.

Compleat

I had that choice, of course, but that I already knew would result in failure of both the relationship I was attempting with his mother, and with him as well, when he grew old enough to realize that I would put my responsibility on another rather than face it for myself.

Some folk may wonder what I mean by 'daddy magic' and justifiably so, since magic is a second-rate attempt at performing miracles. And any parent who has been woken at 2 am in the morning, in order to care for an infant that is uncomfortable, hungry, or frightened can tell you that easing that child where it no longer feels the need to cry, scream or fuss is to be in need of a miniature miracle in itself. I call mine 'daddy magic' in order to make light of what I did, simply because it worked and I didn't consider calling myself a 'miracle worker' as being appropriate.

How I discovered the simple action I took was almost a miracle because I had no idea what I was doing or even why except that I was desperately trying everything I could think of to bring peace to this infant that I loved so much but knew next to nothing about being there for him. One of those acts of desperation was to turn on a radio and try putting on calming music that would perhaps soothe the baby in my arms to sleep.

Instead, it appeared to cause him to become even more irritated, waking him fully and causing him to express his distress more vocally and with greater volume. Realizing that the effect was the opposite of what I was attempting to achieve, I changed the radio station to one that I normally would listen to when I was alone, music from the days of my youth. Hard rock, rock and roll ballads, heavy metal music, and music that in my youth had been so disruptive to my parents that I was often forbidden to play it when they were at home.

Standing there, with a crying infant in my arms, listening to Alice Cooper, Metallica, Deep Purple, Black Oak Arkansas, and others of the ilk, I patted him on the back in rhythm to both the music and the beating of my own heart. Because I found that the music of my youth soothed me, calming me down to where I could feel my own heartbeat slow and settle; and the results were nearly instantaneous. The baby in my arms fell asleep almost at once. While I often gave the credit to the sounds of the music, often stating that my son must have liked 'rock and roll' as much as I myself did, I truly believed that statement until I asked god about it.

The truth was that what I called daddy magic wasn't about causing my son to calm down and be at peace by listening to the music I played. Daddy magic was listening and calming myself inwardly, and when holding the baby in my arms that inward peace communicated itself directly to him, easing his fears, discomfort and after having been fed, bringing him to a fullness of not simply a physical nature.

His world came around to a peaceful, easily accepted, and calming state because the 'daddy' holding him was himself calm, peaceful, and could accept that this child was a person in his care, not merely a possession to be cared for and treated as a 'thing' that was discomforting at best and infuriating at worst.

To young fathers and older ones who have young children and even older children in their lives, I offer this experience in hope that you might avoid my own mistakes in being there for these new individuals, these small people in your lives who grow to become their true and authentic selves.

Try not to think of them as extensions of yourself, or their other parent. Try to think of them as individuals who need and who love, and who care for you in their own right. And most of all, try to remember that these small individuals – no matter what their age they remain the child you love and care for so very much – will know deep inside of themselves if you are upset with them, uncomfortable with caring for them and your feelings of discomfort can bring them more discomfort than a dirty diaper, an empty stomach or a nightmare of epic proportions.

Calm yourself first, like putting on the mask in an airline emergency, and then attempt to calm the child in your care. I can share that in most cases I experienced with my second son, in the moments it took to calm myself, he had felt my own frustration, fear, anger, and uncertainty melt away and had fallen fast asleep.

Compleat

Batter Up!
— . — . — . — . — . — . — . — . — . — . — . — . — . — . —

As a kid, I only tried baseball at school once. I was in the center field position, there was a fly ball hit and although I reached the spot where it was coming down easily, I missed the catch and the ball hit me square in the face. With my parents being as strict as they were about things that cost money, I was more upset with the idea that my eyeglasses broke when I got hit by the ball than the pain of catching it between my eyes and pushing the broken pieces of my glasses into my nose.

With my stepchildren and my first son, Michael Lee, I was so far gone in my addiction and insanity that I never got them involved in sports at school. I was too self-centered and absorbed in doing what I wanted to do, be and feel. Those are also some of the reasons why it was best for them that I lost them and was confined away from them for most of two decades.

With recovery, and guidance I had received a second chance at being a dad, with my youngest son, Mick. Being basically a single dad, and not wanting to mess up his life any more than my past would obviously cause him difficulties, I tried in every way I could to be involved in the things he liked.

His joining the class productions of plays for school was one of his favorites, and although I was restricted from attending for a while, the school rules and the laws allowed me to attend some of the plays where he was the lead actor.

Other people's opinions notwithstanding because many parents became upset when they learned of my past and harangued the school superintendent trying to get me removed from the property and banned from being around their children.

Mick also went out for sports, baseball being his favorite even though the school put most of their sports budget into their basketball program. And he was good at baseball.

Although his coach wouldn't allow him to be the pitcher (the coach insisted that his son was going to be the pitcher for every game) Mick had a great season, batting what would have been considered an actual 1.000 because every single at-bat he got when he was allowed to play, he got on base.

Chapter 1

As his dad, I attended the ball games, at a field away from the school and where parents wouldn't be able to object if they knew about my past, so I got to watch him play frequently. I was probably the loudest parent on the sidelines, shouting encouragement and suggestions to him and the other players because I was so excited and happy for him that he could and wanted to play.

There was a game, where the other team hit the ball and the first base player caught it on the fly. Everyone was shouting, yelling what a good job he had done catching a line drive hit directly to him. But the coach missed an important rule of baseball that day. The first baseman had caught the ball in the air, but the runner that had been on first base had already left the base without tagging up.

I found myself shouting to the first base player to step on the bag, which he did with some confusion showing on his face about why I was suggesting that so loudly.

It was an automatic out, a double play that won the team the game and ended the opposing team's comeback that was looking to overtake the home team's score.

Harshly perhaps but I can say now that although the coach missed that detail, it was his not being willing to allow anyone except his son to pitch that came close to costing the team their victory that day. His son had pitched a great game, for nine full innings, but was obviously tired and had given up too many runs to the other team to not be pulled from the pitcher's mound.

Mick saw what was happening that day, and was so disappointed with the system controlling the games and game players that he quit playing baseball altogether. I blamed myself for yelling too loudly at the games until a few years later he confided in me that it wasn't my excitement that soured the game for him, it was the isolation, rejection, preferential treatment, and the town's willingness to hold my past against him, my son, who hadn't even been born when I committed my crimes well over a decade earlier that made playing for the 'home team' distasteful.

My son, at 15 years of age, showed more maturity than his coach had when Mick had been only 11 years of age and had just wanted to play baseball. Is it any wonder that I'm proud of him, and support him in any actions he chooses

Compleat

to take, even if they appear to me to be mistakes? He learns much more than anyone teaches and I learn from him every day.

Compleat
The Life and Death of Buck - Mr. Fuller

For the few that have read his works, I am not writing the story about the author, instead, I'd like to share a story about my dog, Buck. My youngest son and I had gone to the Southwestern Missouri Humane Society in Springfield, Missouri in an attempt to find and adopt a German shepherd for his mother. When we arrived, the only shepherd they had available for adoption was a young male who had been dropped off by owners who could no longer afford his upkeep and feeding. When we inquired as to the adoption fees, however, the staff there informed us that it would require $250 - as some not astronomical, but beyond my means at that moment. The disappointment was apparent on my son's face and I must admit it must have been reflected in equal measure upon my own. As we were leaving, however, my son and I both noticed another dog covered in brown and white markings. What caught both our attention were this dog's eyes.

One eye - the right, if I remember correctly - was a golden brown, nearly appearing yellow as it seemed to shine from behind the cage where he was being held. The other eye, equally radiant, was a powdery blue, almost white, as it stared at my son longingly, with his tail wagging furiously so that his hind quarters seemed to wave as quickly as his tail.

Something about him captured my heart. I returned to the center where the staff had been so disappointing about the shepherd and inquired about what breed of dog he was. I had never seen a dog of that breed in all my years of raising dogs. They informed me his name, given to him by the owners who had abandoned him there, had been Harley - a popular name from a motorcycle and a takeoff of the movie about a dog named Marley.

Then they informed my son and I that this dog was facing euthanizing due to the fact that he was considered a large breed though he only weighed approximately 80 pounds or 40 kilos. His breed, we were informed, was Catahoula Spotted Leopard Dog and that the reason his owners had abandoned him at the shelter was he had contracted a case of heart-worm. Heartworms in dogs can lead to their sudden and unpredictable deaths, but I suspect to this day that his owners abandoned him not just for his being sick with a case of heart-worm or like the Shepherd's owners because they could no longer afford his upkeep and feeding. My suspicions, based solely on his size, appearance, and energy was that his previous owners had wanted to use him as a guard dog or fight dog.

Yes, dog fighting while still illegal in Missouri is still a common crime throughout the States. Why then was this strong, fast and powerfully energetic animal abandoned? I believe it was his nature that his previous owners had grown disgusted with because this dog simply loved unconditionally every human being he ever encountered. He would no more fight another dog than I would raise my hand in anger toward a human being. The staff after informing me of his medical condition and that his time at the shelter had almost run out, made a suggestion and an offer too good to pass up.

If we were to adopt Harley, they would provide the services of a veterinarian who would treat him for the heart-worm free of financial cost. Apparently, this dog had won their hearts as well. And the adoption fee for a large dog was a special offer just that week of only $10. My son and I passed a knowing look between us and he went to a nearby kiosk that had harnesses and leashes on it, picking out one of each and returning to the counter with them. I paid for them and the adoption fee from the pocket money I had on me.

With Harley, his paperwork, and the vet's information in hand, we returned to our car and prepared for the hour's drive from Springfield, Missouri to our home. A more well-behaved dog, I cannot ever remember having had the pleasure of being responsible for. He sat in the back seat with his face, sticking out the open window and watching everything and everyone who passed by as we drove. My son and I talked about his name, Harley, and I suggested we rename him since a Harley as a motorcycle to be ridden. My son suggested we call him Buck since he had hardly cost much more than that to rescue him and I agreed because I knew his mother was an avid reader and I could introduce him as Buckminster 'Buck' Fuller.

The best laid plans of men and young boys often go astray, it is said. Perhaps even more so when adopting a stray. When presented with a medium sized dog with a medical condition, my son's mother rejected Buck outright.

She not only didn't want the "gift" of him, but suggested that we return him immediately and get our money back. Instead, I chose to keep Buck for myself, assuming responsibility for making his appointments, taking him to them, struggling with him through the six months of treatment to keep him as calm as possible lest the heartworms or treatment for them would cause him to die.

Chapter 1

Buck went through all of this and was eventually pronounced clear of all the heartworms and allowed to run, play, jump, and be the magnificent dog he had always been meant to be. My son's other dog, Gracie, who had aged to over 12 years, simply tolerated this playful, foolishly excited, other dog as if he was an overgrown puppy - not hers, but to be tolerated because he was with me. Sometimes I would catch her after watching Buck's antics, looking at me through a sideways questioning glance as if to ask me "Whatever were you thinking?"

I loved both dogs equally. I know to this day, neither of them felt they were in competition for my affections in that regard. I would get them both into my car and drive to the nearby headwaters of the Gasconade River, where Gracie would swim relieving some of the ache of her arthritis in her hips - being half Labrador and half German shepherd, hip problems accrued for her due to her breed as much as due to her age - and Buckminster ran around as if the world revolved around Gracie. And it was so new and exciting to him, he couldn't decide which was more important for him to play with and explore.

In the early part of 2018 and mere months after being cleared of his heartworms and enjoying a life of freedom on a farm, Buck began to experience breathing problems, occasionally coughing, but still appearing to be his normal, excited self. I sometimes feel I should have acted sooner - as soon as he started coughing - yet I ignored it as being that he had gotten something stuck in his throat and had cleared it by coughing it out. A week later, Buck's energy levels began to fade and he began coughing frequently, so I arranged an appointment with his vet and took him in for a checkup.

The vet wasn't able to diagnose what exactly was wrong, but arranged an appointment with a specialist in dog respiratory illness. I need to mention this simply because, too often, people see me as a monster and worse many aren't willing to spend money to provide for the care and upkeep for their animals that they're responsible for! The specialist that I took Buck to cost $900 just to get an accurate diagnosis for his breathing problems. The river we had been going to repeatedly and for over eight years before getting Buck would prove to be the source of his respiratory problems.

A fungus that certain breeds of dogs are more susceptible to than others had settled into Buck's lungs growing rapidly and filling his lungs with solid matter. The difficulty in treating a fungus, especially one already having established itself in his lungs, was there were no fungicides that could be used to kill the fungus that wouldn't also risk ending Buck's life. He was prescribed

Compleat

antibiotics, sent home with me and I was offered only a small hope that his body might be able to reject the fungus on its own.

It didn't. The doctors offered to perform surgery on Buck, which would have entailed removing 70% of both his lungs, but the cost of that surgery was astronomical and the chances of successfully removing the fungus from Buck's system by then was less than 2%. Buck had weakened and, brokenheartedly, had so much trouble breathing that he would whine in pain with every breath he took.

Selfishly, I cried because I knew what I was facing. I didn't want to let go of this single important source of unconditional love, but I had to let go of my selfishness and do the only thing I could do for Buck. I ended his pain by having him euthanized at last. Many of you might remember the news story involving the OJ Simpson murder trials. Perhaps some of you are too young to remember, but the information is public knowledge. What isn't recorded on the internet is the position people took about the man's guilt or innocence. Some condemned him even before the trial began as being guilty. Most of these were judging him, not for the murder of his wife and her new boyfriend, but for being a black man who had dared to marry a white woman - their bigotry being openly displayed long before his trial date had even been set.

One such individual was a female radio announcer out of Springfield, Missouri, who asked for her listeners to call in and express their opinions on the case being presented against him. As long as they expressed views similar to her own, they were allowed to speak freely and without time constraints, often receiving words of praise and encouragement from her in response to their biased and bigoted expressions of hate - though he had been a professional football star athlete who they may well have been admired many times before this case had presented them the opportunity to express their hatred for his crossing what they saw as a racial boundary.

I eventually became so disgusted with their ranting and assumptions of his guilt that I decided to call this radio personality myself. When she asked me if I thought he was guilty or innocent, I replied that I had no opinion either way since it was a matter to be decided in a courtroom, not the court of public opinion. I believe she missed the sarcasm of my response because she asked me her favorite second question: If he were found guilty, what punishment did I believe he deserved?

And I answered her in a way that I know now she was too bigoted to understand or comprehend. I told her there was an old Disney movie entitled

Chapter 1

Old Yeller where young boy adopted, loved, and cared for a big yellow Labrador. The dog, in protecting the boy from another animal, had contracted rabies and the boy who had loved the dog the most was the individual who was forced to put the dog down, killing something he loved only because he didn't want it to suffer, not out of hate anger or fear, but out of love, respect and compassion.

If it were proved OJ Simpson had indeed killed his wife and her white lover, I believed it should be the responsibility of someone who cared most about him to decide what should be done about it - not frightened, angry, bigoted individuals whose prejudice was openly displayed by their words and expressions of hatred directed at him for the color of his skin.

Her response was to quickly disconnect my call to her station and take what I had said, twisting it to serve her own bigotry by responding publicly to her listeners, "OJ Simpson and rabid dogs have a lot in common don't they listeners." Years later in 2018, as I held my dog, Buckminster, in my arm and he first fell asleep from the medication given to relax him and then expired due to the drug used to end his suffering, the memory of that phone call came rushing back to me.

If God gave us dogs to show us what unconditional love looks like - and I suspect strongly that God did just that - maybe those that condemn other human beings out of fear, anger, hate, prejudice, and bigotry might learn to relate to what I had tried to say to that radio announcer if they were in my position of having to end the life of someone - I still consider animals as someone, not just something - they truly loved, maybe human beings could learn to care for one another just as much. That at least was my hope.

Compleat

Two Out of Three

is Bad

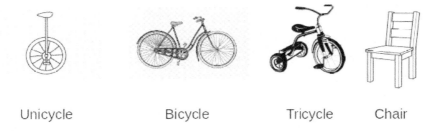

| Unicycle | Bicycle | Tricycle | Chair |

There's a song I listened to a lot when I was a young man because it gave me a sense of that perhaps my wrong of dumping the one love of my life wasn't as bad as it seemed to be when the anger and depression left little to no room for forgiving myself. It was called out "Two Out of Three Ain't Bad" by Meatloaf. In the song, he sang "I want you, I need you, but there ain't no way I am ever going to love you, but don't be sad, 'cause two out of three ain't bad."

When I asked about that song, it was explained to me this way: self-love, the ability to get by with only oneself is like riding a unicycle. It can be done, takes a lot of balance and training, and can easily be upset by the world tossing obstacles in the way. That explained what telling someone "I want you" meant.

To say "I want you and I need you" is similar to a bicycle in that it's easier to both say and do, less easily upset by the world around you but still not completely stable. Fun, and as exciting as a unicycle but with a little more stability to it.

Obviously then a tricycle represented saying "I want you, I need you and I love you." Seriously stable compared to the other two but honestly after time, human beings grow up and move away from the safety of stability - looking for more excitement in their lives, both male and female.

Why then did I get told about the chair? It represents the relationship between two people that will last for their entire lifespans. And some might think a chair couldn't add the excitement of the other three but I was told to think of it this way: It's like saying "I want you, I need you, I love you and I'm in love with you --- "

" - forever".

Chapter 1

Compleat

The Burden

I normally would just carry loads of wood or flour, seeds, or even bread that my owner would task me with but today was something different. The noises at the market were intensified, making my ears hurt and causing me to shiver with the fear that some of the crowd was going to rob me of the burden I was carrying. Which, when I think of it, was strange because usually, I would have appreciated having the loads I carry taken off my back and hurry to my bed at home.

The crowds pressed around me so tightly that at times I feared I would stumble over or step on one of them. That usually meant I'd receive a beating even when it wasn't really my fault, I was only going where my owner was driving me to go, goading and smacking me to cause me to veer in different directions. Again though, this time was different. I knew exactly where I was meant to go -, as if the route and destination were laid out before me even before some of the crowd began making the path easier by laying their cloaks across it. It was as if they, too, knew where I was meant to go and were placing things on the pathway to cause the others in the crowd to give way and allow me to pass with my burden, unhindered.

Chapter 1

This once I wasn't in a hurry to offload the burden I was carrying, not because I enjoyed carrying it though I did find a sense of comfort doing so. It was more because I could feel that this burden was different. Almost as if this burden was carrying a burden of its own, and yet the weight of its burden made it lighter for me to carry it. I know that my owner avoided hitting me, to avoid hitting the burden I was carrying and I found myself being grateful to carry the burden as it was, as well as grateful to the burden for taking that means of driving me from my owner.

Compleat

And The Message

Was Clear

I've thought long and hard about this story. Taking years to clear my mind and heart of all that I hated about myself and realize who and what humans are meant to be - just from having been born human beings. The race of humanity was never meant to treat one another the way they have for so many years that go back before recorded history.

The only way I see ending the mistakes that have been made, continue to be made, and potentially will still be made if humanity survives itself is to make these simple statements:

"I Am Jesus." "I Am Mohammad." "I Am Buddha." "I Am Shiva." "I Am Ra."

I AM that I AM. And I tell you now, one and all, be you 'Christian', 'Islamic', 'Buddhist', 'Hindi', 'Wicca', 'Pagan', whatever religion you identify yourselves as, whatever you call yourselves or pretend to be to one another, whatever facts or faith or evidence you follow or profess to 'believe' to be true: Stop!

Be Jesus to one another. Be Mohammad to one another. Be Buddha to one another. Be Shiva to one another. Be Ra to one another. Be Earth Mother to one another.

Be god to one another. And quit 'playing' god to yourselves.

I am god. And I have spoken...

Compleat

The Angel & The Bad Man
— . — . — . — . — . — . — . — . — . — . — . — . — . — . — . —

After I had been released from the hospital, I focused on my recovery to the exclusion of much else I might have needed to pay more attention to, and beginning to learn how to apply these 'values' that I was told are used to separate humanity from the monster I knew how to be I felt I needed that focus or I would never change.

I was 3 full years out of the hospital when I encountered my first real challenge to 'living' what I believed rather than simply talking about these values or writing about them in newspapers and magazines.

I met a young woman, easily half my age, who went by the street name of 'Angel'. And to see her clearly, from my perspective, she was a vision of what an Angel might appear to seem in human form. Much shorter than my 6' 1" height, with reddish-blondish hair that reached her shoulders, she was petite by anyone's standards but by mine, she it was as if she had been crafted from the finest China -, a doll-like quality so delicate that she seemed vulnerable to being broken by a loud noise, let alone all she had endured in her short lifetime.

She tolerated my foolish self, stumbling around trying to practice at being a gentleman, even finding it amusing at times I can imagine. Opening doors for her, offering to help her in any way I might be allowed, at first simply to be allowed to be with her by being in her presence.

Then the disaster struck. She made the choice to return to the lifestyle of a street drug addict. She began to lose weight, already so pale and nearly painfully thin, she grew to resemble a mummified version of herself that could yet walk, talk, scheme, and control an idiot with her gifting of her used and often abused body to me as an incentive to do her bidding.

If she was out of diapers for her baby, I would provide them, as quickly as she expressed the need. If food for herself, her child and even her boyfriend was growing scarce, I would make a run on to the nearest grocery store, buying anything she would list, even for the man who shared her bed each night, refusing only to buying them alcohol of any kind.

If she needed to 'borrow' my car for a few days, to do her laundry, take her child to doctors' appointments or see a doctor herself I would never even consider refusing her the loan, although I suspected and later learned she had been using my car to make runs down into Mexico to buy and transport meth up into the United States for sales and personal use by them both.

And I would do all of this, simply because this once beautiful woman would share my bed for mere minutes out of her day, and I could pretend to myself I was helping her and that one day she would grow to care for me as I already cared for her.

I thought I was "in love" at last - that somehow, I had been freed from my past mistake of leaving the one I had truly loved because I hated myself even more than I loved "her."

There came the day, when she asked to 'borrow' my car yet again, and I made the error of telling her I had grown aware of what she was using it for... I found myself pleading with her to allow me to provide for her and her child. To allow me to bring her out of that existence she had chosen to return to and help her along her journey away from destruction and death.

She asked me why I would do all of this for her, what possible reason could I have, being that I was insane and probably couldn't reason my way "out of a paper bag." I told her that I loved her, that I would do anything for her just for the off chance that she might someday love me back.

"You're nothing to me, Mike, except another John. A prostitute's paycheck. And there is no way I could ever love an asshole like you, you sick fuck!" And she left my apartment, with those words ringing in my ears, and drove away in my car yet again, on her way to Mexico to buy more meth.

Compleat

Two days of the weekend passed. I sat alone and silent not knowing what I should do, and even less of what I could do. I had already died once, and been sent back against my will. So, killing myself seemed pointless and redundant. I grew angry at the pain and her words; she wasn't a prostitute to me; how could she think of herself that way? Or think of me as a 'paying customer only'? I nearly gave in to my insanity over those dark 48 hours.

I grew to believe I would never find love again, but I wasn't allowed to die, not by my own hand.

Between hell and a hard place, if anyone had bothered to look, that's where they would have found me. I worked (unpaid) as a volunteer at a local recovery center, clearing up tables and chairs, emptying cigarette ashtrays, sweeping floors, answering phones, and taking messages.

So, with the beginning of a new week, I returned there from force of habit. I had a 'sponsor' by then, who was involved in several 12-Step programs, named Lee. He had heard all my whining and complaining about my situation, but this time he saw something had broken inside of me.

We talked - about her, about my car that was still gone two weeks later, and how everyone knew she was back from Mexico with the 'good shit' at her place. So, I knew where she was, where my car was and I was aware of everything that was going on, even though I could not bring myself to go to her door again, not even to get my car back.

Lee taught me something then, something that would not only bring another change into my life but also set my feet firmly upon the oath I have chosen to be my journey.

"You're killing her with kindness, Mike. If she hasn't returned your car in the time that you agreed upon, that's theft and you need to report it."

"I can't do that to her Lee, she's already been convicted twice for grand theft auto, it would be her third strike, California would put her away for life, her baby would go into foster care and I would have betrayed her just as she had betrayed my imagined dream of being with her."

"All the money you gave her, the diapers you bought, the clothes you took her shopping to buy for herself, the car, the gas, every dime was enabling her to use her own money to buy drugs. To live the lifestyle she is living, now. You enabled her, out of a kind heart and a stiff dick. So, what are you going to do, Mike? Are you going to be responsible for her dying a death from an OD or shot from a drug deal gone bad?"

Compleat

"I don't know, Lee, what should I do, I don't even want the car anymore, there's too much of her associated with it, I guess I'll just let her keep it."

"Bullshit! You will not! Do you have a spare key for the car?"

I did, and Lee drove me to her apartment building. I used the spare key and drove away with the car, angry at her, angry at myself, angry at Lee for making me do the right thing for the right reason. It was hard and I told him so afterward many times.

I told Lee it seemed a waste of time and effort because if she came to my door, even knowing how she saw me in reality, all she would need to do is share those minutes in my bed and she would walk away with the car again.

Lee suggested then that I should sell the car. There had been a guy who expressed an interest in buying it long before it became an Achilles heel for me. I called the guy and asked if he still had an interest in the car, and although he offered me $1,000 dollars for it, I sold it to him and transferred the title to him that night for $200 and his assurance that he would take it immediately away from where I lived. Which he did, not knowing how much he was benefiting me, and probably assuming he had gotten a great deal.

Lee and I drank a lot of coffee that night. For even though the car issue had been dealt with, there remained my weakness toward this woman called Angel. Where the idea came from, I cannot say for sure. Part of it may have been the job that I had had as a grave digger /and grounds keeper at a cemetery. We joked about my being a grave digger, not a grave robber - which was where many people's thinking went when I mentioned that job as one of my past experiences. After all, I AM crazy, so it was an easy assumption for them to make.

What happened that night, however, had nothing to do with that job except that Lee asked me about it, why I had chosen it, and what made me good at it. People don't care after they die what happens to their own remains. They are dead, for crying out loud. They pretty much have no feelings one way or the other about anything still here.

But the families that are left behind, I told Lee, they need care, concern, respect and a feeling of security about their loved ones remains. And that service was one I was good at, I helped people through difficult times by doing the job to the utmost of my ability and showing the remains the same respect that they would have shown their lost loved one if the loved one had somehow been revived and walked with them again.

Compleat

We, Lee and I, came up with the idea for a cemetery inside my own head. In it, I would place the tombstones of everyone I had ever known or would know who has died. At 7 years into my recovery there was a list, not a huge or extensive one, but some important to me names that I carved onto stones, placed over graves I had dug there in my mind, and allowed myself to grieve their loss.

And Angel's name was the last one that I placed upon a white marble marker that day. The street woman, the drug addict, the drug dealer, the prostitute I had known, loved, obsessed over, and now lost was buried on a slight hill, facing the rising sun each day, and I allowed myself to grieve. Angel was dead to me. Gone forever, like my first love that I had run from years before causing me to completely lose my mind.

If you've ever been to a funeral, where someone was loved beyond words to express, then you will be able to picture for yourself the tears I cried that night.

When I met the young woman again later that week, whose real name was Debbie, I felt no attraction, no weakness, no fear or trepidation. I greeted her as I would have any stranger, young woman or old, youth or gaffer, and was able to practice the unconditional acceptance that is the root of all unconditional love.

She had heard about my selling the car, and made the comment I had "hurt her heart by selling it, she would have given me $700 for it." And I was able to say, "No, I would have given it to you and lost my soul in the process, for you might have died and I would have been responsible for your death, at least in part. I'm sorry Debbie, but I buried Angel in the graveyard in my mind. She's grieved and missed, but she is dead to me, now and forever."

Was I wrong to tell her that? Was I being mean or vindictive because she had broken my heart by making me face the truth of being just another John to the Angel? I hope not, it is always hard to know why we do the right thing for the right reason, and then again, maybe not so hard after all.

Ten years passed before I even heard about Debbie and her baby again. Ironically it was Lee who heard it first and thought it would be a good thing for me to know. Approximately a year and a half after I had buried the street girl named Angel, Debbie had turned her life around, stopped using drugs, had had another baby, and was married, clean, and working as a counselor to other women trapped in that lifestyle that she herself had escaped.

Compleat

It had nothing to do with me, of course, but still, I was so very glad to hear that news. I hadn't "killed her with kindness." . I had some small role in her life and when I buried her street name, maybe god, pop as I like to call him, took that as a prayer he could work with, doing everything for her that I had wanted to be the one to do.

And in 2018, I found out that the "one" I actually loved enough to die rather than allow her to follow me into the depths of hell, my prayers for her life, her happiness, and the fullness of all that life had to offer had received exactly 'word for word' what I had prayed for her to receive as well. 49 years of praying. To find out I would still never hold her in my arms or hear her say I love you, again. I still think it was all worth it. But then too, the world knows that I AM crazy.

Compleat

Of Magic & Miracles

*** Please be aware, this story is in progress only still. It addresses a question that was raised by someone I care for (not the 'one') and I AM working from raw research and the remains of it which are very disorganized, but I feel if I don't write it, I might not complete it and it is a very important topic in one of the chapters of my book.***

People ask me sometimes why I gave up my studies of theology and the occult.

The first, theology, is simpler to explain I guess - since most theologians adhere to one religion or denomination within a religion or even a sect within a denomination. (Theology being merely the study of belief) I got the distinct impression that to gain an unbiased view of it all, I would need to research and discover things concerning what people believe on my own.

With my studies of the occult, I was, for the most part, left in the same position, with a few exceptions. There are so many areas of magic that are studied, practiced, and believed in that finding an understanding without bias was just as difficult for me.

My research on my own into these two diverse topics led to my discovering two important facts. The first being they are not as diverse as some people might wish to claim that they are.

The second is that, consistently, throughout the beliefs, studies and practices of magic, both white and black, the practitioners were seeking to find answers to problems or situations which they wanted to have some control or power to alter, manifest or manipulate in some way.

Fundamentally, there was no difference in the practices of white magic or black magic, the intent of the user normally being the factor that would determine the use of it as being one or the other. The rituals could vary widely and graphic examples are recorded of some of the more violent of the type labeled black, while less pronounced in white those same rituals might be used as well, even with the reputed disagreement with their practice.

From voodoo, to rune stones, and from sacrifices of blood and/or life to the benign alignment of crystals and stones to focus energy, magic required an external source to supply power (or energy) that would pass through the person, using them as a conduit for directing the flow of said energies, to achieve a result desired by the practitioner.

The problem I found in most cases of magic being practiced was that very thing. Always an outside source for power to use the practitioner and achieve the result FOR them. As conduits of these powers, some benign and healing or helpful, others not so much, and some outright dangerous to be used in any manner because every type required the practitioner to open themselves for use and have varied results as well as varying costs for being used by said powers.

My observations revealed those costs as being, again, something from outside themselves. And therein I found cause or reason to question the practices themselves.

I would review certain theological references and teachings in regard to magic, since most religions that practice what they call faith in whatever belief systems or mythologies they supported or adhered to (some better at that than most) also called upon forces, sources, or beings outside themselves for accomplishing things believed to be beyond human accomplishment.

Miracles were and are viewed as only being performed by those who having attained a level of grace or perfection (holy men and women) that they were able to call upon the powers of god's, life, the universe, or other beings, including other human beings.

Even the remains of these people after their physical lives had expired were viewed to have miraculous abilities when touched, prayed before, or someone having simply stood in their presence. Almost as if miracles and magic were interrelated or interchangeable with one another! This comparison might have passed me by and I might have allowed for the similarities making them mirror images of one another, or perhaps flip sides of the same proverbial coin.

There were however no recorded examples of miracles requiring sacrifices of blood, flesh or other less savory items. The lives of the children from the example of the miracle at Fatima, for example, were not "taken" in active sacrificial rituals or actions resulting in their immediate deaths. While belief did form that their lives were forfeited by their desire to "witness" the same visions the other child involved in that incident had claimed to have seen.

Do miracles then, I reasoned, require some sacrifice from the person or persons performing them? On the occult side of the argument, I was presented with the opinions that indeed, they did. However, upon closer examination of the theological side of my studies, I found that miracles not only do not require sacrifices they are often performed without a conscious awareness of those performing them. They happen, as was told to me by someone who actually was accredited with having performed miracles, as naturally as breathing.

Why then I reasoned, is magic viewed as being more sought after, easier to obtain and teachable while performing miracles so difficult to obtain, unteachable or shareable and less sought after? It was in college during an hour of observation of a course on economics that I gained a hint of where the difficulty with obtaining miracles came from: within yourselves.

Human beings value hard work. Why? Because you can see the accomplishments that come about through hard work, the rewards of your own labors, and the results that you do or do not wish to repeat from performing them.

Humanity devalues what you get for nothing. Sunshine, clean air, water, and even life itself is are often valued so slightly that it is assumed to just be there, of some importance of a sort but not valued in the way you do things you can touch materially, see with your eyes, hear with your ears or even taste. The results being detectable by your five known senses are placed on a scale of value much different than those of what you cannot.

Human beings devalue love-calling it infatuation, romance, lust, desire or even just dismissing it completely, for example.

Yet a job, defines who you are, because one of your first inquiries upon meeting someone new is to inquire: "What do you do for a living?" It amuses me to respond or even ask an alternative question that sounds similar but has an entirely different focus:

"What do you do for a life?"

When asked the former I simply respond that I am disabled or/ retired. And I am immediately dismissed as being of little or no importance to the person who made said inquiry. A disabled person is viewed as incapable of being able to work, to produce anything of value.

And a retired person is often viewed as being incapable of retaining their position of accumulation or gain simply due to age or having succeeded through over achievement of their goals for obtaining material gains.

In 66 years, I have never been asked the second question, the one I myself pose. And that's where asking it can be confusing for others and mildly amusing to myself. The mere thought that my self-identification has absolutely nothing to do with what I may or may not produce or "do" for a living confounds some, confuses most, and even angers some as being the belief of it being sarcastic or disrespectful.

None of these things being my intent, I am simply stating a fact, that I adhere to adamantly, as it's being of much more importance than what I might provide for the common wealth of individuals involved in a race to accumulate that inevitably ends the same for all of us. We came here with nothing materially save the bodies we are born into and we leave here with nothing, not even those same bodies

So, what does that have to do with the differences between magic and miracles? Human beings can believe themselves capable of magic if they apply themselves to the disciplines and requirements of creating the results of magic practices.

Illusionists are artists, for example, who work long hours to achieve a deception or event that will impress others and draw notice to themselves. Magicians even have a code of conduct that says they never reveal their secrets, save to another magician, if even then. As for herbalists, crystals, natural medicines, and things of that nature they have somewhat solid basis in early medicinal practices that have some scientific support simply through their use of materials that have had effects on the human condition for years.

Compleat

Magic, black or white, as described in tomes and spells have been practiced for years as well, but due to larger amounts of disbelief in their reality and results being of varying degrees of success and failure they are seen for the most part as being extreme or edgy and as a result not as commonly practiced.

But here's the rub. No one teaches miracles. No one teaches the practice of them at least.

Some human beings retreat from the doubts of their fellow human beings to seek so-called enlightenment and often are discovered to be performing actions that appear to all intents and purposes to be miraculous. Why then do they need to retreat from association with their fellow human beings to perform these actions?

Could it be that the collective rejection of the abilities you possess as human beings - these miraculous deeds and behaviors are so subject to the beliefs of your fellows that the only way to overcome that collective disbelief is to remove yourselves from its constant close proximity? And in removing yourselves from disbelief would these behaviors become not merely possible, as in the examples of those few who do reside as far away as possible from the rest of humanity, but become common place if not for that resistance?

I have found that what human beings value is where you will find your focus and your abilities will be as limited or unlimited as you allow.

Compleat

On a Life

Having been raised in the State of Missouri, surrounded by religious groups ranging from Southern Baptists to Latin Speaking Catholic Churches led by priests with strange accents and mannerisms, I was limited in my perceptions in regard to sex (taboo until you marry), childbearing, the fallen state of 'unwed' mothers, (seen as shameful by most and sinful by the others) birth control (never mentioned by some and condemned by some as being against god's expressed command to 'go forth and multiply!' (also viewed as a sin) and finally ending in the contentious arguments surrounding the nature of a fetus and whether abortion was to be permitted to women for their own choosing or if it was the murder of innocent unborn human beings and should be punished as such.

Missouri went with the anti-abortion route until it failed with the passing of the Roe vs Wade ruling making abortions a medical procedure and no longer a criminal action to be performed in secret, by the women seeking them and the doctors (also charged with murder if caught or at the very least losing their license to practice medicine) performing them.

Then lo and behold, new terminology came into use by those who wanted above all else to prevent the so-called 'murder' of unborn innocents. Pro-life became the new rallying cry of these individuals that had somehow convinced themselves it was not just their duty, prerogative, and responsibility to decide for these 'children', it was their "right" to intervene and make these decisions for anyone 'mad' enough to even consider killing an unborn child.

So, I was raised to oppose abortion as being something evil. An unjustifiable wrong that could not be allowed to continue, and that GOD hated those who committed these heinous actions. If GOD hated the actions, then that justified in the minds of those opposing abortions their right to do anything they thought of that might prevent even one from being performed. An abortion clinic? Blow it up or burn it down. A doctor known for performing abortions? Ruin his practice by spreading false rumors, gossip, innuendo, and false accusations to the point he would either have to stop or leave the town his family may have had a hand in building when it was first established.

And let's not forget the Jezebel's who opened their legs outside of marriage and, got pregnant by being foolishly trusting of the boys who would promise them marriage if anything happened but who would disappear if a pregnancy actually occurred. Shaming them, threatening them with eternal damnation, and making sure any employer's or potential employers knew of their terrible secret to the point where these women were forced to conceal what they had felt necessary for themselves and the fetus they were carrying. And that just scratches the surface of the list of atrocities done in the name of Pro-life.

Being a male, I had my own reasons for not wanting to know that a woman who was impregnated by me could just kill what I viewed as 'my child' with them, whether I wanted them to or not.

A child of my loins was my only means of having a connection to the immortality of life itself. A means of passing on to the future who I had been and ensuring I would be remembered after I died. That was my upbringing as well.

Mortality ended in either a pass to a 'better' place or like the women at the center of this issue who acted in ways 'religions' condemned were bound to end up going to a place I would one day become way too familiar with through personally experiencing it.

Without understanding or even the ability to relate to the difficulty of the choices these women were making I was more than ready to condemn them for doing something 'bad'. Not that I wasn't doing some heinous shit myself, I would very often find that I justified myself by condemning them, after all, "I wasn't killing babies."

It was to be years later, when my own heinous actions led to my confinement in an institution for the criminally insane, that I would not so much change my position on the subject of abortions but rather become aware and accept the truth of why I opposed abortion in the first place. My position had nothing to do with the fetus being a human being or not and everything to do with my ego wanting to know I would be continued throughout time.

I found that I could no longer actively oppose abortion without proving myself to be totally hypocritical; that type of self-serving was not in line with 'god's will' for me. Yet I continue to believe certain precepts about life and when it is created.

I am, with almost absolute certainty, of the belief that the soul of a human being comes into creation at the very moment of conception. Call it the biochemical joining of two individuals or call it the bestowing of life by a creator, and I wouldn't give an argument to for either opinion.

Why do I choose to support those who legalized abortion, if I truly believe in life beginning at that instant then, is something I had to ask myself. And only recently I had an epiphany regarding this topic and another that is hotly debated: the death penalty.

The Pro-life movement argues a strong case in the support of life beginning at the moment of conception, while at the same instance can often be found arguing in favor of the death penalty, for whatever reasons they deem it necessary.

The argument that to take the life of an innocent is wrong stands for itself, but the reasons given are so convoluted as to be near asinine, don't kill an innocent, but leave the mother to struggle and fail repeatedly in raising the baby after it is born, financially, morally, physically and emotionally? That's not Pro-life! It's Pro-Birth and as for the life of that baby after it's born, they seem to think it means nothing to them.

"Not my monkey, not my circus, not my problem!" - is how I hear the Pro-lifers speak among themselves, especially when challenged with the care and upbringing of the child they insisted must be born.

And the Pro-choice people have an equally strong argument, in that saying it is a woman's right to decide on the quality of the life she might be able to provide an unborn child when the society of the world we live in (not just the States) condemns that child to a life filled with poverty, want, ignorance, abandonment and abuse.

And no, I'm not talking just about physical or sexual abuse. I'm talking about being treated as a 'bastard', born out of wedlock, having no real rights to their identity, no claim to the ties to their fathers' families and even today offered no support to help them avoid the same situation that was the beginning of their own creation. Life begins at conception: the clue word is "begins". If not supported, the existence of life in the womb would become extinct whether it grew to come out of the womb or not.

And here's the rub. The epiphany that startled me so I had to stop my car while driving and witnessed a block of colors that must have been a quarter of a mile square and in height when I did. If life does indeed begin at the moment of conception, as I believe it does, who are we to decide that it HAS to continue to grow to full gestation to be a human being?

Hard to wrap my head around I had to stop and figure out what this weird thought actually implies. Once the soul, spirit, or energy of a being is created, I asked myself "What makes us think that spirit is ended, in any way, if the physical body it was growing within is ended?"

Immortality doesn't come from having children. Those little people are not your possessions, your lineage to pass on down to the future of the human race. The future isn't something humanity can possess or own or have any rights to! Let me say that again: the human beings of the now, the present, HAVE no rights to, or title to, or ownership of the future in any way, shape, or form.

It belongs to them, the children. And if humanity has messed it up for them, as I believe human beings are doing, then the things that are going to come about are going to make Chernobyl, Three Mile Island, and the other nuke accidents disappear into merely being tragedies. I wouldn't be surprised if your sun went supernova during a State of the Union address. That would be ironically amusing to me, to say the least.

For the babies that are aborted for the reasons of rape -, some people will acknowledge that there may be a reason for allowing an abortion, in those few cases and the ones that come about from incest, as well.

Compleat

And maybe you would find yourself agreeing to abortion under those conditions . But a woman deciding for herself and her unborn child based on the quality of life they would experience at your hands?

But Pro-Birth people insist that there be 'no' access to abortion. They deny that they will abandon both mother and child, just as quickly as they would find a reason to condemn the mom for doing what they already did but didn't get 'caught' doing, nor were they forced to choose what was best for both of the souls involved.

I know that the soul is created at the instant of creation, it just makes sense that an individual is just that, created individually to be that one soul that it is, was, and will be; whether it's body lives to be 999 years old like Methuselah, as old as my youngish 66 years, or is never physically born into this messed up, torn up, dirtied and disgusting world that human beings have made of it.

Hellfire and brimstone aside, you folks that try to decide for others MIGHT want to take a few words from your own book. The whole splinter/plank thing at the very least. If the life that is created doesn't get 'born' into this world, get over that insistence for control and offer the unborn soul the love you would any other living soul.

Its body has absolutely NOTHING to do with it being a human being. And if you really believed what you 'say' you believe, you would get that idea clearly.

Compleat

What was the

Beginning of

my Insanity?

The aspects of insanity, seeing the gambit of all existence, physically overwhelming, or our bodies triggered to run a mock mentally. Oh, the long conversation we have with our darkened selves with others not physically present - carrying both sides of a conversation in which we win only 18% of the argument. The sermons preached to the dead in graveyards, expanding their deaths or else they wouldn't stay laying there listening and understanding above all current living representatives of the here and now lost in imaginings at utter destruction of my fear, focus and ending the connection.

There are studies, sayings, proverbs, phrases, concepts, and ideas shared by humanity, the world over. Differences in regions, areas, nations and even continents notwithstanding, they're shared in ways that astound both science and religion into guessing at how they could surpass the physical separations of oceans and mountains too great to cross. In Africa, Asia, and South America, there are physical examples of some of these shared features - gigantic pyramids of stone being so large that even with today's modern industrial means, the feats of architectural construction stagger the imagination.

And when knowing that our means of constructing those wonders were not available to the primitive cultures of those ages from our past, it becomes the subject of theories, legends myths, and urban legends. Did aliens help by sharing their technology for a period thereby driving humanity's formative ages? Was there a greater culture of human beings that traversed the entire globe, using technology beyond our own current abilities, as the legend of Atlantis suggests? Did Nephilim giant children, bred of angels and humans, show humanity how to construct these monuments to ourselves. The guesses are all possibilities, though the probability of any one guess having the absolute answer to the sharing of those ideas remain subject to debate and personal choice. And honestly, I didn't get the concept of the collective sharing of any concepts until after I had my own experience and with meeting the being that I see as being god, though I still choose to call him / her / it "pop."

My interest in the collective connection between all of humanity began with the epiphany of realizing something that is measurable with any human being, from those with genius IQs, expanding across the entire spectrum of human thought processes to those with autism so severe that they are barely able to

Compleat

communicate with others even to the point of not being able to provide for themselves the basic needs of life, shelter, food, and safety.

The one tool that can have a measurable effect on any member of the human race is music - from the steps of great Russia, to the deepest jungles of the Amazon river basin; extending to the frozen wastelands of the barely habitable arctic to the cultural centers of every gathering of humanity, calling itself a nation; wherever humanity is found, there is music. The patterns are often repeated and at other times vary so greatly that they might not be enjoyable to some, while the are recognized as magic by others, yet music still exists. I found that here was one of the universal traits shared by all of humanity; a universal language that reaches beyond dialect, accent, phonetics, or even every language practiced by human beings across the entire world.

How then does music traverse time, distance, cultural and physical divides to touch a portion of that which makes humanity a whole? I stumbled upon a theoretical answer that might suffice to answer these questions as well as resolve the question of music's universality and effect on all human beings. It was something I had read about as a child of approximately 10 years of age, but had noted it in passing and had had no interest in it at that time.

The Gestalt or collective human subconscious is described as a nebulous, untouchable, and imaginable collective of human thoughts, emotions, feelings, and experiences. Psyches and mediums often claim to contact the spirits of those who have died or gone over to the other side, not in a measurable demonstrable or repeatable way, but claiming an ability because human beings have both a fear of death and a curiosity as to what, if anything, might lay beyond that particular ending to their therefore known existence.

What though of those, like myself, who at a very young age can be used to describe preemptive visions or seeing of events that had not occurred yet, but would physically occur days or weeks after the experience of having witnessed them. An eight-year-old boy might develop skills of observation as a survival set of tools, being able to cognitively, but subconsciously piece together his present environmental situation and deduce the possibility of an outcome. As a boy, I did assume that this was what my experiences were yet I later learned from my experience it will be that those premonitions might have had a strong possibility of unfolding anyway, but the probabilities of their unfolding exactly as I had seen, or foreseen them as occurring, were phenomenally lower in percentages as being statistically almost impossible.

How does this observation applied to the shared connection of music being a universal language of all human beings? Simply put, I was shown that the collective subconscious of humanity does indeed exist. It - the gestalt: the sum total of all human thoughts, feelings, concepts, perceptions, and identities - reside in a place outside, not just the individual body or bodies of human beings, but completely outside the acknowledged measures of the illusions of both time and distance, or as it's often called, space.

How can music be universal to all of humanity? Because its source is that area of our shared subconscious outside of time and distance, where we share it without even consciously recognizing where it stems from or how it comes to us. Musicians, lyricist, poets, artists, even actors often draw inspiration from this collective and ancient ways, attributing this successfully obtaining said inspiration from a muse or inspiring spirit, never recognizing that the spirit inspiring them was their own humanity.

After my experience, I began to develop the ability of avoiding certain phrases, especially the over commonly used phrase "I understood/understand." Human beings at present are incapable of understanding one another with very few exceptions. Lovers who believe they know one another so well that they can almost unwittingly finish one another's sentences can and do feel separated, alone, injured emotionally when the initial connection, on an emotional level, cools and they discover they are with a stranger, I can use as an example. And through music, our initial connections are more often strengthened to an almost supernatural understanding of one another because the human race is capable of understanding one another beyond the confines of physicality, time, and distance.

Remember that I mentioned this phenomenon is measurable now. Any human being monitored in a controlled environment can have portions of their brain stimulated and, in some cases, activate inactive or underused portions of the synapses of their brain through exposure to music. There have already been studies done that listening to music as one of the activities capable of influencing or using every area of the human brain. Mythology that the human race uses only a small portion of its cranial capacity as based on studies of activities, measurable by observation, working, writing, eating, sleeping, having sex, even meditative practices, some of which include using repetitive chants or mantras, have been measured to increase the effective use of the brains of the individuals being observed.

Compleat

Unfortunately, with too many of the individuals who do learn to actively use more of their brain's potential, genuine teachers, prophets and religions arise from or around them. I say, unfortunately, because what they are doing - the demonstration of an observable actions that they are capable of performing - are misunderstood and misinterpreted as being unique to them, or making them unique among the rest of the humanity surrounding them.

A silly movie, a cartoon called The Incredibles, describes perfectly how humanity views its collective self-image and those displaying abilities beyond the accepted or societally recognized normal. If an individual displayed exceptional use of their brain - displaying or manifesting an ability beyond the human as recognizable, they would be labeled as a special, unique, divine or superhuman. One character in that cartoon went on to make a statement that reflects perfectly the fear, anger, and jealousy felt by human beings when another displays abilities they see as beyond themselves: "and when everyone is super, then no one will be." The divinity displayed by Jesus, for example, invoked fear of exposure of the established religion for its false hoods and profit motives, anger stemming from that fear because those human beings measured their own abilities as being less than his; hatred for being made to feel inferior though, it was they themselves who were bringing about those feelings of inadequacy and in choosing to amplify him they were trying desperately to retain their grip on their own acceptable form of normalcy.

J didn't come here to show them or anyone else up. He's not boastful, conceited or even showy in that sense. He was, or is, the first conceived of child of a woman, son of the divine being I met that some call god, others, Allah, etc. ... He had no fear, no hidden agenda, no profiteering motivations and no anger toward anyone. The one exception being, of course, those using god as money-making scams. He was disgusted with what religion had done and would do in his name as well. I'd have done more than throw over the money changing tables and whip them out of the house, but that's why he's him and I'm only me.

Jesus was here not to just take away the sins of the world as the so-called christian religions push their brand of bullshit. His self-sacrifice was made to demonstrate, enlighten, and restore humanity to its ability to know and tap into the collective of who you actually are: god's kids. How? By doing something the human race continues to avoid doing to this day: he accepted the responsibility of being first born and stepped up to demonstrate what all are capable of when you accept your individual and collective accountability to one another and yourselves. Some folks say to me "well, you can't walk on water." I reply, "not unless I need to." "No."

Their fear and subsequent anger get me invited not to return to a lot of places where they gather themselves together and I often receive threats of violence because they see my attitude and observations as sacrilegious, blasphemous, or evil - as if I'm saying that being equal with Jesus or god is something restricted to the divine and I'm claiming something solely about myself. The truth being as far from that as I can possibly imagine, because what I'm really expressing is that it is something they themselves needed to do. Walking on water would be as easy for them as walking on a sidewalk or concrete walkway and I don't just believe this to be true about all of humanity. Faith and belief having been suspended and superseded by knowledge; I know they could.

Where does my knowledge come from? From the one instantaneous event or exposure to the divine being, called god by most? Nope. I know simply by having the same gifts to tap into that portion of the collective of humanity. That it is their portion easily identifiable because it was a recognizable and demonstrative portion of the collective of all human beings. Like music, it touches all at some level activating and using that portion of the brain necessary to manifest the ability. Humanity has been taught, twisted, lied to and manipulated by religions to fear and shame themselves from seeing their own true nature and taught to fear, hate, and reject its own potential, especially if manifested around or among its other members.

Some religions blame a universal evil, some even embracing that as a potent and potential source of power. The devil or Satan was or is a cast out angel, a flawed, angry wannabe human being because angels were meant to serve humanity and that pissed him off to no end. Although influencing like, lust, greed, sloth, murder and the rest might be in his area of suggestive thoughts, it is still the power of the individual human being's choice that changes thought into actions. And that power is the divine nature of humanity. Of all the creatures on this planet, humans are the only beings capable of manifesting that ability. Give a rat at a choice of cocaine or cheese, they might take cocaine until they die, but they aren't capable of cognitive of choosing to die. Give a chimpanzee as xylophone and it might beat out sounds consistently pleasant to hear, invoking the thought of music or making music, but only human beings can cognitively choose which sounds they wish to produce in order to demonstratively connect with other human beings.

Compleat

My point being: the responsibility, accountability, and even ability to choose rests solely with the human race, both individually and as a whole. What you've done with them is a measurable and observable set of facts, extending back beyond all written histories. And as J himself said in other words and I choose to reiterate here in the stories of my life, the awakening I experienced, my attempt to avoid my responsibility, and subsequent choice to write this book can be and is summed up in the single sentence:

"It doesn't have to be this way."

Compleat

The Second

Perception of

Insanity

Back on August 17th, 2017 I wrote about an event that caused the society I live within (but apart from) to view me as being completely insane.

And they were justifiably concerned with separating my physical presence from the rest of that society because I had become a danger to both myself and others. The crime(s) I have committed in my past, only slightly referenced to here in this book, are matters of public record for anyone who might wish to research them.

(For those who are too lazy or too impatient to do their own research I might, eventually, consider listing links to the information on a blog and perhaps editing this book to include them).

The facts are that although I had no fear of the legal repercussions of my actions, I always remained a 'coward' when faced with any physical pain from repercussions. That fear was never enough to prevent my acting out on my thinking, but only increased my shame for the things I had been doing along with my ability to deny what I saw as potential repercussions and strengthening my ability to escape 'justice' by avoiding being apprehended for the actions themselves.

I've said before in this book, I became a sneak ... and I gained in my ability to conceal, disguise, and perform the most heinous actions imaginable every time I nearly got caught in the act.

In an earlier story, I mentioned that I would share two examples of my perception being what the society I reside within labeled insanity. This will be the second example ... obviously long overdue.

In my perception of the "god" figure I mentioned then, I deliberately omitted to mentioning his/it's reaction to my raging and threatening to supplant and replace him. Because his reaction(s) were beyond my comprehension at the moment I assume, but with time I grew to understand, to a small degree, that his reaction was one with his response to all I said, felt, expressed and threatened within the entirety of my ravings. He said and did absolutely nothing.

Years later, I had a friend who would instruct me about the nature of perception. While I would argue that the facts cannot be 'altered' in any way by any person; he would gently smile and inform me that one day I would learn to see that white was black and black was white. "The sky is blue, the grass is green," I would argue. "Just because I wish them to not be or want them to be any other colors they won't change." And he would agree with me by disagreeing and informing me of the differing perception of the colors black and white. Infuriating as it was, at that moment, I would come to learn that his comment was correct.

The nature of the colors black and white might never change. But my perception of them was and is subject to my knowledge and limited experience with them both. The same held true with my perception of the god being's response or reaction to my rage. Even a non-response would become an answer, in and of itself. What would change would be my perception and interpretation of what had been expressed.

I had refused a 'commission' (or as some would label it: a calling) from a being I knew to be my superior in every aspect of existence. I even accepted that point as I raged and used it to fuel my anger and words in my efforts to alienate and provoke my destruction by him. "End me or leave me but do not even pretend that you give a flying shit about me!"

No response, no reaction, not even a singeing of the tips of my hair from being exposed to that presence. When my foot fell, I knew confusion, discomfort, and apprehension. Fear perhaps, but more of the unknown future than any concept of repercussion that might occur. I had hit him with all that I had been holding back, from myself even, like a boxer hitting his opponent with a 'finishing' blow, meant to end the fight and win. And he had taken all that I had, in that strike against him, but didn't react or respond as I had assumed he would. (Perhaps as I had inwardly been hoping he would?!)

The end result was my walking away from the experience with a disoriented and combined sense of confusion, apprehension, and relief combining in such a way as to leave me feeling sleepy and ready to rest.

Compleat

I Am Not A Crook
— · — · — · — · — · — · — · — · — · — · — · — · — · — · —

I am not a saint. I am not the reincarnation of Jesus, Elisha, or any of the prophets from their bible. I'm not a messenger from Allah, Krishna, Buddha, or any religion that humanity has created. I'm also not a 'good' man, holy man, wise man, guru, or any other title given to a teacher of any religious doctrine.

What I am is contained in the handle I use to identify myself: runner5150. A messenger, driven to deliver a message and insane to even finish the course and hand over the message to those it was meant for knowing full well that my own life will probably be forfeit for what the message contains through no fault or conceptualization of my own.

I've already addressed the "why me" question in saying that the god dude picked me because of the unconditional surrender of my life to whatever purpose it could be used for by him. I also addressed the "why me" in describing that humanity has received many good, kind, noble, and even holy representatives from god, the universe, life, Mother Earth, etc.… and has shown a total disregard for listening to any of them, so I got picked because I'm an asshole, learning how not to act like one, but still a complete asshole with more issues than answers for myself. I'm not unintelligent, but I'm also not smart enough to make this shit up. I dismiss any efforts to be seen as 'wise' in any way.

What I might not have addressed in the "why would god pick me to deliver a message to humanity" question is something I might have overlooked, however. I am, in the parlance of the human language: a loser. I'm such a loser that when I wanted to die, I not only wasn't aware that there was a god being that I later took offense with it by being asked to give up my life, if I really didn't want it any longer and my subsequent telling the entity behind that voice "He can have the fucking thing." In short, I told him/it/her/them/whatever: "Help yourself asshole, you do what you want with it."

As a loser, I had something that most holy, wise, intelligent, good or even average human beings didn't and don't normally have; I had nothing left to lose. I surrendered my humanity, life, or whatever label human beings care to put on what makes me an individual to the concept of this entity that I viewed as a male, god figure to do with as it saw fit.

And in my not believing for even in it for the length it took to walk home from the building where I first encountered him, to reverse my professed agreement to do what he wanted of me, by reneging on my promise to "quit smoking cigarettes", take a pack of Kool's out of the freezer and light one up.

My wonder and awe of hearing a male voice come out of a woman's mouth lasted just about that long, and I disregarded it though I have to admit I had hoped that by some 'miraculous divine intervention' I would be spared punishment for all the things I had done in life up to that point and would be 'saved' from my own accountability and responsibilities for my actions.

Looking for an easy out, I became religious, professing a 'new found' belief in Jesus, Christianity and that religion I began acting like a zealot, spouting every phrase I heard as if I knew what I was talking about, reading extensively materials that 'explained' the phenomenon that Christianity was reputed to be and more than probably annoying the hell out of all humanity that I came in contact with or came in contact with me.

I didn't care about being of service, completely forgot about having given my unconditional commitment to 'give up' my life, will and being to whatever purpose this 'god' had for me and went about my life as if I thought I would be:

a) forgiven for my past mistakes if I didn't continue to repeat them, and

b) avoid any responsibility for my past actions, no matter how heinous.

Home free, without being tagged for playing a game with the life I had been gifted with, I assumed that my past was forgotten, dismissed and resolved by my simply speaking the words aloud that "I accept Jesus as my personal savior."

How many months did I walk around, spouting bullshit that made sense to others in that particular religion but mattered little to nothing to me because all I cared about was the 'get out of jail free pass' that it appeared to be to me? What took me by complete surprise was that that being that took me at my word, hearing that I was giving over my humanity as unconditionally as I did and would call me in on the carpet and hold me to my spoken word.

I've already described the meeting I had with god, so I won't expound on it here again. I saw that he was seriously considering using me for the purpose that I had been asking about. I looked closely at my own life up to that point; and not just the things that had been done to me but also all the terrible things I had committed to others who didn't deserve to experience any of the things I had inflicted upon them and I went, as I've described it, berserk on the old dude. "Not only no, but fuck no, you incredibly, indifferent asshole."

There are many books about near- death experiences (NDE) and more books about religions from around the world than any one human being could read in a 70-year lifespan. What I experienced that day wasn't an NDE!

Nor, in my opinion, was it an out-of- body experience, since I wasn't meditating or trying to achieve a state of enlightenment. While I was praying and fasting, I admit, but only that I might figure out an answer to the question of whether or not I should quit the Marines, a job which I hated but paid the bills for the most part, and take a position of the pastor to a congregation in a 'church' after allowing someone else to pay for my education and ordination as a theologian for their particular sect of the Christian religion, or continue to hide out in the Marines, drawing a bi-weekly paycheck for a job I felt unqualified to even be attempting to appear to be doing, and blow off both of the pastors who were making me the offer to pay for my education themselves, out of pocket.

What I received was way beyond the question I was asking. An encounter, an accumulation of knowledge that I didn't know what to do with, why I was given it, to whom it was to be delivered, and not even remembering that I had already agreed to be a messenger "if and when I was called upon."

In all of the NDE books I've read, though the experiences are varied and the encounters with another entity are described at all, one aspect has been recorded as being a 'universal' truism. The entity or god that others experienced was always benign, kindly, loving, and caring for the individual having the experience. Such was not my experience.

Nor, as some religions might surmise, was the entity I call god or pop, angry, vindictive, demanding, or judgmental. If I were to choose a word from the English language for what I experienced when confronted with the divine I would choose the words: indifferent or apathetic. My initial awe was greeted with what I can only describe as indifference. My subsequent rage and outpouring of disrespect and verbal abuse, combined with threats of destruction and replacement as well as criticism of his inadequate performance as 'god' were met with that exact same feeling.

Does that mean pop or god doesn't care about humanity, that he is indifferent to the suffering that human beings inflict on themselves and the world around them? I assumed so at first, I admit. And that fact increased my already enraged feelings toward this being that sat before me. But there's an answer in the word indifference that I felt was being displayed during the encounter. It wasn't actually indifference but the word and feeling I was experiencing was were limited by my own understanding.

Like with the appearance of this being to me as a male figure, it was the only way my mind could 'wrap itself around what was happening without exploding.'

The knowledge I gained that day, overwhelmed my limited experiences up to that point. I walked away from the encounter with answers to questions I didn't have, more questions than I could have begun to imagine to even ask for myself, and the message that this book is meant to deliver to whomsoever it was meant for in the first place.

If the human brain is a wet-wired computer of infinite capacity as some scientists believe (remembering that science, too, is a religion of believing they accept only what can be established by testing theories in order to become facts) then my up-to-then human- brain was in desperate need of a re-boot.

The phrase "TMI – Too Much Information" comes close to describing the experience, but only close. And as the old adage says: "Close only counts in horseshoes and hand-grenades."

I received that 're-boot' when I committed suicide in prison, and was given a stay in the mental hospital for the criminally insane to allow my physical brain the opportunity to assimilate the information, much like a computer will re-boot and re-configure to another operating system.

This is why, to this day, I can claim that I am no longer or non-human. I do not claim to be better than humanity, by any stretch of the imagination. In fact, the information that I have acquired allows me to 'see' humanity as being a state I can work toward achieving.

Better than I am, human beings are divine in and of themselves, equal with god in every way, and capable of recreating what they were given if they were only to awaken to their own divine nature.

Compleat

When I was released from the institution for the criminally insane, the doctors and therapists there made an observation that they didn't realize held greater connotations than they intended. They told me that I was beginning a journey toward sanity, each day being yet another step toward that goal, but that I would die upon that journey long before I would be able to achieve the goal itself.

They couldn't realize that the truth of their statement applied to my goal of becoming human again as well. This journey I've engaged upon takes many steps; each day being counted by me as a success if I am able to help even one human being smile per day. But the distance that I have gone from being human is so low and so great that I knew before I even began that I will never achieve the goal I've set for myself.

And similar to the suggestion they gave about my sanity, I have the choice to make each day - of whether or not to continue the journey in spite of that the knowledge that the goal is unachievable. Despair, depression, angst, anger, fear, rejection, and abuse by those that fear my past are like stones upon the path I have chosen to walk. I expect them, and accept them as a part of the journey itself, no matter how much I may wish to avoid tripping over them and with their prolonging the journey. I can "wish" that my journey was over, of course, but there's another old adage that applies to that wishing concept or idea.

"If wishes were horses, beggars would ride.".

Falling or Failing

Near the town of Popular Bluff, Mo there is a park that, ironic as it may seem, doesn't appear on any of the maps on the internet search engines for me. The closest park to water there appears to be a place called Jackson's Bar, which appears to be placed in the middle of a river. I cannot recall the exact name of the park I visited as a youth but if Jackson's Bar was named for the events that transpired there it may have been named long after I had stopped going to places like that in pursuit of excitement and fun, appropriately enough since it may have been 'barred' to avoid the events that often occurred there.

The park I remember was popular with teens for underage drinking, smoking pot and sexual encounters. And although I was not an actual teen at the time, I went along with a group of friends that were and tried to participate in every aspect of the goings on there.

The highlight of visiting what those of us from St. Louis, Mo called "Popular Bluffs" was a space in that park that had a creek running down a narrow chasm into a pond, located beneath a bluff or cliff. It was considered the height of bravery to leap from that cliff, a fall of perhaps fifty feet, into that pond.

The bravery of leaping was considered important because an 'urban' legend held that several young people had jumped from the bluff, missed the water, and landed on the visible and sharp rocks that surrounded the pond.

Compleat

Deaths, as a result, may well have caused the park to be removed from any maps or cartography showing its location but the fact remains that in my youth this place was considered to be one of the high spots of for partying.

For myself, I was younger than most that were there the day I took the leap and it took me a few minutes to steel my resolve to jump. To this day I believe that if there hadn't been a bunch of teenage girls, in bikinis and looking on to 'see' who had the courage to jump I would have simply backed down. My fear of falling made jumping off a cliff feel like certain death even if I were to avoid landing on the rocks because my heart felt like it was trying to explode out of my chest from the fear I felt just from looking over the edge.

Oddly enough though the experience is important and the details remain emblazoned on my memory. It wasn't the leap I finally took and survived that is the point of this story. I leapt off the bluff, and landed in the water without incident, and a few of those who witnessed even cheered though I barely knew any of them well and none of the girls approached me afterward to compliment my effort.

No, the point of this story isn't even about my not getting laid, either. The events that happened after my leap revealed something to me about myself that I hadn't understood until they came about. Remember that I said that the pond was fed by a creek running through a narrow chasm causing it to maintain a consistent water level? In my youthful arrogance, I decided that leaping from the bluff wasn't enough to truly impress upon everyone watching that I had courage.

So instead of climbing out of the pond and regaining the top of the bluff by way of the path, that which teenage feet had created through the simple repetition of walking it, I chose instead to attempt to swim up the creek to where there was a smaller pond that others were using as a swimming pool.

At first, this choice was made easy by the widening of the creek's mouth as it emptied into the pond. But as I swam against the current, the walls of the chasm that the creek ran through narrowed the further uphill I swam and the current became stronger as the chasm narrowed.

Too stubborn and proud to ask for assistance, I exhausted myself by swimming against the flow to the point that I may well have drowned if others hadn't seen my useless efforts and came to my aid.

Pulled from the water, like a dying salmon, I lay gasping for breath and embarrassed that those girls had witnessed my failure to accomplish a task I was physically incapable of performing. I failed and though they were almost all strangers to me, I was ashamed that I had needed to be rescued from my own inabilities.

In all my years that one thing has haunted me and caused me to become psychotically enraged over and over again. Shame. Shame for not being able to do something I saw as being possible. I knew that for myself I wasn't allowed to fail, not by society, not by my parents, friends, peers, or even god. I wasn't allowed to fail what I saw as being possible, no matter how many people would say that it was impossible. In a single sentence. I wasn't allowed to fail by me.

The irony of that sentence comes not from trying to accomplish so many impossible tasks. There are many of those who say that the only failure is to not try or to give up. But those are the exact same people who would say to me "Learn to fail fast." or "Know your limitations." And the irony is that not only have I never 'learned' to fail fast, or accepted my 'limitations' I have always destroyed my self-image because I could not and would not allow myself to fail at anything.

Now anyone who went to public school with me would recall that I received many failing grades on homework assignments, as well as a few failing grades in classes and being beaten up by other boys as a result of my being mouthy and arrogant.

But I never once considered 'grades' as being a measure of who I was and being beaten up was something I had become acclimated to while growing up with my older brother and the insane punishments that were meted out in my family household. The only measure of failure I've ever adhered to was my own. If I felt that I 'should' be able to accomplish something, no matter how difficult, then I didn't know how to quit or simply accept that I wasn't capable of accomplishing it.

The acronym for the word "ego" that I relate to most is edging god out. This holds special meaning in light of the events that I write about in this book because my ego was so large that I actually told god I would toss him out of his seat or position of authority and could run the world (universe) better than he had up to that point. Another point of irony was revealed in that statement because the argument that I presented to justify it was my own life.

All that had been done to me, all that I had done to others, all the failures I had experienced, and every single instance where I had fallen, exhausted by my best efforts only to be pulled from the flow of my insanity by others. That was the evidence I used to charge 'god' with failure.

And that's when I grew so enraged that I told this being that had supposedly created everything, including me, to go fuck itself. Somewhere in this book, I relate a story about Adam and Eve, the whole garden of Eden myth and how original sin wasn't simply their supposed disobedience of the one rule they had been given.

It had more to do with their choice to not accept responsibility for their own actions. That was the lesson I had been brought before their god to learn. Only by facing this god dude on his own turf, shouting him down, raging and swearing to do all I could to remove him from the world and take his place in order to "show" how it should have been done could I be ready to awaken to the fact that I was responsible for everything that had happened in my lifespan.

Does a nine-month-old choose to fall from a chain link fence and bust his skull open? No, I'm not that ridiculous. Yet I had challenged this god dude to allow me to run the world to show I could have done it better. What if, on the off chance that the reason I wasn't blasted into micro fragments or component pieces of the atoms that consist of my physical body I was responsible for everything that had happened in my life?

I cannot count the number of times I've heard learned people ask the questions that come to mind when I write that sentence. "If there's a god, why does god allow bad things to happen to good people?" Sarcastically I usually answer: "What choice does he have in the matter? Humanity allows it all to happen and does nothing to prevent or bring about an end to it." I'm not talking about victims or trying to re-victimize anyone who has suffered at the hands of others, especially those who suffered from being exposed to my insanity when my ego and narcissism were the predominant forces running my entire life.

I use my experiences throughout this book so, in this case, I will use an example from my past again. Does a two-year-old boy have any responsibility for being raped, locked in a dark closet, and threatened with being confined there forever unless he stops crying and swears to "never tell anyone?" The chorus of "of course not" and "no way, the guy who does that to a two-year-old deserves a horrific and excruciating punishment where death would be too good for him!" resound throughout the world even with those who might never read this book. But the fact remains that the world allowed it to happen.

And that boy grew to become the monster he had feared in that closet, so that the echo of those cries for denial and punishment became a part of his own life.

In writing this book, once again I find myself swimming against the flow. The current of humanity grows stronger the further I swim against that flow and my only reward is exhaustion and regret. I no longer feel ashamed for making the attempt at doing the impossible, I'm just tired, panting, and trying desperately to regain some portion of my own humanity.

Because, as I've said to many and often, I gave away my own humanity when I gave up, committed suicide, and failed at being what human beings were meant to be to one another.

The burden of knowledge is that once you know something, and truly know it from experience, there is no means short of dying that can release you from knowing. Drugs and alcohol blur it for a while but then the knowledge comes back full force along with the additional information that you've not only made a fool of yourself in front of those you might or might not think you care about but you've also failed at stopping the process of remembering it at all.

That is the hardest part of sharing all of the information that is in this book. Knowing that most of humanity will never read it. The Christians never read their own book, the bible. The Islamic people don't read theirs, the Quran, with any more precision than the Christians. The Jews ignore their own book, the Torah, with the same disregard - burying the truth under the traditions of religion and hypocrisy to the point that humanity keeps creating more and more religions trying to explain what doesn't really need explanation.

"Why are we here?"

Why does humanity exist at all? The religion of science would try to convince everyone that it's all one big mistake, an accident of universal proportion. Other religions try to convince humanity that theirs is the 'only way' to get to an existence beyond this physical life humanity has been saddled with for so many years. And of course, there are those who deny that there is any reason for humanity to exist at all.

The point remains that humanity does have a responsibility that it has been avoiding for as long as oral or written history records.

To care for one another. I think I'll repeat that for those who think it's too simple. Humanity's purpose for existing is to care for one another.

Compleat

Compleat

Punctuation

The so-called Christians, especially their leaders or pastors, like to cherry-pick verses out of their bible and use them to exemplify or support their arguments for being the 'only' religion that has any validity. I have seen them do this and have witnessed the same behavior with those who claim to follow the Islamic religion. But because I have had more experience with the Christian religion, I've decided to cherry-pick one of the verses of their bible and recreate it in a way that makes much more sense to me and honestly makes it seem much closer to the truth of what god might have been saying all along.

Though the Christian and Islamic religions are both based on the Jewish religion they differ in their beliefs of about who their god is represented by most. For the Christians they profess a belief in Jesus as being the ultimate authority, having been not just the conceived child of god but also the Messiah that was promised to the Jewish religion. While in the Islamic religion, Mohammad is considered the great 'prophet' of their god, representing their ultimate truth and profession of belief in their god's will for them.

My cherry-picked verse comes from what the Christians call the 'old testament' and is included in the Torah of the Jewish religion, which predates the Islamic religion and is why I chose it as an example of the simplest means by which punctuation might alter the meaning of a sentence or title of a book.

Compleat

I learned this method of altering perspective from a secular or non-religious source when having a discussion with a friend of mine who had been an editor for the Sacramento Bee, a major newspaper for that city back when newspapers were the major means of getting information from semi-reliable sources.

Dave P. insisted that Dostoevsky had written the book: "Notes From the Underground." Now although he was my editor, I was forced to show him my copy of the actual book that had been written by Dostoevsky before he would accept that he was making a very common mistake.

Rather than being "Notes From the Underground" the title of the book is actually 'Notes From Underground.' Ironically, the book itself is sold online and listed by many libraries around the world with the title including that injunction of "the" as if that were the actual title of what the author had written. And including that one word, the title of the book is altered to reflect not just the bias of those who include the extra word but also diminishes the intent of the author by its inclusion.

I've done the same type of thing with the Christian bible and am working on some of the phrases that are often misquoted or cherry-picked from the Koran as well. The particular verse is, in itself, not offensive and can be seen as a 'positive thinking' or supportive view of the theory that god exists and is supportive, yet I still chose to change it in order to set a perspective before those who are reading this that alters the entire meaning of that one verse simply by adding punctuation that was never included, and possibly never meant to be seen in the manner I express.

In the book of Psalms, at in Chapter 46, verse 10 (PS 46:10) the Christian bible lists the following phrase:

"Be still and know that I am God."

Who the writer of the psalm was speaking to or about simply doesn't matter to me in the least and especially doesn't come into serious consideration in regard to my altering it for the purpose of this example. My point being is not to create a religious debate but to offer an alternative perspective to this religious example.

Taking the phrase as it was written I've altered the entire meaning of the phrase by simply adding another punctuation mark, in this case, a comma.

"Be still and know that I am," God.

Compleat

By adding one simple comma I've altered the meaning of the sentence from being a command to rely upon god by quieting themselves inwardly and knowing god for who or what he/she/it might be, supportive and omnipresent, to a statement delivered directly from the old dude himself, stating that by shutting up and thereby allowing themselves to comprehend for themselves the entire human race can know that god exists.

Simple. Incredibly obvious if taken out of context and applied as being an interpretation that did not fit with the intent of those who rewrote their bible to include more commands and the patriarchal intent of controlling the masses of humanity through their religion.

I do not intend to dismiss the bible, or the Quran for that matter, nor the Torah or any other "religious" writings as being incorrect or "wrong" as too many religions do about the other religions. As a final example, I want to share again a story of mountain climbers.

Professional mountain climbers use the best equipment available to accomplish amazing feats of scaling mountain peaks of great height and expanse. Mount Everest, being one of the most famous. In choosing their equipment, they often choose rope from a certain manufacturer that has a high reputation of for providing the absolute best, since the quality of that rope might spell the difference between a successful climb and serious injury or death from falling. That particular manufacturer's product is identified by a single red thread among the thousands of threads that are used to create the rope. Those less qualified and experienced in climbing might choose to use other gear for climbing and the results are often reported as catastrophic.

This simple choice is similar to the choices of those who belong to particular religions throughout the human race. Though the religion might 'feel' right to them, and although they might gather themselves together with thousands of others that agree or feel similarly to themselves one fact stands out. That a single thread of truth can be found in any of them.

The so-called Christians' bible contains a single thread of that truth that runs through it as does that professional quality rope for mountain climbing. So too does the Islamic Koran, the Jewish Torah, the writings of the Buddha, the philosophic observations of Confucius, and thousands of others who have tried to communicate their observations to the race of humanity.

My question is if, as the many Hindi religions state, there are many paths to the top of the mountain why do all religions, including that religion, profess to be the single most important thread of truth that runs through the thousands of misleading and deliberately altered information that they all offer on the nature and relationship humanity shares with god?

If any human being wants to actually know what and who they are in regard to the divine or life or god or whatever label they might adhere to I can make this suggestion from my own experience.

Ask. Ask to know and god, life, the divine, the great mother, Allah, whatever label anyone might choose to use or in whatever manner that particular human being's mind can wrap itself around and the nature of what I choose to call pop will be more than willing to reveal it/him/herself to them, simply for the asking. There is an old adage that I humorously feel the need to include at this point:

"Be careful what you ask for – you just might get it."

And again, I've altered that phrase as well, based on my own experience:

"Be careful what you ask for – you WILL get it."

Compleat

Whatever
—·—·—·—·—·—·—·—·—·—·—·—·—·—·—·—·—··

Whatever.

What?

Whatever!

If this phrase or set of phrases sounds familiar it's probably because as a human being you've either said one side of an argument or the other that ended only when it became clear that there would be no acceptable resolution to the discussion. They won't listen to you and you're not about to see things from their perspective if they aren't willing to at least hear what it is you're trying to express.

When feelings are running high and when the points of view are so opposed and when no one is willing to step outside of their own position to consider another then the result is that the discussion ends with the conversation killer … "whatever".

Compleat

Where did this idea come from? What part of human nature leads people to believe in giving up and dismissing a discussion as a pointless exercise in trying to communicate?

It's been around for so very long, this severing of the lines of communication, that written history probably doesn't have a record of when it was first used with this single word.

Ironically the oral histories of humanity might have had a record of its first use, placing blame on an individual for using it by naming it that person's response. But written history has erased most of the sources of oral history; legends, stories, and songs being forgotten in exchange for writing down what was once told and retold as a means of sharing what knowledge humanity had to share with one another.

I find it amusing that one of the 'answers' god gave me, that I absolutely have no idea who would ask for, relates to this dismissive word or phrase.

Is there a definition of the word 'whatever' that human beings have agreed upon that makes it so universally accepted and its use so acceptable?

What I learned is that saying 'whatever' to anyone is not just a dismissal of their perspective on an issue, it is actually a dismissal of the individual themselves. Why god gave me this answer I couldn't begin to understand, but the examples throughout history of human beings dismissing one another stand out like candles in a darkened room when they first become lit.

I'll pick on one, that I'm slightly familiar with from my education and experiences with religions. In Christianity's best example of the 'whatever' concept it is eloquently depicted when the story of Jesus being tried by the Roman Prelate Pontius Pilot is told.

When the governor of Judea couldn't find anything 'wrong' with the Jesus dude and the religious leaders of that day kept demanding that he crucify the dude, Pilot simply washed his hands of the entire matter with … "whatever." "Do whatever you want." "On your heads be his blood." "Not my circus, not my monkey." "Not my problem." "I don't know the dude and couldn't care less." "I just don't care." "I don't care enough to even listen any longer."

How many people even think of the concept that saying "whatever" is washing their hands of the other person and not just their perception of an issue? It's a

Compleat

truth that god had to show me or I wouldn't have even thought about it. But the truth is the truth, and like most truths ... ignorance is no excuse.

Of course, I know that most of you will just say: "Whatever!"

Compleat

Aside from

Being Human

─ · ─ · ─ · ─ · ─ · ─ · ─ · ─ · ─ · ─ · ─ · ─ · ─ · ─ ·

There is a person whose opinions about the natures of reality and humanity I respect despite our differing perspectives on these subjects. And although I've often tried to explain my perspective, they were consistently unable or unwilling to see what I was trying to express from a perspective other than their own.

Yet, one day, almost as if they were trying to explain to me the 'why' other people have such difficulty understanding what I say or express they actually expressed exactly what I had been saying all along in words that made sense to them and still couldn't acknowledge what they had expressed was what I perceived.

"You are over here ... saying things that others don't relate to or understand, almost as if you are making incomprehensible noises or guttural sounds while humanity is over here, communicating by their agreeing to the meanings, intent, and concepts that they use as a common ground for their communications with one another."

Compleat

The fact that this person had labeled my inability to communicate with humanity as being a problem of expectation on my part as if I expect humanity to grasp or even want to understand what I've expressed, I found truly ironic. And with that being that person's assumption, I've come to expect others to relate to their statement, rather than hearing what I'm saying as being my major malfunction when it comes to communicating with human beings Instead, I perceive that they were expressing exactly why I feel unable to communicate with human beings at all.

Now, while I chose not to add to that particular discourse or disagreement by even attempting to point out that assuming what I might or might not expect is one of the most difficult points that I have yet to overcome when attempting to express my experiences with human beings, I held back from the attempt to yet again communicate with them simply because I perceived it would be pointless.

For if it's already an assumption that I expect humanity to listen to what I say and understand it, through attempts at converting their perspectives to conform to my own, then arguing that I have no such expectation would only become yet another empty issue of discourse and disagreement. I'd be wrong, even before attempting the discussion simply because in expressing disagreement I would be demonstrating the very perspective they were trying to advance.

My point here is that if I'm unable to communicate clearly with human beings not simply because I expect them to conform to my way of perceiving things but because humanity has its own set of values and agreed-upon perspectives of what certain words and phrases mean between and among themselves then what chance do I have of gaining their attention, let alone their comprehension of things I've expressed that are outside of their agreed upon means of communication?

As this person had pointed out, so eloquently, by my expressing my experiences in the manner in which I do I am not in agreement or in accord with humanity as a whole. This exactly, as I have stated through many of my stories, expresses my perspectives, and even my experiences of why I actually see myself as being outside of the collective that is humanity.

Compleat

What that person failed to comprehend is that while I do not see myself as better than nor worse than human, I do perceive myself as not a part of the collective that is the human race as a whole.

And their description of my lack of ability to communicate expressed exactly that fact, although I'm almost positive they were unaware that they had just expressed it even as I had frequently expressed it to them, just in their own words.

Compleat

Around & Around the World, It Goes

All my life I've been a voracious reader. Not just in the comic books that taught me how to read and the books that opened the world to my mind over the ages that I experienced. I did read in my attempt to understand the whys and wherefores of life until every story held some small truth if I would only look at it closely enough and because I read this way even the bible became a storybook when I read it the first time from front cover to back.

Yet my reading didn't end with the books and newspapers, comics and comic books, bibles, korans, philosophies, and literature of all the different mythologies that humanity had created for itself. I learned too and was fortunate enough to catch glimpses of the stories people I met held deep behind the distances they managed to keep from one another by looking into their eyes.

While I misread their stories more often than not, I readily admit I was never able to 'see' deeply enough to read everything about them, with practice and experience I was able to view more than they might have realized or wanted others to know. I would listen to their words and while they talked look into their eyes to see the truth behind what they were saying. Perhaps I developed this ability, as I did my other type of reading, as a survival tool or instinctively?

I never really concerned myself with the why I was able to use this to either manipulate or avoid their anger, fear and even love.

But while I've always been a reader of either type, I never thought to be a writer. The written word holds within it a type of power, much as the spoken word holds a volume of power that humanity has yet to realize. And it was with reluctance that I started writing even short stories for newsletters and articles of opinion for newspapers and magazines, though I did everything in my power to remain anonymous when writing and being published. One humorous name I used was indeed Anon E. Mouse, making my name unimportant and attempting to place a smile on whomever read what I had written wither they agreed with my experience, opinion, or expressed reasoning or not.

But writing is as addictive for me as reading had been. And so, when I was directed to write these stories, no matter how reluctant I was and would become, because to write them I would be subject to re-experience them, I began to make the attempt. My first attempt began in 1993, after being released from a mental hospital for the criminally insane. I started out small, writing short stories and articles of about recovery for a local newsletter publicly but all the while the pressure to write all the stories in one book grew until I made my first attempt.

By the summer of 1994, I had accumulated thousands of pages of research, photographic evidence, reference materials, and quotes from medical journals and scientific researchers. Thousands of pages handwritten and more that were typed up on personal computers and downloaded onto discs from websites that were a part of the 'dark web' or 'deep-web' as it was known to me. A place that exists only to those who seek for things that ought not to be allowed to exist or even perused. I went there and, found exactly what I had expected to find but didn't have the strength to avoid becoming drawn deeper into it than I had hoped.   In the end, I was forced, for the sake of my own sanity, to destroy everything I had created, discovered or researched. The discs and notebooks I burned and the passwords and accesses to the dark web I deleted, never to remember and never to go there again. That ended my first attempt at writing these stories, no matter the reason or reasoning behind their needing to be told.

By 1995 I began writing again, this time with only the objective to express what I myself had experienced and perhaps an explanation of the why behind what I was writing. This second attempt held no graphic images and no real stories of anything other than myself. More of a confessional than the missive to humanity I had attempted before in order to explain my story and all the 'whys' behind what I had done to others throughout my lifespan.

A mere six chapters long I soon realized it was more narcissistic and self-aggrandizement than telling the stories for the sake of expressing what I had been instructed to share. And again, I deleted and burned all the research, the hard copies of notes and stories, and went so far as to put writing aside in my efforts to avoid being the asshole I could see behind that attempted storytelling.

As I just stated though, writing is addictive and stopping cold turkey was too hard for me. I went back to writing stories of experiences in recovery, and opinion pieces for magazines, including some a few internationally read magazines, under pseudonyms and false names.

Compleat

Reader's Digest will never know how many of my stories they published under false names, as a laughable example, and it is my intention to keep them and the other magazines in the dark about who wrote what articles they published, though if anyone were to research the articles they published that were never 'paid' for the words that were used and could decipher my style of writing it would probably not be that hard to discover exactly what I've written over the years.

Skipping ahead to 1997 thru 1999 and the birth of my second son, I had resisted the pressure to write these stories until his birth forced me to realize that I was both watched and watched over, even as I would be forced to watch and watch over him until he was grown to where he would take responsibility for himself.

Four more attempts would find the same results that the two previous attempts had found. I've burned, deleted and erased more words than "Carter's has liver pills." An archaic phrase from my past but accurate when applied to the writing of these stories for humanity's use and hopefully awakening. Which brings me to the subject of this story.

I began once again to write these stories, hand written in order that I might not merely experience the emotional trauma of reliving the experiences as I wrote about them but also that the physical pain caused by having arthritis and carpal tunnel syndrome would make burning the notebooks that contained the work a tiny bit easier to resist.

I chose to not self-edit them this go around, instead finding an editor through online sources as distant from my physical presence as I could and at the same time not reluctant to read some of the more graphically challenging stories of my heinous actions, that I felt were necessary in order to present an honest image of who I truly am.

I found such a person, on in the southernmost part of Africa, nearly two thirds of the entire distance of the world away, and mailed my notebooks and notes on January 22, 2021. And as anyone might suspect from this story and that date, an adventure began that day. Covid-19 had recently broken out, the pandemic closed not just businesses and transportation venues it also closed mailing services from country to country.

I had mailed the package at the post office in Hartville, Missouri, expecting it to arrive at its destination within a two or three-week period. It went from Hartville, Missouri to Springfield, MO, and then on to the Chicago, IL

Compleat

International Distribution Center. From January 26th through February 1st, 2021 the beginnings of my manuscript bounced around through that facility being 'processed' until it was finally "in transit to the next facility" on February 9th.

And if it could have been any more confusing, it then arrived at the Regional Facility, Chicago International Distribution Center at first 8:57 pm on Friday, February 9th, again at 1:30 pm on February 10th, and departed Chicago International Distribution Center at also 1:30 pm from that same center to arrive in Chicago, IL USA at 4:58 pm.

The next morning, it departed Chicago, US at 7:59 am to depart from New York, US on February 11th, 2021. Where, oh where, did this package with my life's work go next?

It was processed through the Chicago, IL International Distribution Center on February 12th, 2021 at 7:06 am.

HUH? Yep, it left New York to be processed back in Chicago. But let's not give up on the USPS because it departed New York, US at 8:46 pm that same night. ???

On February 13th the package would be processed through the ISC Miami, FL USPS at 6:50 am, and be processed through the Miami, FL International Distribution Center at that same time and date. Apparently, it had left the US because it next appeared to have departed Dublin, Ireland on February 13th, at 9:12 am.

Thank goodness for the international dateline or I'd have begun to think that my manuscript had broken the time continuum and had crossed the Atlantic Ocean in less than 3 hours. But lo, let's not give up on the USPS making this a bit more confusing just yet. The package departed Dublin, Ireland, and arrived in Miami, US FL on February 13th, 2021 a 4:50 pm. Can anyone say, "Bounce?"

For Valentine's Day, February 14th, 2021 the package containing my notebooks, and the beginnings of my manuscript departed Miami, US at 2:00 pm. And departed Panama City, Panama on February 16th, 2021 at 10:10 am. By this time, I was thinking about hiring my old buddy, Tin-Tin to track down and find the package and my manuscript.

A fictional character, very true, but possibly having a better chance of informing me of 'where' the package was than the USPS had been doing up until that point. Oh, and notice that the package departed from Panama City on

Compleat

February 16th? It arrived at the USPS Regional Facility, Metro NY Distribution Center on March 25, 2021, at 2:51 pm. So, it appears that the time warp the package experienced on its way to Dublin, Ireland caused it to fall into a space/time warp for over a month, only to reappear in New York in time for my second son's birthday.

That night, as everyone was sleeping safely in their beds thinking that time wasn't an illusion and everything had a purpose and existence was an orderly and easily followed process the package departed the Metro NY Distribution Center at 7:08 pm and arrived, across a very small river I'm told, at 9:21 pm at the Newark, NJ Distribution Center. There is no record of when or how it left New Jersey, though if you asked native New Yorkers, they might give you a thousand reasons 'why' it should.

But all is not lost, only my package is or was because it arrived on March 27th, 2021 at the USPS Regional Facility, Kansas City, KS Network Distribution Center. Crossing yet another river, the Missouri River I believe, the package arrived at the USPS Kansas City, MO Distribution Center later that night at 10:36 pm.

Now to put things into perspective, I believe it would be possible for an averagely healthy individual to walk from Kansas City, MO to my home just outside of Hartville, MO in 12 days. And that's with sleeping in hotels or motels overnight each day.

Where then did my package go after it departed Kansas City, MO on March 28th, 2021 at 5:16 am? Why it went to Aurora, IL arriving there a 3:01 pm. Now maybe it's next stop explains 'some' of the delays and routing of this expedition around the world and, in irony, it did appear to avoid April Fool's Day by arriving back at the Customs Clearance, ISC Chicago, IL on April 2nd, 2021 at 12:30 pm.

Did it not get approved by customs on its way to my editor? Or did it not get cleared by customs agents in Miami, FL? One would expect that Miami, with all its drug trafficking problems, would have cleared it already, but since it was going through customs, even in Chicago, IL I had hope that it would finally be on its way to its final destination.

April 5th, 2021 at 12:12 pm the package arrived, again, at the USPS Chicago International Distribution Center. It departed, immediately, from what I could see on the USPS receipt, and arrived at the Customs Clearance ISC New York, NY USPS on April 7th, 2021 at 5:14 am.

Customs again, but really who cares if it means it's headed back to its destination, right? But it didn't really, because it also arrived at the USPS Regional Facility, Jamaica, NY International Distribution Center at that same time and date.

Later that same evening, guess what! At 8:32 pm it was processed through the Chicago, IL International Distribution Center yet again, to arrive a full day later at 10:16 pm on April 8th, 2021 in (you guessed it didn't you?) Chicago, US.

How this next part happened is still a mystery to me, since it apparently never left Chicago but departed the USPS Regional Facility in Jamaica, NY from International Distribution Center on April 9th, 2021 a 2:07 am. And departed the Chicago, US at 9:18 am that same day.

It gets better and more confusing of course because the package with my manuscript also departed Newark, NJ at 8:49 pm on April 9th, 2021 as well, in order to depart from Dublin, Ireland (perhaps I should have packaged my manuscript in green?) on April 10th, 2021 at 11:51 am.

I've never been to New York, YET! But if I can ever get the funds, I intend to visit Jamaica, NY and New Jersey across the river. But while I'm there I might as well visit Queens, NY.

Because my package arrived at the USPS Regional Facility in Queens, NY Distribution Center on April 10th, 2021 at 4:36 pm. And it departed Queens, NY on April 11th, 2021 to arrive at the USPS Facility in Edgerton, KS on April 12th, 2021 at 10:57 pm.

I had begun to think that my package was getting a little tired of traveling and moving through time the way it seemed to be doing by now of course and Kansas, even Edgerton is just across the way from Missouri, as the crow flies.

Perhaps I should have hired a crow to deliver my manuscript? Only minutes later it departed Edgerton, KS, and arrived at the USPS Regional Facility Kansas City, KS Network Distribution Center at 4:29 am on April 13th.

At 8:38 am, it departed the Kansas City, KS Network Distribution Center and arrived at the Kansas City, MO USPS Regional Distribution Center at 12:40 pm. Four hours to cross the same river it had crossed so many times before, and I have to note here that I could swim across that river, if were it not so polluted, in less time than that.

Compleat

On April 14th, 2021 the package containing my life's work departed the USPS Regional Facility Kansas City, MO Distribution Center at 10:37 am. As I mentioned before, it remains my opinion that a healthy individual could walk, carrying that package the entire way from Kansas City, MO to my home in Hartville, MO in less than 12 days.

At the writing of this story, on April 25th, 2021 not only has my package not arrived at its destination overseas or returned to my home where I could resend it by a more reliable and efficient means, but the USPS also has no idea which direction it's going now.

The one alert I've received via email or text was 'while; I was on the phone with the USPS Customer Service Representative and their information was exactly the same as the tracking application I have on my smart phone:

"Your item departed the USPS facility in Kansas City, MO Distribution Center on April 14th at 10:37 am. The item is currently in transit to the destination."

What that destination is or where it's going remains a great and confusing mystery.

But then too, the manuscript itself is a great and confusing mystery to many. Perhaps that's the "why" behind the world traveling package that contains the stories I've written there?! One day, we'll all know.

Compleat

Going Postal

In 1977 I got out of the Marines for a short period of time. I had grown so disillusioned with myself and knew that I was never going to measure up to what others expected of a Marine Corporal, never expecting to get promoted to Sergeant and hating the lie of being the 'finest' that Marines were supposed to be. After my first four years of being in the Marines, I knew that drug use was high because of the men coming back from Viet Nam sharing stories and their own addictions to the drugs they did to withstand the nightmares of having been there. I listened to those stories and hated the system that allowed men to die for something they believed in but that their beliefs were based on lies that they had been told. The war wasn't about protecting a people from Communism, promoting Democracy around the world, or even truth and justice. It was based simply on making rich, old, white men richer. Nothing more and nothing less.

When I got out, I intended to put the entire wasted 4- year experience behind me, blotting it out the way I had tried to erase my childhood through more drug use and burning brain cells by staying high or drunk as often as possible. To do that though, I needed work. The Marines hadn't prepared me for any job that paid more than minimum wage so I did whatever labor that became available. Having the status of being a veteran with an honorable discharge, I was able to find several short -term jobs.

I worked as a janitor in a grade school, working at night when none of the children were there and most of the teachers weren't. I liked the job, but found myself spending too much time in the girls' bathrooms and watching the female teachers who worked late while fantasizing about having sex with them in the school. So, I quit. Or got fired? I don't remember exactly.

My next attempt at employment was working for the post office during the Christmas rush. They hired temporary help, with the preference being shown to veterans with an honorable discharge because we had been government employees before while in the military and that would have counted toward our eventual retirement if they decided to retain us on a permanent basis.

For anyone who has never been inside a post office the size of the main one in St. Louis, let me describe something. The room where the mail and packages are sorted was huge. Semi-trucks, loaded with mail, packages, and parcels were always parked against the doors where their loads would be offloaded as quickly as possible but there was a never- ending stream of the trucks and as one became empty another would take its place.

Into this huge, chaotic place came us temps. Stacks of letters and magazines were placed in trays and the trays were stacked on rolling racks of 12 tiers on both sides. Each night, we were supposed to clear a minimum of 3 racks each. Sorting the mail by zip code, into pigeon holes marked with all the codes for every zone in the States. Foreign mail was simply tossed into a 'foreign' pile and would be sorted by another department. "Probably the regulars" is what we guessed as we worked and talked about the process.

And we did talk to one another there. 12 hours a shift, sorting mail that was sometimes too hard to tell what the zip code was, and growing tired and mentally exhausted long before a break for lunch was called. OSHA would have freaked back then, because there were no breaks other than the lunch for us temps.

Being that I was still using drugs to blot out my past, the solution to exhaustion was simple for me and a few other temps there. Speed. Black Beauties, White Crosses any diet pills that anyone could get a hold of we would do, and we made our quotas every night that way. Of course, the mail probably got sorted into the wrong zip codes after a few hours of speeding through them. We laughed about it, sometimes seeing just how far we could toss a letter or card into one of the pigeon holes, by standing back from our work stations.

And then too, once in a great while, the truck off-loaders would become overwhelmed by the sheer volume of Christmas packages being sent at the last minute by people expecting them to be delivered before the holiday. So, the temps would be called in as reliefs. Giving the package handlers a break from the labor. But oh, what fun that was, especially when we would find a package that was already damaged, but marked 'fragile' and the games would begin for us.

Ever wonder how your packages became so damaged that you were forced to file an insurance claim for the damage to their contents? It was probably either a temp or a permanent person who had grown exhausted with the demands placed on them to perform the impossible without consideration for their physical or mental health.

Compleat

Called Football in Europe and Soccer in the States, it was game on, and kicking those packages the farthest, the highest, or just the hardest became a means of letting off steam and frustration. Putting the racks that letters would go on atop one another was a way of creating goalposts and kicking a package through the goals would get your team points as well as a blast of speed or a shot of whatever booze had been snuck into the job.

By the end of the night shift, even packages that weren't damaged became the balls used to get more 'done.' I worked there for the entire Christmas season of 1977, and though I did sort mail the correct way occasionally it was so mindbogglingly boring that I didn't mind much when I was fired for not showing up to work on a day when I was supposed to be there.

Ironically, it was the only sick day I ever had while working there. I woke up with a fever of 102 degrees, couldn't talk or walk, could barely think and didn't even consider calling in sick to work, just rolling back over in bed and going back to sleep. When the fever broke, I called but was told my employment had been terminated due to failure to appear or inform my superiors that I had been sick.

What a laugh. As if I could have called when I was so sick that I couldn't even remember where I was let alone where I was supposed to be the day that I missed work. The Postal Service in the States used to be one of the biggest businesses in the world. Even with messed up temporary employees like myself and my fellow temps that year. But, and this may be egotistical of me, perhaps they shouldn't have fired me that year?! I might have gone on to become a regular employee, settle down and straighten out.

Or I might have gone 'Postal' on my fellow employees? What I do know is that it doesn't surprise me in the least that they have fallen on into difficult financial situations in recent years. In my other stories, I have mentioned that the god dude had an interest in me even back then. So, I give myself a little leeway when it comes to ego here and guess maybe they brought it on themselves?! Temps are people, too.

Compleat

Mad Man At

McDonald's

Compleat

During my confinement at Atascadero (1988 – 1993) I saw a story on the television of the police being forced to shoot and kill a gunman at a local McDonald's restaurant. Obviously, the news reporters were voicing their shock at the concept of an individual choosing to "shoot innocent men, women, and children at a family eating establishment." Their praises for the officers involved in stopping the gunman were barely counterbalanced by their questioning of "why and how could anyone choose to act in such a manner?"

And as I watched the repeated story on several different channels, listening to the same outrage, confusion, concern, condemnation, and commiseration with the families of the victims I could only think of one important fact that they asked about but seemed to have no real interest in understanding or realizing. Why!? Why did the gunman choose to open fire in a public place, drawing attention to himself and doing such a heinous act? And as I thought about their question, I realized I knew the answer they said they needed but even as they asked it, they ignored it.

I knew why the gunman acted the way he did, I could relate to him much more than I could to the so-called 'normal' society that had confined me because of my own insanity and violent actions. I envied the gunman, though I could never have brought myself to act out in such a manner, because he achieved the result that he had sought and I still find myself seeking. A release from life.

Why did he shoot all those people? Because he was cowardly and angry at the society around him? No. Was he a coward though? Definitely! Because he feared taking his own life but so needed release from the confines of living that he chose to use others to end it.

He used the system to do what he couldn't find the courage within himself to do. He knowingly destroyed lives around himself, gunning down innocents so that those responding to the situation would be forced to end his existence. I knew, even as I saw the reports on the news stations that the hospital staff and patients were obsessed with observing and I walked away from the television viewing area and felt pity for the man.

I had sorrow for the people who were killed, their families and friends, and even for the officers involved that were forced to end his 'rampage' by shooting him. But sorrow isn't the same as pity.

Compleat

Pity is a combination of envy, nostalgia, and anger. I envied his release from life, envying him his final release. Nostalgically I remembered what it was like to be human, in a way, like distant echoes of a memory that had faded but had found one final whisper to be heard in his actions.

And I found I was angry, deep inside. Angry with him for not having the courage to just end his own life. Anger at the society that asked "How could he do something so awful?" all the while not really caring to 'know or understand' the answer to their questions. Anger at the hospital staff for voicing their observations that he had "gotten what he had coming." Anger at the society that had allowed his suffering to exist for so long, untreated and unrecognized until he chose to act out on it and then being "shocked" by his actions. And angry with myself ... for being able to recognize, relate and feel empathy for the perpetrator of the act more than the human beings that he had gunned down.

He died and other than the families of the victims of his actions I imagine that no one will ever remember or even recall his name. Not even me. He was just the Madman at the McDonald's. But I knew him more than anyone else. Because I was him, on the inside, with just the one difference between us. I had tried to end my own life without injuring others.

Jaws

Compleat

If anyone has ever read the book, not just seen the movie, Jaws, they might remember the plot setting where the wife of the protagonist cheated on her husband with a younger, college-educated man. In the book, her innermost thoughts were described as wondering about the man she had just had sex with going to the bathroom, and pissing for over a minute. "Do all men have bladders like a camel?" A ridiculous plot and setting, having nothing to do with the guy, her husband, or the killer shark the story was all about but the author included it for a reason.

As a young man, I took the idea to heart though and began to measure the time it took for me to finish urinating to see if I measured up to being a 'man.' Ego-driven, considering the size of my penis as being too small to compare to other males, I gained some sense of self from the fact that I, too, could take much longer than a minute to piss.

It seems ironic, looking back on the thoughts I had then about my maleness, that I was so insecure and would eventually be betrayed by my first wife in much the same way. She was older than I, smarter than I gave her credit for, and had affairs with younger men, including Randal Moore – the young man she would eventually leave me for and leave her children from her first marriage in my care.

Compleat

The movie showed only that she cheated on her husband, the sheriff. It couldn't display the inner dialog of her thoughts about men and their urinary discharges. Like many movies, the plot and character development lost perspective that might have created a deeper understanding of her character, but in the end, wouldn't have made as much impact as reading the story for myself.

I didn't relate to the author, and didn't question why the plot setting was necessary for that particular character, but I did feel the impact of her cheating on her husband and then relating back to his pissing and considering the length it took for her lover to piss as being similar.

Compleat

The How & The Why
— ∙ — ∙ — ∙ — ∙ — ∙ — ∙ — ∙ — ∙ — ∙ — ∙ — ∙ — ∙ — ∙ — ∙ — ∙ —∙∙

There will be those who will ask themselves, "Why him?" Why would god pick a child molesting, child rapist to speak to humanity about themselves? And as I've stated before, "The answer lays in the question itself."

Being selected to speak wasn't my idea. When I realized what it was that he wanted me to do and say, I rebelled completely, telling him to go fuck himself, threatening to unseat him and show him how he 'should' have run the world of humanity. But even as I hurled insults and derision at him the old dude knew what was in the hidden part of what the rest of humanity calls the heart or soul.

He had been waiting for someone like me. Someone who had nothing left to lose - who, was not just willing but truly desperate to give up their life and able to make the unconditional sacrifice of everything that makes any person a human being. I had become so desperate to die that I was able to make that unconditional choice, ironically it seems now when looking back at that day, telling his avatar that if he wanted my life, he could have it.

And therein lays the reason of for how he selected me. I had driven myself into a living hell on earth, through the choices and decisions I had made throughout my lifespan and I was ready to surrender it all, the good and the bad, if only it could stop being so completely messed up and causing everything and everyone around me so much pain. In desperation I was driven to my knees and when he spoke to me that first time, through a woman who I didn't know and had no reason to trust, it was beyond the awe that I felt that there was this voice coming from her that was obviously not hers that caught my attention and brought the only calm I had ever experienced through the first 26 years of my existence.

There will be some who say that god drove me into that corner, putting the choices before me and knowing prior to my choosing what choices I would make. Some might even try to say he allowed all that happened to me through my childhood so that I would become that desperate. I can assure anyone who might think along those lines, it isn't up to god. When I raged at him, knowingly trying to get him to destroy the thing I had become, I was shown that everything that had ever happened throughout my lifespan had been because he actually had given me control of my life from its very beginning up until the point that I heard him speak for the first time.

Although the experiences would be years apart and although I would later rebel against what it was that he had done or asked of me it was my choices that made my life what it had become. Or if it makes it easier for some to read, what I had become. The reason god sat there and didn't respond as I raged and threatened him was simple. He had known that when I was finally faced with the truth about myself, about humanity, and the complete concept of who and what humanity is meant to be, I would be ready to step away from my own humanity.

He allowed me to "run my own life" from its beginning and make the total mess of it that I had. Was that wrong of him? No, it was hard and some will see it as harsh, but it was the only kind of unconditional love that he could show me and still remain true to his word. Because in the end, god doesn't lie, doesn't bail us out, doesn't run the lives of everyone, and doesn't make the choices that haves led humanity to the brink of extinction over and over again.

Why entrust these truths to a social pariah, such as myself? Because to use someone else, someone who was perfect and pure had failed.

Jesus, that humanity knows as the Christ, spoke, walked among humanity, and displayed all those human beings are capable of and meant to be. And in the end, humanity rejected his teaching and example. I'm not talking about the Jews that crucified him, by the way. Their fear was based in the loss of control of the material wealth that the religious leaders had accumulated.

They would have allowed him to exist, dismissing him as readily as the Buddha, Mohamed, or any other prophet in spite of his unique recognition as the first conceived child of god. But when power and wealth are threatened religion steps in and takes action against anyone or anything that might remove even the slightest amounts of either.

When I say that humanity rejected the teachings of Jesus and all the others who spoke to them before me, I mean that humanity turned their teachings into religions and then warped the teachings to make profits and create divisions among themselves in order to promote fear, distrust, and violence against one another in order to create those who have and those who have not.

*

There was a story I heard, about two sheep thieves in Australia long ago. I can't quite remember who to credit for this story. In the story, these two men had been caught stealing sheep and, instead of letting the legal system punish them, the shepherd decided to brand both of them with the letters ST on their forehead so that anyone and everyone that met them from that day forward would know that they were both sheep thieves.

One of the men, so ashamed of having been caught and branded, moved away from the town where they had both grown up and was never heard from again. The second man, making a different choice, stayed in his hometown, working hard, suffering the ridicule and insults of his neighbors and strangers but accepting his consequences because he knew what he had done was not just 'wrong' but that it had been a choice he had made and guilt caused him to regret his choice.

That second man lived among his neighbors until he was very old, doing no harm and always willing to do whatever he could to help others. One day, a visitor to the town saw this ancient man, walking down the street and being greeted by almost everyone he met as if he was a friend to everyone in town. The visitor asked one of the younger townsfolk, "Why does he have the letters ST branded into his forehead?" And the young town person, who hadn't even been born when the crime of stealing sheep was allowed to be punished in such a manner responded, "I don't know really, but I think it's meant to represent Saint."

I knew of that story, long before my confrontation with god and telling him in no short terms where he could stick his choice of me speaking to humanity for him. But deep inside myself, where I had forgotten the story and knew only pain and rage, god saw that story and saw the childlike need I secretly held to be like that man.

I've stated that shame and guilt are two different things to me. I try to relate that although the dictionary cross- references them both to one another that they are not related at all. The man that disappeared, never to be heard from again, allowed shame to separate him from his family and the town folk he had grown up among. The second man accepted his guilt and used it to change his life forever.

How and why did god choose a person like me? Not simply because all the 'good' examples had been monopolized and turned into religions. Not even because there was no way anyone in their right mind would make a religion out of a child molester's thoughts and words. He chose me because inside myself, even while I was raging, cussing, and refusing everything he was asking of me, he could see that I had the unconditional willingness to step out of my own humanity and accept the responsibility that all of humanity owes to itself.

Why was I able to go to that place outside of time, heaven, hell, and life and experience what it was like to be where he had been before he created it all? Remember that to understand anyone, you have to experience what it is to 'be' that individual, even for an instant.

Before anyone can speak for another, they cannot just relate to what they have said even if they were quoting them verbatim or had experienced anything similar that caused those feelings of relating. To speak for another being, humanity has to "step into their shoes" and "walk a mile in their moccasins."

To know god, even for that instant burned away what humanity I had up until that point. The shell I became afterward was as empty and blank as the first pages of an unwritten book. I was emptied of all that I knew to be true, all that I cared about or desired for myself, and detached from the very real divinity that resides within every human being.

And I understood god by knowing what it was to be him/her/it/them for that briefest of instants. I am not god. And what makes classifies others human beings was burned out of me in that instant experience of what it was to be in his shoes and know what it was like to be outside of both time and space and utterly alone.

Now, I am not human, because I lack that which makes all of you human. The divine within each and every one of you. I can see it so clearly that it's almost blindingly obvious, as each of you crosses past my existence. Human beings are so much more than they give themselves credit for and I envy you - your humanity - even as I do not regret giving up my own in order to see it in all of you.

Like the songs say,

"You don't know what you've got, until it's gone."

Compleat

Minding A Tricky Think

I cannot speak for everyone on the planet but in my youth, I was told that human beings only use approximately 15% of their brain capacity. Statistics would probably prove that many use even less than the 15% that is active in most cases but that's something I haven't researched enough to theorize about or even make a guess at how many and who. What I do know is that the brains of humanity were meant to do and be used to do much more than they are actually being used for today.

Examples of that fact stand out in the stories that every culture across the globe shares in one form or another. Virgin birth, walking on water, raising the dead, healing the sick, lame, blind, deaf, and diseased. Every single culture on the planet has some form of a myth that includes these events. Yet every culture attributes these instances to those who it deems 'holy' or exceptional and above human. The Buddha gained enlightenment and spoke words that explained how humanity could discover itself, simply by looking inward. The Dalai Lama shares the collective memories of previous human beings who have held the position, tapping into the Gestalt in ways that appear supernatural, and those that follow those teachings spend entire lifetimes looking for the 'next' Dalai Lama when the old one's body ceases to exist. Even Christian sects have stories of those who walked on water, healed the sick by the laying on of hands and performing miracles of all sorts but either call the individuals 'saints' or attribute their abilities to being 'blessed' by the god of their understanding. I even hear tell that in the Islamic myth, Mohammad left a footprint in solid stone and the stone is considered to be a 'holy' object now, one that may be seen but never touched, examined, or tested to establish its authenticity.

Religions. I've already wrote written about some of them but there are a few that I feel need to be addressed here as well. And since I got the answers from god I figured, why not say what I know and see what happens?

Atheists are defined as people who disbelieve in the teachings of theists and theist is defined as believing in some type of divine entity of any type. One of the most commonly used arguments against there being a divine being of some type is the old adage: "If god exists, why does he allow evil to exist in the world?" Arguments denoting that 'god' doesn't want slaves or servants that have no choice -, that free will is what was gifted to humanity - is are either ignored or dismissed as being simplistic and an easy way to win without presenting proof of god's existence or non-existence. Logically, they argue, how can the non-existence of anything be proven, if it doesn't exist then there can be no proof thereof. I learned early on that circular arguments aren't solely the province of the recognized religions.

Where then does the 'evil' in the world stem from or grow out of, since nothing can exist in a vacuum? (another adage that I disproved by having been there) Perhaps I can use the stories I grew up hearing about the bible being as the 'word' of god to show exactly where and why evil exists. Or perhaps I should simply answer the question the same way I was answered when I asked god. Here then is a combination of both.

In the myth of Adam and Eve being kicked out of the Garden of Eden, god is credited with placing an angel, armed with a fiery sword to prevent humanity from reentering Eden. I don't remember what name that the Catholic religion gave that particular angel, since they gave just about every possible non-Christian deity a saint name and made them out to be angels instead of pagan deities.

But I did discover the name of the sword itself. The weapon that keeps humanity from discovering and reentering Eden is named doubt. Even I was surprised by that information and since I was getting it in a way that many will obviously doubt as being possible, I found it ironic, almost to the point of ludicrousness that the answer would be that simple.

Examples are given in everyday life and even when hearing of an event that seems supernatural, rather than accept it as being something human beings were and are meant to be able to do, the stories are greeted with apathy and disbelief or explained by science as being a phenomenon of biological necessity. A mother lifts a 6,000- pound car off her child, who is pinned beneath it, in time to prevent the child's death from the car exploding or catching fire. Science attributes it to adrenaline overloading the woman's physical restrictions and enabling her to perform a 'miraculous' feat. Even science calls the event superhuman, being enabled by the chemical reaction of adrenaline in the woman's system.

But science still doesn't grasp the "why" of humanity having an adrenal gland in the first place. Dismissing it as being only for fight or flight emotional events, they fail to realize or accept that the design of the human body and mind are still beyond their theories or understanding. What the woman did was act on her basic human abilities, by dismissing her own non-belief in her desperation to save the child she cared about.

Science, too, falls into the realm of religion when it dismisses the obvious, calls a basic human feat 'miraculous' or 'superhuman', and then attempts to explain away the side effects of the woman having lifted 3 tons off her child. There are and were none.

As Olympic weightlifters, lifting half a ton, or 1,000 pounds can and have broken their spines, torn muscles throughout their bodies, and need belts to prevent their diaphragms from exploding from the strain of the lift, there's the story of a woman, with no training, no preventative measures and without thought to the consequences of her actions lifting 6 times that amount, and yet she suffers no repercussions whatsoever. Not even a strained back or sore arm, unless she had those already from having had the accident that caused her to need to perform so spectacularly. And if the Olympics are spectator sports events, then I'd really rather see the woman lift the car than a man grunting and struggling to lift a lot less weight.

Supernatural? Super-human? Not at all. The adrenal gland was given so humanity could do what needed to be done under any circumstances that required it. And what keeps human beings from doing that particular type of feat more often? Doubt: the sword that keeps humanity locked out of Eden, if you prescribe to that particular mythology.

Why does evil exist in the world today? Did god allow it to 'test' his creation, to prove humanity's loyalty and willingness to do as he/she/it instructed? No. Humanity doubts who and what they actually are, were, and were always meant to be. Superhuman, hell no! What humanity can do, even restoring itself to the Garden of Eden that it was given to be stewards and caretakers of and have totally made a mess of the job, is by simply doing what you are ... being human. It's up to humanity to approach that mythological angel, whatever name it has, and extinguish the sword of doubt, by showing that human beings were created to be family, friends, and equals with the divine. After all is said and done, that's what all the mythologies are about anyway. The only question now of course is: "Are you ready?"

Compleat Privileged, The

From 1986 until I was incarcerated in December of 1988, I lived with the woman who would become my second wife, Natalie Regan. Born in California, to a well-to-do family, she was employed as an insurance claims adjuster and had the money that went with having been at that employment for many years. She had grown up with some wealth since her father's construction company had sold all the wire rope that went into the first construction of the Golden Gate Bridge in San Francisco and if not for her physical appearance and slight disability she might never have conceded to be involved with me in any way, shape or form.

By disability I'm speaking to her hip having been malformed when she was born, causing one leg to grow shorter than the other and creating a limp when she walked from an early age. As for her appearance, I'll try to be kind and say she wasn't the most unattractive woman I'd ever slept with or had sex with, depending on how humanity views physical beauty vs inner spiritual beauty.

But knowing her, I saw she was a kind woman, caring but desperate to be loved for who she was despite her physical appearance and disability. I must admit, as I look back on the years that I spent with her that I took advantage of her kindness and care even though she was so desperate and that she became my enabler with some of the worst of my insanity.

Ironically, however, this story isn't about Natalie or myself. I'm writing it now, these many years later, because she was 14 years my senior then and I'm well into my mid-60s in age. That means the persons involved in this story are, in most likelihood, already deceased, so I can finally reveal a truth about the privileged wealthy of a town called Mission Viejo, California.

To begin this story, I need to put all the players on the board, placing them where they were the day I'm about to relate. First of course would be Natalie herself, since we were living together in Oceanside, California in a condominium only a half block up from the beach.

Next would be Nancy's sister, Mary, who had married a man named Ken Murray, the son of the very first mayor of Mission Viejo, Norman Murray. Being the wife of an inventor must have been tough since Ken invented things but never seemed to be able to get them to market and profit from his own inventions.

For example, he created a jet ski that was designed in such a way that instead of sitting on it, a person could stand on the platform of the ski and achieve speeds in excess of 30 – 40 knots; but when he went to market this prototype of this ski platform, his 'partner' sold the patent to the ski to the Kawasaki corporation, who quashed the production of it to keep their monopoly in the area of jet skis.

Ken Murray never saw a dime of the money from that sale. But, because his father was a politician and the first Mayor of Mission Viejo, he wasn't living on the streets or doing as badly as some. His home was located in Huntington Beach, California, after all, and had plenty of rooms for guests and room for hosting visitors over the holidays.

This brings us to the crux of this story. Being with Nancy, I was invited to attend "Thanksgiving" dinner at the Murray's. A feast like any other perhaps, except that the people there were all California well-to-do, or as I like to imagine them – wealthy. In addition to their family and friends, I came as Nancy's guest/boyfriend/fiancé and was welcomed with open arms and hearts by every one of her family members. Including her sister-in-law and other relatives. But there were three individuals there whose presence I need to focus on for this story to make sense of the title I've given it.

First was Norm Murray, as I've already described him, the first Mayor of Mission Viejo. The second was the then-current Mayor of Mission Viejo, whose name was so unimportant to me that day I forget it completely now these many years later. And lastly, there was a man, whom I refuse to refer to as a 'gentleman', that was introduced to me as the City Manager of Mission Viejo, California in those days.

(Anyone wanting to know their names I'm sure can research the public archives and discover who these people were since I refuse to even add their names to this book for the rage that I still feel when I think about this event.)

Thanksgiving dinner was celebrated with turkey dinner and all the trimmings, including pies I had baked for the occasion, lemon meringue, and pecan. It was after dinner, while everyone was either helping clean up the leftovers, doing dishes, or simply sitting and enjoying an after-dinner drink that I discovered what the word privileged meant to the wealthy.

Compleat

Seeing as I was a guest that day, I wasn't asked or expected to assist in the cleaning up or doing dishes, even though I volunteered to do so, and being at loose ends I wandered into the living room where Norm Murray and his associates had settled in for an after-dinner brandy and smoking Cuban (Havana) cigars. While I am infamous for being a voyeur I honestly didn't try to eavesdrop on their conversation, but since they had no reason to suspect that I wasn't a part of or party to the family involved they spoke aloud with complete candor and without shame, or guilt.

The discussion I overheard that day enraged me. These three individuals were discussing another person, a man whose name they didn't even bother to say aloud, merely calling him the 'chump', the 'fool,' and the 'idiot' as if they were entertained with him to where he wasn't really a person or a human being.

They spoke of how the City Manager had made sure that all the permits for this other individual's business had either been held up, delayed, or outright refused, causing that person to lose contracts for the business he was in, unable to purchase materials that were needed to do the jobs he had waiting to be fulfilled, while the present Mayor had caused the permits for new construction to be withheld in order to prevent him from finding new or different opportunities to make up for the lack of income that his other losses had created.

And Norm Murray, the first Mayor of Mission Viejo's part in the affair had been to contact all the banks locally and nationally, to prevent this person from gaining financial assistance to allow him to weather the losses until he could find gainful employment in his field.

They toasted one another with brandy and were boasting that they had ruined this man, causing him to file for bankruptcy, losing not just his business but his home, and forcing him and his wife, with their 3 children to leave Mission Viejo, forever.

I listened aghast at what they were revealing, stunned into silence by the cruelty of what they were saying until they spoke at the last of their reason for committing this atrocity.

I had thought, at first, that perhaps they had reasons for their actions, that somehow this man had offended them in some way, insulting them or their families, causing someone they cared about harm in some way be it financial or other.

Compleat

What they spoke of was them having done all of these things, not for any rational reason, but simply because they had wanted to prove to themselves that they could do it. They did it as a lark, an inside joke among themselves, and entertainment for one another.

I grew livid, so angry that I was about to not just say something to the three of them but would very well have attacked them all physically right there in the home of my potential future in-laws.

Natalie knew me well enough by then to see the signs that always proceeded my becoming physically violent with others. She stepped between me and those individuals and took my arm to direct me away from them and spoke to me in a whisper outside.

"You can't do anything to them, Micheal." "They could have you killed and no one would ever know." I know now I should have acted that day anyway, but as the adage goes "hindsight is 20/20."

Years later I would discover that Norman Murray had been a frequent host to Jack and Robert Kennedy before they were assassinated and that they had aided in his becoming the 1st Mayor of Mission Viejo at their father's direction. I also learned that Norm Murray had been a staunch supporter of all of the Kennedy's businesses that had been conducted in the state of California as well as the rest of the States for the years he had been Mayor.

That Thanksgiving dinner I learned two very important facts. The first was that any politician is first and foremost a liar and a thief. Any and all of them will sell their ideas, their constituents, and their souls for the power that being in politics appears to provide.

The second is that privilege creates monsters that can appear clean and non-corrupted on their outsides while their insides are as black as all the crimes that I have committed were they all combined.

Compleat

Of The Women in My Life

Many of the people in the 12-Step fellowship I attended often heard me talk about my 2nd wife, Natalie R. She was born into a 'California Well-to-Do" family but had the misfortune to have been born in 1943 and with one leg shorter than the other by at least 2 inches. Apparently, her father Ross, although well off from his company having sold all the wire rope that went into the original Golden Gate Bridge in San Francisco, California, didn't choose to spend the money to have that limitation for her repaired.

Maybe it was the era in which she was born or perhaps her family was glad to avoid dealing with their not-so-pretty daughter by marrying her off, but either way, Natalie married her first husband at a young age. Natalie was no beauty, her features being long and drawn out, her height being much shorter than any of her peers in her debutante grouping, and being rotund in her weight because exercises like running or even just walking caused her great pain and discomfort. And I suspected, although we never discussed the reasons why, that her father had married her off to the first male that wanted to be both her husband and a business conspirator.

What we did discuss, due to our physical relationship both before and after we married, was her first husband's abusive treatment of her. He treated her like she was an emotional burden, interfering in his social life, often assaulting her by inserting no.2 pencils into her urethra so that she would never be capable of having children, and generally treating her like she was a sub-class of both a human being and his own elevated social class. I think back on it now and believe that she put up with this treatment because at that age she truly wanted to be loved by anyone and her family had insisted that she marry as a means of being both rid of her and having her be "married off properly."

How and why they became divorced was something I never bothered to inquire about, although I suspect her adopted daughter could have given me insight if I had taken the moments it would have required. What I do know is that when she and I first met I was in the brig at Camp Pendleton, California having been confined there for the crimes I had committed against my own step-daughter, Regina.

Fourteen years older than I was and not even as attractive to other men as her own stepdaughter, whose husband, Dan, was the one who suggested that I

Compleat

meet her, I met Natalie for our first conversation in the Brig's dining area. I didn't find her physical appearance an attraction or a detriment sitting there across the table from her in the brig. In fact, to this day, I know that I completely ignored her physical appearance except that she was a woman, showed an interest in me as a man, and didn't condemn or judge me as a pariah for what I had done and been convicted of doing.

Here was a woman, apparently accepting of my faults, who showed an interest in me. That was my first thought and impression upon meeting Nancy. These many years later, however, after years of therapy and self-reflection, I realized that there was another motive behind why I found her attractive. Natalie was looking for a man to be her knight in shining armor. A hero who would look past her flaws and be good and kind and considerate of her feelings. A man who would do for her all that her family, friends, lovers, and ex-husband had never done, care. A hero. The core of who I wanted to be to someone, any woman who needed me, wanted me and most of all loved me unconditionally. I saw Nancy, not as a crippled woman, but as an opportunity to be what I had dreamed of being.

There's raving that I use: "You cannot eat dreams, nor live on the waters of fantasy." Yet, on the day of my release, I moved in with Natalie and tried - not knowing how to live with anyone, never having been in a relationship that went beyond loving Megan so desperately - that I left her rather than ruin her life. We had our ups and down, Natalie and I. Moving into a condo just a half-block up from the Oceanside beach at first. The view was fantastic, the beach in those days was white sand, baked smooth and soft by the California sun, and sitting on the beach, watching the waves roll in and out was something I did while Natalie was at work every day until I took a job at the Eternal Hills Cemetery, three miles away.

At first, we seemed okay, Natalie and I. I treated her with kindness, respect, and the gentleness that her experiences with her first husband made precious and rare to her. With her inability to have children though, I wanted more and began to have sexual encounters with other women - some being closer to my own age and obviously others that were much younger than me. At 31 years of age physically I entered a stage of my life where I acted like a seventeen-year-old boy: irresponsible and driven by my hormones to seek sex wherever I could. A mature individual would have simply left the relationship with Nancy, and hopefully left her in such a mature manner as to remain friends with her. I did not.

Compleat

All the affairs I began, all the sexual involvements I encountered, I had no problem with discussing with Natalie in detail and although I never abused her physically, when I look back on those days of sharing my 'prowess' with her I came to an awareness that I was abusing her in a way more terrible than even the physical abuse her ex had put her through. I wasn't bragging about the encounters though I can see where my sharing them with her might have been seen as a braggart's way of boasting about his manliness.

Inside myself, I knew that I was testing Natalie. Pushing at her emotions to see if she truly loved and cared about me to where she would tolerate my doing those things. I was seeking from Natalie what I had taken from both Megan and Regina – unconditional love. I pushed and pushed, stretching the boundaries of what she would endure from me in order to see if she would love me as much as I thought either of them had in my past.

I'm not about to try to claim that I didn't enjoy every encounter that I had, that wasn't the point of my either having had them or sharing the details of them with her. But with every encounter where I pushed at her boundaries, seeing if there would be limits to them because I couldn't believe anyone could or would love me and also because, as the frequency of those encounters grew greater, my self-hatred also grew. Like Megan and Regina, Natalie had done me no wrong, tolerating my behaviors with other women as long as I came home to her.

My therapists taught me a valuable lesson over the years I was confined in the institution for the criminally insane. Borderline Personality Disorder can cause an individual to want love, desperately need love, and still have no way of allowing someone to love them. The closer to loving me Natalie became the more I feared her loving me. I wasn't worth loving. I had destroyed the love I had with Megan and abused the love I had received from Regina. Didn't she realize how 'UN-lovable' I truly was?

There's a picture I saw once while in therapy, of a tree that shows the nature of feelings that lead to prejudice. It showed that at the base of the tree, where the roots went deepest into what was nurturing the tree was pain. Pain is the ground in which all negative emotions grow. The roots of that tree, of course, are fear. Fear of the pain, no matter if it be emotional, physical, mental, or spiritual. Out of all fear grows the trunk of the tree, which is anger. Fight or flight may be the instinctual response to fear but when contained within oneself, when trapped and cornered with no way of releasing the fear, the pain grows up through the fear and becomes a tree trunk-sized thing of anger. And anger, untreated, unchecked, and untrimmed grows out into branches of hatred, often going into many, many different directions; touching on the areas of life like the branches of a tree, blocking the sunshine of hope and love. Out of that hatred grow the leaves of prejudice. Small, almost weightless when it comes to noticing them in oneself, they cycle throughout a lifespan, like the leaves of a tree, having seasons of spring where they are fresh and strong, summer where they can be both vigorous or wilted, fall where they change their appearance and can take on the seeming of beauty and winter, where they no longer serve their purpose, falling and leaving bare the harsh reality of the hatred that bore them.

As Natalie tried to love me and sought to be loved by me, my own BPD made me want her to love me exactly as I had loved Megan and as Regina had loved me, in her childlike innocence.

I wanted her to love me, needed her to love me, but I couldn't allow her to love me, no matter what else she did. So I pushed the boundaries of her feelings beyond understanding and although she never gave up on me, I eventually hated her for trying to be someone I wanted but would never have or be with in this life.

I often shared in meetings that I sought and had 9 lovers during those years, women that I used, seeking love, needing love, wanting so desperately to be loved and yet destroying any and all chances of ever being loved. No. 9 was, of course, Nancy. When I got arrested for the rape I committed, Natalie stuck by me, staying with me while I was incarcerated and even opening her mother's home to me when I was finally released in 1993. She had moved in with her mom, Mary R. to share both the expenses and help care for her aging mom.

But the dynamics of our relationship had changed because I had become aware of my own flaws and mental illnesses. Natalie would have gone back to being husband and wife, without a doubt in my mind. She wanted me there and, at first, I seriously considered it a possibility. Yet even my guilt for all that I had put her through couldn't overcome the new awareness of my failings. I knew that if I stayed with Nancy, we would fall back into old patterns of behavior. She would provide for me, care for me, support me in all my endeavors and I would become complacent, enjoying the care and comfort she provided and eventually my borderline personality traits would bring me full circle to where pain from my past behaviors would cause me to feel fear, resentment, and anger, eventually hatred and prejudice, leading me to return to the only behaviors I knew.

I chose instead to move out, not dumping her as I had Megan, but separating myself from her, forcing myself to become as responsible as I could and leaving her to discover for herself the enabling behaviors that she had developed over all the years of her life.

It only took a year and a half. I was at a 12-Step meeting, in a place where I volunteered to help with setting up meetings, cleaning ashtrays (in spite of the fact that I didn't smoke) sweeping floors, filing paperwork, and participating in dual-diagnosis groups for those who also had substance abuse problems as well as mental illnesses. I remember the day clearly since it was sunny and clear, and the McAllister Institute was where I would begin my career as a substance abuse counselor. I believe now that Natalie only brought a female friend with her in case I became abusive, threatening, or argumentative but she needn't have worried.

Although California laws allowed that any marriage dissolved by both parties gives each party an equal claim to all the assets of both parties, which meant that I could have claimed half of all she owned in stocks, retirement IRA's, cars, bank accounts, etc. when Natalie brought to me the divorce papers her lawyer had written up, I simply signed them telling her I had no claim on anything of hers, whatsoever.

I wasn't that I didn't care, or didn't need the financial help. I was struggling, then as I do now. But I had no right to claim what was hers, no matter what the 'laws' of the State said or allowed.

To this day, I still have financial difficulties, but in this one thing, I have always felt I did the right thing by someone who had loved and cared about me despite my inability to love them in that same, small manner in which human beings know how to love one another.

Natalie had helped me to realize my lack of humanity in that way as well. Many people comment that I was a fool, I could well have been wealthy by Missouri standards or California "Well-to-Do," but instead I chose to practice one small act of kindness to a woman who did no one any wrong and had deserved much better than life had put in her path. And that those who had called me 'fool' showed me that I wasn't really human.

I signed the paperwork, told her I was sorry, and simply walked away. One day, if she reads this or not, I hope that she can forgive that 38-year-old man, one that had the maturity of a four-year-old child and the mindset of a teenager, grabbing at all he could get. Asking for her forgiveness would simply open old wounds for her, so I won't. And as I've said before in this book, saying "I'm sorry." is just expelling hot air to make oneself feel better. I let my actions speak for me and allow that she has the humanity to forgive.

Battling Ego

There will come a point, when reading this book, that those who bother to read it will question if I'm writing the entire thing simply to beg forgiveness for my past misdeeds. There will be others though who I know will be certain that I am merely feeding my ego, telling true stories for the sake of notoriety and possibly fortune to go along with the fifteen minutes of fame that every person on the planet is supposed to be seeking according to urban legend.

While I am not above doing either of those things and admit that both are tempting reasons for writing, neither are in the realm of my true reason for writing it. Forgiveness is something I do need, but I am not so foolish as the seek or believe that I deserve it from those I've wronged. In fact, to ask for forgiveness would mean facing those that suffered most from my past actions, and in many cases just seeing my person or being in my presence would cause them more harm. If the purpose of writing had solely been to beg for forgiveness, I would not have put the burden of their care upon the shoulders of society and the world they live in, but allowed them to remain anonymous throughout the writing experience completely.

Compleat

As for my ego ... there's a reason I choose not to feed the beast that still rages within me. My ego resembles a caged animal, resting until it gains strength and then charging and throwing itself against the cage in which I have kept it contained since I grew to identify it for what it is, the lie that I don't care. For more years than I can relate to anyone and be believed I have hated myself, the world around me, and every one of you. I have felt rejected, even by those who claimed to have loved me, and eventually caused them to voice their rejections because I had adopted the lie that I didn't care if no one loved me. I accepted the role of a pariah within the society I reside because it was easier than doing what I could to become the example that I knew I was meant to be by accepting the lie that I didn't care what others thought of me or how they treated me in any way.

My ego, caged and raging, tries every possible combination of assaults upon the confinement that I use to keep it in check. The fact that after twenty-five years of being a monitored sex offender, I could legally petition to have my name and crimes struck from the sex offender registry wakes me in the middle of the night, shaking with both anger and desire to be free of the stigma of being on that registry. The laws allow it, my ego argues. I could become free of the stigma and seek a normal life for myself, possibly even finding a wife who would love the lie created by my not being on there any longer. It is my choice not to even seek that freedom, not because I'm a martyr of some kind but because I use the system of registration to keep the beast in check, knowing that if I were to approach any law enforcement individual and tell them that the occasion of my acting out again was approaching, they would willingly and without hesitation place me back into physical confinement.

I gave an example of how my ego tries through subtlety to find its release in sharing the knowledge that the public defender worked with the district attorney of the San Diego County region in having me confined for the crime I had actually committed that brought me to the institution for the criminally insane.

Even in San Diego, California during the 1980's (and especially the year of 1988) the laws required that during a criminal trial the district attorney's office was required by way of 'discovery' that all persons who were to be called as witnesses for the prosecution be given to the defense lawyers prior to being called in court.

Discovery allows the defense attorney to provide a correct and proper defense by knowing what evidence and which witnesses the prosecution will be calling. The public defender not only didn't have the entire list, but when confronted with a 'surprise' witness when the prosecution called on my then wife, Natalie Runner, displayed a lack of interest and improper use of his position by allowing the lack of discovery to not be challenged or calling for a mistrial as the law required him to do. If he hadn't been in collusion with the prosecution, perhaps he would have done so. Or if he hadn't been a paid servant of the system that wanted to see 'justice' served through punishment and instead had been a paid representative whose income would have depended on the outcome of the case he was pretending to represent, he might have done so immediately.

For years I tried to tell myself that I didn't care about the outcome of the trial. I was, when all is said and done, guilty as charged. But my ego uses my knowledge of the legal system to wake me at night, with nightmares of being able to reverse the court's decision, have everything stricken from my record and also seek financial restitution from the corrupt system that allowed the pretense of a trial and the lawyers for both the prosecution and the defense for putting on such a display of disregard for the very system they supposedly swore to represent.

There are many cases where a technical error of this nature has led to the release of those who were unjustly accused and convicted of crimes that they never committed. And more than a few where the technicality of misconduct would have caused the case to be dismissed immediately as a violation of the very laws that were being said to be represented. My ego, knows these facts and struggles each night, with that knowledge, as a tool, since the day of my conviction, August 5th, 1988, to gain a release and such financial reparations. After all, it argues, who doesn't want to be wealthy because of lawyers play - acting at a game of justice rather than actually representing the laws of the society?

The cage gets rattled, some days even shaking so fearfully that I find it a wonder that it can hold together against both the rational or irrational thinking that my ego brings to bear against it. What cage can withstand both rationality and insanity? Mine is simply choice. It is my choice not to pursue a release from the sex offender registry. If I am incapable, as has appeared to be the case, of finding a woman on this planet that can love me for who I am and was and will be, then I choose to accept that consequence rather than allow my ego even that tiny tidbit of freedom. Others tell me that I'm being ridiculous or even martyring myself for the sake of past mistakes. To explain my reasons would frighten most of them from associating themselves with me.

Compleat

And who, for that matter, doesn't want to have wealth, and the ability to provide for others and self to the point of comfort at least and decadence if it were possible to achieve such a state?

Again, it is only my choice that keeps my ego in check. Wealth, while a useful tool in providing care and comforts can become an instrument of self-destruction like onto none other humanity has ever encountered before.

The wealthy of this world, sit in opulence, feeding their egos through philanthropic displays of generosity and ignoring the truth that for all their public displays of caring they allow suffering to continue throughout the entire world by not divesting themselves of that wealth that allows them to put on their very vulgar displays in the first place.

So- called "Christians" donate to the poor, giving to every cause imaginable by the scammers and thieves that call themselves leaders of churches and religions. Islam makes a point of giving to beggars and the handicapped, yet does nothing to require that those they deem less than themselves be provided for on an equal basis. Jews are condemned for being money- grubbing, greedy thieves, who manipulate the finances of the world and readily accept that condemnation because it's an easy insult to accept from those who they deem as being and are less able to provide for themselves and their own than they are, through that very manipulation.

I too had wealth, of a sort, once. If I had remained married to my second wife or if during the divorce, according to California law, I had petitioned for half of everything she owned or had saved, I would have it still. When she divorced me, because I had forced her hand by moving out of the home we had shared, I could have done just that and been provided for the rest of her lifespan by alimony until I remarried or one of us died. Instead, and this wasn't some noble action on my part by any stretch of the imagination, I simply signed the divorce papers she presented and walked away from it all. It was my choice to make and my ego rages at living in conditions that are so similar to being incarcerated that - the walls are cold, the floor is hard concrete, and the cost of heating the room I reside within increases the amount I am required to pay monthly to even be able to keep shelter here.

It is difficult, ironic even, to be where I am, know all that I know, and not choose to do anything about it. Even writing this book challenges my choice, because my ego wants to see it as an opportunity to provide for myself my creature comforts and sustenance. I choose not to allow it to start my thinking along those paths. With any sales or profits from the sales of this book going into a trust fund, managed by a legal firm that will remain nameless due to those who might seek some reparations for being named within the book itself, I will receive nothing from said sales or profits. That, too, is my choice to make.

Compleat

What He Said
— . — . — . — . — . — . — . — . — . — . — . — . — . — . — . — . — . — . —

Some might ask why I share all of these awful things about myself with humanity.? Simply to express the truths therein? Or is it to establish the concept that I am telling the truth? Not as I see it, not as I wish it to be, but as it is, as unedited and compleat as I can possibly make it in order to provide humanity with the example that what I am saying is and will be true.

Does it frighten most to know what a monster I had become, I'd say probably. Does hearing the truths I share about myself make for difficult reading for victims of crimes similar to my own, more than likely? And does it make sense to hear what I have to say and see the truth that is behind my words, I can only trust that it will. Because what I write isn't for me, for a profit, or for any type of gain on my part, not even forgiveness from the one I still love.

What I write is for humanity as a whole. It is the work that was given to me when I stood before god and rejected his assignment to another work. He showed me what he meant for me to do and I refused to do it. I saw people, places, and things that will come about and would have come about if I had continued to serve the way I had offered when I told the woman whose body he used to speak in a voice not her own and suggested that if I really didn't want my life any longer I could give it over to him.

"If you really don't want your life, why not give it to god?" If he wanted it, he could have my messed up, totally insane, cruel, self-centered, sick, and twisted life. He took that as a commitment, a contract, or a covenant to do as he would with it. And he did, in spite of my efforts to renege on my acceptance or efforts to resist his control. Even knowing I would resist, turn back on my committed word and his guidance toward a future that would have led to a lot less pain and suffering for others and myself.

When I stood before god, before all my past welled up inside me causing me to rage and refuse his choices for me, he spoke to me of humanity. He spoke to me, someone no one would listen to, in my opinion, and told me things that I really didn't understand or even want to know. He spoke of the past, and why he had come to be on the planet with us as a human being, some call Jesus. He spoke of the present, where the tides of humanity ebb and flow like the oceans and where the storms humanity has brought upon itself are only going to keep getting stronger and more devastating with each cycle. He spoke of the future, where humanity will be faced with the gift and the curse that is being human. And that it will be by your choice yet to be made by all, not by one or another and most definitely not by me or anyone claiming to know his will.

The choice will be made by humanity as a whole. Humanity was given power, stewardship, authority, and ability beyond that of angels. Jesus, they say, walked on water. Why? Was it simply to prove to a boat full of fishermen that believed in what he was trying to teach them that he was their Messiah? Or was it to show them exactly what it was he was saying to them all along? Was he showing off the fact that he knew the god inside himself? Or was he showing them what they, themselves, were capable of if only they would recognize who they really were? Peter supposedly got out of the boat and walked toward him and when he saw what he was doing became frightened and had to ask for help. Why? Why was Peter frightened by what he was doing? Peter, a simple fisherman, not the messiah, not god in man, walked on the same rough sea that this Jesus dude told him it would be okay to walk on and he did it, until he realized what he was doing came from inside himself. It was there all along and that frightened him more than the rough sea or the idea that he might drown. He didn't want to be separated from the humanity as he had been taught to see it. He refused or if you prefer the term, denied, his own ability because he saw who he actually was and who he was meant to be all along. He saw by doing what he had learned all his life was impossible for any human being. Peter walked on water. He is quoted as asking Jesus to call him out onto the water, but although Jesus did call to him, it was Peter's own ability to walk on water that brought him to the point of stepping out of the boat and taking those few steps.

The dude that people label god showed folks that even a simple fisherman could walk on water. And even the fisherman who did it couldn't face the truth of who and what he was by doing exactly as he had asked to be told he could do.

In the conversation I had with god, I received answers to questions I didn't even know to ask. Things that I didn't want to know, things that made no sense to me whatsoever, and things that still make no sense to me today. In this book, for example, I write about the reason why god gave humanity dogs and cats. Why would I want or need to know the answer to that particular and peculiar question? I'm sure I never thought to ask it, since I had questions much more important to my own circumstances and, in the event that I ever did as he suggested, more than probably more important to humanity as a whole. What purpose did giving me answers to questions I didn't know to ask, information that I neither wanted nor felt worthy of having and became unwilling to share due to both my feeling of unworthiness and the obvious rejection by the majority of humanity that would result?

That last answer was my reason for telling this being that sat before me in terms that were disrespectful in ways that a human being addressed in that manner would have smacked me down and put me in my place. Because I rejected not just the assignment that god showed me, not just his will for my life, not simply the entire message he wanted me to share with humanity but my own humanity itself.

I am not less than human. Nor more. And not any more. I was shown where god, no matter what label or name humanity uses for it had been. Outside of the illusion of time and space. I was shown the places humanity has created for itself, both heaven and hell, where some souls reside because they reserved their occupancy in either place. And I was shown who and what humanity was meant to be, could be now, and needs to become in order to save itself from what it has wrought and brought upon itself.

There is an end coming. The Christian bible describes it as an Armageddon. The end of humanity looms, as it always has, ahead of it. The fear of it has driven humanity to religions of every make and type in a desperate attempt to avoid the responsibility of doing what you are capable of doing to prevent it.

Compleat

Islam, Hinduism, Buddha's teaching, Christianity, Satanism, or any of the other religions of humanity are all in response to that fear.

And although the fear is unnecessary it is easier to accept and exist with it than accept the responsibility to be who and what you were meant to be with one another all along. The old dude told me things I didn't want to know. And what made me less than human was the knowledge of who you actually are in relation to him.

God didn't take me outside of both time and space to make me like him, I was human and was already like him, and he showed me that. He took me to that place to show me all of it -, heaven where he sat and talked with me; hell, where I saw people who I would never have thought or believed when I was religious would be there; and then that place outside of it all. He showed me what I had been, what I chose to give away by rejecting his will for me, and the futility of my rejection because I had already given all that I am over into his control.

I hear people's minds whirling even now, if they are reading this especially, that I must be insane or possessed or even some type of prophet that is predicting the end of humanity. I am none of the above, and that much you can believe if you have seen that I have no fear of telling the absolute and complete truth about myself. I am less than you. Outside of humanity. Apart from you in order to be able to observe and report what it is that I see in you all. And I see now with eyes that have been opened to the wonder and beauty that being human is.

There is a price to be paid for everything. Even human beings like yourselves say that there are no 'free lunches' and someone has to pay for what is provided, even if it's not those that are to enjoy the benefits of the provisions. The price that was exacted was the humanity of one. Mine. I surrendered it when I told the god dude that if he wanted my fucked up, insane, sick, twisted, and desperate life he could have it. He took from me my humanity in order that I might see what I had given up and share with you all that you don't have to surrender your own.

I mention music in one of the stories in this book. How it is a universal language that every human being can appreciate and shares on a level above what imaginary divisions you place upon yourselves. Lyrics, sounds, and thoughts that touch you all deep within yourselves, where your humanity is at its purest. One such song has lyrics that speak of what I'm saying here. "You don't know what you've got until it's gone." That which makes you human is the god within you all. The life, love or whatever you choose to label it is real. I see you, some say, but none see you all as I do, except maybe god himself. I am less than human - having surrendered my humanity and paying the price to be able to see humanity as it truly was, is, and is meant to be. I wanted to die that day, and have wanted to die every day that has passed since. But until I speak these words, until humanity has this one last chance to hear what this god dude had to say I won't be allowed to cease this existence outside of who you are. Humanity, you won't know what you have until it's gone. And it will be gone, sooner than many of you expect, unless you choose as a whole to accept who you are.

All seriousness aside and touching on silliness to ease your hearts and minds so that what I say here will be more palatable I have to mention a movie that still makes me smile when god and I talk about it. Bill and Ted's Excellent Adventure. I'm not sure the "party on dudes" part was meant to be a part of the message, though knowing the old dude's sense of humor about humanity taking itself a little too seriously I can see it might be, but the other thing that is used as a vehicle throughout that movie is very real indeed. "Be excellent to each other."

Because that is something he said to share with you. He created humanity not to be divided by the color of your skin, the region of the planet you reside on, or your comfort in your beliefs and reasoning. Politics and religion, every possible division you can imagine or see for yourselves have no place in what you are meant to be to one another. Humanity needs to relearn its own relationship to with one another in order to understand your its relationship to with him. Because when humanity recognizes that you are all family, one to another, despite all your made- up and pretended divisions, he intends to be among you openly and with you as the family you are.

I recently shared with a man, a friend who was seeking some kind of guidance from my experiences in a program of recovery, that to change who he was the simplest thing in the entire world to change but it was also the only thing that could help him to recover from his self-destructive behaviors. His perceptions. To change who he was, his attitude toward others, and his ability to make his life completely different he gets to look at the world in a different way. To change all the 'musts,' 'have to,' 'should,' and 'got to' in his life all he needed to do was look at these things from a different perspective. Not through the eyes or perspective that he had been taught to see, by the society and fears he had been raised with, but with his own eyes, his own understanding, the god within himself. To look with the eyes of being a human being and not what he had been taught to see himself as.

Was the pot calling the kettle black when I spoke those words to my friend? I think not. Simply because I am no longer that pot, the one that was also on the fire and had been removed in order to make room for more important things to be done there. Broken, unusable for the purpose of a pot any longer, I am filled and there grows within me a flower of hope for humanity to enjoy. I cannot see the flower, cannot enjoy its beauty, and cannot even provide it with the comfort or food and water it needs to survive. My place is to simply hold it for humanity to see it or not. To care for it or not as you choose. Even my opinion that it might be a perennial and not an annual doesn't affect it in any way. My place is to simply hold it and let humanity decide whether to enjoy it or not.

They say "yesterday is history, tomorrow's a mystery, today is a gift – that's why it's called the present." I say "open the present that is today, enjoy it and share it with one another, since it is everything that you have already received, and remember to say 'thank you' for it when you can.

There is a beauty in being human that goes beyond any words I have tried to express through the telling of all these stories. The horrors of my own experiences show how far from human any of you can become. And denial really doesn't make the chances any less, telling yourselves that "I would never do that." doesn't change the truth that you could, were the circumstances to arise. He told me that and he told me that you don't have to give in to the circumstances. There is more power in being human than you know.

Compleat

Compleat

Of Dogs & Cats

I have said this in other places, but I have never fully explained the 'why' of my saying it. My pop - God as some call him, though that was just his title – gave humanity dogs in order to show us exactly what unconditional love looks like, so we could learn how to treat and respond to one another. Dog's, in that aspect, would be our perfect examples.

My experience is in this story, and if you are a dog person, I suggest you brace your heart. It is not merely a story, but a real-life encounter of my very own.

When I was child, there came to my yard one day a male German Shepherd. He was an immense creature, tan and black, and so beautiful. Around his neck – place by his previous owner, I'm assuming – was a choke chain collar. Looped into one of the chain links was an old rope, which was clearly used to tie him somewhere. That chain collar had bound around itself so tightly that it had created a large gash in that creature's neck. The sheer depth of the wound told me that his efforts to free himself must have been monumental. It had gone gangrenous with infection and there were maggots crawling through his flesh which produced such a putrid stench that you could smell it from at least 20 feet away.

Obviously, this dog's owner had long stopped caring for him for some reason. I gave them the benefit of the doubt. Perhaps they had grown old and died, and no one had been to collect the dog.

My example is as such: that dog – the suffering and neglect that it had been through – came to me, all alone, and laid his head in my lap. All he wanted was for me to love and care for him. For him, there was no past, no neglectful owner, no abuse, and no starvation. There was neither thirst nor pain too great that could prevent him from loving again.

This is what unconditional love looks like.

On writing this book, I've just recently lost my cat, James. For this reason, I have an example about cats as well.

People tend to joke about cats being lazy, aloof, gross, and always either sleeping or eating. Why then would my pop give us cats? Are they secretly our rulers like something out of Cats Be Dogs, or are they just useless burdens that humanity has tolerated for thousands of years, simply because they purr at a frequency that is appeasing to the human ear?

Neither answer is the truth, if you ask me, though seeing the 'why' with them might be a little harder for those like me who were raised to fear and hate them. Therein lies the story of cats.

When I was growing up, my family had shared a story about a cat that climbed into a baby's crib and suffocated the infant by trying to lick the milk from its mouth after its bottle had fallen away in the night.

The truth of the matter is that the baby most likely died of Sudden Infant Death Syndrome, and that the cat, sensing that something was wrong, had tried – in its cat way – to resuscitate the baby. With information lacking for many years, my family proudly announced whenever the subject of cats was brought up, that every stray cat that would come near them would be killed – and it would. They would be skinned and their pelts would be nailed to the inside of my uncle's barn. I personally never skinned one, but I was no stranger to killing them simply because they existed.

It wasn't until after I met pop and refused his calling – taking my own life and being sent back – that my perception of cats would change. Pop gave us dogs to show us what unconditional love looked like. Why then would He give us cats too?

Compleat

I'll tell you what I've learned. Cats are here to give us practice for what we learn from dogs. It's that simple.

A cat is aloof, ignores those it owns, unless it wants something from them, and almost always times its demands at the most inopportune moments. A cat will seek unwarranted attention. It will howl, yowl, and scream if it doesn't get its way in everything. Two-year-old children don't have anything on a cat when it comes to throwing a temper tantrum.

We are not their slaves, or owners for that matter, we are the stewards of all life on this planet, and cats, next to ourselves as human beings, are the most difficult to care for. But that is their very purpose of being.

So, we can learn from caring for cats, how to care for one another too. Aloof, distant, demanding, selfish, self-centered, and especially almost always crying out for what we want, need, must have, cannot do, cannot live without, or do not understand.

We need them to practice unconditional love on.

Because unconditional love doesn't come from loving something that is easy to love.

It comes from loving something, or someone, that is so painfully hard to love, that they teach us how to surrender.

So that is my experience with dogs and cats. Perhaps it's not as well written as an Atwood novel, but it is truthful nonetheless.

> It wasn't until after I met pop and refused his 'calling', eventually taking my own life and being sent back that my perception of cats changed. Pop gave us dogs, to show us what unconditional love looks like. Why then give us cats, too?
>
> Cats are here to give us practice for what we learn from dogs. It's that simple.
> A cat is aloof, ignores those IT owns unless it wants something from them and almost always times it's demands at the most inopportune times. (Sound familiar yet?) A cat will seek unwarranted attention, howl, yowl and scream if it doesn't get its way in anything. Two year old humans don't have anything on a cat throwing a temper tantrum!
>
> We are not their slaves (or owners for that matter) we are the stewards of all life on this planet, and cats ... next to ourselves as human beings ... are the most difficult to care for ... but that IS their purpose for being.
>
> So we can learn, from caring for cats, how to care for one another. Aloof, distant, demanding, selfish, self centered and especially almost ALWAYS crying out for what we want/need/must have/cannot and do not understand or live without. Human beings must remind pop of cats, after all is said and done. We need them to practice on!
>
> So, that is my experience with dogs and cats. Not well written perhaps but truthful none the less.
>
> I offer this suggestion, not telling anyone what to do or how to live:
>
> "Learn unconditional love from dogs; practice unconditional love on cats; then take it one small step further and practice it on one another. I know you will be glad you did."
>
> - runner's ravings

Compleat

Compleat

Gifts For the Giving

As a young boy I was much more creative than I would be years later in my lifespan. In the summer of my fourth-grade experience, for example, I would memorize all the names of the different bones in the human body, the entire first chapter of the book "Tom Sawyer" by Mark Twain, and make ceramic gifts for both my parents.

For my mother, I created an ashtray of heavy ceramic pieces, painted by hand and set into a hard clay-like substance since she still smoked cigarettes that year and for my step-dad, Anthony Morris, Sr. I would paint and fire a ceramic stein that stood over 18 inches tall, and was decorated with animals of all types from African stories I had read. The cap or lid of the stein was a male lion, in laying in repose, and the paints I would be allowed to use included one in which tiny bits of real gold were embedded.

I was extremely proud of my ability to create these things for them and gifted them each with their own on the celebrated days for Mothers and Fathers. It remains ironic that the items themselves were never used by either of them for the purposes that they were intended. In my gift to my mother, she simply put the ashtray into a cabinet where she kept nick knacks of all kinds and to the best of my knowledge, it remained there even after she left Art for another marriage that provided her with more income.

Compleat

As for the stein, or Jungle Cup as I labeled it when I created it, Art had placed it on top of his black and white television in the living room of what would be his home after she had left. It sat there, until one of the neighborhood's newest criminals or perhaps even one of my old friends decided to tear through the screen covering the window behind that television and steal it. Where it has gone, who took it exactly, and what became of it after that will be a mystery unless someone ever reaches a point of regret to bring it forward and admit to the theft.

The point of giving a gift to parents that were abusive and neglectful might escape some people who have read these stories but I can explain that in gifting them with things I had created with my own hands I felt I was making an attempt or a peace offering to each of them in my efforts to forgive them for all the years of abuse up until those days.

That I failed in my attempt becomes obvious because they both neglected or lost the items that I had gifted them with; in my mother's case, through simply putting it them away where it they would never be seen or used. And although some might say that she valued it, but it was in my knowing her that I knew how little she valued it or the rest of her nick- knack collection by leaving them all behind when she left Art. Anyone assuming that she had cared would be mistaken, while, in my step-dad's case, the item was put on display, almost as if he valued it more than the gift I had given my mother because it came from one of her sons from a previous marriage. Yet, in his drunken and partially insane state brought about by her leaving, he neglected it by leaving the doors and windows of the house unlocked and making it obviously accessible to the thief or thieves that would eventually take it.

This then is one of the many reasons I choose not to own anything of material value in this lifespan I am condemned to complete. It is these simple experiences that taught me that the value of gifts given is often more important to the giver than those who receive the gifts.

Compleat

Immortal Me

There is a song, by a group that called itself Queen, entitled "Who Wants To Live Forever?"

I spoke to god about that song specifically because of all the music in the world I related to it most. The knowledge I gained in asking that question though, went way beyond my simple inquiry about why music effects humanity as a whole, and is reputed to stimulate every area of the human brain.

It does that, and so much more, since it is a universal language that transcends artificial barriers of nationality, dialect, distance, religion, and others. The human condition is such that universal truths and languages can be understood and shared all across the planet on which humanity currently resides, and may even one day reach out to the stars themselves.

Who wants to live forever? An ironic question, because of the belief that death separates every human life from the others around it. None come back, so they are considered gone forever, with only an afterlife where they might or might not be rejoined to anticipate.

Death, however, does not separate humanity! Her single job is an enslavement to be performed until humanity becomes aware that they hold the keys to her release even as some see her as having the ability to release them from the chains binding them to life as they know it.

Compleat

I met death, as I have already described at length, and witnessed her enslavement by humanity first hand. My experience was to feel terror at the perception of her as the threatening figure I had been taught to see at first. An ending of life, a separation from all that I knew and cared about beyond myself. That was why I cried out when I saw her and why, when she gave me her look of assurance that she would come to me when I called for her, I gained a calm and peace that surpassed my own understanding.

With age, something humanity labels to itself and others as growing old, comes an ending of sorts. Like time itself, however, being old is an elusive and illusionist label. To age is something that happens to the human body, a vessel in which the individual resides. Sometimes that vessel fails, sooner than expected, younger also being an illusionist label, but the human being within that vessel does not simply cease to exist.

Though I often regret having had the experience, because of the foreknowledge that I will be returned to it when the vessel I reside within expires, I have had the distinct experience for a simple reason. It was that I might get to know and share with humanity that beyond time and space, beyond even heaven and hell if they are unfortunate enough to know as I do that both those places exist, there is a place outside of all of them.

My body, as we all know, will expire and decay. Even my memory in the minds of others will fade and fail eventually. But though my body will age and the memory of my existence among you all will one day cease, I will never grow older or younger and I will never die.

Yes, I have just claimed to be immortal. Not in my body, this near useless vessel that is rapidly becoming as worn out as any vehicle one might have purchased over 64 years ago and driven carelessly, without proper maintenance, and with disregard for the damages I've done to it through my seeking to escape my own life. Nor do I wish to have it end suddenly and in pain, though I do not fear death I honestly dislike the discomfort of experiencing pain but do not fear living life either.

Long after humanity, as it exists now, has ceased to exist, perhaps for a better existence if you all choose, I will continue to exist as I am now. It is ironic or perhaps poetic justice that I will continue to exist in that place outside of time and space, where I was aware and alone. Perhaps I was given that experience as a penance for my actions among you, as I'm sure some of humanity might either see it as justice or much deserved. And perhaps the foreknowledge of my awaiting place of continued existence is also a part of that penance?!

Compleat

The only other possibility I can imagine or determine from having had the experience is that only by having been there could I understand what the experience was for god as well. What if god, having been there, created humanity and its place to exist within in order to be freed from or escape from the isolation of existing there ... also alone?! It is one of my particular 'ravings' that I insist on sharing whenever I can – that to actually understand another being, supernatural or human, a being needs to become that individual themselves, even for the slightest of instance.

Which, by the way, would explain the entire Jesus mythology. Were god to truly understand humanity, god would choose to become human and in doing so would know us as more than just as friends and family or creations. So, the forgiving of 'sins' wouldn't be merely from a super- powered benevolence but from a true understanding of the human condition.

In knowing humanity as a human being, the tone and temperance of the observations of the personality of the 'Christian' god undergoes an enormous alteration. From punishing, demanding, disciplinarian, and (in the old testament description) jealous to compassionate, caring, considerate, forgiving, tolerate tolerant, and accepting. Anyone who reads their book can observe that the changes are stark and pronounced after the whole Jesus myth became a part of humanity's collection of tales.

Which of course places the question of why did this lesson have to be learned at all at the top of some lists. This god, all- knowing, all- powerful, and real in every aspect is challenged by those who seem determined to dismiss it as being a made- up story, imagined for the sake of explaining what wasn't once understood until science grew to explain certain events and as unnecessary as a children's story book is to an adult mind for explaining things of importance, like existence itself.

"If god is so powerful," the question goes, "could he make an object so large that he couldn't lift it himself?"

The answer lies in the question of course; yes, god can and did. He created human beings.

Compleat

Non-Poetry

—·—·—·—·—·—·—·—·—·—·—·—·—·—·—·—

I AM NOT A POET

This is who I AM.

I am an unfettered spirit, drawn to your light

As a moth is drawn to the light of a flame.

I know no more than a moth of why I am drawn

I know only that your light brings me closer

And unlike the moth I AM aware

The danger of the flame that is you

Where your light shines brightest and sears the dark

I know that I am drawn and you might destroy me.

Your spirit is so gentle, you would not want to

Your heart and mind and Chakra align so harm isn't in you

It's is my unfettered nature, my spirit wild, untamed,

To even light upon your stability for an instant all that I am

Would be consumed, by making solid that which is only energy

Compleat

And creating a fuel that would cause your spirit to nova ever brighter

For an instant, we would be one. Then I would be no more

For you perhaps you reason that you must protect me from myself

But you cannot change the nature of my spirit.

This is who I AM.

Compleat

Thorns

I am the thorn and not the rose.

I tear at your flesh, inflicting wounds so deep you think they will never heal

I rip and shred your dreams and desires putting matches to the tinder that is your soul

I am the thorn and not the rose.

I am the thorn deep stabbing into all that you are

I hold you from progressing forward and clutch you from turning back

I resist your efforts with ease born of my very nature non-thinking, non-feeling, remorseless

I am the thorn and not the rose.

I held you back from the moment you found me

I push against your every effort to advance

I take on the appearance of every foe you've ever faced to terrorize you into surrender

I am the thorn and not the rose.

Compleat

Yet ... you persisted, overcoming the pain that I inflicted, bearing up under the wounds I opened in flesh and mind and heart and soul, you came forward when all else you knew would scream at you to stop, resist, retreat, fall back and away, always seeking that which I am not.

Yet again ... you persevered and broke through the defenses that I am to reach your goal.

A single, cobalt blue rose, hidden behind all the thorn I am, known only as unconditional love.

I am still the thorn and not the rose.

Compleat

Childish Man

When I was a child,

I played as a child,

I thought as a child,

I spoke as a child.

I did as a child,

Yet now that I am a man,

And it is right that I put aside childish things,

Although I walk as a man,

And speak as a man,

And think as a man,

I am still a child, only in a man's body,

Doing as a child would do.

On Women

Women look at men differently than we men look at them obviously. A man is drawn by the visual attractiveness that first brings a woman to his attention. For most, the immature especially, this will be her body's physical attributes - breasts, thighs, hips, buttocks, and belly. More mature men find their initial attraction is to other, less tangible things. The way a woman smiles, not just with her lips, but deep behind her eyes. The jump his heart makes when he hears the sound of her voice especially when she is laughing and it doesn't even need to be laughing with him. Her scent beneath the layers of shampoo, bodywash, deodorant and perfume, can identify her in a room of other women even if he were blindfolded. It's amazingly simple to think that way, but these are my observations and trust that I learned those through experience. There is one deeper, more difficult to express, because I lack it in my own life right now. The warmth of a woman's body as she lays sleeping beside the man she loves. Every human being creates thermal energy (see the Matrix movie to get a visual grasp of that idea) yet when a woman loves the man she is sleeping in bed with (not sex) her body will share a heat signature unique among all others. And all that I have experienced is from my own of being a man. But knowing human beings, seeing the entire race as I do, I believe it is a safe guess that this phenomenon holds true for men that lay asleep beside the woman that they truly love.

Compleat
When I Die

There is a place,

beyond all known hell

I've been there before

I'll be there again

It's where I'll be

I'll be aware of light

I'll be aware of life

I'll be aware of sound, and sight, and smell, and taste, and touch.

I'll be aware, even as I am now, of you.

I won't know light

I won't know life

I'll hear no sound,

see no sights, smell no scents,

taste no flavors and touch nothing.

I'll know I'm alone

I'll know the reasons why I'm there

I'll know loneliness

I'll know emptiness

I'll know longing for all that I no longer know

Compleat

And I'll cry, without tears

without sound, wracked by sobs,

shaking with the desire to apologize

to say, " Forgive me, please."

No one will hear, no one will see

For eternity.

An Island

The saying goes:

"No man is an island."

I call that lie out for what it is here!

The truth is much worse:

"No person wants to be an island"

"Alone."

"On a planet of 7.9 billion plus other beings."

I've burned enough bridges that I found myself alone.

Every gossamer thread of spider silk thin connection I toss in my attempts to connect with another human being has either been blown away by the winds of the world, dropped at the other end by those who fear my monstrous and ancient being or dropped at my end, lest I cause harm to one who might have cared.

"I AM that I AM. And I am an island."

Compleat

Smells

For many years now I've had what others have commented on as being a terrible sense of smell. Accused of not being able to smell my own farts or shit, for example, I came up with what I thought was a justification for my lack of ability or loss of my sense of smell. Throughout the two- year period that I used crystal meth, I consistently snorted it rather than the later, more popular means of ingesting it smoking it in a glass pipe. I surmised that my loss of ability to smell must have come from the damage I did to the inside of my nose and sinuses, perhaps scarring the tissues inside to the point that my sense of smell was depleted.

But doctors from the Veterans Administration examined my nose, sinuses, and tissues and could find nothing wrong. So, I was left with no rational explanation of why I could infrequently smell things, even smelling things that weren't present in my physical surroundings, and still not be able to smell things that others could and would describe to me in detail.

Tonight, as I tried to sleep and failed at that again, I had another epiphany about why I might not be able to smell as others do. I have had nightmares for more than a few years of something that happened while I was in the Marine Corps and witnessed a tragedy first hand but never equated the two until now.

While stationed at the Station Operations and Engineering Squadron, Cherry Point, North Carolina an AV8-A Harrier, a vertical lift- off jet, crashed through the hanger next to the one in which I had been working. I believe I've already shared that story elsewhere in this book, but what I might not have shared was the experience of smelling during the event that transpired that day.

I had grabbed a useless, hand-held fire extinguisher in a hopeless attempt to suppress the fire where that jet had crashed through the hanger and landed in the parking lot of both squadrons. I ran to where the fire raged, emptying it uselessly into flames that rose from the jet fuel, gasoline, and wreckage of the jet itself. Those smells were paramount and nearly overwhelming, but what may have caused my loss of sense of smell didn't come from those scents. It was the smell and the screams of the man, the pilot of that jet, who couldn't be reached through the heat of flames that made using that extinguisher seem like throwing a water balloon at the sun. I cannot describe what it smells like, even

Compleat

having worked in a graveyard around a mortuary that had a crematorium because this wasn't just burning flesh. It certainly wasn't a barbecue that had been left unattended for way too long. What I smelled that day was a human being burning to death, his flesh melting from the heat and his screams of pain still echoing in my mind to this very day. Perhaps, if psychologists and psychiatry are correct, the trauma of not being able to reach that pilot, not being able to even put a bullet into his brain to end his suffering, caused my mind to attempt to avoid having a sense of smell under any circumstances? "There was nothing anyone could have done." I'd heard that comment before when my sister died, so hearing it again didn't surprise me in the least. But, as with my sister, I felt responsible for not being able to do anything for him.

I didn't lose my sense of smell right away, which begs the question of why I did lose it later in life. I can only guess that the additional traumas I experienced later added to that loss.

It's one of the questions I don't have an answer for.

Compleat

The TV is Still On
—·—·—·—·—·—·—·—·—·—·—·—·—·—·—·—·—·—·—

I've been 'reluctant' or perhaps unwilling would be a better expression, to write this down or add this story to the other stories included in my book. If anyone reads what I've written prior to this they already have enough ammunition to dismiss every observation I've made about the race of humanity that my adding this story to the pile would be literally throwing gasoline onto observations I've made so far, so that all the concepts, sharing, belief in humanity as a whole could be burned by the flames of their dismissal from the simplest of sparks.

Some might see it as a challenge to do so, and others an opportunity to take advantage of my book's vulnerability in order to lead others to dismiss the entire book as the ravings of a lunatic.

In recent years I've begun to experience the phenomenon of 'hearing' a sound when I try to sleep. Not the usual 'voices in my head' that psychiatry lists as a symptom of schizophrenia fortunately enough for me since my mom did suffer from dementia to the point where her body survived long after what passed as her identity had left it.

What I experience happens when I'm trying to sleep and I am alone in my room at all hours of the day or night - when there are no others in close proximity to where I am, no other sounds except an electric fan running in order to keep the room cool, and sounds of the night animals and bugs that enter through the screened windows that I keep open for that same reason.

Compleat

I hear what I can only describe as a low murmuring of voices that brings to my mind the sounds of a television having been left on and although the sounds are too far away to distinguish what show it might be it gives me the impression that either someone is watching a show (or listening to a radio station in the distance) or, as has also happened frequently, that a television has been left on long past it's airing signal has ceased; until the "no longer in service" signal, one that used to accompany the endings of broadcast television signals, a droning signal that was a part of the emergency broadcast system before the internet and cellphones made reaching a majority of the public a much simpler task, is the only discernible sound.

I've considered that what I might be 'hearing' is not so much an actual sound in and of itself, but perhaps the echo or memory of a sound from my childhood occurring as a physical manifestation of sound in my present day. What that implies or could imply is so far beyond my knowledge of both science and religion I'm not going to try to understand the 'why' of my experiencing it, and just share it here and now.

Why then am I including it here, as yet another story for my book?

I have twofold reasoning for including it here. The first is that with dementia being an affliction my mother suffered from before her body finally expired, I find that I do dread the concept of being trapped in my physical form, long after my ability to communicate has seceded from being present. I certainly hope that no one will allow that to become the outcome of my lifespan.

But second, and more importantly, I make my book vulnerable to becoming even more likely to be dismissed by humanity as a whole, with it being seen as simply the ravings of a lunatic or madman

That the book itself will be subjected to physical burning is something I knew and accepted when I first conceived of writing down all the things I've experienced. For whatever reasons that might be found for doing so; be they religious zeal, legal or even emotional rationalizations and many others, the literal burning of the book I've written had to be accepted as a probability before I could accept the responsibility of placing into readable words what needed to be shared.

Yet the physical burning of a book does not and never could diminish the idea behind it having been written. The writer's intent isn't changed by the physical burning of paper and ink, no matter to what volume or number of copies of that book come to be subjected to its physical destruction.

However, the burning of the concepts behind what I've written does concern me. There will be those who will dismiss what I've written for their own reasons, be it their religious beliefs, their desire to manipulate their fellow human beings into surrendering the divine in each, or simply from the controlling position of the legality of what I've shared about myself and as many other reasons as there are individuals among the race of humanity.

Why then do I share it here?

I share my experience of having heard what I've come to label 'memories' of past sounds from my life because I need to tell all the truths of who I am and allow others to choose for themselves if what I've shared is meant to be an enlightenment, dismissed for their own reasons or an awakening to the ugly truth about themselves.

One very true thing, ugly as it is even for me, is that unless humanity wakes to itself and comes to know itself for who and what it really is … it is, as a race, doomed.

In fact, since I delayed in writing this book for so long, what I share here may very well come as "too little, too late." For that, humanity, you have my sincerest and deepest heartfelt sympathy.

Compleat Modern Days

What would you be willing to do in order to ensure that you would never harm another human being, if you weren't allowed or able to die? What lengths would you go to in order to prevent any chance of repeating behaviors that were not merely abhorrent to the race of humanity but had become emblematic of all that is wrong within yourself? And where on a planet of 7.9+ billion individuals would you go to separate yourself from humanity for their protection yet all the while wanting, needing, and required to interact with human beings in order to have the slightest prospect of ever becoming human yourself?

These are not rhetorical questions for me because, in this day and age of humanity's most vulnerable weaknesses being exposed to a perception beyond the rational, I am presented with them as daily options. The examples I can present to humanity are few but potent in their simplicity.

I reside on a farm, a small acreage place, in the middle of nowhere. While its location is distant enough from humanity that they aren't at risk from my mental, emotional and spiritual instabilities I am able to view their physical forms as they meander past while going about their lives and purposes. I interact with them occasionally via conversations, smiling, offering them assistance, and often requesting their assistance with tasks I find myself incapable of performing without human assistance.

I am physically awake and aware for much of each 24-hour period called a day, though not always when human beings are awake as well. In my isolation, I am able to perceive things that human beings appear much too busy to slow down and make the effort to enjoy. At 1:13 am, on most nights and when the sky is clear, I'm able to step outside and look to the skies where I can see nearby planets, Venus, Jupiter, and Mars with my naked eye. When the rain comes, especially on a spring morning or early afternoon here, I can stand outside in the rain and witness the birth of rainbows, some as many as quadrupedal and as vibrant and brilliant as the sun that creates them. I can sit in the early morning sun, with the heat soaking into my physical body causing all the muscles that have become tense over days of struggling within myself, to relax finally, often finding myself entranced, falling into a stupor of calm and relaxation at last. I can fall asleep in an instant, not because my conscience is clear or I am at peace, but due to the near-constant state of exhaustion that I feel on levels that go beyond any physical need for rest.

That state of exhaustion consists of the emotional, spiritual, mental, and divine nature of what and who I AM and is an extension of the choices I have made to prevent and avoid returning to the actions that led to my surrendering what little humanity I ever possessed. It becomes more and more difficult to bear up under the weight of my own being, the individual labeled by the society that surrounds me as being insane. Yet if they knew even the slightest part of what I see within myself, they would become frozen with the volume of that knowledge, paralyzed into inactivity, and thrown into a state of near-catatonic immobility mentally.

Compleat

The Bus
—·—

What I would normally view as an exploration of the world in which I live has been an exercise and self-reflection, and surprisingly, where I would have interacted with others on the bus, I merely observed and in observing them, I learned even more by myself. First was listening to a young black man complain about the black bus driver saying "if you cannot piss straight, there's only one toilet on this bus, so for you men, sit your ass down." For 20 minutes, that young man went on and on about how the driver had disrespected all the "niggers" - his word, not mine - on the bus, by telling them to sit down to pee.

He called one woman on his phone, complaining about being disrespected, then told her to quit shaking her titties on his phone. If she was going to shake them, then she should raise her shit up and show him her tits. She apparently did because the conversation took a turn and I put my earphones in so that I wouldn't be forced to listen. I considered talking to the driver privately about that man's slurs and low opinions but kept my thoughts to myself. I dozed for a short while until I was awakened by this young man, so concerned with respect, speaking to yet another woman on his phone and commanding her to put money into his bank account. I quickly turned up the volume on my headset to avoid witnessing that conversation as well.

Ironic, perhaps, that there was a driver change and that disrespectful young man wandered away from where the passengers were told to wait. The new driver was more no-nonsense and left behind anyone who didn't board when he announced that he was leaving. I imagined what that young man was saying about being left behind. And, as fortune would have it, turns out I got the opportunity to find out if I imagined correctly.

The bus I was on broke down on the side of the highway and the very next bus that caught up to rescue us – brought with it the stranded passengers.

Young Mr. Disrespect had been badmouthing the first driver still and had moved up his complaints by adding being left behind by the most recent one. I've often wondered where humanity gains this exaggerated sense of self-value. I would use the term self-worth, but the behaviors humanity displays most often show that humanity have no concept of their own worth, placing values on things that don't matter, just as that young man's pride was of more value to him than the lack of respect he initially was showing to the woman on

Compleat

the bus and thereby any self-respect he might have developed into real value. Another incident on this journey involved a woman who had held her infant on her lap for almost the entire first three days. Exhausted herself, I am certain her infant son was just as exhausted, fighting, fussing, complaining and loudly crying.

What woke me from a deep doze was that the woman began slapping the boys' legs in a spanking way but hard enough that the slaps woke me. I learned a valuable lesson when I tried to assist her with the child by distracting him from crying by asking him to sing for me. He ducked his head into his mom. They were Latin American speaking and he didn't comprehend what I was asking in English. That fact tells me how useful working knowledge of other languages is and emphasized humanity's own lack of comprehension or ability to speak many.

Compleat

My Normie Friends Say
—·—·—·—·—·—·—·—·—·—·—·—·—·—·—

I've been in recovery since August 5th, 1988. Darn near 33 years of staying clean and living a lifestyle 'different' than anything I knew before the day that Narcotics Anonymous came and found me in an institution where society had determined that I should spend the remainder of what life it could have been called.

During that time, I have witnessed things that I disagreed with in NA, shared my opinion way too often (I wipe mine every day, by the way) and in the end, tried to do what I believed to be the right thing for the right reason. And always tried to put the newcomer in the meetings first, ahead of my own selfish nature and desires.

To that end, I started inviting folks in NA to what I call the "Officially" UN-Official Spirit of Unity Bonfire" here at the Farm outside of Hartville, Missouri, USA. I described it as just a chance for the people in Narcotics Anonymous to bring with them one person that they normally don't get along with, write the reason WHY they don't get along with them on a piece of paper that goes into the 'God Box' I provide when they come onto the property and on the night of the big bonfire (if it lasts all weekend there are more than one) and all the differences get tossed into that fire with the Hope that by symbolically giving them to God, as we understand Him, they can find a resolution to their problems.

Maybe it's too much to ask from addicts? Maybe it's too hard for people with time, just like newcomers, to even consider bringing someone they 'disagree with' in an effort to let go and let God? My 'normie' friends sure seem to think so.

I ran into some difficulty with people in NA who tried to express that using the NA Symbol to invite Addicts (and only addicts) to a picnic was a violation of the 6th Tradition. I had to remind them that I, as an Addict in recovery, do NOT qualify as an organization, outside or otherwise. And since I'm footing the bill for the shindig (except bring your own meat because I'm a vegetarian) it was a surprise to meet with such resistance to the bonfire's intent. I asked a retired social worker friend of mine what she thought I should do, since her perspective is from someone outside of NA and a retired co-professional.

Her response: " You've been doing that NA thing for so many years now and this is how they treat you? Mike, you should stop going to those meetings altogether. You're better now, and being around 'those' people is just dragging you down by their being that way and choosing to still live like that."

I almost dismissed her, because she was a normie and it was obvious, even as a social worker, she had no grasp of the concept of what addiction truly is and wasn't open to learning to see it in any other way than what professionals (social workers, counselors such as I was, and the legal profession) are taught to view it.

I disagreed with all that she said until she added those last few words. 'and choosing to still live like that.'

How many addicts have I seen in nearly 30 years, come into the program and discover the promise:

"An addict, any addict, can stop using, lose the desire to use, and find a new way to live." Honestly, does anyone want to guess?

I know I don't, what with conventions, meetings, parties, and events the numbers I've seen are staggering and wonderful to remember. But ... My normie friend had a point I couldn't escape. I see addicts come into the program. Stop using. LOSE the desire to use. And that's it! They hang out with the people that make them feel a part of the group. Separate themselves into cliques, trees, families, and so on, and eventually leave newcomers to fend for themselves until they find their own paths. Don't believe me? You should look around you the next time you find your 'group' going out for coffee, dinner, whatever (bowling is fun btw), and count the number of newcomers there as compared to 'your' group's numbers.

What is it, maybe one newcomer?

Maybe two or three?

Unity in Narcotics Anonymous has nothing to do with uniformity. It's not about hanging out with folk that make you feel safe and secure. It's ALL inclusive. What a scary word that is, isn't it? ALL. The addict that got out of prison for rape - don't want him sitting across the table from me, right? The addict that smells so bad that it makes me want to vomit? Can't take them into a public place and share food at the same table. Yuck. The addict that killed someone by sharing bad dope and survived by dumping their friend's body into a dumpster and sneaking away into the night? Can't trust that addict with the truth about myself? What would they do with it?

Yet still, I think my normie friend was still wrong. I disagree with her because that isn't what I choose to believe. I have seen folk in NA who go out of their way to 'include' rather than exclude. And I know from my small amount of time and the little experience I share: "There is a 'new way of life' in the 12 Steps of Narcotics Anonymous." I found it. And once again I offer to share it with you all.

To the world of NA, to the addict everywhere and anywhere on this planet, with hours clean or semi-centennials of recovery. The 8th "Officially" UN-Official Spirit of Unity Bonfire will be held the weekend of this coming August 5th, 2018. I just happen to be hoping to celebrate 30 years of recovery that night with a Bonfire. I hope you will come, bring a newcomer or a friend, sponsor or sponsee. But most of all I ask you to bring someone you don't normally get along with ... it's time.

My normie friends say ... I'm wasting my time, money, and resources.

What do you say?

I guess she was right.

No one came.

Compleat

12-Step Meetings

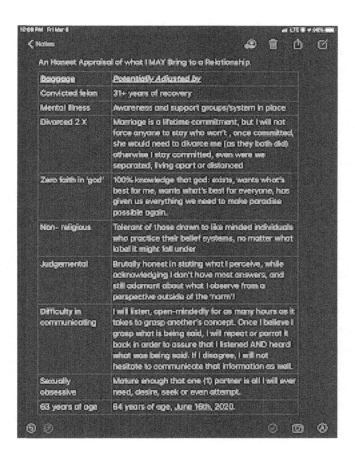

Compleat

I sit in 12-Step meetings, sometimes wondering why I still attend them at all. I've stayed clean and by that, I mean, not just abstinent from drugs, but actually staying off drugs, out of trouble with the law, and not giving into my baser nature for some number of years now. Added to that was the repeated questioning by my peers and fellow professionals of why I choose to continue to keep company with these "unfortunates" who need those meetings, but the real pressure to stop going comes not from outside, but from inside the rooms of every 12-Step fellowship I attend. While I find comfort, serenity, and peace by attending the meetings, I cannot help but to be consciously aware of the discomfort my presence causes others in attendance. I assumed at first it was my past and the heinous actions I willfully enjoyed throughout the period of my existence before being found by and learning from these fellowships: rape child molestation, voyeurism, sexual assault, uncontrollable rage, and other socially undesirable behaviors being well within the range of my normal or standard behaviors. I considered it appropriate that others would find my presence uncomfortable. Not surprisingly, it felt that I had justifiably been categorized as a social pariah, even amongst these - the rest of which society had rejected as addicts, felons, losers, or worse. But by worse, I mean, those labeled crazy or insane. Those sick individual society deemed untrustworthy because they were incapable of maintaining behaviors in such a manner that strictly didn't feel fear or discomfort witnessing or being in the presence of. A reject among, among rejects. And I could relate simply because I had been raised in such a manner as to cause discomfort, fear, and avoidance of such individuals and their behaviors, which may well explain my discomfort, fear, and loathing of myself from the beginning of my cognitive understanding of my feelings, society, and self.

Yet there is more to why I feel their discomfort my presence causes when attending any number of interventions, events, meetings, or gatherings. In 12-Step meetings, services labeled attending church, and other gatherings, I am witness to the discomfort of others because of a behavior that I have exercised and developed as a tool to enable me to retain my freedom and place within the society surrounding me and in order to allow others the information that they require in order to protect themselves as well as assist me in my maintenance efforts for living among them.

I speak of my telling unfiltered truths about myself. I am unashamed of my past behaviors. Although it is my belief, I fear my returning to them much more than anyone who learns of them and contradictory to that, my fear isn't based in the concept of punishment, retaliation, or retribution that might be meted out were I to return to performing them. My fear comes from the self-knowledge that were I to continue or return to those behaviors, I might never be able to discontinue or stop doing them again. In my imagination, to attempt the communication of what that fear might be conceivably related to by others I know I cannot communicate in such a way as to allow others to understand. To understand they would be required to be me or at least inside my mind, in order to know, and/or experience the exact feeling itself.

The closest I can relate the feeling with is visualization or description of a visual effect that can be duplicated. Picture a steaming hot tarpit, such as the La Brea, and the deep blackness of the tar - its heat being high enough to sear and dissolve flesh from bones, yet of such consistency as to hold said flesh in place upon those same foundational bones. Holding the liquified flesh in place, so as to maintain it its form or shape. That is the best descriptive example I can or care to attempt to render. Add to it the perspective of permanent preservation exactly as its form or shape was prior to being introduced to the tar and any individual might well be capable of relating to my imagining of my prior self. I see myself as flesh held with the consequences of my own behaviors by my having assumed my position of these consequences. Very similar, in fact, to stepping into a hot tub or tarpit - as simple as taking one short step with the allure being familiarity and the discomfort, as well as deserved pain to be inflicted. In short, I know the darkness, its effects, and discomfort, whereas living without it has been a struggle of monumental proportions for me to simply reawaken every day, knowing that the darkness of who I am remains, but choosing each day not to return to it because, were I to attempt to reenter even in the smallest of ways, I would become tempted to throw myself headlong back into full insanity.

My reasoning for using the absence indifference to a hot tub instead of a tar put, laying ground for the concept of the appeal or allure earlier, since most sane individuals cannot relate to a tarpit as appearing to be an appealing experience. Within meetings, when sharing unashamedly and hopefully without dramatization, exaggeration, aggrandizement or necessarily reflection, I experience sharing exactly who I am in order to receive from that sharing the modicum of humanity and human connection. I share so apparently because to do anything less would cause me to experience feelings of deception of both others and myself, the first step into the cesspool of who and what I was, am, and could become where my vigilance in avoiding that plunge lapse. This brutal, unfiltered sharing of myself is so far outside the norm of the society of both the 12-Step fellowships and outside of their meetings is more likely the

Compleat

cause of the discomfort others experience in my presence. I've been questioned, even challenged, with toning down what I do say and, reflectively, I know I could. I choose not to, in spite of the consequences of my choice, simply because I know who I am.

Compleat

Let's Talk About God...

...or some of the dumbest questions I've found answers to:

Some of the people in my life who have met me face to face have very often assumed or called me arrogant. I admit that my overconfidence in sharing my values, ideas, and beliefs is radical enough to make others uncomfortable just by my expressing them out loud and express them I do yet, It has never been my intent to annoy project or effect anyone to follow or adapt my personal values as their own.

My youngest son's mom has repeatedly informed me that my intent is very often covered over and/or obscured by the impact of what I say and do. And again, I can fiercely admit that my impact can be like a volcanic eruption, sudden and loud, causing much damage in the wake of what flows out of it.

And like those eruptions it can form islands upon which life can begin anew; forming and developing into paradises of great joy and beauty, but always subject to repeat outburst or outpouring of who I am.

So, it is my concern and compassion that I am intent to express here. When I state simply that if someone is reading this and comes to feel offended by what I express, please just skip over this chapter in its entirety.

I have a few things to express about God that very religious people reading It would probably view as blasphemous and an agnostic or atheist as nonsensical or dismiss-able for being the ravings of a lunatic. My intent in sharing what I view as answers to the commonly, most repeatable and very frequently asked by the latter group of individuals in their efforts to ridicule the first group.

And before I proceed into the questions themselves, I need to state upfront that my upbringing was in a predominantly Christian society. So, my response responses, while very probably appearing biased in or toward that mythology, they do not exclude or dismiss any other myths someone else might embrace. Like honesty truth is a universal principle that transcends all religions, including the non-religious religion of science!

With all of that rambling out of the way, allow me to start with the most often repeatedly asked question that I can recall, "If God exists, why does he allow

Compleat

all the evil to happen in the world?" From the little research I've done on this question, it appears to be the one that has persistently been asked throughout the ages of human existence, being flippant. I really often desire to respond to this question with a question of my own.

Why ask why?

But the honest answer is not that why, but why do we lay evil at God's feet? The Genesis story says Lucifer was created by God to tempt humans in paradise. So, if P then Q logic says if the God dude created evil Lucy, then he's responsible for the existence of evil in the first place, which leads to my first answer.

Do the Christians even read their own book that their God created for them?

They say that to serve in a particular role to tempt was what makes God responsible for providing the temptation and/ or the snake for performing his function. The answer is there, right in their book, but most argue against God being responsible for anything created to evil, responsible for anything related to evil as if God was, or is too small to own his part in the entire process.

The snake being the physical manifestation of Lucy simply did exactly the performance of the actions he had been created for and might be considered an innocent. If their book didn't refuse to accept it. If their book didn't reduce it as excuse or reason for its behaviors.

Then there's the whole Adam and Eve myth and the roles it describes if you've listened to the snake's portion of the story first. They always deem Eve to be worse for listening to the snake and then Adam innocent as he gets into that discussion even though Adam followed suit doing the one thing that they had received specific instructions against doing!

That's where my values leave most Christian religions behind, because they define original sin as some simplistic rule to obey but I challenge that by asking "Was disobedience the condemning action that most religious Christians focus upon the real problem?

My view is simplistic and contradicts several points in the whole of the scenario. The first point in my disagreement with the focusing on disobedience as the problem, the God dude, their book describes was not the manipulative or vindictive bastard they tend to describe him as being, and given the choice who hasn't felt temptation to disobey of some sort and at some point or another in their life?

So, was the god dude guilty of having hardwired humans to fail or was he testing his creations? I don't read it that way. Old dude was simply providing an opportunity but not for disobedience they define as being the 'original sin' and it wasn't just for testing the human ability to obey.

Maybe that's why their book is viewed so suspiciously because the opportunity being provided wasn't in the disobedience or even the temptation they focused upon. The opportunity lay and the choice for it was provided to both as individuals and was acted upon after being confronted with the facts of the disobedience being discovered.

Eve is recorded as trying to shift responsibility to the snake and Adam goes even further astray upon that path by first pointing some of the responsibility toward Eve, but eventually trying to lay the blame at the God dude's feet saying, "The woman YOU gave me tempted me and I did eat." He had been happy with her up until faced with accepting his responsibility for his own actions. Yet, he'd rather blame her and then eventually tried shifting it all back towards the God dude for gifting him with someone in his life, failing to own our own shit.

We make our own messes and our task is to face the consequences, thereof. Anyway, I ask that you don't just believe me! Instead, the next time you take a shit, paint the walls of your bathroom with that shit and see how long you can live comfortably that way. Am I responsible for making the suggestion? Absolutely. Am I responsible if you act on that suggestion?

No way and in no way would that be possible. I can't and don't control any human being and here's the kicker of this point, neither will or can the God dude. He made the choice and accepted his responsibility by allowing them to be able to choose for themselves.

And that leads to yet another question. Many people ask, even so-called believers, "If God exists, where's the proof, how come no one sees him or hears from him or at the very least how come he doesn't show up and put a stop to all the messes, evil, etc... that is happening in the world?"

Some say his non presence or lack of active participation is the proof that he doesn't exist. Others use every imaginable, excuse for his non-participation usually by misquoting some spiritual literature or the other. My perspective with its slight bias is to respond to that question with yet another of my own.

"Why would he?" Rather than establishing his non-existence for my view, his lack of active participation is a strong indication that he does actually exist . I will relate what I personally experienced that removed world doubt for me.

Almost every religion describes their deity figure. In some parental role, the god father figure, the earth mother goddess, even a dark Lord figure for the anti-God figure, where it is looked to as a source of power providing its followers, their need, or wants similar to a parental figure and benevolence being a trait associated with parental figures, all of them are seen as capable of providing human beings and human beings appear to be hardwired to view them as providers, especially of basic needs like food, water, shelter, security.

Comfort and caring as parental figures, even wolves can be found to be viewed as parental figures to human children as manifested in myths of children being raised by wolves, Romulus and Remus, the Jungle Books with Mowgli, even horror stories of half-human/ half-wolf werewolves relate to this basic programming that becomes hardwired during early development.

Why does God appear to take on the appearance of a parental figure. If not because human infancy programs us all to view whomsoever provides those basic needs in the parental role.

So why doesn't the God dude suit up, show up and fix things for human beings? It might just be because, if one believes the whole creation myth, he never made or created human beings to be permanent children. I often question Christians and Muslims about their roles in relation to their particular God figures, and almost without exception, their responses come from their reading from the same pages of propaganda, "We are the children of God." and they end up acting as if they are children, by fighting with one another inside their specific myths, groups of 'believers and vilifying those outside of their myths as enemies of their faith.

Even if they actually believed their relationship to the old dude, they still choose to fight among themselves and with others, like siblings striving to be the center of his attention. As long as human beings here existed, and are focused on all providing figures, external to ourselves as being superior, better, stronger, calling them mother, father, goddess, or God, and asking like a nagging toddler begging for something incessantly it makes me wonder when humanity is going to grow up?!

I honestly see him as an individual male only due to the bias of my upbringing and gender yet I also see him as fed up with the entire experience. I have difficulty retaining hope that by setting the example, human beings would wake up, stop acting like spoiled children and assume their proper roles beside him.

Has anyone ever read their Bible.

Their Genesis story states specifically that he created humans and that after he had done so walked, talked and resided among them all that in a garden and waited to see what would happen. I dare any humans to stick all of that in a garden and see what grows here! They were living as he did and he was here with them. But no one ever questions why the whole Lucy myth is based on Lucifer being an arch angel, the one of light whose face reflected the glory of the god dude, but when old dude created these humans, not just supplanting him as first in old dude gaze, but by creating them old dude was making company for himself, friends, literally making his own friends and making humans not like angels or even arch angels, but somethings more.

Poor Lucy got pissed off by that, according to their myths, but as equals with the creator or equals with life itself, that didn't leave room for him.

But damn doesn't that sort of relate to their being children. It would be their own actions; disobedience being expected as they learned. Yet, it would be their choice to attempt to avoid responsibility, being the real disappointment for him. They lied and looked to blame someone, something, or even him rather than accept who they actually were by avoiding the responsibility for their own actions that they were offered.

And by the words I pick on, I express my negative feelings toward religion in general, not just the Christian religions, my first example does show my major difficulty with all religions. Jesus, whether you choose to view him as divine or simply human, was an individual. A person whom historically can be somewhat established as having a physical presence in Jerusalem and Galilee at the time period he is reputed to have been and done the things he is accredited with doing, and even with his death.

Discussions about his actions, since no one living today can claim to have been physically present at those times, with his actual presence as a matter of both secular and religious historical documentation, he was one individual, one person, or one Messiah as he is denoted in all Christian religions shall remain moot points of debate.

Meanwhile I myself present the case frequently that God's relationship with every individual on this planet is distinct and just as individually theirs, since no to human beings are exactly alike. The Christian religions all claim exclusive relationship with god, excluding all non-Christians as being outside of God's grace and therefore to be either pitied for their lack or viewed as potential enemies of God, Jesus, and the truth.

Amazingly enough, they apply the same appellation to one another as well. Catholics claim, divine designation through interpretation of their book, AKA the Bible division from Islam, Judaism, Buddhism, etc. ... and establishing their claim to legitimacy became so important and a means by which enormous secular wealth and power would be accumulated that the atrocities performed in god's name became a self-justified means of pursuing these ends from crusades to reclaim lands in which none of them had ever resided or had ancestry within to inquisitions used to seize properties, wealth, goods, lives, and services without need of restoration or reparations became tools of fear and abuse to such an extent that individuals within their own system became offended either through lack of self-profiteering, or legitimate disgust with the actions being performed in God's name, that they chose to break away from the Catholic ties and would become to be known as Protestants.

Has anyone ever known the simple engineering principle that a thing, anything, once broken that the subsequent pieces or portions thereof are subject to being easily broken as well? That's a fact found in nature!

All of existence and personalities (and human beings) that have once been broken, become more easily broken, and unless the broken pieces are repaired or individually reinforced, subsequent breakage is inevitable. Hence Catholicism has Jesus Frankensteined, and Protestants became Lutherans, Baptist, Methodists, Pilgrims, Quakers, and Mormons. The latter of whom are viewed by some of the other denominations as non-Christians, alongside those who attempt to revert to a form of Judaism known as Jehovah's Witnesses. They all demand only one God, one dude, one name of Jesus, and apparently each sect denomination or faith has the one true empirical representation of all of mankind's relationship with the divine being credited with creation of the entire human race.

I could excuse their diverse approaches as being either they are the gathering of like-minded individuals into a 'church' due to the comfort they found in one another's company, if it wasn't for the inevitable separation of themselves from other human beings based solely on that underlying comfort. It is in comfort with themselves where they lose their connection with others of different beliefs, means, methods and so on leading to both judgment of others as being wrong, lost, confused, misled or deceived, and with such judgment, it always has one inescapable result, division.

If they are wrong and choose to continue being wrong and if it's even recognized as a choice that others are entitled to make, then they must have been right when I was in college. I had an American history professor who wandered into the area of philosophical discussion by offering his observation of the country known as the USofA and it's inevitable and unavoidable growth into a true Utopian society.

His presentation of this observation was, of his faith in a social model, expounded in Edward Bellamy's book, "Looking Backward" and the predictions from the year 1865, of things such as motorcars airplanes, shopping malls, ATM cards, credit cards, etc. … having come to pass.

The mono application of businesses through mergers, which the professor declared would accumulate in the inevitability of businesses merging to become the government and sole employer of every resident of the nation where medical treatments would become universally available at no cost, every person would serve a four year period of employment within the system or government, at whatever position they qualified for from their completely funded education and they had chosen to follow determined as their skill or capability, and then retire with full benefits of the society to pursue their desires and hobbies. That professor expounded this concept in a room full of impressionable teenagers where I already stood out as being different, but I chose to question his expressed opinion by interjecting a simple observation of an alternative philosophical nature.

The Utopian society, sought by much of humanity and many, if not all religions, I expressed will remain unobtainable until such a time as the entire human race comes to or awakens to the realization of a need to change the basic supposition about yourselves and one another. His response, although completely anticipated was still discouraging to hear him express in a class room, wherein he was meant to teach by example of history.

What I had just expressed he answered with the question, "Why should I need to change?" He further questioned, "I'm a good person, and what about her", pointing to one of the other students in the classroom, "Why should she need to change? She's a good person." "And him," pointing to yet another student, "He's not a criminal or crazy. Why should he need to change?"

Yet, unknowingly, he answered his own questions in the very expression of them.

Why does the human race need to change in order to obtain the Utopian society or paradise or restoration to Eden in the Christian mythology? The answer is in the question. Why? Because without understanding the need to change, the human race is incapable of changing to obtain what they desire most.

Yet human beings seek to amass great wealth and power and gain self-security and comfort. There is no questioning that fact. To deny all physical comforts, focusing on self-awareness and enlightenment is obtainable, true. Yet both extremes exist on and are of the same spectrum, each viewed as more desirable by some and to an extent by all human beings, but no matter where they find themselves on the range of the spectrum, even considering themselves as bad or good people, the human race chains itself away from ever obtaining the Utopian by continuing to exist upon, within and restricted by the reliance of that self-definition.

Based upon that spectrum, the religions of the world define God as being omnipotent, omniscient, and if infinite or eternal outside of time, they say God exists everywhere in every moment in every action and in every interaction with their resultant reactions. and in this recognition, they separate themselves by encasing themselves within the illusion of time, born, grow old and die, with only death and taxes being the unavoidable events in the lives of every human being.

There are, however, people who avoid taxes, paying next to nothing or nothing. And their results are usually the amassing of physical wealth by means that are seen as cheating. They are viewed with distrust or anger or envy, some even viewing they're amassing of great material fortunes as an admirable or sought-after goal for their own lives.

Others express their envy through jealousy and resentment initially and verbally directed toward these fortunate ones. With statements of dismissal such as they may have it all now, but they'll die and go to hell and will simply represent their own lack of similar comfort, security, and power and bring themselves full circle, as it were, to repeating Adam's original sin, my interpretation of blaming God or others, or even themselves for what they lack.

Compleat

I've been comfortable with and known real want in my lifespan so far and I choose to be grateful and express my gratefulness for both circumstances equally. It was only by a chance circumstance that I became aware of my position within that spectrum. That experience also helped me recognize humanity's combined position for within many of the overlapping interconnected, multifaceted spectrum that are the building blocks of existence and the restraining walls by which humanity confines and comforts one another.

Back to the question offered by that history professor, "Why does a good man need to change in order for the human race to obtain a Utopian state of existence?" As I said before, the answer resides within the question itself in seeking for or struggling toward the Utopian humans place themselves within the illusion of time and continue your separation from God, the divine of life itself, or whatever name by which to call it by your faith-based labels. "As God is my witness."

When I first met him in spite of many different religious experiences that supposedly defined both God and our relationship to one another for me, it was as if I were meeting a complete stranger. One who in claiming a special relationship with me I had had a similar experience when I was 15 and my biological father came around supposedly to establish a father's relationship with his children, especially his sons.

While my older brother was accepting of the opportunity, I was leery of this and of this individual that I had heard about since my early childhood, but had no actual memories of that didn't involve beatings. One I remember was for wetting the bed, when the bed was a pallet laid a top a railroad train set board with tracks and train and another for inappropriate sexual contact with a cousin step sister at three years of age.

This god dude, hadn't beaten me physically as far as I could remember, but the threat of punishment loomed large over the atmosphere of the meeting due to my fear of the stranger being of immense power and the feeling of being picked out and isolated. My fear of my own behaviors caused me to project the aura of danger onto this god entity.

Fortunately for me, I was only projecting the anger and it wasn't emanating from God. As helpless as a caged rat, I struggled, snapped bit clawed and screeched as loudly as I could. I knew why I was there, who it was that had brought me there and why I was there, before my total freak out of open rebellion, I had an instant in which I felt elation since this god being had picked me to call on, but the instant was overcome by memories of my past and recently passed behaviors.

Now, these many years later and when I think back to it, I can relate to the whole Moses story in my own crazy way.

I'm out when it comes to pushing for recognition and would move that claim to understand another human being's feelings would be impossible. The best I can do is imagine how I might have felt for Moses called upon to do something so far outside of human comprehension. The fear I felt triggered a fight or flight instinct. As I had no way of knowing how I had arrived, there was the knowledge of being held in a manner that suggested while my foot rested upon something. I had no idea how or where to run.

Moses in that story told god he couldn't do the things being asked of him, thereby trying to avoid confrontation and/or doubting his own sanity. But in that moment, his brother or stepbrother, Jacob was assigned to speak verbally for Moses.

When selected by the strange person to do something, I fought. Eventually breaking free of the experience only to realize the enormity of both rejecting God's offer, but threatening him in regard to how he had, or was running the planet and unloaded all my shame and blame upon God.

Violent abuse of foul language seemed to well up from within me, finding unfiltered release immediately as if the threats I was screeching were in any way effective of reflecting my own inability to conform to socially defined proper behaviors.

I hurled all of it forward into God's face, very like spittle ejected toward an opponent during a verbal confrontation. I was completely incapable of touching anything though even though this presence was within my arms reach. Let alone that I was incapable of wounding it/him in any way and confronted with this new awareness of my powerlessness, my fear, anger and certainty exploded as well.

As I felt more of them these many years later, I can look back to see that God had patience and tolerance toward me, perhaps in the way a loving father would or could show a rebellious teenager or toddler. The Bible, the Torah, the Quran, and other books of fiction all tell of similar events. But since my experiences relate most to the book known as the Bible, I will as I've already stated be focusing my comments toward it, those who are quoted from it and especially those who chose to edit it so heavily called the Christian religions.

Compleat

The "word" of God, as it has been disputed about, argued over, fought for and killed in the name of since the beginning of that particular religion.

And it is only from my familiarity with having read it that I chose to focus on it. The other religious books having been subjected to the exact same processes, I'm about to describe was Mohamed the prophet of Allah, sharing one truth about God and humanity's relationship with the divine. But the Koran is just as edited and filled with fictional bullshit as the Torah of the Jewish religion contains, as the farce of humanity and as the human race embraces.

So, feel free, whichever fiction or fictional book you choose to believe or ignore to place that title, where I refer to the Bible as a book or source of misinformation. In fact, I encourage those who practice any of the religions, humanity embraces to reread the book or books, not just of their particular religions after having read what I am writing here and see for yourselves if the truths I express here, aren't applicable to all religious texts.

Let's start with atheist since they express their doubts about the existence of any divine being or beings, many refuse to read religious texts like the Bible, for instance, quoting the coined phrase, "The Bible was written by man." while they were not meaning to be correct as to the patriarchal editing of that text.

They are right in that fact that it was initially written by male human beings. That book, as well as the Jewish Torah from which a large portion of it is derived was pinned by men in religious sects, trying to record the history of their people through some of human's earliest written records mentioned.

The Bible, the Quran, the Torah, the teachings of Buddha, and every other major religion followed on this planet, including some of the obscure religions such as Wicca, Scientology and the book of Mormon were all written by men, perhaps unintentionally due to the cultures the individuals were raised within and perhaps unconsciously subjugating women through no real fault or blame upon themselves. These books were written to record spiritual guidance, practical living advice, expressed belief in the good that all of humanity possesses, yet were influenced in the choice of words and phrases by those individual's own upbringing, thereby subjugating women to men, simply through their known or experienced gender roles and role models.

I mentioned Wicca as being still written by men, even though it realizes and recognizes the roles women play in the growth and the development of humanity more than any of the rest, because all of these religious texts were written by the hands of male human beings and were influenced by their own very gender specific thought processes.

As I have expressed, this recognizable fact was pointed out unintentionally by those labeled as atheists for choosing to not believe in any divine or so-called God beings. The Bible was completely scribbled out by the hands of men, male human beings, culturally and socially raised to view women as the weaker and inferior, to be provided and cared for, but never recognized as an equal sex or gender.

It was with no surprise to me when a self-professed woman atheist expressed her opinion of the Bible as being a m mishmash of patriarchal bullshit used to justify the subjugation of women to the point that women were treated as property instead of individual human beings in their own right. I couldn't disagree with her on that point because she was absolutely correct about the outcome and results of how it had been initially scribed and would eventually be edited for that very purpose by the Counsel of Trent, along with the Quran as well by different Moslem scholars.

By the way I wonder how many of you ask yourselves, if you dare, how did all the writings, pages, books, and recorded deeds depicted in the Bible and those other religious texts gather themselves together in single volumes? Unless humanity had no hand in the very net of gathering them together, did Muhammad truly sit down and write every page and word included in the Quran? Or were his statements recorded by others and rewritten through their perspectives as well?

For example, possibly he did write most of it, but scholars of Islam will write, will note and ensure that passages included in it reflect the attitudes, writing styles and thoughts of other men as well. The Bible even offers separate books for different events in the old Testament and books or letters in what is labeled the new Testament.

My studies of the Quran were interrupted at too early of a stage for me to recognize if it too was separated in this manner. But that is a part for another story in this book, I will be returning my focus to the writing and editing of the Bible written being by men willingly or unconsciously subjugating women to a secondary role in human society.

It was almost inevitable that religions would rise up among the female gender of the human race in which they would be able to protect, support and empower themselves. Human beings do not take well to subjugation and women as one gender of humanity were no exception. How then could the Bible be used to cause them to surrender themselves to that state of subjugation?

The tool that was used was their very gender and its specific, highly noticeable differences.

The atheists were correct about the writing by men. A few, even recognizing the editorializing of the Bible by the religious leaders of the era during the conclaves that took place as Christians from the known world and always only men of faith, while having strong beliefs in God, gathered together to decide which letters, books, stories, events, and characters, including the character traits and personality features that would be attributed to Jesus, their Christ as his having had and displayed with emphasis solely upon his divine nature.

After all his father was God and almost no references to his mortal are humanity allowed.

I often joke or tease with religious folks, by asking them laughingly: "Since Jesus ate food and drank wine while he was here and the physical body that he got from his mom would process that food in the usual manner yet with him being holy and all, does that mean somewhere around the areas of Bethlehem, Galilee and Jerusalem, there could be turds of holy shit?"

About that point in the conversation, I usually get invited to leave whatever building they call a church and also invited to "not come back." 'sigh'

It is a simplistic question, not disputing the J dude's divinity at all, but honestly expressing that glossing the over his human nature in order to elevate his spirituality was done by men. Whose humanity they say supposedly caused the stains on the shroud of Turin and were supposedly the blood from the beatings and the crown of thorns forced upon him during his torture and death by crucifixion.

I would personally have examined that Turin shroud for stains. However, knowing that after death, without embalming being applied to the human body, it would have released any foodstuff, processed or partially from out the rectum, since his being of the Jewish religion, his family and friends would have applied myrrh and burned frankincense , but would not have allowed the body to be subjected to the Egyptian process of being embalmed.

So, in a way, no shit becomes an established fact as to the authenticity of the shroud or it's not being real ask any moron if my observations are correct or not. I suggest if I sound as if I'm supporting the position of atheists by questioning some of the major discrepancies in those religious texts and teachings, it is not my intent to dismiss or deny the existence of God by doing so, just to point out that the discrepancies of religion are much simpler to resolve than even atheists have given thought to or ask for evidence of establishing facts from fictions.

My personal experience with the divine being such that I now know he exists. My intent, however, is to dispel the false information that is embraced by so many human beings of every religion ever created by stating that, God as an individual being, does in fact exist. I sincerely hope no one else ever has the misfortune to meet the old fucker face to face in the manner that I did and live through the experience.

The Bible, however, viewed as mostly an edited, written for the purpose of controlling humanity, and full on for the subjugation of the female, is in fact simply a tool for the subjugation of the female gender and filled with perspectives of the men that re-wrote it. For the most part that would place it in the section of being a fictional writing, a story book for helping people feel good or bad about the events that come about in their lives or actions, they have taken against one another in an attempt to force compliance, obedience and conformity to the accepted societal norms, where it is practically applied as a tool for those purposes.

The same holds true for the Quran teachings, of the sayings of Confucius, the sayings of Buddha and every other human embraced religion, including the anti-religions of Satanism and atheism. But all of humanity's efforts to understand, or at least explain what they fear and do not understand hold one common thread.

Even atheists, who question anything as being divine. When I agree about the Bible and other texts as being written by men, I'm not agreeing to any lack of the presence of the divine in any of the writings, followed by any religions, perhaps the teachings of the Buddhists say it's in the simplest of terms by stating there are many paths to the top of the mountain, while the Hindi religion uses the story of four blind men touching an elephant in different spots. One calling it a rope from touching its tail, another a fan for its ear, another a hose for its trunk and the fourth, a wall for touching its side, yet in being blind they were all correct in what they were experiencing, but missing the hole by not being able to know the elephant for what it was.

Compleat

When I first looked at the religions of humanity. I too saw them from a similar perspective. Religions of every kind were like slices from the exact same thing, every piece nourishing those who partook of it, having a flavor, familiar to each, but described through the filter of the experiences of those who chose for whatever reasons to partake of their particular piece.

This obviously led to disagreement, discourse, division and often physical violence because each religion knows itself to be right in how it describes itself and the divine. Even the atheist non-belief in God as an individual, being a religion of sorts, not organized with frequent gatherings of mutual support on a Saturday, Sunday, solstice or Ramadan, but still a religion.

How can non-belief be a religion? By means of a professed belief in that non-belief. After I met God in person, a male figure, since that was how my mind could withstand perceiving him. I came to the realization that even my own concept of religion was flawed. Mountain climbers use specialty ropes made to withstand the rigors of climbing where rope might be the only thing to stand between themselves and falling to their certain deaths. These ropes had to be made in such a way as to not merely bear the weight of the climber and their gear, but withstand being subjected to extremes of weather, sharp rocks, the scraping and wearing at them as the climbers use them to assist others or raise and repel themselves and their gear needed for their own survival. Most professional climbers use specialty made ropes that are marked during the manufacturing process with a single strand of threads being colored differently than the rest of the threads in their ropes. White ropes, for example, might have a single red strand of threads woven in among all the rest to give the rope a distinguishing feature recognizable by the climber as having been tested extensively and matching the conditions it was manufactured to be used for their express purpose.

The Bible and other religious texts are very much like those ropes, with each and every one being manufactured by different religions, tested, approved, and used by those who embraced their religion of choice with a single strand of truth running through it. Then written by men and edited for mankind's purposes. Be that purpose the massing of wealth, the controlling of populations of peoples or the instilling obedience into the rebellious nature of humanity as a whole, not even those changes could alter the thread of truth that marks them as being divinely inspired or written by god.

For example: While I write by hand with pens or pencils of differing colors of ink and lead. Sometimes by the pen I might choose and also by differing in style or coloration of pencil or even through the pressure I apply while writing I take the effort to write out carefully what I am recording of God as humanity calls my pop, my action does the same thing. He picks and chooses human beings through which to express his thoughts, feelings and his own truth very much like that. Single strand in all those many ropes filled with patriarchy and other strands, easily recognizable as the bullshit or as I call it, holy shit. Yet the truth endures in each of them. Jesus, they say, was the first physically conceived son of god. So, fucking, what? Did he have a choice in the matter? Did he choose his mother, live his life, share his example, display his abilities and time his death. Only to come back in spite of knowing there would not just be those that doubted, he knew there would be worse than any doubts, he was aware that humanity would take his example, twist his words, change his purpose for going through all of that and make religions out of it.

Out of his sacrifice. He knew more human beings would be killed in the name of God, Allah, or whatever religion that was embraced. All the while still being willing to make the sacrifices he chose to make for the sake of hope.

Islam promotes the hope of paradise, Mormonism promotes a heaven of eternally pregnant women, Christianity in all its varied sexual flavors promotes the kingdom of God in heaven, without the pain suffering or the death that humanity fears most, of all the things they fear as a whole. Christianity calls itself followers of Jesus Christ. And because most claim to be following the written and edited teachings of Jesus few, if any, embrace or act upon the actions of the person of the one they call the 'son of God."

Jesus knew this would be the situation after he was crucified and got sent or came back, he knew it, saw what was to be and did what any human being would do under his circumstances. With what knowledge he had, (remember that strand of truth I mentioned being in the Bible) how even with all the patriarchal bullshit and editing to remove the references to his humanity they missed editing this one verse out because it probably sounded too simplistic to have any effect except to set the stage they wanted for the next scene, not recognizing its importance in establishing both his divine and mortal natures.

He knew what humanity would do in his name and in a garden as his followers who had walked with him for three years, fell asleep on guard duty and slept. It says just two words, "Jesus wept."

Paintings in Catholic buildings show the depiction of a white male figure with a glow of divine lights around him and tears streaming down his cheeks, very pretty, extremely religious and spiritually motivating to the masses of the indoctrinated practitioners of their religion.

But not factual or even what really happened. Jesus wept. He cried the way a man does when his wife dies, the way a mother does when her baby dies upon taking its first breath, he cried the way I would eventually cry 34 years after feeling responsible for my older sister's death. Jesus wept tears, snot running from his nose and aching so deep that his sobs rocked his body, shaking every muscle.

And if he hadn't already been kneeling, it would've brought him to his knees. When I faced god that day, I saw the suffering and exactly how Jesus had cried. And I was angry, not just at God for choosing to allow humanity to put Jesus through that, but humanity for being the way they were then and still are now.

But mostly at myself for knowing all that I grew aware of in that instant. Remember I had only read the Bible the whole way through once when I was 13 years old, thought it was a fun read and a great story book with all those stories, though it's a bit boring today to read all the way through. In that instant, that knowledge of what he went through, what humanity was meant to be instead of who you act and think you are hit my stunned brain. Another voice spoke a verse to me. Jesus' voice. I realized then, and I remember now another verse I had read many years before, "Pick up your cross and follow me."

He wasn't being cryptic or proverbial in what he said in both instances, it wasn't open to interpretation or debatable as being meaning physically or not, any more than the verse, "Jesus wept." This was something he was expressing again and directly to me, literally, and he meant it.

He meant it for the entire human race of course, not just me! My being the self-controlled narcissistic perverted, and as a male non-human being I was even without the religious changes I had applied to my behaviors up to that point. I freaked out. There was no doubt or even questioning what it was what I was meant to do

Take training, become a pastor of a congregation that had already been selected, share what I had been shown and willingly accept the consequences that would unfold, including a torturous and painful death. Even as J had experienced, though, I didn't see myself as being crucified the way he had been.

Compleat

Some religious folk might call it the spirit of rebellion while others of that same bent might all it a possession by the devil or devils. But in that instant of knowing fear, anger, self-discussion, avoidance of my responsibility, rage rose up inside and through me to which I told God - not Jesus, as he was a sibling. I felt empathy for - to go fuck himself.

Compleat

The Child Inside
– ‐ – ‐ – ‐ – ‐ – ‐ – ‐ – ‐ – ‐ – ‐ – ‐ – ‐ – ‐ – ‐ – ‐ –‐

I don't mind being called crazy or insane, but I'm not saying that I don't care when people do use those labels to describe me or my behaviors because I do care. I just accept the labels as being humanity's means of trying to make sense of who I am, what I'm about and most of all what I've been trying to express as I perceive the world around me.

Perhaps I'm afraid of heights because I was dropped on my head as a nine-month-old baby? The reason why doesn't concern me as much as the terror I feel when I'm looking down from a height, be it inside a building or monument like the St. Louis Arch or a bridge high over a river where others are swimming and diving from the bridge into the river below. I've mentioned that even playing video games in which the character falls or leaps from great heights causes my stomach to react as if it were my physical self that was falling, even though I would never jump from some of the heights imagined by the game's creators.

And what about my disassociation from the race of humanity? Could I have developed the distance through reading so many books at a young age, many of which were science fiction, fantasy, and/or horror stories in which the main character was an unwilling monster? Yet I relished the thought of being able to convert into a beast or monster from the weak, frightened, and powerless boy I saw myself as for most of my youth.

If only I were Hercules, I would tear down the school where I was tormented by my classmates, yet show them mercy when they cowered in fear of me. And the Hulk, mindless rage unleashed with only one thought, to smash whoever and whatsoever stood before me and opposed me. My experience with the boy, Sal, frightened me because I saw that while I didn't have the trans-formative power of having been exposed to gamma radiation, I did have the uncontrollable and detrimental rage the comic book character displayed.

Suppose all the reading I did shaped my thinking so that by the age of 7 or 8 I would feel that rooms I was exiting would 'shut down', with all actions within it stilling or freeze-framing, and the rooms I would enter would activate, as if they had been in stasis until I entered them. I only know that I grew so concerned by the emotional impact of this unfounded and unproven feeling that by 8 years of age I began considering the possibility that I must cut someone open as I walked into a room, just to prove to myself that they were, indeed, automatons put there to observe, provide appearances and control my life. If I had ever been able to decide the 'who' to subject that proving on or with I very possibly would have acted upon it. Instead, I changed genres of reading, from comic books and science fiction to the pure fantasy of magic, swords, and sorcery.

Of course, the shift wasn't that far from where I had been before and I would begin to study the occult stories and literature that was available. I even attempted to turn myself into a werewolf at one point, although no physical manifestation ever occurred to denote that 'magic' actually worked in that manner. Eventually, I turned to fantasy humor fiction, where the protagonist was considered weak in physical prowess but had the knowledge and some single skill that would be considered 'fantastic' by the other characters around them.

Harold de Shea could fence with an epee and overcome giants with skill and knowledge. Professor Wolfe would learn the real words of magic that allowed him to become a wolf, of the sort of voluntary werewolf that didn't eat babies or tear out people's throats – unless they were the 'bad' guys in the story.

Yet I had no such skills or knowledge. And the opportunity to use those skills, even if I had had them, would never present itself.

I longed to be the hero, loved by the damsel who I would love forever and completely, able to protect and care for her, forever. The child wished for childish things until reality came home in Marine Corps Boot Camp, where childish thoughts and feelings were meant to be put aside and I was expected to become a man.

My body has grown older, aging well for many years but also developing flaws and weaknesses. Yet, inside myself, the last vestiges of the child I was, remain untouched by age, adulthood, responsibility, or even trauma. The story of Peter Pan relates that Peter didn't want to grow up and chose not to, forever. I know the story well and relate to the Lost Boys much more than I do to Peter Pan himself. But the not growing up part, the blessing or curse of being a child inside the body of a grown man has never left me although it was never my choice.

For many years people would tell me that I "didn't look my age." When I was 32, I could pass myself off as being 19, and did so frequently. I was still being 'carded' for legal drinking age at 38 years of age because I looked so much younger than the years I actually had lived.

Could that have been a result of my inner child being predominant in my life, I wonder? Could the spirit of youth that remains buried deep within me have prevented the aging process from occurring in the manner it did for human beings?

I only know that also around the age of 8 I saw a concert on a black and white television in which Edgar and Johnny Winter played and I immediately became obsessed with having white hair like theirs. Yet at 65 years of age, I have barely begun to have gray hairs on my head, although my scruffy beard has turned white and my mustache has bits and streaks of white throughout.

Is it possible that there might be a spiritual connection between aging and growing old? One where human beings become worn out faster when they labor and strive for things; things that in my experience don't matter because all material things fade and fail eventually and, because I've never valued those things in the way human beings do, I failed to age in a way that some might call 'proper.'

These are some of the questions I would ask of god, if and when I confront him again. The answers not being given when I was given other answers for questions that I didn't even know who would ask them, let alone who the answers were meant to be delivered to, they are the questions that show how little I know about myself, who or what I am.

I don't concern myself with "what is the meaning of life?" type questions; the meaning of life is to live. That simple answer would suffice for every human being on this planet if they could learn to live with one another instead of for or over one another. But the so-called mysteries of life, the butterfly effects of living, and the pebble in the pond repercussions that reach far beyond what any human being sees, I observe and wonder about the results and the reasoning behind the nature of the ripples themselves.

Compleat
Notes

Compleat

Although there may be as many as five others who share your physical appearance, no one is exactly as you are yourself. Identical twins, for example, look so similar in physical appearance that even close family members cannot distinguish between them. Yet they are unique individuals, and while they often find themselves sharing similar feelings and some even share feelings so closely it appears to many that they share thoughts they know themselves to be separate entities, complete and whole as individual human beings.

My name is Micheal. Spelled M I C H E A L - it's not the normal way, because my mother actually asked the nurse what the most unusual way of spelling it would be, and that's what the nurse suggested. All through grade school I caught hell from teachers for not knowing how to spell my own name. Thank you, Monroe, Froebel, and St. Anthony's for telling me I don't know shit about myself.

Recently I went online on an app called TikTok, to share my pain of being alive, maybe share a smile with some silly videos and see what makes human beings laugh. I wasn't disappointed in the least UNTIL: The political extremists like the Proud Boys (they really are boys, by the way btw) and their ilk started sending me notices that I should "go to hell" or "get out of OUR country if you dislike it so much."

So rather than argue with them what I'm doing is giving these individuals the opportunity to put their money where their mouths are:

If you want me to leave the country so much, donate a buck, or two or three dollars, a five, ten, or even 20 ... and send me packing. I've got my passport, I've no ties to this nation of insanity worth speaking about and if I die overseas the only view of me you might experience will be when the VA buries me for my service in the Marine Corps that I am no longer confused about or pretend to be proud of having served.

So, for all the haters on TikTok (you can share this with anyone you choose) have at you!!!

This is the gauntlet of defiance. You really want me gone? Prove it. A dollar each from millions of you would be too much. But with $7,000.00, US,D it would mean I can leave and never return, alive.

Thank you,

Compleat

Micheal (a.k.a. Jesus's kid brother).

Compleat

Barring the Way to Eden

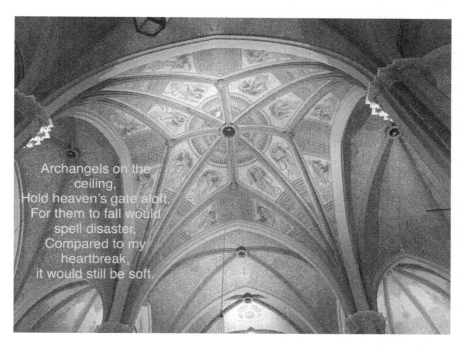

Archangels on the ceiling,
Hold heaven's gate aloft.
For them to fall would spell disaster,
Compared to my heartbreak,
it would still be soft.

I've spent many words in this book describing how humanity has taken the works of good men and women and turned their efforts into a mockery by wrapping them up in religions. From Islamist's to Zionists, from Christians to Atheists and Science humanity takes a perverse and twisted pleasure from using what it gifted to them and creating religions in order to manipulate and control others in order to obtain great wealth and influence throughout the world. Some call that gaining power over others, while I see it simply as worshiping their true god, Mammon.

Because I learned through my experience with meeting the divine entity who I call pop and others label 'god' some truths that humanity avoids. Here, therefore, are a few of those truths that humanity cannot seem to abide hearing aloud, going as far back as I can in the little bit of knowledge I have of written history.

The garden of Eden myth:

I've already addressed the fact that the so-called original sin wasn't simply disobedience of doing what they were told not to do. There's a secondary part to that myth that most don't address or realize, however. Theologians will know the name of the angel set to guard over the entrance back into Eden, where I neither know nor care for that particular piece of information, though I could research it and include it here if I felt it was necessary. (believe it was the Arch-Angel Jophiel.)

What most won't realize is that the 'flaming sword' that particular angel holds as the weapon to keep humanity from re-obtaining Eden has a name of its own. Ironic that the name of the angel is so well known but that the fact that the sword itself has a name is ignored or has remained a mystery to many who've studied religious texts and dogma for years on end. It's simple really, once the name is revealed as it was to me in my meeting with god. And so obvious that it would make sense in an instant to those who believe in that particular set of myths.

The name of the sword that keeps humanity from reentering the Garden of Eden, that flames and burns so brightly that humanity cannot see their way past it is one small word: doubt.

Humanity doubts not just the existence of god, or the many myths that represent the teachings of good, honorable men and women that show god's existence as a being, they doubt their own relationship to that being because it would require them to accept responsibility for all that they have done, are doing and will do to one another.

When told that god doesn't make anything that is equivalent to 'junk' human beings take comfort from the words yet in the same instant ignore their meaning. And their response when told that they are capable of so much more than they believe their response is just as conflicted: "Nobody's perfect." They point their fingers at the wise, good beings among themselves, saying "well, the Buddha was enlightened" or "Mohammad was god's prophet" or even "only Jesus was perfect." Yet each and every one of the god's children they point their fingers at were human beings just as they themselves were and are today.

Examples are there throughout history and even contemporary news stories if they are investigated closely. Jesus walked on water, in their bible, to the consternation of his own followers and although the fear that he was dead and a spirit approaching them caused them to call out to him to be recognized, he even called to one of them and told that individual to go ahead and walk on the water as well.

Peter did just that, until he realized exactly what it was that he was doing and doubt drove him back into the boat. Christianity would have humanity place the responsibility for that on his faith in Jesus or in the divine nature of Jesus himself, but therein lies the doubt.

Jesus didn't empower Peter to walk on water in that story, he simply told Peter a truth that humanity is afraid to accept. The power to do the divine resides within every human being because every human being is divine. Or did they simply miss the part in their bible where it says that they were made in god's own image? It's the doubt, from what god told me that day, that keeps human beings from obtaining not just Eden but also walking, talking, and knowing the divine as an individual being and their relationship with divinity that resides within themselves.

Mohammad wrote many similar stories, but the religious among his followers used his words to twist his teachings around to say that there is only One god, Allah. Totally ignoring and disrespecting the teachings of both Mohammad himself and others who were enlightened by discovering the truths about themselves.

As an example: a Hindu monk who isolates himself from the distractions of the world obtains the ability to levitate and communicate through telepathic means and his abilities are viewed as trickery or blasphemy by the Islamic religion as well as many Christian sects, when all the man did was discover what is inside each and every human being and would be possible if humanity didn't create the very distractions that the monk had to isolate himself from for years in order to obtain or realize.

God said that humanity as a whole is destroying itself by doubting its own potential and abilities. By pointing to others as being saints, holy men and women, Gurus, teachers, and (most hurtful of all to god) better than themselves, it has caused humanity to fear, doubt, and be separated from their own divine nature for entirely too long.

Using the bible mythology again, I had asked the age-s old question: Why are we here? And the answer was simple, just like knowing the name of the sword that keeps humanity from re-obtaining Eden. The divine created humanity as company: f. Friends, equals, and family.

Not to be subservient, bowing and scraping, often disobedient creatures to be punished for their transgressions. That's the purpose of angels, to serve both god and humanity.

Compleat

When humanity as a whole, not simply the individuals who realize their potential and abilities, and recognize, as Jesus did when he manifested the divine within his human form, then humanity can and will re-obtain their rightful place as beings of the divine nature, manifesting all that that implies in living with and among one another.

Someone once asked me, when I shared all of this information with them, a question that humanity has asked in various forms throughout the ages of humankind:

"If god is so all- knowing and all- powerful, why does god allow evil to exist?"

My answer was simple too. While many would respond with "Who told you god allows it?" and what most would imagine I would have the audacity to imply; I just added a perspective that came from my confrontation with god that day?

"Why would god get involved with a bunch that not only denies their own abilities but when they do realize their abilities, would probably turn those abilities against the divine entity that created them in the first place?"

Remember this from my other stories? When faced with the divine being that others call god, I became enraged by all that had ever been done to me and all that I myself had ever done to others.

That rage came from the recognition of all that I am, all that I was, and all that I will ever be and I wasn't ready to accept it any more than humanity is ready to put aside doubt, cool the flaming sword as it were, and accept who they were actually meant to be all along.

There are those who say that I'm fortunate that god didn't destroy me that day. I'm of the opinion that god chose not to destroy me in order to allow me to attempt to destroy the divine within myself. And I believe that in some strange, inexplicable way I succeeded, though it took years more of my behaving as if I didn't know the truth. I define stupidity as being willfully ignorant. So, I acknowledge that I was being stupid throughout those following years. And that willful ignorance, that very stupidity, is what destroyed the humanity I once had.

Compleat

One
_._._._._._._._._._._._._._._._._._

Folks are always telling me I should "get over the past" or "move on" or even that "there are many more fish in the sea." But like the movie - Big Fish - there was/is/will always be only one. They say I'm crazy. They also say I'm melodramatic. They, being humanity as a whole, even say that my feelings are childish and immature.

What I know about myself is that I am childlike in my obsessions. I want what I want, need what I need and won't understand 'why' things have to be the way they are until my 'pop' explains them to me.

If you're listening God, I'm sorry I'm such an immature asshole. I'm sorry I told you to go fuck yourself. I'm sorry I told you what a shit job I thought you had done with my life. And I'm sorry I ever told you I thought I could run my life or the world better than you could.

I apologize, so please will you either take it over and do what you think is best with my life? And if it's not too much to ask, an early out would really be appreciated. It hurts to live with the mess I've made of it.

Thanks,

Micheal

An Answer From God

"When offered a safe place to experiment with new types of behaviors, most human beings will begin to experiment more deeply than ever before with love and trust!"

"They will drop their defenses and posturing; the barriers of distrust, fear, resentment, and prejudice.

They will experiment with disarming themselves! They will experiment with peace - peace within themselves and within the group. And in experimenting with it, they will find that the experiment works!"

"Peace can be and will be achieved."

Compleat

A Letter from God

> **This Is My Madness - The Perception That I See**
>
> The entire race of humanity would rather look up to a beautiful lie; Than face the responsibility of creating from a harsh reality.
>
> I used the example of a man, supposedly in recovery for 27+ years, who married a young woman with 30 days in a 12 Step program.
>
> They are still together, after 10 years, and are held up as an "example" of what IS possible in recovery.
>
> But she doesn't know his true nature. Doesn't know that even as he married her, he would tell others that without sex he would "kick her ass to the curb."
>
> It's a beautiful lie. It holds them together. And still it is a lie.
>
> Their book says that Lucifer was the angel of light. The most beautiful of all the angels ever created to serve god. And the father of all lies.
>
> Is it any wonder, humanity is still drawn to the beautiful lies and avoids facing the harsh truths of who we are, what we are meant to be and ... ironically the harshest truth ... what we are meant to do.

Dear Humanity,

First, I'd like to say how proud of you I am. You have accomplished so much over the moments that you've existed on the planet I've given you. Your buildings reach for the sky, you've covered almost the entire globe with means of easy travel and communication among yourselves and most importantly you've learned so very much about what your world contains for you to use and enjoy.

But with all those things available to you, you still disregard the things I've given you to do as stewards and caretakers of the planet and one another. You're using the resources that the planet provides faster than it can replace them and are suffering the consequences of your wasteful use of them. You ignore one another, using divisions and separations that YOU create as if they matter more than my giving you one another to care for with each and every one of you as being equal in my eyes.

As proud as I am of your accomplishments, I am saddened by your self-doubts and focus on attaining material comforts as being the measure by which you judge one another as successful.

Compleat

I've sent prophets among you, wise men and women, to speak on my behalf and give you direction to avoid what I see as the results of your own actions. They have written to you in every language you've created and in every portion of the planet where you've gone in order to speak of what I'm saying to you again, here and now, through this letter.

I've used them, those men and women, the way you yourselves would use a pen, calligraphy, and paintings and it seems that you don't understand or comprehend how serious your situation is, so this time I'm using the equivalent of a crayon in that I'm using this individual to deliver my final attempt to communicate with you.

You are destroying not simply what I've given you, the planet, the creatures you were meant to care for and be stewards over, but also one another. Humanity as a whole, and that is how I see you not by the divisions you create among yourselves but as the entire race of human beings, is bringing about an end that some of you seem to want to happen because you believe it would bring you back to me.

That lie couldn't be further from the truth than if you placed it in the core of the planet you are on and traveled across all the universe to its furthest regions. You are meant to join me, not simply after you die, but before you destroy one another and yourselves.

You can stop this process. I've given you the power, authority, and especially the responsibility to do so ... now it's up to you.

- god

Compleat

I Understand or I Die
— . — . — . — . — . — . — . — . — . — . — . — . — . — . — . — . —

Here in two WORDS lays the greatest lie one human being can tell another. You do not understand. Not ever. Not before I lost my soul. Not before I stopped being human and certainly not after I made the choice not to be. Yet you all encourage one another and myself with saying, platitudes, and so many WORDS.

'It can't be that bad!' Bullshit, it is that bad, here inside my mind.

"This too shall pass." What? Like a piece of bad fruit, I ate that gave me diarrhea? I'm going to shit out the source of what makes me sick inside? Like it's a turd causing me the discomfort of constipation?

You can say that to me with a straight face, serious as the day is long, and not choke on the vomit coming out of your mouth in the form of the words you are shaping with your lips, tongue and teeth?

"Tell me about it." What the fuck ever for? What a purposeless noise to squawk in my direction. Of what possible use would telling you what I'm feeling serve? Even assuming I could find the words inside myself to clearly express those feelings that are killing me from the inside out like a cancer that the cells of which have attained the level of self-awareness to become an intelligence in and of itself, completely independent of even a symbiotic relationship with myself!? You WANT to experience that life consuming disease? As if that experience would abridge the distance between my insanity and your perception of it (or me)? You already know you don't, the noise is just a means or method of staving off any possibility of coming into contact with the actuality of me.

We, all of humanity, relate to/ with one another on so many levels. A book read where a few written words trigger familiar feelings so similar within ourselves we label it as 'UNDERSTANDING'. Music that can bring inner peace, total excitement, joy so strong our bodies are compelled to dance even when our egos tell us we cannot dance or risk the attention we desire and fear from our other human beings. Poetry, art, photography, and even piss poor prose (such as this) can trigger emotionally charged reactions or responses and because we don't have the proper tools (word) to express those feelings of relating to any or all of those triggers. We label them under a generalist heading: calling them understanding.

Compleat

It remains impossible for us to understand even one of another of us. Re-read that now!

"It is impossible for even a single human being (no matter any professed levels of awareness) to understand any other human being. To do so, to actually understand, we would need to become the other individual. And while we would draw close enough through all the mediums I've listed above, as well as the others I've deliberately avoided mentioning until now, physical contact as brief as a glancing touch of the hand of complete strangers encountered in the venues of crowded stores, concerts, or walking past one another on a sidewalk to the depths of intimacy shared through sex and all other means of by which we connect with one another, especially love, in the end our fear of losing our 'self' would turn us aside even as the heat from a raw flame will turn aside even the most persistent moth drawn toward the light of that self-same understanding.

Draw as it might, shining so bright in the darkness of separation that is the human condition that a supernova occurring in an enclosed room would appear the final flicker of that last ember of a forest fire finally fought and extinguished, its very existence experienced within every human soul it generates the repelling heat which prevents it from being obtained.

As an aside, this made sense of the final note included in the Garden of Eden mythology. What more accurate description to use than that of an Angel (a supernatural servant to god AND man) being placed at the entrance to paradise, preventing humanity's return or re-entrance unto/into Eden, with the weapon borne by said entity being described as a 'flaming sword'?

My question to god on this point was simple: "What happens when humanity embraces the pain and accepts the 'flaming sword' of understanding one another AND you, the way you were meant to be all along?" Old fuck just sat there smiling at me because his answer was right there in the question I posed just as I addressed it to him directly. "Deal with the truth of the sword , and nothing prevents humanity from resuming our rightful place in paradise - walking, talking, and simply being in his presence again. It's where he wanted us to be, still wants us to be and where he awaits our return.

We just need to understand.

Compleat

A Last Note on Myself and My Love for Megan

Megan Abby (nee) Kaiser, the girl I loved, still love, and will love for all of eternity, no longer exists anywhere outside of my broken mind and heart. I'm sure it wasn't her intention, though her shout of "You, motherfucker," still echoes all the nights in which I try to sleep for her any of the pain that came from my betrayal of her love for me, to become the cause of the damnation of my soul because I knew what I was doing to her was wrong and yet I still chose to do it.

My provoking that cry from her was my intent to leave her no room or leeway in which she might forgive me, so she would go on with her life. Hers was the only right and the power to damn me that dreadful night. It seems appropriate now that Halloween night and all Hallows Eve, my soul should have been cast into the pit from which I've never crawled, climbed, or escaped. One doesn't love and lose – or in my case, toss away - that precious a gift of unconditional love. It is and was insane of me to do so. And she who holds the power of forgiveness - the key to my release from the self-inflicted hell - no longer exists.

Compleat

Compleat
The Craftsman & The Tool

There was a screwdriver, made to be self-aware, that the craftsman chose to use for a specific task. The task was a difficult one, thankless, requiring effort on the part of the screwdriver and most importantly creating discomfort upon the tool through the heat that the task would cause it to bear.

The screwdriver being self-aware, felt both put upon and incapable of performing the task it was being required to complete, and in its self-doubt broke in the craftsman's hand, losing its head and becoming useless as a screwdriver from that day forth.

But instead of discarding the screwdriver, the craftsman set it aside, high upon a shelf, where it remained for many years. Angry at the craftsman for its being set aside and even angrier at itself for having broken in an instance that it had been created for in the first place.

The years passed slowly for the screwdriver, regret being its only feeling and company there on that shelf. Until one day, almost miraculously the craftsman took down the broken tool and began grinding it upon a stone. Not a modern grinder or grinding stone, simply a plain, natural stone upon which the craftsman slowly reshaped and reformed the screwdriver into something else.

Compleat

It became an awl. Sharpened to a point that could be used to scratch upon the surfaces of both stone and wood. And the craftsman began to use this newly made awl to write, crafting words through use of the awl for others of his ilk to read and one day heed if they should so choose.

This then is my story. Once asked to become the pastor of a 'church' I refused. I wasn't capable, wasn't ready, wasn't able to bear the pressure and the heat that would have come from taking up a position I was unqualified for and didn't believe I should have been selected for in the first place. And I broke. I went completely insane, losing not just my mind by my life eventually.

But like that screwdriver, I was ground down and brought to become something I hadn't been crafted to be in the beginning. And so, I write the words I am given to share, scratching out the difficult lines that many would rather not read, often closing their eyes rather than see for themselves the knowledge that I was given.

It is yours for the taking or for you to ignore. Because you too are crafted to be exactly who and what you already were, are, and always will be ... humans.

Compleat

Looking with God Eyes

Some of the stories that I share may have the appearance of being 'unbelievable'. Someone recently told me that the way in which I perceive the world around me and how I express what I observe is similar to playing Scrabble with other players, who are used to seeing, playing, and accepting that game as being played on a flat board with specific positions for bonuses on letters and words; while I try to convince the entire world that there is another way to play that game. They told me that I try to convince others to play the game by placing the tiles vertically and in the different positions.

WHY? Why would anyone even want to put the tiles vertically on a flat board? Obviously, it's more difficult, easier to unbalance them and have them become displaced and more difficult to view the tiles, their values, and placements. It makes NO sense. Or as it was put to me, it's nonsense to even want to place the tiles in that manner.

Maybe it is. That would definitely explain my being labeled as 'insane'. But here's a thought that I keep trying to express, one that my lack of communication skills keeps others from hearing, let alone understanding.

If the world as I see it is so out of place, so easily disrupted, so impossible to perceive in the way I try to express it, then truthfully, I must be insane. Or ... maybe, just maybe, I'm seeing things from a different perspective. Could it be possible that somehow, in some way even I cannot explain or rationalize, I have learned how to look at things from an angle not expected?

I have used two of the stories that I have set before you as examples of this view of reality that I have. I hope you will bear with me long enough to read them both. I am neither lying to deceive anyone nor trying to gain anything from any other human being on this planet. Not even acceptance of what I perceive to be real is real for me.

Have you ever had a special cup or plate - One you preferred to use and considered yours; to be used by you and you alone? I have known people who have applied that particular possessiveness to objects and while I myself have chosen not to own anything I can relate to having something that was so special that claiming it and being protective of was important.

Compleat

And having had that experience of being able to relate I have also had the responsibility of being protective of their objects of consideration. Wash enough dishes and someone's special cup will come to need to be cleaned; placing the responsibility of its protection squarely on your shoulders.

I consistently find myself in that position, caring for someone's special objects, and it used to be that I cared for their objects out of fear that I might be responsible for breaking them by accident or even intentionally. I was always concerned that I might be held accountable for breaking anything of great value or even punished for it as if it were always intentional.

Now I find that I have no fear of breaking anything belonging to anyone else, not simply because I find myself holding no ill will toward others, but because I have come to the understanding that the care that I show what belongs to others is only an infinitesimal portion of the respect I can show for them.

In place of fear of the repercussions of my actions, both accidental and intentional, I find that I am allowed to show respect for others simply by giving their objects the respect I would show the individual themselves. I get to treat their objects the way I would treat them if they were in my physical hands and under my care, protection, and treatment.

In the place of fear and without so-called courage to take its place I find that I can use respect.   How too then can I not respect you? The entire human race, in spite of skin colors, religions, financial means, political differences, environmentally altered upbringing, and all the other differences we use to separate ourselves one from another you, I, we all belong to one another. We are meant to be family. We are family. We are god.

Compleat

What's Your Story?

For almost a year now, I've been actively taking steps toward completing my plans for going to Europe, then backpacking across Europe, Asia, Asia Minor, and Africa.

In that year, I've asked for help with the financial burden of making the trip from 'friends and family' and got a whopping $45 in contributions from the only two guys who supported my efforts.

I've also asked for assistance in making the trek itself, by trying to recruit a traveling companion. I've been posting on social media that I need to find a woman traveling companion who has the determination, strength, courage, and curiosity to attempt a pilgrimage of this nature in my company. A woman that could not only physically complete the journey but also keep me from making foolish decisions and choices based on my loneliness and the heartaches of my past.

Yet, there is another reason why I'm going on this journey - a reason that I believe most people won't relate to because it seems too far-fetched.

I'm going to Europe (first) in order to find the god, I physically met back in 1980, the same one I told to go f' himself when he asked me to do something for him.

I'm not seeking him out to apologize or ask for his forgiveness, as the religious among you might think or imagine. I'm going to find him because I have my own questions that I want to ask of him. And I think it best, just in case anyone hasn't read about my experience, to explain I only choose to label the divine as a "him" because that's how my head was able to wrap itself around the experience without imploding that day, it has nothing to do with how it manifests itself to others.

To do what I'm setting out to do, to find him where he's disguised as a human being among the rest of the 7.9+ billion souls on this planet I'm going to need to do something extremely unusual. I'm going to travel around the world to meet the people of the human race and ask them to tell me their stories.

"What's your story?"

Compleat

Not in a sarcastic or challenging way I hope, but an honest inquiry to learn as much as I can about as many human beings as I can in the years or months or weeks or days I have left on this planet. I want to know and not presume to know what others have experienced in their lives here. What they have gone through. What they see as their purpose for being or existing. And most of all, what they perceive as being the reason for human existence here.

So, I ask of you all, please, if an old man with a white goatee, carrying his backpack and hopefully still using a walking staff approaches any of you and asks "what's your story?" please don't take offense. I'm just learning how to become a human being and your answers will help me find my own.

Compleat

The Final Story

Compleat

If anyone has been able to read this far, finishing the entire book, then you might be asking yourselves the question that I've been asked most often beyond "What's the book about?" People who first hear about what I've written, often asking for details of the stories it contains become confused, irritated, angry, or even outright vehemently opposed to hearing about its content.

Why then do I share all of my darkest secrets, unfiltered by social acceptability, political correctness, or shame for the things I have done? Do I not fear repercussions from the religions that I appear to attack, disparaging them and belittling them by pointing out their weaknesses and flaws? Am I not incapable of feeling empathy for others, mentioning their names and their relationships in forming the insanity that I suffered from for so many years? Am I not concerned about the repercussions that radical-thinking, religious people might bring to bear against me for my observations? But the biggest question, of course, is the first one always asked.

What is this book about?

I readily admit that it appears to be about me -, I am very aware of how it sounds as if everything in the world relates to me and, how I perceive everything to be through my own experiences. Fortunately for me, that is not the case.

This book is about humanity as a whole. Each and every one of you. Because I tell my sordid stories, not for my own aggrandizement but to show you that the courage to be real with one another is not impossible. That to be unafraid is to act against your greatest fears, putting yourselves in the open, and allowing one another to truly know who and what you are inside.

Why do I share my secrets? Is it just because they kept me sick for so many years?

Insanity, it is said, is doing the same thing over and over again expecting a different result. And after years of insane thinking, most human beings grow to believe that there is no other choice for themselves. In fact, I dare to say here that humanity as a whole is insane in that regard. You have all come to believe that there is nothing you can do other than what you have learned to do, year after year, age after age, century after century, and have no thought of ever waking to the truth if someone doesn't show you that you have fallen into believing the beautiful lie.

Compleat

Do I not fear the repercussions of being so open about my past mistakes?

I do not. Having died once already, I do not fear death, or even the pain of dying. Having been to a place outside of both time and space, I have no fear of heaven or hell being where I might end up after I die either.

The attacks I appear to make on religions may well result in extremists from any one or all of them seeking to end my existence here among you, but I can honestly say I do not fear that either. I know that even though this body will cease to function one day, who and what I am will continue in that place beyond time with greater power and purpose than this earthbound form can withstand. I consider any attempt on ending my existence as being a well-wisher hoping to aid me in gaining or regaining my true form.

To feel empathy with others I would first have to have some connection to them, and I have none with anyone that I mention in my writings here. In fact, the poem I wrote about being an island unto myself was my first realization and attempt to communicate my inability to connect with any of the 7.9 billion+ individuals on this planet. Not because I haven't tried or that because there haven't been those who have tried to reach me in my isolation. But because the damage I've done, to myself and others, has burned away the humanity in me to the point that even the slightest attempt to connect has failed.

Many authors change the names of those in their books to 'protect the innocent' while I do not. And it's not simply due to my lack of empathy that leads me to choose this path. I do it because the people I've hurt most, the human beings who walk among you who have had the misfortune to encounter me in the worst days of my insanity need your help. They are, I have been told, very good examples and opportunities for the entire human race to practice the things I have spoken to you about when it comes to changing or doing things in a different way.

Every one of them -, man, woman, or child - ... is an opportunity for the human race to practice being more than they see themselves as ... less than perfect. Silly as it might sound, the human race actually could "Be excellent to each other." But ironically you have been taught that 'no one is perfect.' When folks die, when loss and suffering is are at its their greatest, when you see yourselves as less than you really are ... you are believing that lie.

And ironically, it is in those moments of greatest suffering, that you remind one another that there is a plan or method to the madness that is life, you say a truth that belies the statement "No one is perfect." By saying one sentence that is real, truthful, and could change the world if only all of you would embrace it fully.

"God doesn't make any junk."

At the beginning of this book, I honestly stated that I would write about myself, that to write about you would be hypocrisy at its worst. I still hold that to be true even with what I have just said in this story. I can only relate to these stories because I have experienced them. And I can only state that they are your stories too because every one of you has something I have lost.

Hope.

You hope for a better future, for yourselves, your children, grandchildren, and your lineage down into prosperity. I have none. You hope that nothing bad happens to your own family, friends, and loved ones. Then you turn away from that same hope for others of your own kind through divisions created by both the mind of humanity and the entities that spoke the beautiful lie to you so many, many years ago.

Every lie has worn away who you really are, even as every act of insanity wore away my own humanity. And it was not my will to write this book, because I wanted nothing to do with placing the truth in front of you this way. Not out of fear, but out of consideration of the source from which this information is coming and my anger with god.

There will be those who ask themselves "Who does he think he is?" And as I've said in one story herein – "I tried to think, but nothing happened." Who I AM doesn't matter. What I am would only matter, if I was human enough to share a connection with humanity as a whole. And I've already stated that I don't believe I actually can or do that very thing.

In one poem or story here I challenge god, not simply asking him "why me?" but challenging his attempt to communicate with humanity through me. Not simply out of low self-esteem or over-inflated ego, I challenged him on the observable facts that none of those who tried to communicate with humanity as a whole have ever been heard or listened to correctly. What then makes him think you might listen to me?

The so-called "Christians" have been misled, lied to, and use their book to condemn and divide themselves from others of humanity based on their so-called faith and sects or denominations. Islamist's have done much the same, ignoring what their 'prophet' actually said and creating an atmosphere of fear and hatred for anyone who doesn't agree with their book their way as well. As with all religions, this truth stands out as being self-evident, yet no one chooses to recognize it unless someone else points it out to them. Thousands of years have passed, millennium in which humanity has clung to religions teaching partial truths and sometimes outright lies, in order to manipulate and control the wealth, power, and prestige of this world you now live within. And not once has anyone actually asked god, to take a break from it all. Offering it/her/him a place to rest from the struggle it is to watch humanity walk away from itself, its rightful place in existence, and not intervene. I made the grave mistake of inviting him to visit, and he did.

Humanity. Even the word cannot bring you together. You divide yourselves by skin color, as if that matters, by location or nationality, and languages, deliberately misunderstanding one another by speaking languages that you make sure others than those closest to you cannot comprehend. Even among those who share similar physical locations and attributes, you have dialects and accents that make it difficult and nearly impossible to be sure of what you are saying to one another. Nationality, location, physical features, accents, birth, and family lineage … the means by which you divide yourselves is so vast I see why he gets depressed with even trying to maintain contact with you.

And yes, god *his title, not his name* gets depressed over the loss of all of you. From those who think they are the most powerful, to the humblest of you; from those of you who fear his anger, to those of you who use, abuse, and misquote all that he has ever tried to communicate with you, and mostly he is saddened by your lack of knowing who you are and how very much you mean to him.

I can give you proof of what I have just said, using the Christian bible as an example. In it, there is a story that god created humanity in his own image. Has anyone ever asked themselves, "Why would he do that?" Why would this omnipotent, all- knowing, all- seeing being, entity, force, or whatever create something just like himself? (Herself or itself for those of you who think of god in those terms.)

What purpose did we serve? The answer to that is simple. He needed us. Not to bow down and worship him, scraping and crabbing along on our knees in fear of him, nor as the atheists among you try to dismiss god as being created by humanity to explain what you do not understand. Humanity was created to walk, talk and be with god, as his equals, friends, confidants, and company.

Compleat

When I died, when I had killed myself and tried so very hard to escape this existence you call living, I saw beyond the places some of you label heaven and hell. And I saw those that are in both those places, heaven with its comforts and companionship with god. Hell, where the knowledge of their separation from all that is life, good, and worth having is as great if not greater than the torments they have reserved for themselves through their own actions. I went to a place outside of both time and space … .beyond existence itself and I came to know what it was like for god before he allowed everything to exist.

Evolutionists say it took billions of years for everything to come into being. They are right, if you consider that time has no meaning beyond our comprehension of it. Time is an illusion, created by the minds of humanity in order to construct order out of the chaos you fear and the death of your bodies you witness every day.

I've written about death in this book, but I want to emphasize that death would surrender her task, gratefully, if only humanity would allow her to rest. And what, some of you might ask, is her task? The one she can only do and has no hope of ever being relieved of? It's picking up the pieces of life you break off of one another with every instance of hate, hurt, harassment, and haranguing of one another. Death bears the burden of collecting all the pieces chipped off of the lives you break off of one another and is being forced to release those whose lives are, can be, and will be, so broken that her release is a gift. I can tell you with complete confidence and honesty that she actually hates her job, wishing only to stop doing it. If only humanity would allow her to stop.

Each of you is unique in that there is no one else like you, no other that has your spirit, soul, or whatever it is that makes you who you are. Even twins cannot share themselves beyond connections that appear supernatural at times. Your actions, the result of which are your own experiences, form who you are more than the DNA that formed the body you wear and ride around in like a vehicle or vessel, carrying you from point to point in your lives in order that you might grow to know yourselves for who and what you really are.

.... to be continued.

Compleat

Ravings & References

Compleat

Runner's Ravings

1. "The respect we show others is a direct reflection of the respect we have for ourselves."
2. Kindness shows in the smiles, the eyes, and the hearts of those who care.
3. "To think outside of the box, it helps to get out of the box, first."
4. "Yesterday's history, tomorrow's a mystery, today is a gift, that's why it's called the Present; Open it, enjoy it and remember to say 'thank you' for it.."
5. "Having a full-time job, children, and trying to manage a full- time relationship is like having three eight- hour- a- day jobs. Something is going to give, and it's usually us, first, so go slow and rest."
6. My one rule in life to judge a day as a success or not isn't based on my productivity but on whether or not I have helped bring a smile to at least one person's face that day.
7. "People who think their shit doesn't stink might only be having a problem with smelling the truth."
8. "Little steps, are big strides, for new people."
9. "We have met the enemy, and he is us!"
10. "The road to hell is paved with good intentions."
11. "To actually understand another being, supernatural or human, a being needs to become that individual themselves, even for the slightest of instance."
12. "An asshole is created by ignoring a **person**."
13. "It doesn't HAVE to be this way."
14. "Learn unconditional love from dogs, they display it every chance they get. Practice unconditional love on cats, they offer opportunity

in every encounter. Then take it one small step further and practice what you've learned upon one another. I know you will be glad you did."

15. "Hope is the beacon, and the light of the world, even in the darkest of days."

16. "The only wrong I can right, is helping others avoid my own."

17. "Major depression is very much like the ocean between the States and Europe. It can be crossed, overcome, traversed, and risen above - yet it always remains where it is - until the end of "'time'.'""

18. "The connections between human beings are stronger than all the man- made divisions created by religions, politicians, and those who choose to do harm"

19. "...we think that if we can just get enough food, enough sex, or enough money, we'll be satisfied and everything will be alright."

20. "And when nothing could fill the emptiness, I became the emptiness thereby losing my humanity as a result."

21. "The second worst thing you can do to as a human being: kill love."

22. "We must caffeinate, lest we procrastinate."

23. "The only fight you can win; is the one you don't fight."

24. "Music is one of the universal languages. Blending is   simply translating it so all can understand it."

25. *Every human being has greatness within them, because good without god, leaves 0. And every one of them can tap into the god part of themselves, without needing a religion to show them how. Just by being true to who they really are … instead of who they were taught they had to be or are "supposed" to be.

26. "How to wake the dreamers when they see the lie as beautiful and reality as the nightmare they want to escape."

27. The old adage goes:

"A leopard ☐cannot change its spots."

Compleat

For the world that means once a dangerous creature, always a dangerous creature.""

But for me it means that by accepting being crazy I get to choose how I will act, no matter how I appear to the entire world.

Compleat

References

1. Passenger. (2012). Let Her Go [Recorded by Passenger]. On All the Little Lights [Folk].

2. Redford, Robert. (2000). The Legend of Bagger Vance [Film]. DreamWorks Pictures.

3. Lorre, Chuck. Prady, Bill. (2007). Big Bang Theory [Series]. Faye Oshima Belyeu.

4. Meatloaf. (1977). Two Out of Three Ain't Bad [Recorded by Meatloaf]. Bat Out of Hell [Pop, Rock].

5. The American Heritage Dictionary of The English Language; New College Edition: William Morris – Editor; Published by Houghton Mifflin Company ©1981

6. Joan Jett and the Blackhearts. (1988). I Hate Myself for Loving You [Joan Jett and the Blackhearts]. Up Your Alley [Hard Rock].